Natural Hazard Mitigation

Natural Hazard Mitigation

Alessandra Jerolleman and John J. Kiefer

CRC Press
Taylor & Francis Group
Boca Raton London New York

CRC Press is an imprint of the
Taylor & Francis Group, an **informa** business

CRC Press
Taylor & Francis Group
6000 Broken Sound Parkway NW, Suite 300
Boca Raton, FL 33487-2742

Printed in the United States of America on acid-free paper
Version Date: 20121011

International Standard Book Number: 978-1-4398-3493-0 (Hardback)

Library of Congress Cataloging-in-Publication Data

Natural hazard mitigation / editors, Alessandra Jerolleman, John J. Kiefer.
p. cm.
Includes bibliographical references and index.
ISBN 978-1-4398-3493-0 (hbk. : alk. paper)
1. Emergency management. 2. Natural disasters. I. Jerolleman, Alessandra. II. Kiefer, John J.

HV551.2.N383 2013
363.34'6--dc23 2012031516

Visit the Taylor & Francis Web site at
http://www.taylorandfrancis.com

and the CRC Press Web site at
http://www.crcpress.com

Contents

Introduction

This text is intended to focus on hazard mitigation from a practical perspective, including questions such as: What needs to be considered when engaging in hazard mitigation planning and related activities? What alternatives are there to the federally funded mitigation projects? How can a community get the most use of a hazard mitigation plan and involve constituents actively in the process?

There is no shortage of technical publications on hazard mitigation, most of which are very useful, and many of which can be accessed online. However, there is a lack of guidance regarding the implementation of hazard mitigation. This text attempts to begin to address that gap. Many individuals currently involved in hazard mitigation have little to no formal training in the field beyond that provided by the various technical publications that outline potential measures. These professionals come from a wide variety of backgrounds, including engineering, planning, sociology, public administration, business, and so on. Often, hazard mitigation is only one of the many different roles that they play in their community or place of employment, and may be one of the least-related to their previous formal training.

As a result of the above, we felt that there was a need for a text that can assist these professionals in better understanding hazard mitigation conceptually, beyond potential measures and federal funding requirements. There is a need for practitioners to be able to better educate themselves in the value and potential of mitigation, as well as how to convince others of that value and how to better

involve the community and avoid one-size-fits-all answers to unique local situations. As academic institutions begin to focus more on emergency management and hazard mitigation, there is also a need for a text that can provide these students with a thorough understanding of the various issues involved in hazard mitigation, along with how mitigation fits into the emergency management cycle.

This text covers a range of topics including the history of hazard mitigation, how to involve the public in mitigation planning, and some of the tools available to practitioners.

Chapter 1—A History of Hazard Mitigation in the United States

An overview of the history of hazard mitigation with a focus on the Disaster Mitigation Act of 2000.

Chapter 2—Mitigation and Emergency Management

An overview of where hazard mitigation fits into emergency management.

Chapter 3—Intergovernmental Relations and Hazard Mitigation

A discussion of some of the challenges that can arise in navigating the various intergovernmental relationships involved in hazard mitigation.

Chapter 4—Public–Private Partnerships in Mitigation Initiatives

Public–private partnerships can be a very useful and effective way of getting hazard mitigation done at the local level. This chapter explores some model partnerships.

Chapter 5—The Growing Role of the Private Sector in Mitigation

A discussion of the role currently played by the private sector with a look at how communities can best make use of contractors.

Chapter 6—The National Flood Insurance Program and the Community Rating System

The National Flood Insurance Program and the Community Rating System can both be very effective tools for promoting hazard mitigation. This chapter provides information on how to maximize their use.

Chapter 7—Risk Communications

Risk communications is a key component of encouraging hazard mitigation. This chapter provides a basic overview.

Chapter 8—Natural Hazards and the Law

A discussion of legal issues relevant to hazard mitigation.

Chapter 9—Involving the Community in Mitigation and Outreach

Involving the community in hazard mitigation can be a daunting challenge for emergency managers. This chapter looks at some ways to more actively engage with the community.

Chapter 10—Persuasion and Policy

A discussion of how to advocate for hazard mitigation policy.

Chapter 11—Non-FEMA Mitigation: Local Government Actions

As federal mitigation budgets are reduced, it is critical to look at ways in which local governments can promote and even fund mitigation without utilizing federal dollars. This chapter discusses hazard mitigation at the local level.

Chapter 12—State Initiatives

This chapter discusses hazard mitigation at the state level.

Chapter 13—Leveraging Nonprofit Organizations and Volunteers in Hazard Mitigation

Volunteers can be a very useful resource, but can also pose certain challenges to emergency managers. This chapter discusses how best to make use of this resource.

Chapter 14—Area Analyses

The area analysis is an innovative means of addressing flood risk at the block or neighborhood level. This chapter illustrates the process of conducting an area analysis and includes a case study.

Chapter 15—Tools for Hazard Mitigation

This chapter covers some tools that local practitioners can use.

Appendix—Compendium of Links and Resources

The Appendix includes a wide range of links and resources for additional information.

Editors

Alessandra Jerolleman, MPA, CFM, is a program specialist on the Gulf Coast with Save the Children USA. Jerolleman is also the executive director of the recently formed Natural Hazard Mitigation Association. She sits on the board of the Greater New Orleans Disaster Recovery Partnership and is the secretary for the Executive Committee of the American Society of Public Administration's Section on Emergency and Crisis Management. She was recently awarded the 2009 Petak Prize by the American Society of Public Administration for the best paper in emergency management presented in 2008. Jerolleman has acquired wide-ranging experience in the private, nonprofit, and academic sectors.

Over the past few years, she has worked with five Louisiana parishes that are participating in the Planning Pilot Grant Program. The Planning Pilot Grant Program is the first of its kind in the nation and is intended to provide communities with the funding to not only update hazard mitigation plans, but also to undertake preliminary engineering, environmental, and benefit–cost analyses to "scope" specific hazard mitigation projects. In particular, she served as the project manager and lead senior hazard mitigation planner, assisting these Louisiana parishes with mitigation project identification and scoping, as well as plan updates under the Planning Pilot Grant Program.

Jerolleman played a key role in the 2008 update of the State of Louisiana Hazard Mitigation Plan and is currently serving as project manager for the 2010 update. She has also been involved in the update of the State of Louisiana's

Hazard Mitigation Administrative Plan, as well as Louisiana's accreditation under the Emergency Management Accreditation Program. She also worked on several community college and university plans in Mississippi and Louisiana, as well as several other plan updates in the State of Louisiana.

Jerolleman has also worked with six New Jersey counties on hazard mitigation project identification, as well as plan review, the City of Tulsa's Hazard Mitigation Plan, and the 2009 Update of the Polk County, Iowa Hazard Mitigation Plan. She recently worked on the University of Louisiana Disaster Resistant University Plan, the Chatham County, Georgia Hazard Mitigation Plan Update, the Mississippi State Plan Update, and the Alamo Area Council of Governments Hazard Mitigation Plan Update in Texas.

In previous positions, she has conducted applied research related to mitigation, community outreach, and disaster planning with select Louisiana communities and for the University of New Orleans. She has been involved in crafting and delivering the community outreach in both Jefferson and Orleans parishes related to the Hazard Mitigation Grant Program. Jerolleman played a key role in the development of the University of New Orleans Hazard Mitigation Plan and served as the coordinator for several area analyses in suburban New Orleans neighborhoods with severe repetitive losses. Additionally, she has assisted on Repetitive Flood Loss Area Analyses at the Center for Hazards Assessment, Response and Technology in New Orleans, Louisiana, and the Disaster Resistant University Project at the University of New Orleans.

John J. Kiefer, PhD, is an associate professor and director, MPA Program in the Department of Political Science at the University of New Orleans (UNO). He is also a faculty associate at the Center for Hazards Assessment, Response and Technology, UNO's applied hazards social science research center. In his applied research, Dr. Kiefer specializes in the development of outcome-focused collaborative networks to create disaster resilience, especially focused on vulnerable populations. He is currently either principal investigator or a research team member for several projects that include elderly evacuation, technology initiatives for vulnerable populations, repetitive flood loss mitigation, and a disaster resilient university project. He has been principal evaluator for a broad range of programs funded by the U.S. Department of Education, State of Louisiana, and several cities. He has delivered numerous papers and chaired panels at professional meetings in the United States and Canada. John is past president of the Section on Emergency and Crisis Management of the American Society for Public Administration. His current research interests include hazard policy, emergency management, and program evaluation.

Contributors

Robert Anderson is a senior engineering geologist at the Alfred E. Alquist (California) Seismic Safety Commission in Sacramento, California. He is a licensed geologist and certified engineering geologist in California. Anderson provides advice to the governor, legislators, and the public on issues related to seismic safety. He serves on the California Multi-Hazard Mitigation Plan development team and has been active in the development of the seismic hazards portion of the plan since its inception. His emphasis on seismic safety issues is focused on seismic and tsunami hazard and loss reduction to the built environment, including energy infrastructure, ports, and harbors. His main areas of interest are in earthquake forecasting, earthquake and tsunami early warning, and loss reduction from natural hazards. He also helps to monitor and coordinate advanced applied earthquake research and mitigation among the California Earthquake Authority, the Commission, and the seismic hazard, earthquake engineering research, emergency management, and insurance communities.

Prior to joining the commission, Anderson worked on natural hazard and resource issues for power plants, landfill design, residential and commercial developments, and faulting and landslide hazard assessments. During his 25 years as a geologist, he has worked in California, Oregon, Washington, Nevada, Alaska, Turkey, Taiwan, Mexico, the Republic of South Africa, Kyrgyzstan, and the Republic of Indonesia and Jamaica. He has a BA in geology from California State University, Sacramento, and an MS in homeland security from San Diego State University.

Frances L. Edwards is director of the Master of Public Administration Program, professor in the political science department at San Jose State University, and Deputy Director of the DHS National Transportation Security Center of Excellence at the Mineta Transportation Institute. Her main research interests are emergency management, terrorism, transportation security, and public policy development and implementation. Her work has been published in the *Journal of Contingencies and Crisis Management, Public Administration Review, Administration & Society, State and Local Government Review,* and *The Public Manager.* She teaches emergency management, public policy, and introduction to public administration. She was the director of emergency preparedness for the city of San Jose, California, and the emergency services manager for Irvine, California, and a member of the California Seismic Safety Commission.

Tammy Barnett Esteves, PhD, brings both practical and academic experience to the field of public administration. She received her BA in American government from the University of Virginia and has an MPA from James Madison University and a PhD in public administration and public affairs from Virginia Tech. She is currently a full-time faculty member with Troy University's MPA program and is also active with the United States Coast Guard Auxiliary, where she volunteers in the area of contingency preparedness. She is very active in the American Society for Public Administration (ASPA), where she serves on the boards of the Section on Democracy and Social Justice and of the Section on Emergency and Crisis Management. She is also on the board for the ASPA Evergreen chapter in Seattle/Tacoma. Her main research interests are in the areas of sustainability in communities, particularly, how it is impacted by social justice and disasters, and the role played by social media (crisis informatics).

Monica Farris, PhD, is an associate professor of research and the director of the Center for Hazards Assessment, Response and Technology at the University of New Orleans (UNO). She earned her MA from Louisiana State University and PhD from UNO, both in political science, the latter with a public administration/public policy specialization. Her current applied research focuses on education and outreach emphasizing mitigation. She has published on the subject of building internal capacity for disaster resilience and has presented multiple times on hazard risk reduction and disaster planning.

Vener Garayev, PhD, is an assistant professor in the Department of Political Science and Public Administration at Gediz University, Izmir, Turkey. His main research interests are emergency and crisis management, decision making under uncertainty, collaborative governance, and networks. His work has been published in *Public Administration Review, Journal of Emergency Management and Homeland Security,* and the *International Journal of Public Administration.*

Daniel C. Goodrich is a research associate at the Mineta Transportation Institute. He has also worked for emergency management offices at the city, county, and private sector levels and has ten years of active duty military experience in security forces. His research interests are emergency management, transportation security, and terrorism. He also teaches transportation security at MTI.

Jerry V. Graves, Jr., is the chief administrative officer for St. Bernard Parish, a coastal Louisiana community still recovering from Hurricane Katrina. He is a founding member of the Natural Hazard Mitigation Association and is a Certified Floodplain Manager. Graves is PhD candidate at the University of New Orleans (UNO) and previously earned an MPA from UNO and a BA in political science from the University of Louisiana at Lafayette.

Naim Kapucu, PhD, is an associate professor and founding director of the Center for Public and Nonprofit Management in the School of Public Administration at the University of Central Florida. His main research interests are emergency and crisis management, decision making in complex environments, collaborative governance, and organizational learning and design. His work has been published in *Public Administration Review, Journal of Public Administration Research and Theory, Administration & Society, American Review of Public Administration, Public Administration, International Journal of Mass Emergencies and Disasters*, and *Disasters: The Journal of Disaster Studies, Policy, and Management.* He teaches public and nonprofit management, emergency and crisis management, and analytic techniques for public administration courses.

Richard L. Krajeski has served the Presbyterian Church and the ecumenical community as an ordained pastor for over 40 years and the disaster response community for 30 years. He spent 40 years as a pastor in the mountains of Kentucky and West Virginia and now lives and works in the delta area of Southern Louisiana—all places of "economic, environmental, and human extraction."

His disaster-related publication coauthored with his wife Kristina Peterson titled "'But She Is a Woman and This Is a Man's Job': Lessons for Participatory Research and Participatory Recovery" appeared in the *International Journal of Mass Emergencies and Disasters.* He has written a chapter "The Big Thompson Flood: Twenty Years Later" in the journal *Church and Society*, a chapter in a recently published *Women and Disasters: From Theory to Practice*, and "Women of Faith" in *The Women of Katrina.* Krajeski was awarded the Disaster Response Meritorious Service Award by Church World Service (CWS) in 1999 for his work in developing the long-term response of the religious community and his advocacy with marginalized people. He has been elected a fellow in the International Society for Applied Anthropology.

Krajeski was a founding member of the International Gender and Disaster Network and a founding member and board member of the Natural Hazard

Mitigation Association. He does policy and program analysis with the Center for Hazard Analysis Response and Technology at the University of New Orleans.

Mary V. McCarthy is a native of the Washington, DC area. She earned her BA degree in history from the University of Mary Washington in Fredericksburg, Virginia, in 2006 by writing her thesis on Michael Collins' role in Ireland's independence from Britain in the early twentieth century. She worked briefly at the Coalition for Smarter Growth, a DC-area nonprofit organization advocating for smart growth in regional planning, before moving to the Virginia-based American Waterways Operators (AWO) in September 2006. At AWO, she served as manager of government affairs, advocating for the national tugboat, towboat, and barge industry. Four years later, she was accepted into the Masters in Public Administration Program at the University of New Orleans, where she expects to graduate on the Hazard Policy track in May 2013. Mary currently works for Canal Barge Company, working in communications and regulatory affairs.

Erin Patton Merrick received her BA from Louisiana State University in 2007 and her MA from the University of New Orleans in 2009. In 2010, she became a Certified Floodplain Manager through the Association of State Floodplain Managers. Erin has been working with the University of New Orleans' Center for Hazards Assessment, Response and Technology on their Repetitive Loss Project since 2008. She has extensive experience working with local officials and resident leadership in communities in the process of completing Repetitive Loss Area Analyses.

Betty Hearn Morrow, PhD, is professor emeritus at Florida International University and former director of the Laboratory for Social and Behavioral Research at the International Hurricane Research Center. Her focus on the effects of human and social factors on the ability of individuals, families, and communities to respond to hazards is reflected in *Human Links to Coastal Disasters* published by the Heinz Center for Science, Economics, and the Environment. She is the coeditor of *The Gendered Terrain of Disaster* and, more recently, coeditor of *Women and Disasters*. She was part of a team of social scientists who analyzed the effects of Hurricane Andrew on South Florida, funded by the National Science Foundation and resulting in the coauthored book, *Hurricane Andrew: Ethnicity, Gender and the Sociology of Disaster*. She was the 2003 recipient of the Mary Fran Myers Award from the Gender and Disaster Network. Retired from academia, she continues an active research agenda as a consulting sociologist, primarily focusing on issues related to risk communication (warning messages in particular), household response to hazards, evacuation behavior, social vulnerability, and community resilience.

Dorothy Norris-Tirrell, PhD, is a professor, researcher, and consultant in the areas of nonprofit organization governance, volunteerism, university–community partnerships, and cross-sector collaboration in a variety of policy areas including community resilience. She currently teaches at the School of Public Administration, University of Central Florida. Her research is published in the book, *Strategic Collaboration in Public and Nonprofit Administration*, and in book chapters and journals such as *Policy Studies Journal*, *American Review of Public Administration, International Journal of Public Administration*, and the *Journal of Health and Human Services Administration*. She has extensive experience as a nonprofit agency manager, board member, consultant, and volunteer. She received her PhD in public administration from Florida International University.

Maggie Olivier, MA, CFM, is a full-time research associate at the University of New Orleans' Center for Hazards Assessment, Response and Technology. She earned her BA from the University of Louisiana at Lafayette and MA from the University of New Orleans, both in sociology, the latter with a focus on disaster studies. Maggie has two years of experience writing Repetitive Loss Area Analyses. Her current applied research includes projects geared toward community education and outreach around hazard mitigation. She is also recognized as a Certified Floodplain Manager by the Association of State Floodplain Managers.

Ann Patton is a Tulsa-based consultant and author with 45 years of experience in local program management, consulting, and writing about community affairs issues. A former *Tulsa World* reporter, Patton has worked across a broad spectrum of issues, from disaster management to social justice. National clients have included federal agencies and nongovernmental organizations.

She is the founding director of award-winning local programs in Tulsa, including Tulsa Project Impact, Tulsa Citizen Corps, and Tulsa Partners, Inc. She also volunteers on national and local boards and policy committees. Her focus is on helping create whole communities that are resilient, disaster resistant, sustainable, and committed to justice.

Patton just published her second book, entitled *Dan's War on Poverty: A Grassroots Crusade for Social Justice*. This nonfiction book recounts the story of a crusading priest who fought for the poor in the 1960s. Her first book, *Fifty Years Remembered*, is an illustrated coffee table book recounting the history of water resources in this region. She is working on a third book, *Unmasked! The Rise and Fall of the 1920s Ku Klux Klan*. She has also authored hundreds of articles, technical reports, and other publications.

Inés Pearce, chief executive of Pearce Global Partners (PGP), launched PGP with the dream of a disaster-resistant world. Her vision is to increase each community's capacity to address its local hazards through developing partnerships, creating

solutions, and building/enhancing relationships. This vision is called Community Legacy®. As no one sector of any community has all the resources necessary to fully minimize its risk, each sector must be tethered to the other in order that lives can be saved, property damage lessened, and economies protected. Through shared information and the application of the best available science, PGP works with clients to create and develop best practices to enable "Education into Action."

Kristina J. Peterson, PhD, has had a lifetime of professional and academic work based in citizen participation for problem solving as it pertains to reducing social and environmental vulnerability and increasing sustainability especially following disasters. The current emphasis of her work is with traditional and indigenous Louisiana coastal high-risk communities. Peterson is a founding member and has served on the International Steering Committee for the Gender and Disaster Network. She was also a founding board member of the National Hazards Mitigation Association.

Peterson received the 2010 William Gibson Award for Individual Leadership in Environmental Justice, was elected a Fellow in the International Society for Applied Anthropology in 2003, and received a Maryland State Legislature Honor in 1990 for community and social development in response to multiple plant closures in Western Maryland. She is a member of APA, AMS, NHMA, IASC, IAEM, SFAA, and ISA and regularly participates in the Natural Hazard Workshop. She is a senior research associate at the Center for Hazards Assessment Response and Technology at the University of New Orleans.

Edward A. Thomas, Esq., is the president of the Natural Hazard Mitigation Association and is the chair of the Hazards Sub-Committee of the Land Use Planning and Zoning Committee and American Bar Association Section of State and Local Government Law. He also serves on the Advisory Committee of the Natural Hazards Center of the University of Colorado. He is a former board member of the Association of State Floodplain Managers and now serves as the liaison for that organization on the No Adverse Impact Committee. He is employed by the Michael Baker Jr., Inc. Engineering Corporation, working on the development of partnerships to better map natural and man-made hazards in the United States. He retired from the Department of Homeland Security-Federal Emergency Management Agency after nearly 35 years of public service. During his time in government, he worked primarily in disaster mitigation, preparedness, and response. He also was involved in the construction and management of housing developments for the Department of Housing and Urban Development. He worked on about 200 disasters and emergencies, serving as the President's on-scene representative, the Federal Coordinating Officer, dozens of times.

French Wetmore is the president of French & Associates, a floodplain management consulting firm. Prior to consulting, French was chief of Local Floodplain Programs for the Illinois Division of Water Resources and State Flood Insurance Coordinator, 1976–1988. Before his state work, he was a city administrator. French's consulting projects include assisting communities with their floodplain management ordinances and administration, preparing mitigation plans and programs, and helping to design and administer the Community Rating System. He is the author of several guides for local officials, floodproofing handbooks, and planning references. He has served as chair of the Association of State Floodplain Managers (1985–1987), president of the Certification Board of Regents (2001–2004), and on the board of directors for the Illinois Association for Floodplain and Stormwater Management (1989–2007). French has a BA in government from Indiana University (1968) and an MPA from Syracuse University (1972).

Chapter 1

A History of Hazard Mitigation in the United States

Mary V. McCarthy and John J. Kiefer

Contents

Learning Objectives

- The reader will be able to trace the evolution of hazard mitigation in the United States.
- The reader will be able to correctly define the concept and scope of "mitigation."
- The reader will be able to understand the significant extent to which effective mitigation efforts depend on functional and effective intergovernmental relationships.

Introduction

Human beings are becoming more vulnerable to catastrophic disasters due to both an increase in population and the resultant need to find places to settle, which leads to the development of disaster-prone areas (Mileti and Peek-Gottschlich 2001). In the past 50 years alone, natural disasters have increased threefold, leading to the rapid multiplication of disaster losses (Handmer and Dovers 2007). Because of this, mitigation of disasters has become a crucial activity to protect people, property, and the economy (Burby 1998). Today, Americans look mostly to the government to protect them from disasters (Birkland 2006).

This was not always the case. The set of federal disaster mitigation policies we currently have in place is the result of 150 years of lessons learned from successes and failures, and subsequent policy development. Gaining a full appreciation for this historical context is invaluable for teaching emergency managers, legislators, and policymakers what has worked, what has not, and why, so that they can continue to create and refine mitigation policies to best protect their constituents.

What Is Mitigation?

There are almost as many definitions of "disaster mitigation" as there are types of disasters, but three common themes emerge from such definitions: For one, the mitigation of disasters is a sustained and ongoing event unlike disaster relief, which is a short-term event (Haddow et al. 2008). Second, mitigation is designed to lessen or diminish the negative impacts of a disaster on people, property, and the economy (Birkland 2006; Clary 1985). Finally, mitigation is a strategic activity that involves identifying the specific risks posed by disasters and developing policies to alleviate them (Bogard 1988; Sylves 2008).

There are four phases of emergency management: (1) preparedness, (2) response, (3) recovery, and (4) mitigation (Peek and Mileti 2002). Many believe that mitigation is the foundation of emergency management because

of its long-term and strategic focus (Clary 1985; Haddow et al. 2008; Sylves 2008). Nonetheless, these four stages are interrelated and all of them are focused on loss reduction (Clary 1985; Peek and Mileti 2002).

Mitigation should not be confused with preparedness, which simply prepares a community for the shorter-term functional stages of response and recovery (Haddow et al. 2008). According to the Federal Emergency Management Agency (FEMA), mitigation "focuses on breaking the cycle of disaster damage, reconstruction, and repeated damage," and it results in safer communities, faster recovery from a disaster, and saved resources (FEMA 2011). The saved resources include a significant return on investment: According to the National Institute of Building Service's Multihazard Mitigation Council, three FEMA hazard mitigation grant programs implemented between 1993 and 2003 resulted in $4 in savings for every $1 spent, resulting in $14 billion in benefits (MMC 2005).

Although the foundation of emergency management is mitigation, the cornerstone of mitigation is policies. According to Clary (1985), mitigation regulation is "the attempt by government to mitigate hazards through comprehensive planning requirements, zoning, building codes, and other forms of control" (p. 25). It is important to remember that citizens expect their government officials "to learn from disasters and to prevent repeat disasters" through policies aimed at fixing mistakes, closing gaps, and making improvements to processes and structures (Birkland 2006, p. 29).

There are many obstacles to sound mitigation. Government officials are often hamstrung by the need to provide immediate relief; budget restrictions; and the inevitable shift in focus to other, more urgent issues (Birkland 2006). Real estate and insurance markets can not only prevent mitigation policies from being enacted but also promote ways of rebuilding that actually make a community more vulnerable to disaster (Platt 1998). For example, after the Oakland, California fire of 1991, various policies allowed homes to be rebuilt larger than before in the same patterns that had contributed to the quick spread of the fire and the difficulty of evacuating (Platt 1998).

Hazard Mitigation as an Intergovernmental Policy

All levels of government are involved in the development and implementation of hazard mitigation policy, and these levels of government, often involving multiple agencies, are interdependent (Petak and Atkisson 1982). For example, the U.S. Army Corps of Engineers builds levees to protect communities from flooding, and it in turn relies on the U.S. Geological Survey for maps identifying the best places for building those levees (Petak and Atkisson 1982). The private and nonprofit sectors also have roles to play in hazard mitigation, and these sectors are intertwined with the government

entities responsible for formulating the disaster policy (Petak and Atkisson 1982). Mitigation activities are usually initiated at the federal level, but both states and localities are responsible for implementing these measures and many take the initiative to enact their own policies to protect their communities (Clary 1985).

One important note is as follows: Mitigation policies do not always achieve their goal of lessening the impact of a disaster. One reason is that mitigation cannot remove all disaster risk, although, unfortunately, some people assume that it can (Burby 1998). For example, structural forms of mitigation, such as levees, do not offer full flood protection, although home and business owners often assume that they do and settle in areas that could be hazardous (Burby 1998). Sometimes, mitigation policies effective in some areas can cause harm in other areas (Burby 1998). Continuing with the levee example, such structures can have environmental consequences (such as loss of wetlands) and can even cause a community to become vulnerable to disaster in other ways (without wetlands to absorb floodwaters, a flood can inundate the communities that the levees were designed to protect (Burby 1998). Some mitigation initiatives, such as canals and levees, split or cross traditional neighborhood boundaries, resulting in weakened neighborhood identity and a commensurate loss of community social capital. This in turn serves to increase the vulnerability of affected communities, particularly those that are made up largely of poor and minority populations.

Fortunately, evidence suggests that government officials learn from past events and mistakes and subsequently develop more effective mitigation policies (see Figure 1.1) (Birkland 2006). Another heartening factor is that

FIGURE 1.1 Photograph of the seawall construction site, Galveston, Texas (ca. 1909–1915): It could be argued that Galveston, Texas, undertook one of the biggest mitigation projects in U.S. history by erecting its great seawall in the wake of the Galveston hurricane in 1900. (Courtesy of Wikipedia Commons.)

lawmakers and policymakers increasingly see mitigation as a way to reduce disaster relief and recovery costs; therefore, it has found its way into more and more hazard policies (Birkland 2006; Platt 1998).

Next, we examine the history of mitigation in federal disaster policy. We clearly trace the evolution of mitigation in the United States along with showing the successes and failures of various government policies in reducing the risks and impacts of disasters. Understanding the history provides an important foundation for subsequent improvement of mitigation policies and their goal of protecting communities from the hazards they will inevitably experience.

Early History: Flood Policy before the 1936 Flood Control Act

Mitigation has a long history, not only in the United States but also in other regions of the world. One could argue that mitigation began with Noah building his ark to survive the biblical flood (Platt 1998). We will start our study from a somewhat more recent period. In the United States, disaster policy began soon after the country was formed, when Congress passed a bill in 1803 to provide relief to a New Hampshire town that was decimated by a fire (Haddow et al. 2008). Yet, mitigation policy in the United States did not begin to develop for another half a century. In 1861, two engineers, Henry Abbot and Andrew Humphries, published a report that advocated for a system of levees to keep the Mississippi River from periodically rising over its banks and flooding the surrounding areas; Congress eventually discarded other flood control proposals on the table to implement this "levees only" policy (Arnold 1988). (John Barry's formative book, *Rising Tide*, outlines the full history behind this decision and should be regarded as required reading for anyone who seeks to understand the evolution of hazard mitigation in the United States.) Since 1825 the organizations that would eventually become the U.S. Army Corps of Engineers have been granted the authority to conduct waterways improvement projects, but those were primarily focused on navigation and not flood control (Arnold 1988; Platt 1998).

One of the few non-flood-related hazard mitigation policies from this era stemmed from the devastating 1906 San Francisco, California, earthquake and resultant fire. It was America's worst urban natural disaster until Hurricane Katrina hit New Orleans, Louisiana, in 2005, and the 1906 disaster was marked by a collapse of San Francisco's critical infrastructure, including the water supply (Platt 1998). Following the disaster, the main mitigatory measure implemented was the development of an outside source of water, created by damming the Hetch Hetchy Valley (Platt 1998). However, similar to many mitigation measures that were implemented

after it, the dam raised both environmental concerns and the possibility that vulnerability was actually increased as it could fail in the event of another earthquake (Platt 1998). Unfortunately, hazard mitigation was not a concern when the city was rebuilt; not only did the city decide not to alter its pre-earthquake/-fire land-use and building policies but it also built on top of the rubble of the destroyed buildings, which made those structures even more vulnerable to damage during later earthquakes (Platt 1998). This is a good example of the all-too-common propensity of communities to fail to implement critical mitigation measures in the wake of disasters.

The catastrophic flooding of the American Midwest and South in 1927 led Congress to abandon its ineffective levees only policy and explore a wide range of engineering techniques to mitigate Mississippi River flood hazards (Platt 1998). The next year, Congress passed the Mississippi Flood Control Act, which authorized a number of flood mitigation projects using some alternative techniques, including dams, flood storage, channels, and floodways (Arnold 1988; Platt 1998). This illustrated the newfound importance that Congress and the nation placed on flood mitigation (Arnold 1988; Platt 1998). In the 1930s, dams began to be built, including the Hoover Dam between Arizona and Nevada, and the Grand Coulee Dam in Washington State, thanks to funds and workers provided by President Franklin D. Roosevelt's New Deal policies (Platt 1998). Another New Deal initiative was the creation of the Tennessee Valley Authority (TVA), whose projects included flood mitigation programs such as the management of river main stem systems, multipurpose reservoirs, and floodplain management (Arnold 1988; Platt 1998). According to Platt (1998), TVA's programs illustrated for the first time that flood mitigation policies and regional economic development could go hand in hand.

The Flood Control Act of 1936

Flooding in 1936 in the Northeast and the Ohio Valley prompted Congress to build on the 1928 Mississippi Flood Control Act and develop measures to mitigate flood hazards nationwide by enacting the Flood Control Act (Arnold 1988; Platt 1998). The bill marked the beginning of a federal movement toward structural projects designed to mitigate both the likelihood that floods will occur and flood damage to property (Clary 1985; Haddow et al. 2008). The authority for designing and creating these projects was given to the U.S. Army Corps of Engineers who also became responsible for "softer" mitigation strategies, such as advising states and localities on floodplain and flood hazard issues (Petak and Atkisson 1982). In order to illustrate the key role played by the Corps in this flood

mitigation policy, consider the following: In the first 18 years of the program, Congress allocated $11.1 billion for flood control 90% of which went directly to the corps (Platt 1998).

According to Haddow et al. (2008), the 1934 Flood Control Act "reflected a philosophy that humans could control nature, thereby eliminating the risk of floods" (p. 2). However, the bill has been criticized for its narrow focus on structural mitigation technologies (Clary 1985). As noted earlier, these structures permanently modify the environment, which can change the risks posed by disasters instead of reducing them (Clary 1985). Furthermore, traditional structural mitigation projects are extremely expensive and have been criticized for not being cost-effective in reducing the costly impacts of floods (Haddow et al. 2008). What cannot be disputed is that the 1936 Flood Control Act had a major impact on disaster mitigation policy in the United States. The Corps' work today is a direct result of the mandates in this seminal legislation.

Years 1937–1965: Federal Policy Pays Little Attention to Mitigation

During the early to mid-twentieth century, the federal government paid little attention to enacting measures to mitigate the impact of disasters. Still, the government did not completely abandon the concept of mitigation as an important disaster policy; there were a handful of developments worth noting that took place during this time.

In 1938, Congress passed another flood control act mandating full federal funding for all northern dams, reservoirs, and channel improvements but required levees to be funded by localities (Arnold 1988; Platt 1988). In 1950, nonstructural mitigation strategies caught the attention of federal legislators and policymakers in a report by the Water Resources Policy Commission, which was created by President Harry S. Truman (Burby 1998). The report recommended mitigating the risk of flood damage through land-use planning and zoning, which, instead of trying to control where flooding occurred, attempted to control how close to flood-prone areas people were allowed to settle, as well as to make buildings damage-resistant (Burby 1998). In 1955, various hurricanes and floods nationwide prompted the passage of the Federal Flood Insurance Act in 1956, but no money was ever appropriated to implement it, due to both disagreements with insurance agencies and concerns over the effectiveness of its programs (Petak and Atkisson 1982).

In the 1950s, the federal government also began a program of producing manuals to train state and local governments, as well as the general citizenry, about how to locate and design buildings to mitigate the chances that they would be damaged by floods (Burby 1998). The 1950s also saw an increase in the use of floodplain management through land-use planning

thanks to a mapping and information program initiated by the then head of the TVA, James E. Goddard (Platt 1998).

In the following decade, as emergency management was beginning to be recognized as its own discipline, the National Governors Association commissioned a study that identified the four main elements of disaster management: (1) preparedness, (2) response, (3) recovery, and (4) mitigation (Haddow et al. 2008). However, despite its inclusion in the report, mitigation was not widely recognized as important for decades even after the mitigation-focused National Flood Insurance Program (NFIP) was launched later in the 1960s (Haddow et al. 2008).

In the early 1960s, the federal government tried an interesting spin on hurricane mitigation: It conducted experiments on how to physically weaken hurricanes by "seeding" the outer clouds with silver iodide (Willoughby et al. 1985). The project partially stemmed from Project Cirrus in 1947, but it was discontinued in the 1980s after questions arose over its effectiveness (Willoughby et al. 1985).

In the 1960s, two other events occurred that spurred future hazard mitigation legislation. First, in 1964, a large earthquake hit Alaska. This spurred President Lyndon B. Johnson to create the Federal Reconstruction and Development Planning Commission, which eventually led to the 1977 Earthquake Hazards Reduction Act (to be discussed later in this chapter) (Birkland 2006). Second, in 1965, Congress commissioned a study of alternatives to structural flood control and disaster assistance (Platt 1998). Two resultant reports, one written by Marion Clawson and the other written by Gilbert F. White (the father of floodplain management), recommended the creation of a national flood insurance program based on land-use planning and building codes (Platt 1998). This helped to set the stage for the passage of the 1968 National Flood Insurance Act, a pivotal piece of hazard mitigation legislation.

The 1968 National Flood Insurance Act

Hurricanes in the 1950s and 1960s, including Hurricane Betsy in 1965, which caused severe damage in Florida and Louisiana, combined with the Clawson and White reports, prompted Congress to pass the National Flood Insurance Act in 1968 (Petak and Atkisson 1982; Platt 1998). Championed by Congressman Hale Boggs (D-LA), the bill established the first (and best known) true federal disaster mitigation policy in the United States, that is, the NFIP (Birkland 2006; Petak and Atkisson 1982). As Haddow et al. (2008) put it, it was the first federal disaster bill that "sought to do something about risk before disaster struck." It also marked the beginning of federal involvement in land use and planning on private land (Petak and Atkisson 1982).

The purpose of NFIP was to solve problems associated with development in floodplains, and it had three objectives: (1) to limit home and business

development in flood-prone areas, (2) to distribute some flood loss burdens to all inhabitants of flood-prone areas, and (3) to create maps of floodplains (Petak and Atkisson 1982; Platt 1998). With the NFIP, for the first time, the federal government "linked the prevention of future floods with the availability of disaster recovery funds, in the form of flood insurance for insurance for individual property owners" (Clary 1985, p. 21). The NFIP used the concept of "community-based mitigation" to support local action on flood control by providing localities with subsidized flood insurance and helping them to create floodplain maps (Haddow et al. 2008). In return, communities were required to limit development in flood-prone areas (Haddow et al. 2008). This was done by requiring buildings located in floodplains to pay higher insurance premiums (Petak and Atkisson 1982). Thus, mitigation was achieved by lessening the likelihood that structures would be in the way of a flood in the first place (Petak and Atkisson 1982).

Although the creation of the NFIP was a formative moment in the history of disaster mitigation policy in the United States, the program is not without its flaws. As originally written, the NFIP was voluntary, which meant that only a handful of localities chose to participate in it during the first few years (Petak and Atkisson 1982). Furthermore, there was little research available on floodplains in communities at the time, which hampered the setting of insurance rates for those communities and made it impossible for many communities to participate in the program (Petak and Atkisson 1982). In 1969, Congress amended the NFIP to allow participating communities to receive discounted flood insurance while the research was being conducted, but this move did not measurably increase involvement (Petak and Atkisson 1982). Another criticism of the NFIP was that it delegated responsibility to local planning departments, which fragmented the process, calling its efficiency and effectiveness into question (Haddow et al. 2008). Finally, some argue that the NFIP is flawed in that it allows for rebuilding in high-risk, flood-prone areas. The result is increased community vulnerability, which can often run counter to the principles of mitigation (Platt 1998).

The Early 1970s: Feds Make State Grant Money Contingent on Mitigation

The early 1970s were marked by new requirements that made federal disaster aid to states and localities contingent on the implementation of local mitigation measures. First, reflecting the nationwide growth of the environmental protection movement, Congress passed the 1972 Coastal Zone Management Act (CZMA) (May and Deyle 1998). The CZMA provided coastal management grants to states as long as they submitted plans for land and development management that took floodplains and flood damage risk into account (Petak and Atkisson 1982). In 1976, the Act was expanded to require coastal

states receiving aid to submit erosion plans as well (Petak and Atkisson 1982). Overall, CZMA signaled a shift toward local responsibility for land-use planning in a way that mitigated hazards (Clary 1985).

Second, Hurricane Agnes's landfall on the East Coast in 1972 and resultant damage propelled Congress into making NFIP mandatory (Haddow et al. 2008; Platt 1998). The purpose of the 1973 Flood Disaster Protection Act was to reduce federal and private expenditures for disaster relief, which is, at its heart, mitigation (Petak and Atkisson 1982). The bill required any community receiving federal disaster aid to participate in NFIP and establish ordinances restricting development in flood-prone areas (Platt 1998). Also, the bill required the federal government to identify flood-prone communities and required those communities to either participate in NFIP or prove that they were not flood-prone (Petak and Atkisson 1982). Furthermore, any citizen borrowing money from a lender affiliated with the federal government for a home in a flood zone was required to purchase flood insurance (Platt 1998).

As expected, this bill dramatically increased participation in NFIP; however, some criticized the new program's mandatory penalties as being too harsh (Platt 1998; Petak and Atkisson 1982). In 1977, the bill was amended to eliminate the prohibition of federally insured lending institutions from making loans to homeowners in flood-prone areas that did not participate in NFIP (Petak and Atkisson 1982). It was replaced with a requirement that lending institutions notify lending recipients who did not participate in NFIP that they were not eligible for federal disaster relief should a flood occur (Petak and Atkisson 1982). Also in 1977, President Jimmy Carter further strengthened flood hazard policy by requiring each federal agency to identify and implement ways to minimize national losses to floods and maximize the value of floodplains (Petak and Atkisson 1982).

Another way through which the federal government linked state aid to the implementation of mitigation policies was the 1974 Disaster Relief Act. This legislation acknowledged the need for more mitigation measures and encouraged them by requiring any state or locality receiving federal disaster assistance to identify hazards and develop ways to mitigate those hazards (Sylves 2008). However, not many states obeyed this requirement until the federal government started filing lawsuits in the early 1980s against non-compliant jurisdictions (most notably, Jefferson Parish and St. Bernard Parish in Louisiana) (Clary 1985).

The Late 1970s: Earthquake Hazards Reduction Act and FEMA

Another federal law that recognized the importance of natural disaster mitigation was the Earthquake Hazards Reduction Act of 1977, which established the National Earthquake Hazards Reduction Program (NEHRP)

(Haddow et al. 2008). The bill explicitly called for the mitigation of the risk of earthquake damage to life and property through both research on earthquakes and new building codes (Haddow et al. 2008). Interestingly, part of this research was dedicated to the question of how to actually predict earthquakes after a 1975 earthquake in China was accurately predicted, spurring an evacuation that saved thousands of people (Birkland 2006). However, research on earthquake prediction was not subsequently translated to earthquake mitigation policies (Birkland 2006). Some criticized FEMA (which became responsible for NEHRP after FEMA's creation in the following year) for unnecessarily delaying its evaluation of earthquake hazards to be used to develop mitigation policies (Clary 1985; Platt 1998). Two decades later, this was still the case: In 1993, the former head of the Federal Insurance Administration, George Bernstein, publically reported that the program was ineffective and inadequate due to its voluntary nature (Petak and Atkisson 1982).

The closing of the 1970s marked another watershed moment for U.S. disaster policy when, in 1978, President Carter sent Reorganization Plan Number 3 to Congress, which proposed combining the disparate emergency management functions, scattered throughout several federal agencies, into one single organization, that is, FEMA (Haddow et al. 2008). One of President Carter's goals for FEMA was that it would "incorporate federal hazard mitigation activities, linked with state and local activities, into preparedness and response activities" (Sylves 2008, p. 56). Congress accepted Reorganization Plan Number 3, after which Executive Order 12127 formally established the agency, whereas Executive Order 12148 outlined the reorganization (Haddow et al. 2008). John Macy was FEMA's first director and he immediately created the integrated emergency management system (IEMS) concept, which was an "all hazards" approach (Haddow et al. 2008). Although FEMA was not initially as focused on mitigation as one might argue it should be, its creation as an agency responsible for all federal emergency management activities was a major step in the history of U.S. hazard mitigation policy.

Lead-up to the 1988 Stafford Act

In the 1980s, the federal government continued the trend toward greater recognition of the importance of hazard mitigation. The focus on flood hazards also grew with a 1980 requirement by the Office of Management and Budget (OMB) that federal agencies must further explore ways to mitigate flood losses (Platt 1998). In addition, the 1982 Coastal Barrier Resources Act was enacted to mitigate flood damage on barrier islands (May and Deyle 1998). The bill strongly disincentivized the construction of new structures on barrier islands by making them ineligible for flood insurance (May and Deyle

1998). Furthermore, FEMA's Unified Program for Floodplain Management, which was initiated in 1986, set objectives to reduce flood losses and established methods to achieve those objectives (Sylves 2008). Finally, the agency's community rating system, initiated in the late 1980s, continued the trend of offering incentives to communities for not developing floodplains (May and Deyle 1998).

In the 1980s, the growing appreciation of the need to implement mitigation measures was challenged by the property rights movement. This movement opposed government regulations limiting development on private property, including restrictions to mitigate the risk of disaster damage to buildings, as well as government "taking" of private land in disaster-prone areas (Platt 1998). In 1987, the property rights movement achieved a win from the Supreme Court who ruled in *First English Lutheran Evangelical Church v. County of Los Angeles* that property owners could receive damages if they were wrongly restricted from developing their land by the government (Platt 1998). The property rights movement continues to serve as a counterpoint to the mitigation movement to this day (Platt 1998).

However, the mitigation movement won a victory with the passage of the Stafford Act in 1988. This bill established the Hazard Mitigation Grant Program (HMGP), which was the "largest source of funding for state and local mitigation activities" at the time (Haddow et al. 2008, p. 84). Specifically, HMGP provided 10% of money given to states and localities for aid after a presidential disaster declaration for disaster mitigation programs, as long as they prepared a long-term mitigation plan in accordance with section 409 of the legislation (Birkland 2006; Sylves 2008). Also, the legislation allowed owners of flood-prone properties to sell them to the federal government (Birkland 2006).

Unfortunately, for the first 6 years of its existence, HMGP was not utilized by most states due to widespread state fiscal troubles (Haddow et al. 2008). That hurdle was overcome after the devastating 1993 Midwest floods, which prompted Congress to change the cost-sharing ratio (to be discussed later in this chapter) (Haddow et al. 2008). In addition, the mitigation planning requirements under section 409 were discovered to have "little relationship between mitigation planning and actual mitigation projects," so that this section was replaced by a new planning program under the Disaster Mitigation Act of 2000 (to be addressed later in this chapter) (Birkland 2006). In 2002, the OMB recommended that HMGP be discontinued and replaced with a new pre-disaster competitive grant program; however, to date HMGP is still in effect (Haddow et al. 2008).

The Stafford Act is an important piece of legislation, not only for disasters in a general sense, but also specifically for mitigation. The act signaled FEMA's move away from its focus on the Cold War and nuclear weapons in the 1980s toward disaster mitigation, disaster relief, and the threat of human-made disasters due to the actions of "nonstate" terrorists (as opposed

to traditional warfare) (Birkland 2006). However, the act still requires that a disaster must have occurred to encourage mitigation measures, which is somewhat counterintuitive (Birkland 2006). Clearly, the best time to implement mitigation policies is before a disaster strikes.

Early 1990s: Mitigation Trends Continue

The beginning of the 1990s saw a continuation of the mitigation trends that began in the late 1980s. Overall, federal disaster policies included mitigation provisions more often than they did before the passage of the Stafford Act (Birkland 2006). For example, in 1990, President George H. W. Bush made the government a mitigation leader by issuing Executive Order 12699, which required that new buildings either constructed or rented by the federal government meet standards for withstanding earthquakes of certain strength (May and Deyle 1998).

The early 1990s also saw the private insurance industry starting to play a growing role in promoting better land-use and building codes after Hurricane Andrew decimated the East Coast and put nine insurance firms out of business (Petak and Atkisson 1982). The property rights movement that began in the 1980s continued to strengthen in the following decade. It successfully lobbied to block amendments to NFIP that would have strengthened the program's building restrictions and won a series of court battles such as the 1992 decision by the Supreme Court, which ruled that the government may be required to compensate owners for regulations that remove most of their property's value even if the original legislation was intended to do so (Petak and Atkisson 1982).

Mid- to Late 1990s: Stafford Act Amendments and FEMA Programs under James Lee Witt

There were two major disaster mitigation developments at the federal level in the mid- to late 1990s. The first was the Hazard Mitigation and Relocation Assistance Act, passed in 1993, which amended the Stafford Act (Birkland 2006). As mentioned in the previous section, floods devastated the Midwest that year, and numerous studies were commissioned to determine why the flood mitigation measures in place thus far had not adequately prevented the damage (Petak and Atkisson 1982). The leading report was the one produced by the Interagency Floodplain Management Review Committee, which was chaired by Brigadier General Gerald E. Galloway, Jr. (Petak and Atkisson 1982). The major findings of the Galloway report were as follows: (1) Often, people located

in floodplains who experienced the most property damage were low-income individuals, who therefore could not afford to live anywhere else; (2) restoration of wetlands helps to mitigate smaller floods much better than it does larger floods; and (3) developing and implementing land-use policies to mitigate flood damage is the responsibility of states and localities, although the federal government should provide leadership and guidance for such efforts (Petak and Atkisson 1982; Galloway 1994). The floods and the Galloway report (unfinished at the time) prompted Congressman Harold Volkmer (D-MO) to sponsor the Hazard Mitigation and Relocation Assistance Act, which changed the program's cost-sharing ratio to make it easier for states to implement flood mitigation activities (Haddow et al. 2008; Birkland 2006).

The second major disaster mitigation development at the federal level in the mid- to late 1990s was the initiation of Project Impact: Building Disaster-Resistant Communities, which was created by FEMA Director James Lee Witt in 1997 (Haddow et al. 2008). Witt was appointed by President Bill Clinton to lead FEMA in 1993, and his leadership ushered in a new agency emphasis on natural hazard mitigation, a departure from FEMA's previous focus on natural disaster relief (Birkland 2006; Haddow et al. 2008). His creation of Project Impact was partially due to the spate of disasters that occurred early in the 1990s, such as Hurricane Andrew on the East Coast in 1992, the Midwest floods in 1993, and the Northridge, California, earthquake in 1994, which initiated years-long, expensive recovery processes (Haddow et al. 2008; Platt 1998). Besides Project Impact, Witt also founded the Mitigation Directorate within FEMA (Platt 1998).

Project Impact's goal was for communities to incorporate risk assessments and measures to mitigate those risks in their already-established decision-making processes (Haddow et al. 2008). The program encouraged communities to accomplish this by creating partnerships with all area stakeholders, including private businesses, which was a novel strategy at the time (Haddow et al. 2008). This way, mitigation measures had a better chance of being effective because they were both tailored to and integrated into the communities (Haddow et al. 2008).

Witt's Project Impact was deemed a success by many. First of all, the project was popular: It began with three pilot communities, and within 4 years the number of communities grew to 200 (Haddow et al. 2008). In addition, it was commended for its community-based approach focused on building partnerships, which had value beyond disaster mitigation (Haddow et al. 2008; Sylves 2008). The public-private partnerships were especially lauded as they were seen as fostering a deeper, community-wide dedication to hazard mitigation, rather than an effort confined to the local emergency management agency (Birkland 2006). The success of Project Impact was underscored when, in 2002, an earthquake hit Seattle, Washington, an original participant of Project Impact, and only caused minimal damage (Birkland 2006).

As with any mitigation program, Project Impact had its critics. Some claimed the program was never really tested; the Seattle earthquake is usually the only disaster mentioned that occurred in a Project Impact community (Birkland 2006). Others point out that Project Impact's success has been limited because "it is difficult for the federal government to compel county and municipal governments to take mitigation steps" (Sylves 2008, p. 69). These criticisms about Project Impact's effectiveness led the Bush administration to eliminate it in 2002 (Haddow et al. 2008). Although the project's supporters in Congress attempted to keep it alive by authorizing funding for it, it eventually died due to an overwhelming focus on homeland security legislation in the wake of the September 11, 2011, terrorist attacks (Birkland 2006; Haddow et al. 2008).

The Disaster Mitigation Act of 2000

The Disaster Mitigation Act of 2000 was a pivotal piece of federal disaster mitigation legislation (Haddow et al. 2008). The bill established a National Pre-Disaster Mitigation Fund in which states and localities could apply and compete for funding for public-private partnerships, vulnerability assessments, and mitigation project prioritization; this was known as the competitive grant Pre-Disaster Mitigation (PDM) program (Haddow et al. 2008). This program has shown real benefits: In 2007, the Congressional Budget Office (CBO) issued a report finding that the competitive grant PDM program saves more money than it expends. For every $1 spent by the program, $3 are saved, totaling tens of millions of dollars in savings (Birkland 2006; CBO 2007).

The Disaster Mitigation Act also strengthened the Stafford Act by no longer tying mitigation funding to a presidential disaster declaration (Haddow et al. 2008; Sylves 2008). States were required to develop two different levels of mitigation plans before a disaster occurs in order to receive both aid in the event of a disaster and new pre-disaster aid established by the Act (Birkland 2006; Sylves 2008). In addition, localities were required to create their own mitigation programs to supplement those at the state level and such programs were required to include such elements as hazard mapping and establishing building codes (Birkland 2006; Sylves 2008). Finally, the Act increased the amount of funds available to states and localities under HMGP (Birkland 2006).

Unfortunately, the funding allotted for these mitigation activities has varied from year to year, and in 2003 the omnibus bill reduced HMGP's funding due to concerns by the Bush administration over the program's effectiveness (Haddow et al. 2008). The reduction was strongly opposed by some: For example, the Oklahoma Floodplain Managers Association argued that HMGP was "extremely effective in reducing the impacts of natural disasters" (Birkland 2006, p. 129).

Early to Mid-2000s: A Focus on Security until Hurricane Katrina

Although the Disaster Mitigation Act of 2000 was a seminal moment in the history of U.S. hazard mitigation policy, the terrorist attacks of September 11, 2011, dramatically changed policy priorities government-wide, including in the area of emergency management (Birkland 2006). Unsurprisingly, a newfound broad and deep commitment to homeland security came to dominate both legislation and regulation (Birkland 2006). The 9/11 Commission was chartered by Congress in 2002 to develop ways to protect against and prepare for terrorist attacks (Haddow et al. 2008). Although, in fact, most of the commission's resultant policy recommendations had been proposed before September 11, 2011, the terrorist attacks opened a policy window that facilitated their implementation (Birkland 2006).

The renewed focus on mitigating a terrorist attack, coupled with the fact that "the Bush administration's attitudes toward hazard mitigation [were] less sophisticated and informed than those of Bill Clinton and James Lee Witt," meant that the growth of natural hazard mitigation measures slowed considerably, and the existing measures were incorporated into "the broader context of homeland security policy" (Birkland 2006, p. 115). This incorporation was formalized by the 2002 Homeland Security Act, which established the Department of Homeland Security (DHS) and moved FEMA into it (Birkland 2006). Subsequently, in 2005, DHS Secretary Michael Chertoff reorganized FEMA, and under the new structure mitigation was not recognized (Haddow et al. 2008).

Many have pointed to this security-focused restructuring as one of the reasons why Hurricane Katrina in 2005 had such an incredibly devastating impact on the Gulf coast (Haddow et al. 2008). In the early 2000s, funding that used to be funneled toward states for mitigation programs under the various policies outlined earlier in this chapter went to other DHS departments instead, severely weakening the ability of communities nationwide to mitigate potential disaster damage (Haddow et al. 2008).

However, the federal government did learn mitigation lessons from Hurricane Katrina. In 2006, Congress passed the Post-Katrina Emergency Management Reform Act, which sought to remedy some of the administrative barriers for the destruction caused by Hurricane Katrina and "strengthen [DHS's] ability to prevent, prepare for, protect against, respond to, and recover from all hazard threats" (DHS 2008). Under the bill, the FEMA director became an administrator (Haddow et al. 2008). A 2007 Government Accountability Office (GAO) report found that although DHS and FEMA had implemented a number of the bill's provisions, including those related to mitigation, there were a number of areas that either had not yet been addressed or had only been partially addressed (GAO 2008).

Summary

Although it is too soon to analyze and assess the Obama administration's mitigation policies, there has been a positive development in the area of U.S. hazard mitigation policy recently. In December 2010, Congress passed the Pre-Disaster Hazard Mitigation Act of 2010, and President Barack Obama signed it into law in January 2011 (Public Law 111–351). The bill reauthorizes the PDM program, allowing states' and localities' mitigation programs to continue to be funded (Public Law 111–351).

Hopefully, the passage of the Pre-Disaster Hazard Mitigation Act of 2010 signals a continuation of the trend toward emphasizing disaster mitigation at the federal level. As an examination of U.S. hazard mitigation policy reveals, one of the best ways to save lives and property in the event of a disaster is through the creation and implementation of measures that reduce the specific risks of the disaster before it occurs, in other words, through mitigation policy. If for no other reason, the proven economic benefits of mitigation programs should compel the federal government to enact more of them and encourage states and localities to do the same.

End-of-Chapter Questions

1. What was the impetus behind the Flood Control Act of 1936?
2. What prompted Congress to pass the National Flood Insurance Act of 1968? What was its significance?
3. What is the purpose of NFIP?

References

Arnold, J. L. (1988). *The Evolution of the 1936 Flood Control Act*. Washington, DC: U.S. Government Printing Office. Retrieved from http://140.194.76.129/publications/eng-pamphlets/ep870-1-29/entire.pdf.

Birkland, T. A. (2006). *Lessons of Disaster: Policy Change after Catastrophic Events*. Washington, DC: Georgetown University Press.

Bogard, W. C. (1988). Bringing social theory to hazards research: Conditions and consequences of the mitigation of environmental hazards. *Sociological Perspectives*, *31*, 147–168.

Burby, R. J. (1998). Natural hazards and land use: An introduction. In R. J. Burby (Ed.), *Cooperating with Nature: Confronting Natural Hazards with Land-Use Planning for Sustainable Communities*. Washington, DC: John Henry Press.

Clary, B. B. (1985). The evolution and structure of natural hazard policies. *Public Administration Review*, *45*, 20–28.

Congressional Budget Office (CBO) (2007). *Potential cost savings from the pre-disaster mitigation program*. Washington, DC. Retrieved from http://www.cbo.gov/ftpdocs/86xx/doc8653/09-28-Disaster.pdf.

Department of Homeland Security (DHS). (2008, October 7). Implementation of the post-Katrina emergency management reform act and other organizational changes. Retrieved from http://www.dhs.gov/xabout/structure/gc_1169243598416.shtm.

Federal Emergency Management Agency (FEMA). (2011, July 28). Federal Insurance and Mitigation Administration: About FIMA. Retrieved from http://www.fema.gov/about/divisions/mitigation.shtm.

Galloway, G. E. (1994). *Sharing the Challenge: Floodplain Management into the 21st Century*. Washington, DC: U.S. Government Printing Office. Retrieved from http://www.floods.org/PDF/Sharing_the_Challenge.pdf.

Government Accountability Office (GAO) (2008, November 21). *Actions Taken to Implement the Post-Katrina Emergency Management Reform Act of 2006*. Washington, DC. Retrieved from http://www.gao.gov/new.items/d0959r.pdf.

Haddow, G. D., Bullock, J. A., & Coppola, D. P. (2008). *Introduction to Emergency Management*. New York, NY: Elsevier.

Handmer, J., & Dovers, S. (2007). *Handbook of Disaster and Emergency Policies and Institutions*. Sterling, VA: Earthscan.

May, P. J., & Deyle, R. E. (1998). Governing land use in hazardous areas with a patchwork system. In R. J. Burby (Ed.), *Cooperating with Nature: Confronting Natural Hazards with Land-Use Planning for Sustainable Communities*. Washington, DC: John Henry Press.

Mileti, D. S., & Peek-Gottschlich, L. (2001). Hazards and sustainable development in the United States. *Risk Management, 3*, 61–70.

Multihazard Mitigation Council (MMC) of the National Institute of Building Sciences. (2005). *Natural hazard mitigation saves: An independent study to assess the future savings from mitigation activities*. Washington, DC. Retrieved from http://www.nibs.org/client/assets/files/mmc/Part1_final.pdf.

Peek, L. A., & Mileti, D. S. (2002). The history and future of disaster research. In R. B. Bechtel & A. Churchman, (Eds.), *Handbook of Environmental Psychology*. New York, NY: John Wiley & Sons, Inc.

Petak, W. J., & Atkisson, A. A. (1982). *Natural Hazard Risk Assessment and Public Policy: Anticipating the Unexpected*. New York, NY: Springer-Verlag.

Platt, R. H. (1998). Planning and land use adjustments in historical perspective. In R. J. Burby (Ed.), *Cooperating with Nature: Confronting Natural Hazards with Land-Use Planning for Sustainable Communities*. Washington, DC: John Henry Press.

Sylves, R. (2008). *Disaster Policy and Politics: Emergency Management and Homeland Security*. Washington, DC: CQ Press.

United States Office of the Federal Register (2011, January 4). An Act to Amend the Robert T. Stafford Disaster Relief and Emergency Assistance Act, *Public Law* 111–351.

Willoughby, H. E., Jorgensen, D. P., Black, R. A., & Rosenthal, S. L. (1985). Project stormfury: A scientific chronicle, 1962–1983. *Bulletin of the American Meteorological Society, 66*, 505–514.

Chapter 2

Mitigation and Emergency Management

Naim Kapucu and Vener Garayev

Contents

Learning Objectives

- Have a general idea about hazard mitigation as well as the related concepts of hazard, vulnerability, and risk analysis.
- Have a snapshot of hazard mitigation in emergency management.
- Distinguish between physical, structural, and social vulnerabilities and understand their relationship with hazard mitigation.
- Comprehend the process of hazard mitigation as well as the types of related interventions.
- Evaluate the link between hazard mitigation and community resilience and sustainability.

Introduction

The classic cycle for emergency management consists of four quarters: mitigation, preparedness, response, and recovery. Mitigation is defined as a sustained action taken to reduce or eliminate risk to people and property. Preparedness is defined as a state of readiness. Among the many activities used to get people ready, the most effective tools are training and education. The primary readiness document used today is the National Response Framework (previously National Response Plan), which introduces the public to the sequential terminology of prevention, preparedness, response, recovery, and mitigation.

The devastating historical impact of Hurricane Katrina in 2004 in New Orleans, Louisiana, has revealed the need for and priority of disaster-related research on vulnerability measures, which can also be considered a rational factor and predictor of effective mitigation, planning, and response. Infrastructure, flood, and population vulnerabilities were especially critical for New Orleans (Caruson and MacManus 2008; Kapucu and Van Wart 2006). Geographical discrepancies and social inequalities necessitate a different approach to mitigation, response, and recovery actions (Cutter and Emrich 2006). It is of crucial importance to perceive that effective mitigation planning defines the scope of future actions of emergency managers and leaders. Therefore, "decisions made about mitigation will determine the safety of the region in the face of inevitable future storms" (Godschalk 2007, 90). The interpretation of mitigation "refers to sustained action taken to reduce or eliminate risk to people and property from hazards and their effects" (Bullock et al. 2006, 267). Reduction in the vulnerability would have a cause and effect relationship and decrease disaster cost, create more resilient and more sustainable communities, and reduce the loss of lives and property.

As with every other aspect of emergency management, the successful mitigation plan requires the involvement of collaborative partners at all levels to address the needs of a community as a whole. Therefore, an effective mitigation planning and precondition process requires the engagement and collaboration of multiple individuals as well as entities that have a stake in mitigation (Col 2007; Godschalk 2007; Kapucu and Van Wart 2006; Rubin 2007; Sylves 2008). Hence, hazard mitigation is of crucial importance for the emergency management community because it addresses the clarified view and development of fundamental steps of effective vulnerability assessment and planning, which in turn will establish the strategy for saving a significant amount of money for both federal and local governments, and also reduce the size of the risk to property and life. If implemented correctly, hazard mitigation can also be a model or a case study for the other states or communities that face the same flooding problems.

Mitigation Goals and Objectives

To understand what mitigation goals and objectives entail, it is important to understand the difference between the two. According to the Federal Emergency Management Agency (FEMA 2003), goals are general guidelines that a specific community would like to achieve, while objectives are the steps or strategies used to implement those goals. The former are usually more general and abstract, while the latter are often specified and measurable. For example, minimizing wildfires in California is a possible goal, while educating the public about wildfire protection strategies might be an objective for that goal.

The goal of any mitigation strategy is usually one or a combination of three main activities. First, mitigation may be targeted at changing the nature of the threat. This includes efforts to contain or modify the hazard (e.g., dikes or seawalls). Second, mitigation might involve efforts to decrease community vulnerability to damage, including such activities as building levees and elevation against flood. Finally, mitigation may target the reduction of exposure to the threat of possible disasters, such as putting regulative restrictions on the use of hazardous areas (Perry and Mushkatel as cited in Godschalk and Brower 1985). While all of these goals entail proactive measures to reduce risk to life and property, these goals are generally chosen based on the type of disaster expected. For example, while natural disasters require strategies to reduce the risk of a disaster cycle, man-made disasters require focusing on eliminating the cause, or reducing the chance of occurrence of a disaster (Godschalk and Brower 1985).

It is also important to note that mitigation goals and objectives do not have universal tenets. In other words, mitigation is viable and effective only if it is based on the values, identity, culture, and principles of the community at hand (FEMA 2003). This issue is especially crucial in terms of the acceptance of the implementation measures at the community level. Citizens would be reluctant to be involved in activities for which they have never given approval. Likewise, they would object to and possibly prevent those measures if they feel unsatisfied, unconvinced, or uncomfortable about those activities. Therefore, in order for mitigation to be effective, it is necessary to get buy-in from the respective communities before establishing wide-ranging goals and community-specific objectives.

Value of Mitigation

While all phases of emergency management are of crucial significance, mitigation plays a particularly important role in pre- and post-disaster situations. Ironically, mitigation is the least visible concept, despite it being the most important tool for protecting communities from disasters. The main goal of creating resilient communities is attainable to the largest extent

through effective mitigation measures. While it is impossible to prevent all disasters, emergency situations can be effectively managed through community-based initiatives (James Mullen, president of NEMA, as cited in NEMA n.d.). Such initiatives would help to break the cycle of disasters, as well as minimize their potential risks to communities (FEMA 2009c).

By minimizing the influence of potential disasters, mitigation offers several benefits. First, mitigation reduces direct damage to property, namely, buildings, bridges, and the main infrastructure. Second, it reduces direct damage to business activities, whether retail facilities or industrial complexes, by preventing the interruption of those activities. Third, it reduces indirect damage caused by business interruption in the form of economic ripple effects, thus preventing the domino effect on the loss. Fourth, mitigation provides protective measures for the nonmarket environment, creating safer natural environments for parks and wildlife. Fifth, hazard mitigation protects other nonmarket facilities like historic sites. Sixth, it reduces damage to society in the forms of human casualties or homelessness. Seventh, and finally, mitigation reduces the need for basic emergency first response, be it fire rescue, ambulance services, or law enforcement (Multihazard Mitigation Council 2005).

The previously mentioned benefits of mitigation can be further detailed; however, the general range and scope of the benefits can be summarized in three main functions. The first function is that mitigation creates resilient communities by protecting lives and property (NEMA n.d.). This is perhaps the most important factor, because damage to individual lives and property can hardly be compensated for. The second function is that mitigation creates a more prepared community, which reduces uncertainty, confusion, complexity, and loss of time when and if an emergency strikes. In a sense, a plan for faster, more secure, more reliable, and viable response is being promulgated through mitigation measures. The third function involves the minimization of the financial impact on communities as well as governments responsible for bringing "normal life" back. This function specifically targets the reduction of potential financial burden during response and recovery phases (FEMA 2009a).

According to the Multihazard Mitigation Council (2005), on average, a dollar spent by the FEMA on hazard mitigation saves four dollars in terms of future benefits. When one thinks of multibillion dollar response and recovery costs like those in the case of Hurricane Katrina, this proportion presents a significant opportunity for respective governments. In a sense, it is the governments' responsibility to implement mitigation measures that would save citizens' tax dollars.

Despite the approximation of savings stated above, one should note the difficulty in capturing the whole value of mitigation due to several reasons. First of all, disasters do not differentiate between segments of society. Thus, they strike every entity belonging to the affected areas. Therefore, it is not

only individuals and businesses that are affected, as is often assumed; rather, government entities, basic functional infrastructure facilities, and public services (e.g., police, schools, fire rescue, hospitals, and utilities) are impacted by disasters as well. Secondly, it is impossible to account for, and measure, all damages of a disaster because some of them are simply abstract. Loss of life and individual value attachment to loss are among the unmanageable concepts during disasters. Lastly, disasters produce long-term impacts via ripple effects across affected communities, thus making it difficult to account for a significant proportion of damage. The inclusion of only disaster-time and immediate impacts, and exclusion of long-term effects on community would cause misleading results about the value of mitigation. In this regard, it is important to capture as many disaster-time as well as potential variables and factors representing disaster damage in order to have a complete picture about the value of hazard mitigation (FEMA 1997).

Another important point regarding hazard mitigation is related to the time line of the process. Since the overall benefit of mitigation is the prevented losses that would have otherwise occurred, a question of cost-benefit analysis comes to mind. In this regard, one should distinguish between the costs and benefits incurred by the mitigation hazard process. The main point here is that mitigation costs are relatively certain and take place primarily during a short period, with the exception of operating and maintenance costs that are usually lower when compared to costs incurred by construction. A related example is the construction of a bridge or a levee. On the other hand, mitigation benefits are comprehensible only in the long term, and usually only if a disaster strikes. In other words, mitigation benefits stretch across time, which may or may not reveal the true value of mitigation due to the inherent dilemmas in the process itself. The dilemma primarily consists of discrediting mitigation measures by stakeholders when no damage occurs, while those measures may, in fact, be the real reason for a respective community's minimized damage (Multihazard Mitigation Council 2005).

This problem results in another dilemma in the political context. This is the line where a distinction between a public administrator and a politician should be noted in regard to hazard mitigation. In other words, mitigation comes with administrative burdens that may hurt the political agenda of the respective governments. Since government officials, in many ways, represent a political party or entity, political agendas mainly characterized by the short-term goals of related entities may conflict with long-term aspirations and plans that every individual should possess as a public administrator. While political realities have a power to dictate conditions, and thus, may restrict government officials, it is of utmost importance for every public administrator to embrace a long-run approach and proactive mitigation measures for the benefit and good of the communities he or she represents (NEMA n.d.).

Role of Mitigation in Emergency Management

Emergency management is a concept that entails a wide range of efforts and activities to deal with disasters, crises, and emergency situations at all levels of the community. The goal of the discipline is to protect citizens, government, and private parties as well as their properties from all possible hazards. Effective emergency management is characterized by a functional all-hazards approach to emergencies, cooperative and community-based planning, efficient and proper use of resources, and shared responsibility among all levels of government (FEMA n.d.a). Success in attaining these goals is very much dependent upon correct and manageable distribution of duties and responsibilities as well as resources among all relevant stakeholders. It is with this aim that the FEMA classified emergency management activities in four phases, namely, mitigation, preparedness, response, and recovery.

Mitigation is the first phase of emergency management and, as has already been discussed, it deals with reduction of the threat of hazards to life and property. In a sense, it is a long-term preparation to prevent future disasters or minimize their effects when and if they strike. The implementation of mitigation strategies and use of resources is especially stretched across time in this phase. Buying flood insurance or planting trees to minimize the impact of strong winds are examples of mitigation activities.

Preparedness, on the other hand, is an aggregate of pre-disaster efforts aimed at the minimization of the damage of an expected disaster. When compared to mitigation, the preparedness phase is relatively shorter because this stage is considered when there is an immediate reason for, or possibility of, certain disaster, and thus, it presents less opportunity in terms of time. It is also a more loaded stage characterized by extended and increased efforts and activities to respond to upcoming disaster. It is, in fact, certainty about a disaster that results in loaded preparation activities during this phase. Stocking food and water before a hurricane or use of sandbags to prevent flooding are examples of preparedness activities.

The response phase involves efforts and activities targeted at saving life and property during emergency situations. In a sense, this phase is putting the preparedness phase into action (FEMA n.d.a). Due to the immeasurable value of human life, response operations' outmost role is to save the lives of affected citizens; all other activities are secondary, including saving or preventing further damage to property. The response phase is also perhaps the most complex stage, due to time pressure, lack of necessary (or load of unnecessary) information, and uncertainty—all of which contribute to the complexity of the situation. An effective response phase is characterized by a controlled situation, comprehensive role, accountability distribution, and

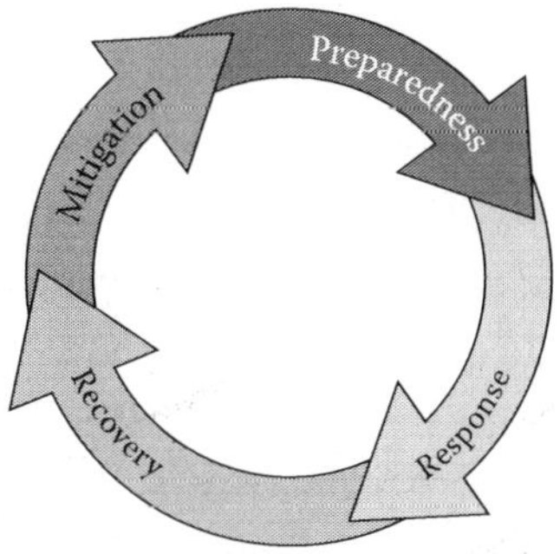

FIGURE 2.1 Phases of emergency management.

proper and efficient use of resources at hand. Providing shelter to homeless people after an earthquake and rescuing people during a flood are examples of response activities.

Recovery is the fourth and last phase of emergency management, and it deals with bringing "normal" life back. This stage is characterized by activities aimed at restoring the previous functionality of infrastructure, businesses, and services as well as the individual property of citizens affected during emergency situations (FEMA n.d.a). Perhaps the only loss that cannot be restored or recovered during the recovery stage is the loss of life, which is hard to handle due to emotional and psychological factors attached to such loss. The recovery stage is relatively symmetrical with the mitigation phase in terms of duration, use of resources, and cost. Repair of damaged houses and removal of debris after a hurricane are examples of recovery activities.

It is important to note that while the four phases of emergency management are theoretically ordered as previously mentioned, those stages are not necessarily ordered in practice and are characterized by a cyclical pattern. In addition, the stages are not necessarily mutually exclusive, but can be overlapping (Figure 2.1). In this regard, mitigation, for example, can be part of the preparedness, response, and recovery stages. For instance, buying home insurance for a house that is being constructed after a disaster is a mitigation activity taking place during a recovery stage. In fact, such overlapping is inevitable as well as necessary.

Types of Mitigation

Generally speaking, mitigation activities are grouped in two categories: structural and nonstructural. The former deals with physical "hard" engineering measures and adjustments characterized by efforts to avoid or reduce damage, including building levees and dams; protecting coastal infrastructure, strengthening, elevating, or relocating buildings; and securing fuel tanks and facilities with high risk of hazard. Nonstructural mitigation activities, on the other hand, focus on "soft" engineering measures such

as the use of wetlands to buffer against floods or the use of forests to prevent landsliding (Sylves 2008).

A similar classification is proposed by the Multihazard Mitigation Council (2005), which makes a distinction between project activities and process activities. While project activities involve physical measures and efforts to minimize the risk of hazard, process activities focus on government efforts to manage, facilitate, and/or control the use of, and investment in, hazard-prone areas. The basic distinction is whether the mitigation measures require substantive physical involvement and investment versus policy adjustments and regulations to protect from future disasters (McCarthy and Keegan 2009).

FEMA/Department of Homeland Security and Mitigation

To understand how mitigation is related to FEMA and the Department of Homeland Security (DHS), it is important to know the history of reforms that occurred over the past century. Those reforms are generally of a structural and methodological nature, and have had significant implications on subsequent disasters. Up until the 1950s, there was very little federal involvement in responding to disasters; in fact, disaster response was primarily a local activity. More than that, there was no national policy to deal with nationwide natural disasters (Haddow, Bullock, and Coppola 2008).

After World War II, the Disaster Assistance Act of 1950 was signed into law and was aimed at assisting communities in responding to disasters at the federal level. Several major disasters that occurred between 1950 and 1979, including Hurricane Carla in 1962, Hurricane Camille in 1969, and the San Fernando Earthquake of 1971, led to further organizational and intergovernmental arrangements. This resulted in the creation of several additional agencies: Housing and Home Finance Administration (1951–1953); Federal Civil Defense Administration (1953–1958); Office of Civil Defense and Mobilization (1958–1961); Office of Emergency Preparedness (1961–1973); and the Federal Disaster Assistance Administration, Defense Civil Preparedness Agency, and Federal Preparedness Agency (1973–1979). During these years, there was a growing belief that disasters were not coped with properly at the federal level. One of the reasons for this belief was the structure of the federal emergency management system being made up of several fragmented agencies that lacked coordination (Sylves 2008).

This approach continued until the end of the 1970s, specifically until the creation of FEMA in 1979 under President Carter's administration. Several of the above-mentioned agencies were merged to create a single and centralized federal agency that would be responsible for emergency management functions. FEMA was the first agency to embrace a unified mission of disaster management at national level. The federal Disaster Relief Acts of 1969 and

1970 presented an opportunity for federal disaster funding, which led to an explosion of federal grants and aid in the subsequent decades of the 1980s and 1990s. The Robert T. Stafford Disaster Relief and Emergency Assistance Act, signed in 1988, set forth provisions for mitigation grants at the state and local level (Sylves 2007) and was the cornerstone of any related legislations.

Generally, since the creation of FEMA in 1979 up until the end of the Cold War at the beginning of the 1990s, the federal government was a strong supporter of disaster preparedness. In other words, disaster mitigation was still not a formal policy advocated by federal emergency management agencies, and the focus was still on disaster preparedness, response, and civil defense. In April 1992, the federal government issued the Federal Response Plan (FRP), which aimed at a more systematic, coordinated, and effective system to provide federal assistance during emergency situations and disasters. The major disasters of the 1990s, including Hurricane Andrew in 1992, the Loma Prieta earthquake of 1989, and the Midwest floods of 1993, were a test for programs and initiatives initiated during the late 1980s and early 1990s, and these disasters showed that existing policies and approaches at that time were both inappropriate and ineffective (Schwab, Eschelbach, and Brower 2007).

Though ineffective at that time, perhaps the most important development after the creation of FEMA was the establishment of an all-hazards approach that considered all disasters similar, and required a unified policy to deal with all kinds of disasters (FEMA n.d.b). The main goal of the approach was essentially to develop a more responsive and inclusive emergency management policy responding to potential threats to human life and property as well as national and foreign attacks. However, the natural disasters of the 1990s proved that additional reforms were needed to prepare and prevent disasters. It is with this aim that the federal government shifted from the focus on preparedness and civil defense to emphasize the role of mitigation after the end of the Cold War, which led to the creation of the Mitigation Directorate under FEMA. The primary mission of the Directorate was to enhance mitigation planning and measures across the nation. Additionally, the first National Mitigation Strategy was published in 1995 by FEMA under President Clinton's administration. In a sense, the policy of FEMA has evolved over the years from noninvolvement to response, primary financial provision, and hazard mitigation championship (Platt as cited in Schwab, Eschelbach, and Brower 2007).

In the years following, FEMA's primary goal was to advocate for emergency management and mitigation at the national level. The Project Impact program of 1997 was an initiative that fostered community-wide mitigation planning and activities. The program envisioned the inclusion of all stakeholders in the mitigation phase of emergency management. The initiative was replaced by the Disaster Mitigation Act (DMA) of 2000, which amended the Stafford Act and set mitigation as the centerpiece of the respective

legislation (Godschalk 2007). The DMA aimed at reorganizing and streamlining disaster relief and mitigation programs offered by the federal government. It explicitly emphasized the role of pre-disaster mitigation (PDM) and set specific requirements for state and local governments. One of the crucial prior requirements for state and local governments to receive federal grants was that they develop a viable multijurisdictional mitigation plan for implementation. The DMA was established as a checks-and-balance system on the federal government side as well as an authority to reward abiding communities and governments if appropriate mitigation plans were developed and implemented (Schwab, Eschelbach, and Brower 2007; Sylves 2007).

The year 2001, and specifically the terrorist attacks targeted at the United States on September 11, became a turning point for emergency management in the country. The event resulted in advocacy and support for creating a new DHS amongst congressional leaders. Some 22 agencies, including FEMA, were consolidated into one large DHS via enactment of the 2002 Homeland Security Act, with the department beginning its operation in January 2003. This reorganization and rearrangement of agencies resulted in an immediate increase of emphasis put on defense and law enforcement and a decreased role of emergency management agencies with an all-hazards approach (Sylves 2008). Terrorism became the main type of disaster that all departments within the DHS focused on to align their practices at the expense of federal grants allocated for mitigation programs.

With the issuance of Homeland Security Presidential Directive-5 by President Bush in February 2003, a National Response Plan (NRP) was enacted to replace the FRP. Additionally, the National Incident Management System was proposed as a general framework to manage domestic incidents. The directive's main goal was to unify domestic emergency management under one umbrella and make it applicable across all levels of government. What is more, the NRP assumed the DHS secretary was the only entity responsible for dealing with domestic disasters (Sylves 2008).

The international disasters around the globe, as well as the 2004 hurricane season and Hurricane Katrina in 2005, were a reminder that mitigation practices were still not at the desired level and that disaster relief and mitigation should receive its previous attention (Schwab, Eschelbach, and Brower 2007). According to Gall and Cutter (2007), the failure to effectively deal with those disasters, especially with Hurricane Katrina, is attributed to several reasons. First, FEMA degraded when its status was changed from cabinet-level agency to a directorate under DHS (Gall and Cutter 2007). Second, FEMA lacked its all-hazards approach when dealing with Hurricane Katrina. Finally, it lacked as much focus on natural hazard mitigation as existed prior to its absorption by DHS. Additional reasons mentioned in the literature are ambiguity in terms of agency roles, FEMA's lessened influence and prestige in comparison to other agencies' prevalent antiterrorism programs (Sylves 2008), and

change from all-inclusive and coordinative practices to command-and-control type practices (Tierney as cited in Sylves 2008).

In 2006, President Bush signed into law the Post-Katrina Emergency Reform Act, which reaffirmed FEMA's role in disaster management but allowed it to remain under the authority of DHS (Gall and Cutter 2007). Another important reform occurred when the NRP was reissued as the National Response Framework in early 2008, which aimed at strengthening and improving the existing system to cope with domestic disasters (Sylves 2008). While these post-Katrina reforms sought to reestablish FEMA's previous position as an effective emergency management agency, the agency still lacks its previous autonomy and strength.

Federal Mitigation Programs

As a result of the increasing belief in the 1990s that mitigation is an area that should be considered more seriously, the Mitigation Directorate was created under FEMA in November 1993. The main goal of the directorate was to advocate mitigation as the cornerstone of emergency management and as the primary strategy if long-term efforts of risk reduction are considered (Multihazard Mitigation Council 2005). Today, there are several programs and grants offered through the directorate to encourage local and state agencies to invest in mitigation. The mitigation programs are mostly shaped by the DMA of 2000 (Godschalk 2007). The Mitigation Directorate is composed of three divisions, namely, the Risk Analysis division, Risk Reduction division, and Risk Insurance division. The programs and grants offered by FEMA are grouped under these respective divisions (FEMA n.d.c).

The Risk Analysis division focuses on applying engineering and technological techniques and tools to identify and analyze natural hazards risk and to develop strategies to prevent them. The programs and activities administered by the division are as follows:

Flood Hazard Mapping/Map Modernization: Closely related to the National Flood Insurance Program (NFIP) (see below), this project focuses on the creation, maintenance, and update of flood hazard maps. The project is maintained in conjunction with Cooperating Technical Partners, an initiative by FEMA to create and maintain partnerships between FEMA and local, state, or regional agencies interested in flood hazard mapping.

National Dam Safety Program: Created through the Water Resources Development Act of 1996, the program focuses on dam safety projects against natural and man-made hazards. It offers grant assistance to states, dam safety technical and archival research, and dam safety training for state staff and inspectors.

National Hurricane Program: Established in 1985, the program focuses on hurricane risk assessment and provision of relevant tools and technical assistance to local and state agencies in regard to the development of hurricane evacuation plans. The program is a partnership of several agencies, including the National Oceanic and Atmospheric Association, National Weather Service, U.S. Department of Transportation, and U.S. Army Corps of Engineers.

HAZUS: HAZUS is FEMA's basic risk analysis methodology and technological tool to analyze potential losses from natural disasters like floods, hurricanes, and earthquakes. The methodology comprises the latest engineering as well as geographic information systems (GIS) knowledge and tools. HAZUS mainly focuses on the physical (e.g., basic infrastructure, residential, and commercial buildings), economic (e.g., unemployment, business interruptions), and social (e.g., shelter requirements, displaced households) impacts of potential disasters.

Mitigation Planning: The subdivision focuses on creating long-term community strategies to break the cycle of, and also reduce the impact of, the disaster damage. Its primary goal is to enhance and facilitate the planning process of local, state, and tribal communities so that they create viable mitigation plans that would provide a framework for risk-based decision making to reduce damage from future disasters (FEMA n.d.c).

The Risk Reduction division focuses on pre-disaster and post-disaster projects and activities related to land-use control, building codes, and similar tools for existing buildings, as well as on future developments. The programs and activities administered by the division are as follows:

Hazard Mitigation Assistance

1. *Hazard Mitigation Grant Program (HMGP)*: Created by the Stafford Act, the program is intended for post-disaster declaration cases and offers grants for long-term mitigation projects before and after a disaster. The program is the largest source of federal funding for communities after a disaster declaration, which is distributed proportionally with the damage loss estimates. The projects funded through the program are expected to be cost-effective, environment-sensitive, regulation-based, and to contribute to the reduction of future damage or loss (FEMA 1997; Schwab, Eschelbach, and Brower 2007).
2. *Pre-Disaster Mitigation Grant Program (PDM)*: Established by section 203 of the DMA of 2000 (first authorized by the Stafford Act), the program provides funds to communities and universities to reduce future disaster losses as well as minimize the reliance on grants claimed under the HMGP following a disaster

declaration (FEMA 2007). The funds are provided on a competitive basis with no specific formula for distribution and are primarily intended for natural disasters but are also used for man-made disasters (FEMA n.d.c).

3. *Flood Mitigation Assistance Program (FMA)*: Created by the National Flood Insurance Act of 1968 and amended as part of the National Flood Insurance Reform Act of 1994, the program's main goal is to provide grants to states and communities for long-term flood damage reduction projects in order to reduce or eliminate the claims under the NFIP (see below) (FEMA 2009b). The grant types available for communities under the FMA program are classified as planning grants (aimed at development of flood mitigation plans), project grants (aimed at implementing measures to reduce flood losses such as elevation or relocation and are only available to NFIP-participating communities with approved flood mitigation plans), and technical assistance grants (up to 10% of project grants to states for administrative purposes) (FEMA 2007).
4. *Severe Repetitive Loss Program (SRL)*: Authorized by Bunning–Bereuter–Blumenauer Flood Insurance Reform Act of 2004 and amending the National Flood Insurance Act of 1968, the program provides funding for long-term flood damage and the risk reduction or elimination of projects encompassing severe repetitive loss structures (as defined by the National Flood Insurance Act). The program also aims at reduction of claims under the NFIP (FEMA n.d.c).
5. *Repetitive Flood Claims Program*: Similar to the SRL program, this program was also authorized by the Bunning–Bereuter–Blumenauer Flood Insurance Reform Act of 2004 and amended the National Flood Insurance Act of 1968. The program envisions providing up to $10 million for states and communities to reduce damage to properties with one or more claims to the NFIP (FEMA 2007). The program is voluntary and has no mitigation planning requirements; the main requirement is to meet FEMA's Repetitive Loss Property criteria (FEMA n.d.c).

Floodplain Management and Community Rating System: Implemented under the NFIP, the program is on a voluntary basis and aims to recognize and encourage the NFIP-participating communities' floodplain efforts and activities as well as increase the awareness of flood insurance and facilitate accurate insurance ratings. The main advantage for the participating communities includes discounted insurance premium rates reflecting reduced flood risk. However, communities that are experiencing an emergency situation are not eligible for this program (FEMA n.d.c).

National Earthquake Hazards Reduction Program (NEHRP): Established in 1977 by Congress, the program is a coordinated approach to address, identify, reduce, or eliminate the earthquake-related risks through basic or applied science and engineering measures. Specific goals include the development and implementation of earthquake loss-reduction policies and strategies, improvement of techniques to reduce seismic vulnerability, improvement of seismic hazard identification and risk-assessment methods, and improvement of understanding earthquakes and their impacts. FEMA collaborates with several agencies to implement the NEHRP, some of which are the National Institute of Standards and Technology, the National Science Foundation, and the United States Geological Survey (FEMA n.d.c).

Building Science: Being a technical bureau with highly skilled subject matter experts, the branch seeks to develop technical guidance and tools to enhance disaster-resilient communities. The branch's main goal is to reduce risk to life and property through advanced measures for buildings and facilities (see Figure 2.2). Activities performed by the Building Science branch include, but are not limited to, developing publications, guidance, and tools with the latest building codes, floodproofing requirements, and seismic design standards;

FIGURE 2.2 Pascagoula, Mississippi, February 28, 2006—Robert and Sandra Harris returned to their Pascagoula neighborhood days after Hurricane Katrina to discover theirs was the only house left standing. They previously had mitigated their home in 1999 with $30,000 in Increased Cost of Compliance funds through the National Flood Insurance Program. (Photo courtesy of Mark Wolfe/FEMA.)

providing technical support to the public as well as related private sector stakeholders; outreach activities to communicate about the branch's issues; and providing technical support for the NFIP and related FEMA agencies (FEMA n.d.c).

Finally, the Risk Insurance Division comprises the NFIP, which was established by Congress through the National Flood Insurance Act of 1968. The main goal of the program is to provide flood insurance to participating local communities if they adopt and enforce a floodplain management ordinance with the aim of reducing future flood risk and damage. The program also is an alternative to reduce possible repair costs upon flood damage (FEMA 2002) and is the largest insurance provider in the nation (Schwab, Eschelbach, and Brower 2007). The program consists of three components, namely, flood insurance, floodplain management, and flood hazard mapping. The program is voluntary, and today some 20,000 communities across the United States participate in it (FEMA n.d.c). The estimated reduced flood losses in the United States through the NFIP are around $1 billion each year (Schwab, Eschelbach, and Brower 2007).

Mitigation Planning

In order for communities to be involved in and implement effective mitigation strategies and measures, it is vital that respective governments or entities have a viable mitigation plan first. The main goal of the hazard mitigation plan and the planning process overall is to educate the public about the hazards they encounter, to develop respective goals to minimize those hazards, and to develop strategies and actions to prevent those hazards (Schwab, Eschelbach, and Brower 2007). In order for state, local, and tribal communities to receive federal pre-disaster assistance grants, including mitigation grants, they have to develop a hazard mitigation plan specifying goals and strategies to reduce future disaster loss. The legal basis for this approach is provided through the Stafford Act as amended by the DMA of 2000 (FEMA n.d.d).

Schwab, Eschelbach, and Brower (2007) define hazard mitigation planning as the "process of determining how to reduce or eliminate the loss of life and property damage that can occur as a result of hazards" (446). This process is intended to implement an all-hazards approach with the purpose of identifying all possible risks, natural or man-made, and developing strategies to minimize their possibility of occurring. It also seeks to consolidate and streamline community mitigation efforts to avoid gaps and redundancies, as well as to effectively manage limited resources. In a sense, the mitigation plan and planning process provides an all-inclusive and future-oriented vision for key policy and decision makers. While the goal is promising, the programs provided by the DHS are far from being an all-hazards

approach because of the specific and tightened focus on natural rather than man-made and technological disasters (OIG 2009). The ultimate goal of the planning process is to develop a viable mitigation plan that is facts-based, environment-sensitive, and community-driven, resulting in resiliency and sustainability of the communities involved.

As identified by FEMA (n.d.d), the traditional mitigation planning process consists of four phases, namely, organizing resources, assessing risks, developing a mitigation plan, and implementing and monitoring the plan. Organizing resources is the first step of the planning process and includes the mobilization of resources, knowledge, and human capital. The main goal here is to involve the community in the process and get its support for the plan. All relevant stakeholders are expected to come together for the design of a community mitigation roadmap and provide political buy-in on their sides. A typical arena for such discussions is the respective local emergency management department. Because there is a possibility of resistance from the community due to such factors as low political support for mitigation, public complacency about disasters, and public belief that mitigation is an engineering and not a community tool, respective emergency management officials should extensively invest in much-needed informative and educational tools about the risks and potential damages of hazards in case mitigation activities are not implemented (Godschalk 2007).

The risk assessment phase of mitigation planning seeks to identify the characteristics and potential threats posed by disasters with the aim of understanding the magnitude of the possible impact on facilities, property, and human life. FEMA (n.d.d) groups risk assessment activities into four basic components, namely, identifying hazards (via historical records, contacting experts, etc.), profiling hazard events (hazard event–based loss estimation using technology like GIS or FEMA's risk assessment software HAZUS-MH), inventory assets (quantification of potential threat in terms of facilities, assets, and demographics in hazardous areas), and estimating loss (quantification of potential losses in financial and nonfinancial terms). One should be aware that completion of these steps does not guarantee elimination of all potential threats because uncertainty about the source and magnitude of disasters is always present. Nevertheless, community involvement is a necessary factor to reduce future political accountability, to justify existing and future mitigation activities, and to buffer against future claims by respective communities. Ideally, the risk assessment phase should be inclusive, future-oriented, and technology-informed (Godschalk 2007).

The mitigation plan development stage seeks to identify community priorities and establish a strategy to attain those priorities and long-term sustainability. This phase comprises four steps: (1) setting goals and objectives (risk assessment-based expression of ultimate expectations and relevant

intermediate actions), (2) identification and prioritization of actions (creation of actions document based on feasibility, community values, timing, political viability, and resources), (3) preparation of implementation strategy (detailed description of actions and their timing to create an efficient, coordinated, coherent, and understandable course of actions), and (4) the write-up of a mitigation plan (resulting document with concepts, principles, analysis, and actions of the whole planning process). An ideal plan should be clear, concise, accurate, comprehensive, and complete with linkages established between the goals and objectives, and the actions intended for implementation (Godschalk 2007).

Lastly, the plan implementation and monitoring stage of the mitigation planning process includes realization of actions specified in the mitigation plan and periodic evaluations and updates with the purpose to maintain a relevant and up-to-date community mitigation plan (FEMA n.d.d). This stage consists of four steps: adoption of the plan (formal adoption of the plan by respective communities as required by DMA of 2000), implementation of plan recommendations (inclusion of the plan into administrative, budgetary, and regulatory processes of the local governments as well as establishment of performance evaluation criteria), evaluation of planning results (analysis of progress and identifying which tools and strategies of the mitigation plan are effective), and revision of the plan (amendments of, additions to, or replacement of existing mitigation plans to account for regulatory changes, emergency situations, and lessons learned) (Godschalk 2007).

Mitigation Strategies

Shcwab, Eschelbach, and Brower (2007) provide a detailed classification of mitigation strategies by dividing them first into natural versus man-made (technological and terrorism-related) hazard mitigation strategies. The natural hazard mitigation strategies include structural engineering projects, prevention, property protection, natural resource protection, and public information. Structural engineering projects involve efforts to minimize the risk and impact of hazard by modifying the environment or development of the hazard event. Dams, levees, and beach nourishments are some examples in this category. While this is an effective way of dealing with hazards in the short run, the tool may ultimately result in vulnerabilities in the long term, especially through environmental degradation. Prevention activities aim at avoiding hazard by noninvolvement in related areas. This is an effective tool in terms of long-run policies because it prevents the development and investment in hazard-prone areas ahead of time. Land-use planning, zoning, taxation, and floodplain regulations are examples for this category. Property protection intends to prevent damage and impact to already established

facilities and property by modifying and/or strengthening them. This strategy is a relatively weak tool because it aims only at existing structures, which means less flexibility. Flood- and wind-proofing and building codes and construction standards are examples in this category. Natural resource protection focuses on preventing impacts of natural hazards through the preservation or restoration of natural resources and areas that naturally possess mitigating functions. This tool is essentially against structural development and may also serve as an environmental protection and community interest tool by creating recreation areas and greenways. Beach preservation, habitat protection, and erosion control activities are examples in this category. Lastly, public information strategy utilizes informative and advisory tools to educate the public about issues to be considered when buying a house or property, establishing a business, or visiting hazard areas. Education programs in schools, public outreach projects, and real estate disclosures are examples in this category of hazard mitigation activities (Schwab, Eschelbach, and Brower 2007).

Man-made hazard mitigation strategies, on the other hand, include site planning and landscape design (e.g., limiting entrances/exits, providing adequate lightning), architectural and interior design (e.g., restricting roof access, locating service spaces in secured areas), structural engineering (e.g., creating blast-resistant exterior envelopes and structural elements), security (e.g., developing backup systems, installing screening systems), mechanical engineering (e.g., protecting utility infrastructure by burying, concealing), and electrical engineering (e.g., securing primary and backup supply areas, implementing separate emergency and normal power systems). While these target-hardening strategies are important to establish a protected environment with structures that can withstand a technological disaster or an attack, it is likewise crucial to educate the public about self-protection strategies through public awareness campaigns and deliberate and informative tools (Schwab, Eschelbach, and Brower 2007).

It is important to note, however, that the previously mentioned strategies and tools are not used by all communities at the same level. In other words, there is no single universal strategy that governments or individuals should or would pursue, because certain factors are more important than others in choosing a mitigation tool. Depending on the nature of the problem, availability of resources and funds, commitment of the respective community, and the level of government support and involvement, different sets and levels of mitigation tools are utilized in communities. Perhaps the most important factor in regard to this is the cost incurred by mitigation activities. This is partly determined by the duration as well as the scale of the investments. Relatively immediate and short-run initiatives draw more attention on community but less support on the political side. On the other hand, investments and development initiatives requiring long-run

commitment, and thus resulting in higher costs, receive less political support. A balanced approach is needed on the governments' side to meet the communities' interests, on the one hand, and follow a political agenda, on the other (Schwab, Eschelbach, and Brower 2007).

Marrying Mitigation with Resiliency and Sustainability

Communities that do not invest in mitigation strategies, especially if they are threatened by a disaster cycle, are prone to be vulnerable in many aspects. It is impossible to create resilient and sustainable communities if disasters keep breaking the "normality" of living conditions. A sustainable community characterized by balance among economy, environment, and equity should be the centerpiece of a mitigation plan, which envisions two things: recognition of and commitment to reducing the risks of hazards and development based on the cognition of hazards and commitment to prevent future vulnerabilities (Godschalk 2007).

A resilient community, in turn, means a community that incorporates mitigation in all direct and indirect programs concerning community and community development. It is a "sustainable network of physical and social systems that are redundant, diverse, adaptable, and interdependent" (Godschalk 2007, 110). Disaster resistance is not only about emergency management. It also links healthier communities in terms of economy, social well-being, and environment (Witt 2000). Mitigation is the tool to link sustainable development practices with daily planning and development at all levels of government.

Project Impact

Several regulatory and legislative changes resulted in the 1990s during the Clinton administration, due to an increased emphasis on mitigation by Congress. One of those changes was the establishment of Project Impact in 1997, which was a concrete step by the federal government to stress the importance of mitigation in emergency management. The project was created as a pilot program to advocate mitigation measures as a tool to prepare communities in advance of disasters. FEMA's approach to the selection of communities for the pilot program was based on criteria such as previous experience, ongoing risk encountered by specific communities, and the level of collaboration entailed by the program at the local level (McCarthy and Keegan 2009).

Despite the government's commitment for a PDM program, especially in the aftermath of disasters that occurred in the 1990s, the level of appropriations by Congress specifically for this purpose was not at the desired level.

After the establishment of the pilot program in 1997, subsequent years were characterized by some $25 million appropriations. The PDM program became a basis for, and part of, the 2000 Robert T. Stafford Disaster Relief and Emergency Assistance Act in 2003. After the September 11th terrorist attacks, the federal government changed its focus from mitigation to prevention and preparedness measures, which resulted in diminished attention to PDM and the overall concept of hazard mitigation along with variations in appropriations for each year. The 111th Congress of 2009 introduced a legislation that intended to stabilize the amount of appropriations with $250 million for each fiscal year up until 2012 (McCarthy and Keegan 2009).

The initial Project Impact is very much identified with the then FEMA Director, James Witt, who considered the initiative to be protection against future disasters and a tool to create disaster-resistant communities (see Figure 2.3). The project, in a sense, was an attempt to create a national mitigation strategy to reduce the risk to lives and property in future disasters (Sebring 2009). While this attempt was partly successful, especially in the form of the adoption of a federal mitigation strategy in the late 1990s and early 2000s, subsequent years were characterized by a shift in congressional interest from mitigation to prevention measures focusing on antiterrorism strategies. Today, the PDM offers grants to states, tribal, and local

FIGURE 2.3 FEMA Director James Lee Witt and then President Bill Clinton discuss Project Impact. (FEMA news photo.)

governments with the purpose of reducing the potential threat of disasters and reliance on post-disaster mitigation grants. The mitigation measures, tools, and activities offered by the grant range from voluntary acquisition of real property to localized flood control projects (FEMA 2009).

An example of effective mitigation measures implemented through PDM can be seen in Brenton, Wyoming County, West Virginia. The repetitive floods in Vance's Trailer Park since 2001 had created a damage-repair cycle for the residents in that area. In 2004, the Wyoming County Emergency Services decided to relocate the residents through the PDM program. The PDM grant was received and implemented, and the park was converted to a recreation area maintained by a voluntary church. In May 2009, when a flood destroyed the banks and covered the area with 3 feet of mud, no families were forced to leave and no damage was observed to homes. Relocation to new houses in a different area and establishment of a recreation park area were just examples of what PDM is willing to do (FEMA n.d.e).

Today, there is an effort for a nationwide mitigation strategy by several scholars. The main goal of the effort is to create an effective national mitigation strategy that would guide national mitigation efforts. The strategy would envision commonality of objectives, risk-oriented practices, inclusion of mitigation in regulatory documents, and mitigation education and knowledge pool (NEMA n.d.).

Summary

Mitigation is a long-term but politically sensitive issue. It is important to convince governments as well as include all stakeholders to be involved in mitigation practices if damage from future disasters is to be reduced. It should also be demand-driven, and culture- and environment-sensitive to get the highest buy-in. Both communities and governments save via mitigation measures.

End-of-Chapter Questions

1. A group of community leaders has asked you to describe the mitigation strategies that a local government could implement without any outside assistance. What would you recommend to your audience?
2. Why do collaboration and coordination have significance in mitigation in emergency management? What are some challenges? How can we overcome barriers preventing multisector and multijurisdictional agencies from working together in disaster response and in recovery from disasters?
3. How might the information you gained from this reading affect you personally and professionally?

4. Why do people generally show little concern for environmental and technological risks?
5. What communities or states do seem to show more concern for such risks, and why?

References

Bullock, J. A., Haddow, G. D., Coppola, D., Erdem, E., Westerman, L., & Yeletaysi, S. (2006). *Introduction to homeland security*, p. 267. Burlington, VT: Elsevier Inc.

Caruson, K., & MacManus, S. A. (2008). Disaster vulnerabilities: How strong a push toward regionalism and intergovernmental cooperation? *The American Review of Public Administration, 38*(3), 286–306.

Col, J. M. (2007). Managing disasters: The role of government. *Public Administration Review, 67*(1), 114–124.

Cutter, S. L., & Emrich, C. T. (2006). Moral hazard, social catastrophe: The changing face of vulnerability along the hurricane coasts. *The Annals of the American Academy of Political and Social Science, 604*(1), 102–112.

FEMA, Federal Emergency Management Agency (1997). *Costs and benefits of natural hazards mitigation*. Washington, DC: Federal Emergency Management Agency.

FEMA, Federal Emergency Management Agency (2002). *National Flood Insurance Program: Program description*. Federal Emergency Management Agency. Retrieved September 18, 2011, from http://www.fema.gov/library/viewRecord.do?id = 1480.

FEMA, Federal Emergency Management Agency (2003). *Developing the mitigation plan*. Federal Emergency Management Agency. Retrieved September 18, 2011, from http://www.fema.gov/library/viewRecord.do?id = 1886.

FEMA, Federal Emergency Management Agency (2007). *Grant program comparison: Mitigation division grant programs*. Federal Emergency Management Agency. Retrieved September 18, 2011, from http://www.fema.gov/library/viewRecord .do?id = 2128.

FEMA, Federal Emergency Management Agency (2009). *Pre-disaster mitigation grant program: Building stronger and safer*. Federal Emergency Management Agency. Retrieved September 18, 2011, from http://www.fema.gov/library/file;jsessionid=3E0E931B365DA1C45AE34B1373728CB4.WorkerLibrary?type=publishedFile&file=pre_disaster-mitigation_active_04_2009.pdf&fileid = b3339020-2abd-11de-9100-001185636a87.

FEMA, Federal Emergency Management Agency (2009a). *Mitigation's value to society*. Federal Emergency Management Agency. Retrieved September 18, 2011, from http://www.fema.gov/library/viewRecord.do?id = 3031.

FEMA, Federal Emergency Management Agency (2009b). *Flood Mitigation Assistance Program: Building stronger and safer*. Federal Emergency Management Agency. Retrieved September 18, 2011, from http://www.fema.gov/library/viewRecord.do?id = 2056.

FEMA, Federal Emergency Management Agency (2009c). *FEMA's mitigation directorate: Mitigation works*. Federal Emergency Management Agency. Retrieved September 18, 2011, from http://www.fema.gov/library/viewRecord.do?id = 3032.

FEMA, Federal Emergency Management Agency (n.d.a). *The four phases of emergency management*. Federal Emergency Management Agency. Retrieved September 18, 2011, from training.fema.gov/emiweb/downloads/is10_unit3.doc.

FEMA, Federal Emergency Management Agency (n.d.b). FEMA History. In Federal Emergency Management Agency. Retrieved September 12, 2011, from http://www .fema.gov/library.

FEMA, Federal Emergency Management Agency (n.d.c). Mitigation directorate. In Federal Emergency Management Agency. Retrieved September 12, 2011, from http://www.fema.gov/library.

FEMA, Federal Emergency Management Agency (n.d.d). Multihazard mitigation planning. In Federal Emergency Management Agency. Retrieved September 12, 2011, from http://www.fema.gov/library.

FEMA, Federal Emergency Management Agency (n.d.e). Brenton, Wyoming county pre-disaster mitigation. In Federal Emergency Management Agency. Retrieved September 12, 2011, from http://www.fema.gov/library.

Gall, M., & Cutter, S. L. (2007). 2005 Events and outcomes: Hurricane Katrina and beyond. In C. B. Rubin (Ed.), *Emergency management: The American experience* 1900–2005. Fairfax, VA: Public Entity Risk Institute.

Godschalk, D. R. (2007). Mitigation. In W. W. J. Waugh & K. Tierney (Eds.), *Emergency management: Principles and practice for local government*, p. 90, 110. Washington, DC: ICMA.

Godschalk, D. R., & Brower, D. J. (1985). Mitigation strategies and integrated emergency management. *Public Administration Review*, *45* (Special Issue), 64–71.

Haddow, G. D., Bullock, J. A., & Coppola, D. P. (2008). *Introduction to Emergency Management*. Burlington, MA: Elsevier.

Kapucu, N., & Van Wart, M. (2006). The emerging role of the public sector in managing extreme events: Lessons learned. *Administration and Society*, *38*(3), 279–308.

McCarthy, F. X., & Keegan, N. (2009). *FEMA's pre-disaster mitigation program: Overview and issues*. Washington, DC: Congressional Research Service.

Multihazard Mitigation Council (2005). *Natural hazard mitigation saves: An independent study to assess the future savings from mitigation activities*. Washington, DC: National Institute of Building Sciences.

NEMA, National Emergency Management Association (n.d). The white paper: Recommendations for an effective national mitigation effort. National Emergency Management Association. Retrieved from http://www.nemaweb.org/?3190.

Office of Inspector General (OIG) (2009). *FEMA's progress in all-hazards mitigation*. Washington, DC: Department of Homeland Security.

Rubin, C. B. (Ed.) (2007). *Emergency Management: The American Experience 1900–2005*. Fairfax, VA: Public Entity Risk Institute.

Schwab, A. K., Eschelbach, K., & Brower, D. J. (2007). *Hazard Mitigation and Preparedness*. Hoboken, NJ: Wiley.

Sebring, A. (2009). *Recommendations for an Effective National Mitigation Effort*. EIIP Virtual Forum Presentation.

Sylves, R. T. (2007). Federal emergency management comes of age: 1979–2001. In C. B. Rubin (Ed.), *Emergency Management: The American Experience 1900–2005*. Fairfax, VA: Public Entity Risk Institute.

Sylves, R. T. (2008). *Disaster Policy and Politics: Emergency Management and Homeland Security*. Washington, DC: CQ Press.

Witt, J. L. (2000). *Planning for a sustainable future: The link between hazard mitigation and livability*. Federal Emergency Management Agency. Retrieved September 12, 2011, from http://www.fema .gov/library/viewRecord.do?id=1541.

Chapter 3

Intergovernmental Relations and Hazard Mitigation

Jerry V. Graves, Jr.

Contents

Learning Objectives

- Describe the importance of the role of local government in the field of hazard mitigation.
- Have a working knowledge of the federal grant-in-aid system and of some specific hazard mitigation grant opportunities.
- Understand the difference between risk reduction, risk sharing, and risk elimination.
- Identify key components and functions of the ideal local hazard mitigation team.
- Explain the typical role of state government in the field of hazard mitigation and identify the opportunities and challenges associated with the relationship between local and state government.
- Explain the typical role of the federal government in the field of hazard mitigation and identify the opportunities and challenges associated with the relationship between local and the federal government.

Introduction

The most opportune time for local government to implement a robust hazard mitigation program is immediately following a major natural disaster. At this time, hazards are a highly salient issue among the general public, and local officials and citizens alike are more willing to engage in the public policy processes necessary to plan for future disasters and to ultimately become more resilient. Otherwise, the overwhelming scientific evidence is that people are typically unaware of the hazards they face, underestimate those of which they are aware, overestimate their ability to cope when disaster strikes, often blame others for their losses, underutilize pre-impact hazard mitigation strategies, and rely heavily on relief when the need arises (Mileti 1999, 136–137).

Because it is often easy for a community to "discount ambiguous future benefits for short-term costs," it is critical for local government to take advantage of the saliency of hazards issues following a disaster and to engage disaster-stricken communities in planning for hazards while risk and vulnerability do not seem so ambiguous and while the future of the community hangs in the balance (Gerber 2007, 231).

A willingness and ability to navigate complex intergovernmental processes in the volatile post-disaster/recovery environment is critical to local government taking advantage of hazard mitigation opportunities (Rubin et al. 1985, 57). This chapter will use flood hazards, nonstructural and structural hazard mitigation, and the 2005 Hurricane Katrina event to highlight the complexity of the intergovernmental processes associated with hazard mitigation and the inherent challenges and opportunities that exist for practitioners in local government. Because natural disasters are first and foremost local events, the analysis will be presented from a local perspective and has been designed as an abbreviated body of guidance for local practitioners. As a hazard mitigation practitioner in local government, I will also include excerpts of my own personal experiences in the field in order to illustrate certain points. Such excerpts will be primarily focused on hazard mitigation and intergovernmental relations in post-Katrina St. Bernard Parish, Louisiana, which borders the city of New Orleans to the south and east. Over 95% of the 27,000 structures in St. Bernard were damaged or destroyed during Katrina (see Figure 3.1). Additionally, approximately 130 lives were lost and nearly 100% of the parish's 67,000 residents were dislocated. Although St. Bernard Parish had not been aggressively engaged in mitigating flood hazards prior to Katrina, the municipality initiated a number of hazard mitigation projects following the hurricane which totaled over $25 million in grants alone. Navigating various intergovernmental processes and utilizing an array of federal funding streams was critical to the initiation and completion of said projects, and ultimately to the overall increased sustainability of the community going forward.

FIGURE 3.1 (See color insert.) New Orleans, Louisiana, 9/19/2005—Aerial view of flooded homes in a subdivision in St. Bernard Parish following Hurricane Katrina. (Photo courtesy of Andrea Booher/FEMA.)

Articulating the Local Burden

When a major disaster strikes the United States, there is a period of time immediately following the disaster in which affected parties and concerned onlookers gaze at the devastation before them and ponder how the effects of the disaster might have been mitigated or otherwise avoided altogether. In the aftermath of Hurricane Katrina, much of this attention was focused on the failure of hurricane protection levees and the delayed federal relief response. This focus was the product of national media coverage that provided non-stop footage of citizens taking refuge at the New Orleans Convention Center and Louisiana Superdome, the U.S. Army Corps of Engineers (USACE) scrambling to plug broken hurricane protection levees throughout the New Orleans metro area, and the Federal Emergency Management Agency (FEMA) seemingly being unaware of the severity of the situation.

The perception of the disaster was such that one would be inclined to believe that doubling structural mitigation efforts (building bigger and better levees) and improving the federal post-disaster response would be the "silver-bullet" approach that would eliminate the possibility of future Katrinas. Undoubtedly, there is much room for improvement in each of the aforementioned areas and doing so would certainly help. However, engineered structural mitigation measures such as levees are always subject to failure. In fact, a 1976 study prepared for the U.S. Department of Housing and Urban Development found that approximately two-thirds of all flood

losses in the United States resulted from catastrophic events that exceeded the design limitations of engineered structural hazard mitigation works (Sheaffer et al. 1976). Furthermore, the federal response to a disaster provides relief only after devastation has already occurred. Relying solely on structural measures and the FEMA response as a means of mitigating hazards would certainly be an exercise of futility on the part of local government, as it has no direct control over the engineering and maintenance of federal levees and will never directly command a FEMA relief response.

What the local government does have direct control and command of is land use decision making. As chance would have it, land-use planning also happens to be the most effective means of mitigating future flood hazards in an at-risk community. The major critique of many accepted hazard mitigation techniques is that they are shortsighted and have a tendency to "postpone losses into the future rather than eliminate them" (Mileti 1999, 35). However, unlike levees (risk reduction) and disaster relief (risk sharing), land-use planning is focused on risk elimination. Following a disaster such as Katrina, nonstructural hazard mitigation opportunities abound and although local government may autonomously make land-use decisions and implement land-use controls, getting funding for large-scale acquisition/greenspace and/or acquisition/relocation projects will require venturing into the intergovernmental arena. To be certain, mastering the federal grant-in-aid system is a plus. However, local consensus building is also vital to successfully mitigating hazards via land-use planning.

The federal grant-in-aid system has been described by David Kennedy as a "vertical flow of funds and administrative regulations (in which)... the federal government decides policy and supplies money; the local governments face the problems; and the state government, if involved at all, reluctantly goes along with the whole thing" (Kennedy 1972, 136). This assessment is quite cynical. However, it illustrates the essence of the challenges associated with shared governance. Kennedy goes on to say that "shifting the financial burden while retaining control is central to understanding the intergovernmental system" (Kennedy 1972, 139). In terms of nonstructural hazard mitigation, opportunities to retain local control while keeping a great deal of the financial burden on the federal government certainly exist. For example, the FEMA-administered Hazard Mitigation Grant Program (HMGP) provides mitigation funding opportunities to localities so long as the proposed project is consistent with state and local hazard mitigation plans. This arrangement offers local government an excellent opportunity to enact its choice of hazard mitigation measures at the expense of the federal government. Because the federal and state governments are reluctant to intervene in local land-use decisions, they are not averse to funding locally designed nonstructural acquisition mitigation projects so long as the benefit-cost analysis shows that the projects are worthwhile. However, the catch is that the acquisition of private property for

a mitigation project is often an unpopular proposal at the local level and that local government must bear the political burden of pursuing the project.

In addition to HMGP, there are various other federal programs which local government may utilize as a means of funding its hazard mitigation efforts. One of the more unique federal programs is the FEMA Planning Pilot Grant Program (PPGP). The PPGP provides a funding source for localities to not only update their existing comprehensive hazard mitigation plan, but also to scope and prioritize hazard mitigation projects and to essentially prepare said projects for federal grant applications such as those of HMGP. The program provides local government with an excellent opportunity to not only plan ahead for future hazards, but also to plan ahead for future hazard mitigation funding opportunities and their associated deadlines. Certainly, one way to capitalize on the opportunities afforded to local governments via programs such as HMGP and PPGP is to use such opportunities to engage in land-use planning practices with the most ambitious goal in mind—risk elimination.

The political burden associated with pursuing hazard mitigation via land-use planning is largely the product of the market (and growth interests) that have historically guided local land-use decisions (Clary 1985, 23). Because of this phenomenon, regulating land-use for the purpose of hazard mitigation is often viewed by even the most at-risk communities as being economically imposing (Mushkatel and Weschler 1985, 52). Certainly, there are several cultural challenges to consensus building at the local level when it comes to land-use planning for hazards, including capitalism and market competition, Western thought and individualism, and democracy and the "majority rules," winner/loser mindset (Mileti 1999, 34). Despite these challenges, eliminating risk is paramount in the hazard mitigation game; local government has a great deal of control in doing so through land-use planning for hazards, and the federal government will likely foot the bill for acquisitions that the local government is committed to so long as such projects are consistent with state and local hazard mitigation plans.

A good starting point for initiating an aggressive hazard mitigation plan at the local level is to review the existing plan and to take inventory of the most desirable and feasible hazard mitigation projects included in the plan. You can then seek funding for said projects through the HMGP or some other FEMA source. If no plan exists or if there are no desirable or feasible projects to initiate, then building a hazard mitigation plan which includes a robust docket of projects should become priority number one. Utilizing the PPGP to do so would be ideal, as this program will allow you to build a comprehensive plan and to scope and prioritize potential projects. You can then simply seek funding for said "prepackaged" projects as opportunities arise. Following a major disaster, you can anticipate that a certain amount of federal hazard mitigation funding will be designated for your community, allowing you to seek approval and funding for the projects of your choice. It is critical that you have an idea

of which projects you would like to pursue, because when the opportunity to get funding arises, you do not want to be forced to desperately scramble to meet deadlines and you certainly do not want to miss the opportunity to initiate the projects while hazards are still a salient issue in your community.

In the case of St. Bernard Parish, $7 million in HMGP funding for Katrina and $4.2 million for Rita had been designated specifically for hazard mitigation projects in the community. However, even with $11.2 million lying in wait, the parish did not have a solid comprehensive hazard mitigation plan in place and did not have any specific hazard mitigation projects scoped and prepared for approval. This cost the parish valuable time while it scrambled to design and scope a project for the funding, and ultimately caused it to lose some degree of public buy-in on the somewhat controversial acquisition/demolition project that it ultimately had approved and funded. This situation could have been avoided had the plan and specific scoped projects already been in place. PPGP funding ($150,000) was also designated for St. Bernard Parish following Katrina and would have certainly helped the parish in terms of scoping the HMGP project. However, the HMGP money was made available before the PPGP money was, and the opportunity to scope and prioritize a number of projects before accessing the HMGP money was foregone. This perhaps prevented the parish from utilizing the $11.2 million allocation on the most desirable and feasible project possible.

The Local Hazard Mitigation Team

The composition of the local hazard mitigation team will certainly vary from municipality to municipality. However, there are several key offices that should be included in any local hazard mitigation team:

1. Emergency Management/Homeland Security
2. Planning and Zoning/Safety and Permits
3. Public Works

Local emergency management/homeland security officials are typically most familiar with the hazards that a given municipality faces, and are often very much involved in devising all elements of local hazard plans. Furthermore, such offices usually have a substantial amount of experience in coordinating with FEMA and the state and in navigating the FEMA and state grant-in-aid systems (most emergency management/homeland security departments are funded to a large degree via FEMA and state grants). This component of the team will contribute greatly to hazard mitigation efforts in terms of the substance of plans and projects, as well as in terms of the administrative and intergovernmental processes of securing funding.

Planning and building professionals are another crucial element of the local hazard mitigation team, as they should be most familiar with the

development patterns and building code requirements of their municipality. Such professionals are especially useful when a municipality decides to use land-use planning as a hazard mitigation tool. Because they are responsible for plan review, permit issuance, and inspections, planning and building officials have much to offer the local hazard mitigation team in terms of regulating and monitoring development in a manner that is consistent with hazard mitigation plans and projects.

Public works professionals are typically the most familiar with the location and design of public infrastructure, and can be extremely useful to the local hazard mitigation team in terms of either relocating or rebuilding said infrastructure in a manner that makes it more resilient and thereby mitigates future hazards. Public works professionals should definitely play a leading role in managing all FEMA Public Assistance (PA) projects (which will be explained in greater detail later in the chapter) following a disaster, and should primarily be involved in structural hazard mitigation efforts such as elevating fire stations, libraries, and so on. Public works departments usually have a great deal of experience in managing large projects, grant monitoring and reporting, and public bid laws and processes, making them excellent partners for helping navigate intergovernmental processes and administering hazard mitigation funds.

The efforts of the aforementioned civil service departments will not be successful without the support of the public. Since elected officials serve as a buffer between the local bureaucracy and the general public, it is important that such officials be heavily engaged in all activities of the hazard mitigation team. Presenting findings and reporting progress regarding hazard mitigation plans and/or projects at various council/commission meetings where both elected officials and the public are present is a good way to gauge support and secure public buy-in on hazard mitigation efforts. As previously mentioned, hazard mitigation is often a politically contentious field, especially when there is private property involved. Therefore, it is critical that elected local officials are fully aware of the actions of the hazard mitigation team and that everyone is engaged in keeping the public informed as well. Elected local officials will also assist the hazard mitigation team in terms of facilitating the intragovernmental coordination which will be required to keep the team working in unison.

Local government may not operate in a vacuum when engaged in hazard mitigation efforts. Partnerships with other local public offices, such as the fire department or school board, and with local civic and business organizations, greatly improve the chances of success. Because hazard mitigation plans and projects will inevitably affect various local political subdivisions, businesses, and neighborhoods, it is extremely important to have them all involved in the process, if only as a sounding board for ideas. Such partnerships are likely to generate valuable resources for the hazard mitigation

team and will certainly help in terms of feeling out precisely which elements of the plan/projects are most desirable and feasible for the community.

Following Katrina, St. Bernard Parish established a diverse hazard mitigation team which included representatives from various municipal departments and local political subdivisions. The HMGP grant application process was headed by the Grants Department with support from the Department of Emergency Preparedness and Homeland Security and the Department of Community Development. The St. Bernard Parish Council (the governing body of the parish) also established the Housing, Redevelopment, and Quality of Life Commission (HRQL) for the purpose of guiding and monitoring the efforts of the local hazard mitigation team and providing a forum in which the public could become engaged in the process.

After obtaining PPGP funding in 2009, St. Bernard Parish also established a more formal hazard mitigation committee to guide the hazard mitigation planning process going forward. With the assistance of a private contractor, the Hazard Mitigation Committee (HMC) has begun the process of updating the hazard mitigation plan and scoping and prioritizing specific hazard mitigation projects for future funding opportunities. The HMC consists of representatives from the Department of Emergency Preparedness and Homeland Security, the Department of Community Development, and the Grants Department. The HMC will be presenting its findings to the HRQL, the St. Bernard Parish Planning Commission, and the public during various public meetings throughout the course of the next year.

In late 2009, St. Bernard Parish formed a partnership with the University of New Orleans Center for Hazards and Response Technology (UNO-CHART) in order to generate more resources for the HMC and to further engage the public in the planning process. UNO-CHART is currently working with St. Bernard Parish to facilitate communication between the local hazard mitigation team and business and civic associations.

For the purposes of the parish's structural hazard mitigation efforts, St. Bernard Parish established the Department of Recovery, which coordinates directly with FEMA and the state on FEMA PA projects and FEMA Project Worksheets (PWs). The Department of Recovery has worked hand in hand with the Department of Public Works in administering FEMA PA funds and managing public infrastructure projects. The St. Bernard Parish Council established the Building Mitigation Committee (BMC) in order to oversee the efforts of the Department of Recovery and to provide a public forum for feedback.

The State's Role

A coercive intergovernmental policy mandate describes a situation in which policy is prescribed by the federal and/or state government, and state and/or local agencies are charged with implementing and achieving the goals of

the said policy (May and Burby 1996, 173). This arrangement acknowledges the tension resulting from shared governance and presumes that conflicts will arise between federal/state policy goals and state/local implementation. Consequently, tools such as sanctions are utilized as "sticks" to ensure state and local compliance (May and Burby 1996, 173). Conversely, the grant-in-aid system may be viewed as the "carrots" that are used as a means toward those same policy ends. It is typical for states to have such arrangements with municipalities within their jurisdiction when it comes to hazard mitigation planning.

The Coastal Zone Management Act of 1972 gave states a great deal of authority to get involved in hazard mitigation planning and spawned a slew of state-enabling statutes, which required the adoption of hazard mitigation plans at the local level (Clary 1985, 22). However, due to an awareness of the dynamic and highly contentious nature of local land-use decisions, states are often reluctant to be very coercive vis-à-vis local government in the arena of nonstructural hazard mitigation (May 1994, 5). A case study involving Florida (which has enacted "strong" nonstructural hazard mitigation policy mandates) showed that state mandates may actually have little impact on local land-use decisions regardless of how coercive they were intended to be (Deyle et al. 2008, 366). This study once again highlights local authority over land-use decisions and the latitude that local government has with respect to mitigating hazards via land-use planning.

Despite the challenges associated with state mandates, Raymond Burby points out that they may be useful in alerting localities of the cost associated with development in areas threatened by hazards, persuading localities of engaging in land-use planning which recognizes the threat of hazards, and making hazard mitigation a higher local priority (Burby and Dalton 1994). Burby goes on to state that studies have shown that local awareness of hazards leads to local demand for political action vis-à-vis hazard mitigation and that experienced losses due to hazards may create a demand for property in hazardous areas and stimulate policy adoption (Burby and Dalton 1994, 230–231). Burby's findings are critical to this analysis because they underscore how crucial the period of time immediately following a disaster is to galvanizing local constituents and implementing hazard mitigation policies. The same could be said of state policies and mandates, as "policy makers' perception of the seriousness of a hazard and beliefs about appropriate intervention appear to help shape the level of mandate coercion vis-à-vis local government" (May 1994, 15). Although the evidence suggests that high levels of coercion are frowned upon by local government and are often ineffective, if they simply function as a catalyst for local awareness (as described by Burby), progress has been made.

Some of the common complaints local government has with states is that the state fails to provide adequate technical and financial assistance during

a recovery and that having to deal with the state is simply an added layer of bureaucracy between the local and the federal government (on which the local government heavily relies upon for hazard mitigation funding) (Rubin and Barbee 1985, 58). Undoubtedly, such complaints are typically the product of the pressure that is put on local government by constituents to have a "speedy" recovery. However, most state regulations are specifically aimed at increasing the capacity of local government to implement hazard mitigation programs on their own, and the added layer of bureaucracy does have advantages at times (Cigler et al. 1987, 120). For example, when a locality applies for HMGP funding, it must do so through the state and FEMA, with the state ultimately functioning as the grantee and the locality as the subgrantee. Because of this arrangement, applications are filtered through the state and state personnel are typically available to help locals navigate the process. This certainly affects the turnaround time on getting funding for a project, but having a larger scope of experienced professionals shaping the HMGP application (and the project) will likely result in a better-designed project and will increase the likelihood of funding. It is critical that localities get access to a full range of state resources during this process.

During the Katrina recovery, Louisiana enlisted the services of James Lee Witt Associates (JLW) to assist both the state and local governments in navigating the hazard mitigation federal grant-in-aid system. Because Witt was the former director of FEMA under President Bill Clinton, and many Witt employees were former FEMA officials with much experience in the field of hazard mitigation, JLW was an excellent resource for localities seeking hazard mitigation funding. Although the turnaround time on project funding was slow for many Louisiana parishes, in most cases the funds were ultimately allocated and projects executed. There were many fine examples of localities capitalizing on state resources throughout this process.

States have been enabled to intervene in local hazard mitigation planning by mandating local plans. State mandates may not always be very effective outside of forcing localities to devise plans and thereby raising an awareness of hazards and building local capacity to address hazards. Raising awareness is valuable in its own right and is critical to mitigating hazards, particularly in the recovery phase immediately following a disaster. However, states are very reluctant to become entrenched in local land-use decision making and typically concede nonstructural hazard mitigation plans almost exclusively to the discretion of localities.

Utilizing federal grant-in-aid hazard mitigation funding sources such as HMGP is critical in bringing local hazard mitigation plans to fruition. The role that states play in this arrangement is that of the "middle-man." Localities may view the states' position as simply being an additional layer of bureaucracy between them and federal funding. However, a more positive perspective on states' role in the grant-in-aid process is that of an additional

layer of resources and a filter through which hazard mitigation projects pass before they are federally scrutinized and funded. Naturally, each locality's experience in dealing with the state in the hazard mitigation arena will differ.

Leading up to Katrina, St. Bernard Parish had almost no experience in dealing with HMGP applications or with large-scale hazard mitigation projects in general. However, in late 2006, the Louisiana Governor's Office of Homeland Security and Emergency Preparedness (GOHSEP) hosted a number of seminars aimed at familiarizing local government with how to apply for HMGP funding and administer HMGP grants. After attending a couple of seminars, I (then an employee in the St. Bernard Parish Grants Department) and another grant writer began the process of applying for the HMGP funding, which had been designated for our community following Katrina and Rita.

The process of applying for HMGP funding with a limited amount of time before the deadline was the equivalent of trying to learn a new language just before venturing off into a foreign country. However, assistance was available through GOHSEP and JLW. Our office utilized said resources and was able to satisfy the requirements of the grant application before the deadline. I am not ashamed to say that we would not have completed the application had we not worked closely with state officials during the application period. Learning how to navigate the HMGP application process proved not only useful for that specific round of funding (the $11.2 million allocation for Katrina and Rita), but also for future opportunities. Having built our capacity to apply for HMGP funding and to administer the HMGP grant, St. Bernard was subsequently awarded an additional $3 million in noncompetitive HMGP funding in late 2008 and $10 million in competitive funding in mid-2009. What started off as an $11.2 million acquisition/demolition project had grown to a $24.2 million acquisition/demolition project that allowed St. Bernard to eliminate risk in a floodplain that had previously included over 150 housing units. The funding for the project would not have been acquired had St. Bernard Parish not taken advantage of the state resources (especially the assistance from JLW) that were made available to us. The Grants Department now has the capacity to seek and apply for hazard mitigation funding on its own, and has actively done so since 2007.

FEMA and the PA Program

Federal policies regarding flood hazard mitigation are flawed in that there is an obvious tension between actions such as funding structural mitigation projects, subsidizing flood insurance through the National Flood Insurance Program (NFIP), providing an enormous amount of disaster relief, and the goals of nonstructural hazard mitigation (Burby et al. 1999, 249–250). Certainly, such actions may be classified under the aforementioned phenomena of risk reduction and risk sharing. In terms of the ultimate hazard

mitigation goal of risk elimination via nonstructural hazard mitigation, federal efforts have by and large been counterproductive.

The NFIP has proven to have some impact on land use, but its impact can either be amplified or subverted by local land-use decisions (Holloway and Burby 1990, 259). Many critics of federal hazard mitigation policy point to the NFIP approach of site-by-site (rather than comprehensive) mitigation as an example of the federal government's failure to enact any sort of comprehensive land use policy which is aimed at risk elimination. Furthermore, when coupled with enormous structural mitigation efforts such as levees and so on, property values in at-risk areas increase and future attempts at acquisition in the name of hazard mitigation are either greatly complicated or forgone (Holloway and Burby 1990, 262).

The pros and cons of federal hazard mitigation policy notwithstanding, we arrive at the same conclusion—local decision making regarding land-use and the willingness and ability to use land-use planning as a means of nonstructural hazard mitigation are very powerful tools. As with state policies and mandates, there are "openings" in federal policies and mandates where local control over land use is conceded. Funding opportunities such as HMGP are there to meet local demands for hazard mitigation and states may bring various resources to bear on the HMGP process. Once again, it is crucial that such opportunities be taken advantage of immediately following a disaster and that state resources are utilized to the fullest extent (and are approached as resources rather than constraints). This explanation largely reinforces what has already been discussed regarding the state's role in hazard mitigation and the dynamics of the federal grant-in-aid system in the nonstructural arena. However, hazard mitigation efforts via the post-disaster FEMA Public Assistance (PA) program and the associated intergovernmental processes are critical to disaster recovery for local government and are worthy of further discussion despite the fact that they do not always foster risk elimination.

Following a natural disaster, FEMA provides funding opportunities to repair or replace damaged public infrastructure through its PA program. There is a hazard mitigation component to the PA program which may be helpful in repairing/replacing public infrastructure in such a way that it is more resilient in future similar disasters. This is an excellent opportunity to bring older buildings and infrastructure into compliance with NFIP and other standards and to protect public assets going forward (see Figure 3.2).

Aside from structural measures such as elevation (risk reduction), PA provides the opportunity for public infrastructure to actually be relocated into areas that are not as exposed to the associated risk. For example, a locality may choose to relocate a substantially damaged (by flood) fire station out of the floodplain completely rather than to simply repair and elevate the

FIGURE 3.2 New Orleans, Louisiana, March 8, 2006—The level of flooding from Hurricane Katrina is evident by the water line across the awning and pillars of this house in Gentilly. The homeowner has coverage from the National Flood Insurance Program (NFIP) and is eligible for the Increased Cost of Compliance (ICC) benefit since he lives in a high risk area and is elevating his home above the base flood elevation in compliance with the community's floodplain ordinance. (Photo courtesy of Robert Kaufmann/FEMA.)

structure in its original location. Actions such as these taken by local government are an example to the community and may even redirect private development away from the floodplain.

The downside to the PA program is that the bureaucracy surrounding the project worksheets (PW), which must be completed, submitted, and approved for PA funding, is famously dense. Using substantial damage and benefit-cost analysis tools, as well as operating under restrictions in terms of eligible costs, can all be cumbersome to local government and can frustrate post-disaster hazard mitigation efforts. There is a fine line which must be walked between mitigating infrastructure from future hazards and outright improving infrastructure, the latter being explicitly prohibited. The state may or may not be a good partner in navigating these processes. However, like other mitigation funding sources, FEMA PA will only approve projects which are consistent with the applicable state hazard mitigation plan. Consequently, it really helps if a locality is operating in a state which has a comprehensive and coherent plan to follow.

Once again, we see that the burden on local government is substantial. While operating in the demanding recovery environment, localities must take

the time to explore hazard mitigation opportunities through the PA program and to make tough decisions regarding public infrastructure. The pressure to rebuild and to begin providing public services to a returning population cannot be overstated. Therefore, it is critical at this time to be as patient as possible and to utilize all available resources. In terms of funding (like HMGP), there may be a 25% nonfederal cost-share associated with PA projects. The state may be a useful resource in covering the cost-share, covering a portion of the cost-share, or providing guidance as to how the cost-share may be covered.

In summary, the federal policies that have resulted in a heavy reliance on structural mitigation measures (the construction of levees, dams, etc.) and have fostered risk sharing (the NFIP) pose challenges to what should be the ultimate goal of hazard mitigation—risk elimination. However, engaging in nonstructural hazard mitigation measures and working toward eliminating risk may be achieved by local government within the federal framework. It is a matter of having solid, locally designed nonstructural projects which are consistent with local and state plans carried through the federal grant-in-aid process.

In terms of the PA program, opportunities to replace or repair existing public infrastructure in its previous location abound. Doing so has value in terms of hazard mitigation because it is mandated that all infrastructure be brought up to current standards (such as NFIP elevation requirements) when PA funds are used. However, FEMA PA also affords local government the opportunity to relocate infrastructure out of harm's way and such nonstructural opportunities should always be taken advantage of whenever possible. The challenge associated with considering the nonstructural relocation route on a PA project is that the pressures of a recovery on local government are great and that time is always of the essence. Patience and political will are key in seeing nonstructural PA projects through, and utilizing state resources during this process may also be quite helpful.

Summary

It is quite advantageous for local government to engage in mitigating hazards and hazard mitigation planning immediately following a disaster, when hazards are a salient issue and local stakeholders are willing to engage in the intergovernmental processes necessary to make the community more resilient in the future. Using nonstructural hazard mitigation techniques such as land-use planning is the most effective means of eliminating risk in the community, and programs such as HMGP and PPGP are excellent tools in utilizing federal funds to do so.

The local hazard mitigation team will vary depending on the structure of a given local government. However, it is critical that certain departments and professionals be involved in the process. It is also critical that elected

officials and the public be involved in the process, as hazard mitigation efforts will likely affect a wide range of local stakeholders.

State government will play a vital role in getting hazard mitigation funding at the local level, as it often functions as the grantee for many federal hazard mitigation grant programs and has the authority to enact its own hazard mitigation plan and to mandate local hazard mitigation plans. The state is often viewed as an added layer of bureaucracy between the local and federal government. However, a more positive approach to this relationship is to view the state as an added layer of resources between the local and federal government, and as a filter through which only the most desirable and feasible hazard mitigation plans and projects will be evaluated and funded. The state also has the potential to increase the local capacity to seek and administer its own hazard mitigation grant funds in an effective manner, as we have seen in the case of St. Bernard Parish.

Not all federal hazards policies are effective or especially conducive to risk elimination. However, the federal grant-in-aid system and programs such as HMGP and PPGP are an excellent way to receive funding for desirable and feasible local hazard mitigation projects, particularly those which are nonstructural in nature. The FEMA PA program is also an excellent means of mitigating public infrastructure following a disaster, and although many of the PA opportunities are structural in nature, they will ultimately contribute to an increased level of sustainability in the community. Navigating the bureaucracy and "red tape" of the PA process can be cumbersome, but it is nothing that a well-staffed and motivated local hazard mitigation team cannot handle, particularly when the team is using all of the state and federal resources available to them.

Navigating the intergovernmental processes associated with hazard mitigation is not easy. However, opportunities for success abound. Utilizing the full range of local, state, and federal resources is crucial, as is keeping the public informed and involved in the process. Always keep in mind that the future of your community may depend on your hazard mitigation efforts, and that the work that you do is an investment in the sustainability of a community that people care for and depend on.

End-of-Chapter Questions

1. When is the most opportune time for local government to engage in hazard mitigation planning? Why?
2. Why is the role of local government so critical in terms of utilizing nonstructural means of mitigating hazards?
3. What are the advantages of local government having a sound, comprehensive hazard mitigation plan and a list of specific scoped hazard mitigation projects prior to a major disaster striking?

4. What are the key components and functions of the ideal local hazard mitigation team?
5. What are the pros and cons of the state's role in hazard mitigation?
6. What are the opportunities and challenges associated with the FEMA PA program?

References

Burby, R., Beatley, T., Berke, P. R., Deyle, R. E., French, S. P., Godschalk, D. R., ... Platt, R. H. (Summer 1999). Unleashing the power of planning to create disaster resistant communities. *APA Journal, 65*, 247–258.

Burby, R., & Dalton, L. (1994). Plans can matter! The role of land use plans and state planning mandates in limiting the development of hazardous areas. *Public Administration Review, 54*(3), 229–238.

Cigler, B. A., Stiftel, B., & Burby, R. J. (Fall 1987). Rural Community Responses to a National Mandate: An Assessment of Floodplain Land Use Management. *Publius, 17*(4), 113–130.

Clary, B. (1985). The evolution and structure of natural hazard policies. *Public Administration Review, 45*, 20–28.

Deyle, R., Chapin, T. S., & Baker, E. J. (2008). The proof of the planning is in the platting. *Journal of the American Planning Association, 74*(3), 349–368.

Gerber, B. (2007). Disaster management in the United States: Examining key political and policy changes. *The Policy Studies Journal, 35*(2), 227–237.

Holloway, J., & Burby, R. (1990). The effects of floodplain development on residential land values. *Land Economics, 66*(3), 259–271.

Kennedy, D. (1972, March/April). The law of appropriateness: An approach to a general theory of intergovernmental relations. *Public Administration Review, 32*(2), 135–143.

May, P. (1994). Analyzing mandate design: State mandates governing hazard-prone areas. *Publius, 24*(2), 1–16.

May, P., & Burby, R. (1996). Coercive versus cooperative policies: Comparing intergovernmental mandate performance. *Journal of Policy Analysis and Management, 15*(2), 171–201.

Mileti, D. (1999). *Disasters by Design: A Reassessment of Natural Hazards in the U.S.* Washington, DC: Joseph Henry Press.

Mushkatel, A., & Weschler, L. (1985). Emergency management and the intergovernmental system. *Public Administration Review, 45*, 49–56.

Rubin, C., & Barbee, D. (1985). Disaster recovery and hazard mitigation: Bridging the intergovernmental gap. *Public Administration Review, 45*, 57–63.

Sheaffer, J. R., Roland, F. J., Davis, G. W., Feldman, T., & Stockdale, J. (1976). *Flood hazard mitigation through safe land use practices.* Prepared for the Office of Policy Development and Research, U.S. Department of Housing and Urban Development. Chicago, IL: Kiefer and Associates.

Chapter **4**

Public-Private Partnerships in Mitigation Initiatives

Robert Anderson and Inés Pearce

Contents

Learning Objectives

- Describe the two principal types of mitigation.
- Describe how mitigation issues are interrelated with preparedness, response, and recovery.
- Describe in a general sense why mitigation is not carried out unless a mitigation champion and justification are well presented to both the public and private sectors.
- Provide examples on how the public and private sectors collaborate on mitigation issues.
- Locate information about mitigation on the Internet.

Introduction

This chapter concentrates on the mitigation of natural hazards in the United States supported by examples of public–private partnerships (PPPs). PPPs are defined as collaborative, cooperative groups with the aim of proactively addressing community issues, such as pre-disaster mitigation, which includes a governmental agency working in tandem with any private entity (nonprofit, chamber of commerce, a club, etc.), as no one sector can accomplish the task in question on its own. On the private side, where mitigation is concerned, individuals, families, businesses, and organizations that have taken mitigation actions in advance of a disaster event (mitigators) are better prepared to recover more quickly during a disaster. They help their communities in several ways during the response and recovery phases: mitigators require less community resources, as they have already reduced their exposure, which strengthens the workforce tax base. Owing to their proactive measures, they have the ability to provide volunteers and donations to assist their community after a disaster. A special word about one particular segment of the private sector: The private sector is greatly complemented by nongovernmental organizations that help provide expertise, personnel, funds, and/or educational resources to conduct general types of mitigation. The public sector side is led by governmental emergency management offices from the local to national levels (e.g., the Federal Emergency Management Agency [FEMA]). By facilitating the community to become disaster-resilient, emergency managers help the local economy as residents and businesses are able to resume operational activities after the disaster and keep their doors open, so the community may survive and thrive. In some cases, the public sector can seek or provide financial support for community mitigation that may not have been accessible to residents or business owners on their own. Depending on who is involved from the community and their determined priorities, these collaborative mitigation activities can take on many shapes, such as hazard identification, retrofitting existing structures, the changing

of building codes, or changes in construction practices. The reality is that mitigation reduces loss of lives and property, reduces injuries, and helps communities recover more quickly. In fact, when mitigation activities are not undertaken and the acceptable level of risk for a community is exceeded, an increase in needless fatalities, injuries, financial losses, and duress may be expected by a community. Such losses may affect not only the local economy but also the economies of the state, territories, and, in extreme cases, the national or global economies. Thankfully, such extreme consequences are preventable, as impacts can be reduced at the local level through proactive mitigation activities.

The general concepts of PPPs can be applied to addressing all hazards, risk issues, and even nondisaster topics, although specific information on these is beyond the scope of this chapter. In addition, the motivation and process to get the private sector engaged favorably and consistently with the public sector while focusing on all risks identified for a community is beyond the scope of this chapter.

Mitigation Background for Discussing PPPs

Mitigation of natural hazards, like preparedness, starts from the bottom up at the individual level with a decision to take action and is supported from the top down through leadership and funding at the national, state, or local level. However, unlike mitigation, which seeks to minimize or eliminate hazards, preparedness is about addressing what could not be mitigated and being ready for what will happen during those events. For the purposes of this chapter, the authors are breaking mitigation activities into two classes: structural and nonstructural (Phillips 2009). Structural mitigation typically involves physically increasing the resiliency of a building, structure, or system, including infrastructure, whereas nonstructural mitigation involves loss reduction by loss avoidance through well enforced planning practices; code changes to improve the resiliency of buildings, structures, and systems to some defined or implied levels of acceptable risk; using tools such as insurance, education about hazards, vulnerability, and risk management options, as well as warning systems for hazards such as tornadoes, hurricanes, and tsunamis; planning evacuation routes; and the posting of signage and the education of the public and private sectors on how to follow posted signage. Mitigation is typically needed because of the development and use of land, infrastructure, buildings, and businesses with or without fully taking into account hazards or the interactions of development and changes in use. In many cases, mitigation may not be accounted for by individuals, businesses, or agencies doing an actual mitigation activity, as they just see that they are simply following a more robust and updated version of the laws, ordinances,

regulations, and standards required for the siting, design, construction, and operation of new buildings, structures, and systems. Mitigation may also be appropriate or required as new information is developed about hazards, vulnerabilities, or risks, or as new levels of acceptable risk are established or changes in use occur. Finally, mitigation may also be required if regulatory dictums mandate it or the vulnerability of sites, buildings, infrastructure, and equipment change with age and buildings or sites are rehabilitated, upgraded, or remodeled.

A complete survey of the mitigation for any one specific natural hazard in the United States does not exist. For instance, a detailed survey of corporate mitigation activities is not known to exist for any one state and may not exist in detail even at the operations area level. There are several reasons for this lack of documentation. First, businesses are not required to provide mitigation data to emergency managers; second, in many cases, private companies do not participate or share data consistently with local governments, states, or even each other on mitigation matters; third, some corporate activities are considered proprietary and confidential. This does not mean that corporate America does not carry out mitigation activities. In fact, business carries out a great deal of mitigation activities, but may keep the information quiet if the company is privately held. Most mitigation activities are intended to reduce risk and allow companies to quickly recover from unplanned interruptions and resume business operations shortly after a disaster.

On average, most state multihazard mitigation plans do not elaborate on mitigation activities and/or plans that have been developed by individuals or companies. These companies, industries, and utilities typically do not share hazard exposure, vulnerability, and risk data much less mitigation and preparedness information, excepting perhaps with their local emergency management agency. This is because sharing of information can be seen as giving a competitor an advantage or could provide critical information on security matters to the public. However, this is contrary to the new perception of viewing the public sector as a resource instead of a liability in areas of hazard and vulnerability exposure.

Why Do PPPs Matter?

PPPs matter since they allow the collective effort of mitigation activities to be shared between all stakeholders, where everyone benefits from a safer community. Working collaboratively can drive down the cost of mitigation. Cofunders take on a greater sense of responsibility for the mitigated site or activity, and an existing hazard can then be lessened or removed entirely. Because PPPs are using community resources, they can implement sustainable measures that will mitigate their risk for the long term.

Infrastructure is mostly owned by private entities in the United States. Although preparedness and timely response help reduce the time lost due to damage or loss of function after a natural disaster, it is mitigation spurred by a PPP that helps increase the resiliency of infrastructure as well as factories, businesses, and homes. Increased resiliency helps communities, businesses, and individuals recover more quickly. A business's ability to recover more quickly than a competitor helps the business to lower its potential for lost revenue and possibly increases market share. It can take the place of businesses that cannot recover equally as fast (or potentially ever), as they have been isolated from their customers, perhaps only because they have lost utility services after an event. Conversely, the public sector also benefits from these partnerships, as they rely on the private sector for a variety of critical services and products. By creating a dynamic PPP and working together in advance, relationships can be built that increase trust and lower false expectations that could have either sector making erroneous decisions based on assumptions. As no one sector can address community hazards on their own, PPPs are a solution-based tool for pre-disaster, during disaster, and post-disaster in which the entire community benefits.

The Importance of Mitigation to Protect a Community

Mitigation needs to be balanced between levels of acceptable risk and the needs of a community. For the purposes of this chapter, risk is the product of hazard and vulnerability, and the unit of measurement for any losses will be in dollars. For example, the 7.0-magnitude earthquake that occurred on January 12, 2010, in Port Au Prince, Haiti, had a widespread and devastating effect. The loss in U.S. dollars for the Haitian earthquake was estimated at between 7 to 14 billion. Haiti is one of the poorest countries in the Western Hemisphere. Many of Haiti's buildings were built out of cement or concrete with little or no reinforcement, and in some cases, there was no quality control in any phase of construction. In the United States, most structures and permanent buildings require a construction permit that includes inspections by the building department to ensure that the structure meets the appropriate building codes. These buildings and structures require knowledgeable supervision during siting, design, and construction. In contrast, Haiti did not have a viable building code and especially one that emphasized some level of acceptable risk, like holding builders to a life safety standard such as we have in the United States. This has resulted in Haiti experiencing more than 212,000 fatalities, 300,000 persons injured, 1 million people made homeless, and an unknown number of persons displaced. Although the United States has experienced a variety of major disasters in the last 30 years, including floods, hurricanes, tornadoes, wildfires, and earthquakes,

the impact has not raised to the level of destruction in Haiti due to what we have defined as structural and nonstructural mitigation in the form of improved building codes and improved construction. Similarly, the 8.8-magnitude earthquake that struck off the coast of Chile on February 27, 2010, caused damage, collapsed structures, and created a tsunami, but the people did not experience widespread devastation thanks, in part, to their stricter building codes in the well-known highly active seismic area.

What has been learned over the decades is that collaboration between all levels of government with professionals that deal with the built environment has helped to establish various law ordinances, regulations, and standards, including building codes and standards that reduce the potential loss of life in the United States. Although the depth and magnitude of the Haiti earthquake differ from those of the Loma Prieta and Northridge earthquakes (magnitudes 7.1 and 6.7, respectively), the California earthquakes can serve as general indicators of the usefulness of building codes and mitigation done as a function of siting, design, and quality control during construction. In the two California earthquakes, the overall performance of buildings, structures, and infrastructure resulted in a lower number of buildings destroyed (or heavily damaged), less than 130 combined fatalities, and a combined financial impact estimated at less than 0.1% of the U.S. gross domestic product. This damage was significantly less than that reported by the post-disaster data of Haiti, where the initial loss was estimated to be above 100% of Haiti's gross domestic product. This highlights the degree to which mitigation can make a difference.

It is interesting to note that in the case of seismic hazard mitigation, the state and local agencies and private communities have far outspent the federal government in California from 1990 through 2002 (CSSC 2003). This trend continues today. The Hazard Mitigation Grant Program (HMGP) can help by funding a state or local government through FEMA, but these funds are not available unless a disaster has already occurred. However, these funds alone are not enough. Local and private sector funding and participation are needed. This can be a perfect opportunity to bring in a PPP to fill this gap. Some typical major private-sector participants can be insurance and reinsurance companies, and these can include the building and banking industries, which all have a vested interest in the success of their community, where they operate and where their employees live.

What Are PPPs?

PPPs are described as collaborative, cooperative groups with the aim of proactively addressing community issues, such as pre-disaster mitigation, as no one sector can accomplish this on its own. The public and private sectors do play vital roles in PPPs, but unlike the name suggests, partners are not

limited to just the public and private sectors. They also include representatives from nonprofits, science, and academia, and benefit most when they also include community groups, neighborhood organizations, technical experts, media, researchers, and many others, depending on the focus of the partnership. In particular, the private sector can provide a wealth of expertise, services, and support to partnership efforts. This may come directly from a company or representatives who participate on their behalf. How contributions are tailored will vary from one community to another, even if they come from the same company, unless they are specifically mandated from a corporation's headquarters. However, the cookie-cutter approach is not always the best one, as a PPP needs to match the unique culture of its community to be successful. The private sector's role can vary from one of leadership to one of support, to a provider of an expert service or a funder, but most importantly, to participate and contribute to the effort in whatever way makes the most sense to the business. The same must go for any other partners, as a true partnership is about both give and take.

Many PPPs are launched due to an influx of funding such as a grant, but successful partnerships are not designed on just the exchange of funds. A key element of a PPP is the value of its partners' contributions, including nonmonetary contributions such as experts' time, which is considered an in-kind donation. The goal of a successful PPP is to institutionalize programs for long-term risk reduction, so it must be designed to surpass initial grant funds and should find ways to be self-sufficient through a combination of partners' support and contributions, both direct and in-kind.

PPPs will vary from one community to another, as the hazards may differ as well as the makeup of local expertise. Therefore, partnerships should reflect their community. For example, a partnership launched by leadership in science/academia and government is California's statewide Earthquake Country Alliance (ECA) whose mission is to foster a culture of earthquake and tsunami readiness in California. The ECA was created to present common messages, to share or promote existing resources, and to implement activities and products all geared toward people taking action. A core focus of the ECA is to educate people about securing the structure of their home and interiors and about what quake-safe actions need to be taken in advance of a temblor.

The ECA, originally focused on the southern California region, was launched in 2003 by the Southern California Earthquake Center (SCEC) to create a one-stop shop for earthquake science and preparedness resources in preparation for the 10-year anniversary of the Northridge earthquake. Some of the early developments by the ECA at that time included the first update of the *Putting Down Roots in Earthquake Country* handbook along with a Spanish version and partnerships with Spanish-language media, the development of the www.earthquakecountry.org website, and coordinated

responses to misinformation that could harm people if followed. The ECA began working in earnest on broader public education initiatives in 2006 led by SCEC, along with cochairs from the U.S. Geological Survey and the City of Los Angeles Emergency Management Department, with the launch of the "Dare to Prepare" and "Secure Your Space" campaigns, and the development of the Southernmost San Andreas Fault Scenario, which is what led to what is now known as "ShakeOut."

A major public education and outreach campaign created and conducted by the ECA was "The Great Southern California ShakeOut" (ShakeOut) held in 2008. All ShakeOut activities were coordinated by a steering committee made up of ECA's partners with the effort divided into two main areas. First was the ShakeOut Scenario development led by the U.S. Geological Survey, which included the coordination of more than 300 scientists, engineers, and technical experts to create a comprehensive scenario detailing a 6.7-magnitude earthquake on the Southern San Andreas fault, including expected effects to everything from housing to infrastructure and community recovery, and the creation of animations and a movie to tell the "earthquake story" to everyone from schoolchildren to elected officials and business leaders. The scenario was developed into two printed forms: one is the complete detailed open-file report, and the other is an overview chronology of expected experiences to walk anyone through what may occur after an earthquake of this size and get them thinking about how to become better prepared. All of it was geared toward becoming the basis for full-scale exercises and simple drills by first responders, businesspeople, and homeowners alike. The second area was taking the ShakeOut Scenario and bringing it to the public. This included partnership building; educational information, website, games, and online tool development; a speakers' bureau; handouts, flyers, posters, presentations, and other promotional materials; drill manuals for basic to advanced participation; public service announcements, videos, and animations; and audio and video drill broadcasts to be played at the start of the ShakeOut to encourage all participants to take the quake-safe action of "Drop, Cover, and Hold On" the moment the earthquake begins. This second area was led by the SCEC at the University of Southern California, with support from a variety of partners and supporters such as State Farm Insurance and the City of Los Angeles, which also brought additional events to the ShakeOut calendar, such as the International Earthquake Conference and the "Get Ready Rally."

The 2008 ShakeOut was so successful that communities requested that it be expanded to include the entire state. The ECA now holds an event called "The Great California ShakeOut," where among a variety of mitigation messages that governments, schools, businesses, neighborhoods, nonprofits, neighborhoods, individuals, and families receive, all are invited to participate in the largest public earthquake drill in the U.S. history. In 2008, the

drill had 5.47 million participants, in 2009 it had 6.9 million, and more are expected each successive year in California. This program has expanded to other earthquake-prone areas of the United States and abroad, such as with the 2009 ShakeOut in New Zealand.

Originally, the ECA was specific to the southern California region, but has now grown statewide as an alliance to include other alliances within its structure. For instance, four of the first alliances in the ECA are the Redwood Coast Tsunami Workgroup, the Bay Area Earthquake Alliance, the Central Coast Earthquake Alliance, and the Southern California Earthquake Alliance, with room for more. Ostensibly, these are PPPs within a PPP. The purpose was to make collaboration and partnership run smoothly as the ECA plays the role of coordinator, fundraiser, marketer, organizer, and supporter. Projects at the ECA's statewide level are agreed upon by all the alliances. The individual alliances have more autonomy to make decisions about their own organizations and events at the local level. This is not to say that the PPP is rigidly structured; it is, in fact, quite flexible, and everyone benefits from shared messaging, websites, materials, and events such as ShakeOut. Success will be measured first by the number of registrations, which reflects the efficacy of campaign messages that have reached the public; second, by the numbers of increased sales for nonstructural products with partnering retailers; third, by the stories and information shared by the public as to what they did before, during, and after the drill, followed by researchers documenting activities; and finally, the lessened impacts after an earthquake, which would demonstrate the success of this mitigation effort. The ECA is not waiting to reach out to the public only through ShakeOut, as mitigation needs to be an ongoing push to keep complacency from taking hold. Thus, success continues to be measured in participation at the PPP level, and the number of residents who share what they have mitigated to be ready for an earthquake. These activities are expanding to other states including those who are planning something similar to the Great California ShakeOut for their region or state.

An example of PPP led by governmental local emergency management offices is FEMA's 1997 Project Impact initiative. The goal of Project Impact was to support, from the federal to the local level, the development of mitigation programs to reduce or eliminate community risk. FEMA grant funds and support through the 10 regional offices allowed each community to fully focus on mitigation for the first time. Some of the handful of pilot communities that launched Project Impact were Seattle, Washington; Oakland, California; Deerfield Beach, Florida; and Pascagoula, Mississippi. FEMA quickly grew the initiative within 3 years into more than 250 Project Impact communities across the United States. These jurisdictions were focused extensively on mitigation solutions in their own communities as well as sharing information and lessons learned between communities.

While initially launched with the government as the lead, some communities selected their own leadership from the private or nonprofit sectors, but were always inclusive of all partners. Examples of Project Impact communities that were still operating after more than 10 years are Tulsa, Oklahoma; Seattle, Washington; Miami-Dade County, Florida; and Jefferson County, West Virginia.

For an example as to why some jurisdictions were chosen for Project Impact, one only needs to consider Tulsa, Oklahoma. The community of Tulsa had faced years of flooding disasters, and by 1987 had faced nine Presidential-declared disasters within 15 years. Into the late 1990s, the community was determined to strengthen itself against this repeating hazard and had been organizing and championing changes to lessen their risk.

Due to the participation of key partners and collaboration to mitigate their flood hazard, Tulsa was perfectly positioned to become a Project Impact community in 1998. The idea was that the FEMA initiative should build upon what existed, and enhance current mitigation efforts, which was exactly what occurred in Tulsa and other successful communities. Tulsa Partners, a PPP that led the initiatives that were launched under Project Impact, now permanently manages the mitigation efforts in the community, which has instituted widespread community programs that affect real change (Bullock et al. 2009). As a nonprofit, Tulsa Partners has established mitigation in the community supported through grants and long-term relationships to provide additional funds.

FEMA's Mitigation Division

FEMA is actively engaged with all aspects of natural and human-made hazard mitigation. The FEMA's Mitigation Directorate was established in 1993 and for the first time, created mitigation as a cornerstone of emergency management. The Directorate's range of programs, such as the National Flood Insurance Program (NFIP) and the HMGP, are significant elements of the American emergency management system. These programs are statutorily authorized and designed to address impacts from floods, earthquakes, tornadoes, and other natural disasters. To assist in addressing all hazards, the Mitigation Directorate has three divisions working to reduce future losses to homes, businesses, schools, public buildings, and critical facilities: Risk Analysis, Risk Reduction, and Risk Insurance.

The Directorate engages in many PPPs, such as their launch of the national Project Impact initiative in 1997, which grew from seven pilots to over 250 communities in all 50 states. Partners include a broad spectrum of stakeholders in private, nongovernmental, media, and volunteer organizations; universities; academicians; federal, state, tribal, and local government; and professional organizations. The Directorate also fosters partnerships with

nongovernmental groups involved in public policy and administration, insurance, higher education, the building sciences, and urban planning, all with an eye toward proactive, pre-disaster mitigation.

Addressing Flooding: Mitigation Projects

The City of Quincy, Massachusetts, also was a Project Impact–designated community and had a significant flooding issue. Quincy was situated with 27 miles of coastline, 15 miles of tidal shoreline, and nearly three square miles of the town in the 100-year floodplain. Very little attention was paid to the potential for flooding at the time that many of the houses were built more than 60 years ago. By 2001, more than 150 residential properties in Quincy had experienced repetitive flood damage due to serious rainfalls or snowstorms. In addition, some neighborhoods were at risk of flooding due to hurricanes, storms, and surges coming in from the coast, while others were at risk from river, creek, or wetland overflows. Building upon their PPP to connect the community and focus on mitigation efforts, Quincy was able to focus on high-risk areas. Through HMGP and city funding for one such project, a pumping station was constructed and activated for serious storms and high tides; it prevented flooding in low-lying areas. After these disasters were averted, additional HMGP funds were used for various mitigation projects, such as building seawalls, retrofitting houses, drainage improvements, acquisitions, and demolition. The City of Quincy experienced the success of mitigation actions built upon the foundation of their PPP and community outreach (FEMA 2001).

The City of Pascagoula, Mississippi, was selected as one of the pilots for Project Impact in 1997. Their PPP identified one priority to create a database of structures in the local floodplain, which would hold critical information for preparing mitigation plans. This selection was made because of the risk of the community to hurricanes, storm surge, and flooding. Then, through Federal Housing Administration Title I loans that provided below-market rates, partner Merchants & Marine Bank offered a special home improvement program for homeowners to use for retrofitting work that included mitigation projects such as workable shutters and tie-downs. Other Pascagoula Project Impact business partners, BellSouth and the Mississippi Power Company, announced special incentives and services that aided customers in the event of a disaster as well as a series of steps that mitigated damage to their own facilities (Witt 1998).

As a way to increase community education and decision making, Pascagoula Project Impact held a Hurricane Awareness Day. There were over 30 exhibits, awareness activities, and displays. One of the biggest attractions was a risk assessment hot air balloon ride over Pascagoula, an

educational ride that showed the floodplains and surge-prone areas of the city. It was reported that "the success of this exposure was dramatic. By providing an aerial vantage point, citizens could see the interface of development and vulnerable areas and could better understand the need to protect these important, protective land barriers" (Vorel 2001).

Unfortunately, Pascagoula was a community hit hard by 2005's Hurricane Katrina, but due to their established PPP, city manager Kay Kell cited their partnerships as a key to their faster recovery. Kell said that from attending partnership meetings she realized that the "best thing was the partnerships and getting people together." This is because governments and communities were doing things for each other and sharing information with each other they never would have done otherwise. Kell stated that Pascagoula did not have money to hire consultants, so in addition to their local partners, new outside partnerships were formed that assisted their recovery, such as many free resources provided by universities and other cities not in the disaster area. A city management association also provided a retired city manager who provided onsite mentoring during recovery. Existing and new partnerships became an important element to Pascagoula responding to and recovering from this devastating disaster (FEMA 592 2007).

Addressing High Winds: SafeRooms and Key Partnerships

Tulsa was also an example of a successful program that addressed the tornado hazard through the addition of SafeRooms in all new construction. Thanks to a partnership with the Home Builders Association, Tulsa Partners were able to popularize SafeRooms to protect homeowners from tornados and successfully expanded the practice across Oklahoma, as most houses did not have basements to protect them from this high-wind hazard. Tulsa's long-term mitigation success was borne out of repeated disasters that took their toll, community collaborations aimed at solutions, the benefit from federal programs/initiatives, and funding combined with forward-thinking champions. This was also the recipe of success for two pilot projects: Pascagoula, Mississippi, and Seattle, Washington.

Addressing Earthquakes: Regional Home Retrofit and Code Master

Seattle Project Impact was one of FEMA's seven pilot communities for Project Impact. Their PPP brought together representatives of the entire community to develop three programs: Home Retrofit, School Retrofit, and Better Hazard Mapping. One of the area's vulnerabilities is to residential construction that

did not use sufficient bolts to keep the house in place during strong ground shaking. The Home Retrofit program, which began initially in Seattle, was actually designed by regional building officials, architects, engineers, contractors, trainers, and building professionals. In doing so, the Home Retrofit program developed pre-engineered plan sets and created expedited permitting, training for contractors and classes for homeowners, tool-lending for do-it-yourselfers, and special loan packages that fit not only Seattle's specifications but also the region's specifications. Contractors would not need to attend different trainings in different jurisdictions, as the standards were adopted by all participating jurisdictions. Within 8 years, 21 jurisdictions were participating in the Regional Home Retrofit program. Nearly 500 building professionals attended trainings on these new standards, and thousands of homeowners sat through a two-hour class. More than 1000 houses have been retrofitted and more are still being strengthened today. This was all accomplished through the Seattle Project Impact PPP.

Currently, the Regional Home Retrofit program is still educating and bolting vulnerable houses against earthquake damage 12 years after inception. Those aspects still managed directly by the city are covered under general funds, but in order to institutionalize the mitigation solutions, elements of Regional Home Retrofit are now a part of everyday operations for local government, like the building department, or addressed by community programs such as the classes managed by the Phinney Ridge Neighborhood Association. Mitigation success was achieved through long-term partnership support in the community to maintain program initiatives.

Another partnership example focusing on structural mitigation is how FEMA's National Earthquake Hazard Reduction Program (NEHRP), in collaboration with the International Code Council, has produced an educational publication called *The Code Master: Seismic Residential Rehabilitation*. Other partners included in the development are the Applied Technology Council, state and local agencies, and other professional organizations. This document provides basic information and example graphics of seismic mitigation/rehabilitation details for wood-framed one- and two-family residences. *The Code Master* is intended to reduce losses observed in similar buildings from earthquakes. This document is not based on a specific code or standard; instead, the mitigation examples are based on vulnerabilities and damage observed after earthquakes. The document also provides web addresses for documents and codes that may be useful to those working on reducing seismic risk to single-family residences or upgrades to local building practices and was found to be the most understandable and user-friendly approach to presenting the information. The steps are simple and designed to guide the user through the table of information. *The Code Master* may be ordered from NEHRP or from the Builders Book Source.

Addressing the Economy: Disaster Resistant Business Toolkit®

A unique PPP focused on one entire sector of the entire economy is the Disaster Resistant Business (DRB) Toolkit® Workgroup. Over 99% of business employers in the United States fall under the category of small (U.S. Small Business Administration 2007), and when disasters strike, community recovery times are prolonged as these businesses struggle to reopen or maintain operations. Inspired by the positive experience of Seattle Project Impact partners, an unfunded effort was launched to focus on small businesses after observing serious impacts due to events in 2001: the Nisqually Earthquake in February and the 9/11 terrorist attacks in September. As in most disasters, smaller businesses commonly experienced a greater financial impact as they have less resilience due to having fewer resources. Partners had seen how many communities had tried to engage their small businesses with limited success. So, the DRB Toolkit® Workgroup initiative was launched as a partnership with private, public, and nonprofit sectors to create a clearinghouse of resources to assist vulnerable businesses in taking mitigation actions. The Workgroup quickly found that even good information was not organized for easy use, and many publications or tools promised to result in a plan, but never got beyond the basics. The DRB Toolkit® Workgroup began culling information, materials, and best practices of the partners, but found that it was best to start fresh and develop what became the DRB Toolkit®.

By working together with government planners, business continuity professionals, nonprofit trainers, and a variety of experts from small to large organizations, a new approach was developed. The DRB Toolkit® demystifies the process for small businesses with limited time, resources, and experience to develop their own disaster plan. The Toolkit uses a simple but comprehensive process that integrates risk assessment, impact analysis, mitigation, response and recovery solutions, training of employees, how to partner with local government, and much more. Small businesses are provided a guided DRB approach to build or enhance their disaster plan, train employees, and exercise their actions to ensure resilience. In a natural progression, the DRB Toolkit® Workgroup has now progressed into a 501(c)(3) nonprofit public charity consisting of both public and private representatives, and is currently working with sponsors to provide the Toolkit to all U.S. businesses at a low cost with the ultimate goal of making it free. When small businesses have mitigated and planned for possible disruptions, when the inevitable happens in the community, they can rebound more quickly and limit the long-term impacts on local, regional, and possibly national economies (DRB Toolkit® 2009).

How to Develop a PPP

If a community were interested in building a PPP, the following contains some practical information to accomplish this. These steps are intended as guidance as every jurisdiction is unique and needs to address the area-specific hazards while incorporating the community culture.

When beginning this endeavor, one should note that there are special components in order to establish a PPP. They are as follows: agreeing to a purpose, invitation and makeup of partners, defining the leadership structure, goal-setting, formalizing the partnership, program development, recognition of partners, and institutionalization of the partnership.

The first decision that must be made is the purpose of the partnership. What is bringing about this impetus? It might be that a disaster event has just occurred, a new hazard has been discovered, or new information has been released. Many times the cause is an influx of funding or some change in personnel, possibly of a political or other nature. Regardless of the cause, it provides a unique opportunity to pull together disparate initiatives under one umbrella of public safety, disaster risk reduction, or mitigation. If the cause is funding, those dollars can have specific strings attached, so that the funds must be directed toward a specific hazard or issue. These types of requirements can help define the purpose of a partnership and highlight natural partners for such an endeavor. This is not to say that the purpose cannot change in the future, but it is best to begin with common ground, build momentum, and expand efforts over time.

With the initial goals in mind, natural partners should be invited to participate. The actual partners should be representative of the community at large and should not be limited to only the local level; disasters cross geographical and political boundaries, so leveraging will bring additional resources to the mitigation efforts. Again, partners should represent government at the local, state, and national levels; small and large businesses; academicians; nonprofits; volunteer organizations; neighborhood groups; individuals; researchers; media; and so forth. An important aspect to the invitation is not only the right organizational structure, but also the right people. A successful partnership will need participants who are willing to try, to take risks, versus the people more likely to say "no." This is where value needs to be determined. While PPPs may be the right thing to do, participants will be contributing their time, resources, and potentially funding to this initiative. Therefore, while partners are giving something to the cause, they will need something in return. This may be as simple as organizational name recognition, access to other partners, or even the opportunity to investigate new business opportunities. As partnerships are about both give and take, the invitations need to be inclusive and understanding that acceptance to participate is just the first step in

the partnership dialog, which will develop over time. The bottom line for businesses is that they need to make money, whereas governments need to be fair in appearance and fact. All will need to understand these bottom lines to enable the continued participation of essential organizations in the partnership. This is not to say, for instance, that the private sector should make money from the PPP, but that they cannot lose money and still be expected to participate.

The leadership of a PPP can also change over time, but begins with a structure directly tied to the original goal. The initial drive could be sparked by the receipt of funds or simply momentum developed by an organization where partners are already members. A natural leader in many such efforts is the local office of emergency management where the legal and moral mitigation authority resides to protect a community, but it does not have to end there, as the emergency management office may not have enough community clout based on its placement in the governmental hierarchy. Thus, leadership could reside, or be shifted, to a nonprofit or a business organization. The leadership structure will vary from one community to another as partners will represent the unique culture of a community, but in order to be successful, emergency management needs to always play a vital role in some aspects of the leadership, be it only a supporting role for some. While there is a leader who keeps projects on schedule and manages funds, the structure needs to be based on a participatory one such as a steering committee with subcommittees. This simple approach allows for a manageable core group, which can expand or contract the number of subcommittees as needed, yet allows for innovation and participation from a broader pool of local experts. A steering committee can be the decision-making body that drives the overall partnership, with subcommittees who perform the more detailed tasks and program development. The leader is important in a partnership as there will be times that "no" is the best answer, so it takes that head of the organization to have the respect of partners and credibility to have others follow through with decisions. This is not dictatorial leadership, but instead involves engaging others in a participatory organization with the ability to enforce rules. Without that type of leadership, partnerships can slip into a decision-making paralysis where no one has the authority to decide.

Setting the leadership is quickly followed by goal setting and formalizing the partnership. With the structure in place, the partnership next needs to set short- and long-term mitigation goals that the group wants to accomplish. These should start at a high level and then work down to specific projects such as to earthquake-retrofit 2000 vulnerable houses in the next 3 years or to update flood maps for the region by the fourth quarter. Goals should be tangible and specific for each program area or subcommittee, but

in the beginning can be for the general partnership to keep everyone in sync, especially as new partners are recruited.

Next comes the time to formalize the partnership. This is an opportunity to create a date from which all benchmarks for the partnership can be set. Formalizing the partnership involves defining the activities of all individuals and organizations so that it is clear how partners will be accomplishing the set goals. Creating a voluntary, nonbinding memorandum of understanding (MOU) is the easiest way to formalize relationships, as it allows all participants to know what is expected to be given and received, which also assists when new partners come aboard to understand the definitions and assignments. One aspect to this that should not be overlooked is how it is made public. The official signing of the MOU, or a signing ceremony, should be a celebratory event as it brings together all partners. The recognition and celebration of partners and their accomplishments are important parts of a PPP. It is a way to keep people engaged as this is not a part of the normal activities of most organizations and they need to be lauded for making it a priority. The bottom line is that risks are being reduced through mitigation activities, and the PPP is the avenue to saving lives.

During the design phase, as the PPP is developing programs, there is an important element that should be implemented: how to institutionalize the effort. If programs are only developed to exist until recently provided funds are spent, then long-term risk reduction cannot be achieved. Instead, methods should be established to provide ongoing support for programs or elements that can be incorporated into the existing activities of organizations. For instance, activities related to the earthquake strengthening of buildings need to include the local building department that manages permits and inspections. It is only natural that this eventually be a part of its existing seismic strengthening program, so a building department should be one of the partners, although it should probably not lead the subcommittee in the beginning, as it will likely be primarily focused on the efficacy of existing standards rather than invested in changing or updating them. That leadership transition can happen later. The building department's involvement, however, is critical to the program's success if not addressed at the beginning. Therefore, partnerships should not only be resource-driven, but they should also be strategic.

Once the PPP is at this stage, it is well on its way to reducing long-term hazards and establishing successful mitigation programs in its community. While there may be some challenges in establishing a PPP, the benefits to the community far outweigh any issues. Some were mentioned earlier, such as bringing in the right individuals to the partnership. One such roadblock can be caused by a limitation in viewing the mitigation big picture. There are partnerships that get started due to an influx of money, which is a good, but some communities arrange the partnership activities around

the funds, so once they are expended, the partnership dissolves. There is a considerable amount of time required to get a partnership to that point and for it not to be institutionalized is a disservice to the community. One of the largest contributions to the success of a PPP is the time provided by partners, experts, and the community. Attending meetings, shaping programs, developing materials, and holding trainings are all examples of how partners can contribute to initiatives and they are likely not paid for these activities. Materials cannot be developed without participation from local experts, and their time is often overlooked as a key resource. People want to make their communities safer, so partnerships can provide an opportunity to give back. With a little recognition of individuals' endeavors, further success is more likely as they commit to additional participation.

Funding

This chapter has already discussed two grant programs that provided money through FEMA, HMGP and Project Impact, but that is only a limited scope of the mitigation opportunities. The NFIP, one of the largest and most established of FEMA's mitigation programs, provides insurance to individuals and communities with the stipulation that these communities will legislate and enforce ordinances that eliminate new construction and restrict other developments in the floodplain. FEMA's Hazard Mitigation Assistance (HMA) Grant Program provides funding opportunities before and after a disaster for mitigation from natural hazards. The HMA grant programs include HMGP, mentioned earlier, to fund state, tribal, or local governments, following a Presidential disaster declaration; Pre-Disaster Mitigation as a competitive grant process to be applied toward hazard mitigation planning and the completion of mitigation-specific projects for any hazard; Flood Mitigation Assistance, which provides funds for actions that will eliminate or reduce the flood risk damage to buildings insured by NFIP; and two other programs for repetitive flood loss properties. In addition to federal funds, some corporations and wealthy individuals or families have formed foundations that may provide grants to communities for use in increasing their resiliency with respect to natural hazards.

U.S. Small Business Administration

The U.S. Small Business Administration (SBA) has many programs to assist businesses on a daily basis to begin, enhance, or continue operations. When it comes to disasters, their programs will help not only businesses, but homeowners and renters as well. After a disaster strikes and it is presidentially declared, the SBA offers two loans: physical disaster loans and economic

injury disaster loans. Both are available to businesses, but only the physical disaster loan is available also to homeowners and renters. The interest rates for these loans cannot exceed 4%. Teams of SBA personnel will travel around disaster areas sharing information about the loans, many times in concert with FEMA, to ensure that those directly impacted are getting the best information to help them recover. As the hope is that businesses and individuals do not have to experience a disaster by mitigating, a portion of their loan funds may be used for mitigation purposes. In addition, the SBA has brought many resources to the table on a variety of PPPs around the country. The SBA was so vested in the idea of mitigation that they created the pre-disaster mitigation loan program for businesses to use specifically for mitigation and without experiencing the effects of a disaster. As the SBA operates at the national and regional levels, they are perfectly poised to provide perspective to the varied disasters across the United States. A current PPP is one where the SBA has entered into an MOU with the U.S. Chamber of Commerce Business Civic Leadership Center (BCLC). The BCLC provides the National Disaster Help Desk for Business, which will coordinate with state and local governments and businesses who are hit by a disaster. The SBA and BCLC will coordinate and collaborate with information sharing and resources to facilitate a faster recovery for the local businesses. By using the 1-888-MY-BIZ-HELP number, the BCLC provides a resource for businesses who are not sure where to go for information, and through their coordination, affected businesses can be directed to the SBA or other needed agencies for assistance.

Other Funding

Other funds in recent years have gone primarily to address homeland security issues across the United States. One of those programs, also provided through FEMA, is the Urban Areas Security Initiative (UASI), which targets funds into jurisdictions that have a more significant terrorism threat. Since the aftermath of Hurricane Katrina in 2005, the program scope has been modified, so some communities began using these funds to address the all-hazard approach if these initiatives also assisted in protection against terrorism. Such examples of this can be found in New Jersey, New York, Chicago, and Los Angeles, where nongovernmental organizations may not be at the decision-making table, but are working with these homeland security and emergency management agencies in determining priorities. This has been aided by a special UASI grant for nonprofits that may also be at specific risk to terrorism. Communities can build partnerships under the terrorism umbrella that increase benefits by mitigating against other risks.

The Role of Insurance as a Fiscal Tool to Reduce Loss

Insurance is a risk transfer tool and not a traditional mitigation tool, even though certain activities encouraged by some insurance companies may actually provide premium discounts for mitigating very specific risk of insured buildings or infrastructure. Insurance does not usually directly result in a reduction of loss of life or injury over an extended period. The California Earthquake Authority, a publically managed but privately funded instrumentality of the State of California, does, by state law, encourage seismic mitigation activity for certain aged houses with cripple walls. It is now engaged with Cal EMA in developing a mitigation program for all residential housing in California.

A Case Study in Mitigation: The Pacific Gas and Electric Company Activities

The Pacific Gas and Electric Company (PG&E) is an investor-owned utility that has a complex and large gas and electric system. PG&E is the largest combined gas and electricity utility in Northern California. It serves 15 million Californians. The company has been working on seismic safety issues, including mitigation for its electric and gas activities for many years. It has provided funding and in-kind resources for all levels of seismic hazard assessment, vulnerability, risk assessment, and mitigation projects either on their own or with partners ranging from FEMA and the Bonneville Power Administration to the National Science Foundation earthquake engineering laboratory, to manufacturers of electric equipment and independent testing facilities and many different kinds of engineering consultants.

The utility's major elements include power generation, transmission, distribution, and gas transmission distribution and storage. Major components include hydroelectric power generation facilities at dams, the Diablo Canyon Nuclear Power Plant, major electric switchyards and substations, as well as office buildings and a supervisory control and data acquisition system. The PG&E Company was in service in portions of Northern California during both the San Francisco earthquake of 1906 and the Loma Prieta earthquake of 1989.

PG&E realized that in order to reduce the downtime of its electric and gas transmission and distribution systems, it needed to invest in understanding the hazard presented by earthquakes and related effects, as well as component and system vulnerability and risk from direct and indirect effects. PG&E participated and helped to develop industry standards for seismic design of substation components. Management at PG&E as well as the California Independent System Operator and Cal EMA have realized

that the timely restoration of electric power service helps in emergency response. The resumption of electric power and gas service, where safe, helps the utility to reduce customer interruption and loss of revenue to the utility as well as to businesses. This in turn helps to mitigate the loss of revenue to the utility from lack of customers and lower claims for loss of service.

PG&E models loss of service against industry loss models with input files keyed specifically to their utility and a specific scenario earthquake. By updating the resiliency of select components to the PG&E system, revised loss of service estimate may be obtained from which a benefit–cost estimate of the seismic mitigation update can be conducted. Examples of recently completed or initiated seismic upgrades include the seismic retrofit to the PG&E headquarters buildings in San Francisco, California, as well as replacement of natural gas transmission pipes that were clay or cast iron and replaced with high-density polyethylene pipe. The exact nature of the seismic updates and vulnerability issues addressed by the utility are not disclosed to the public under the Critical Infrastructure Protection Act.

At present, there are over 7000 ready reserve members made of 700 engineers and 6000 building inspectors available to Cal EMA in California as a ready reserve to respond to major disasters. The members come from both the public and private sectors. It seems reasonable to train and certify all ready reserve members in different approaches to mitigation for structure, nonstructure, and contents of residences, businesses, and industrial facilities. The idea is that as the ready reserve members help communities take advantage of various mitigation activities, the sites that are mitigated may suffer less damage than if they had not been retrofitted. Such residences, businesses, and industries may also be more likely to have and maintain preparedness plans and supplies that can be used during a disaster.

Summary

In conclusion, a PPP is a community-based solution consisting of representatives and expertise from the public, private, and nongovernmental sectors working collaboratively. In mitigation, PPPs are used to address structural and nonstructural hazards, and their effort may be driven by federal or other grant funds enhanced by the problem solvers who make up the local partners. The goal is for sustainable, long-term risk reduction that can be supported by the PPP. This chapter has provided many examples of successful PPPs developed to address one or many of a community's hazards using a range of partners, leadership types, innovation, and funds. We cannot stop most disasters from occurring, but we can minimize the impacts on our communities through PPPs, so that when an event does strike, the community can recover more quickly.

Acknowledgments

The authors wish to thank Ms. Alessandra Jerolleman, Dr. Richard Krajeski, and Mr. Ryan Walker for their review of this chapter; Dr. Brenda D. Phillips for inspiring thinking used in the preparation of the text from her text *Disaster Recovery*; and Mr. Richard McCarthy, Executive Director of the California Seismic Safety Commission, for his patience in the development of this chapter.

End-of-Chapter Questions

1. Describe the two principal types of mitigation.
2. Describe how mitigation issues are related to preparedness, response, and recovery.
3. Describe in a general sense why mitigation is not carried out unless a mitigation champion and justification are well presented to both the public and private sectors.
4. Provide two examples on how the public and private sectors collaborate on mitigation issues.

References

Bullock, J. A., Haddow, G. D., & Haddow, K. S. (2009). *Global Warming, Natural Hazards and Emergency Management*, p. 94. Boca Raton, FL: CRC Press.

Disaster Resistant Business (DRB) Toolkit Workgroup (2009). DRB Toolkit®. Retrieved October 1, 2009, from www.DRBToolkit.org.

FEMA (2001, May). Hazard mitigation success stories, dated May 23, 2001. Retrieved October 1, 2009, from www.fema.gov/news/newsrelease.fema?id=5256.

FEMA 592 (2007, June). Robert T. Stafford Disaster Relief and Emergency Assistance Act, as amended, and related authorities. Retrieved October 25, 2008, from www.fema.gov/pdf/about/stafford_act.pdf.

Phillips, B. D. (2009). *Disaster Recovery*, p. 54. Boca Raton, FL: CRC Press.

U.S. Small Business Administration, Office of Advocacy (2007). *The Small Business Economy: A Report to the President*, p. 9. Washington, D.C.: U.S. Government Printing Office.

Vorel, M. (2001, September. Forum on Risk Management and Assessments of Natural Hazards—Proceedings, p. 3-1. Retrieved July 15th, 2012, from www.ofcm.gov/risk/proceedings/pdf/chapter3.pdf.

Witt, J. L. (1998). *Disaster Recovery Journal*, Vol. 11#1. Retrieved July 15th, 2012, from www.drj.com/drworld/content/w4_107.htm.

Resources

California Seismic Safety Commission (2003). Progress Report on the California Earthquake Loss Reduction Plan 2002–2006. The Progress Report indicated that from a limited sampling of known seismic mitigation projects that took place in the state from 1990 (the year after the Loma Prieta earthquake) through 2002, over 50 billion dollars had

been spent in the state on seismic hazard mitigation activities. Very little money was expended by FEMA in the state for seismic hazard mitigation during this period. This included seismic retrofitting for many structures, an expensive proposition compared to the design and construction of seismic resilient features in a new structure. Over the same period, 575 billion dollars was spent on the construction of new structures in the state. These activities were carried out mainly by the state and local governments and companies. It also indicated that insurance, which is typically not counted as a mitigation tool, accounted for a significant amount of loss reduction from earthquakes. www.seismic.sdsu.edu/pub/CSSC_2003-06_Progress Report 20_CA_ELRP.pdf

California Seismic Safety Commission (2007). The California Earthquake Loss Reduction Plan 2007–2011. This publication is the second loss reduction planning document series for the state of California and predates the State Multi-Hazard Mitigation Plan. It is now incorporated by reference into the State Multi-Hazard Mitigation Plan. www.seismic.ca.gov/pub.html

Community Action Plan for Seismic Safety (CAPSS). This project addresses seismic vulnerability of soft-story buildings in the City and County of San Francisco. It is leading up to a recommended ordinance for the city to increase the resiliency of such buildings through improvements to their ability to resist interstory drift by being seismically retrofitted. www.sfgov.org/site/dbi_index.asp?id=84209

Disaster Resistant Business (DRB) Toolkit® Workgroup is a 501(c)(3) nonprofit public charity consisting of public, private, and nonprofit business continuity and emergency management representatives. Essentially, the DRB Toolkit® Workgroup develops educational products to promote disaster-resilient organizations and individuals; advances knowledge and capacity of groups to plan for survival and recovery from disasters; and provides training. The Workgroup developed the DRB Toolkit® software for small to mid-sized businesses and nongovernmental organizations to assist in creating or enhancing their disaster plans, training employees, mitigating, and practicing their readiness. The Workgroup is also developing toolkits for other sectors. www.DRBToolkit.org/

The National Earthquake Hazard Reduction Program (NEHRP) under FEMA, and in collaboration with the International Code Council, has produced an educational publication called the *The Code Master: Seismic Residential Rehabilitation*. This document provides basic information and example graphics of seismic mitigation/rehabilitation details for wood-framed one- and two-family residences intended to reduce losses observed in similar buildings from earthquakes. The document is not actually based on a particular code or standards, and the rehabilitation and mitigation examples are based on vulnerabilities observed after earthquakes. This document also provides Internet addresses for other documents and codes that may be useful to those working on reducing seismic risk to single-family residences or upgrades to local building practices. *The Code Master: Seismic Residential Rehabilitation* may be ordered from NEHRP or from the Builders Book Source at www.buildersbooksource.com/cgi-bin/booksite/24843.html.

U.S. Chamber of Commerce BCLC is a nonprofit affiliate of the U.S. Chamber, the world's largest business federation. BCLC's mission is to promote better business and society relations and improve long-term social and economic conditions by communicating the U.S. private sector's unique and valuable contributions; cultivating strategies and practices that achieve positive results; and coordinating PPPs and coalitions. BCLC works with leaders from the business, government, and nonprofit sectors to address and act on shared goals. BCLC addresses social issues that affect business,

including corporate social responsibility, philanthropy, nonprofit and social service effectiveness, globalization, community investment, and disaster assistance. www.uschamber.com/bclc/

Institute for Business and Home Safety (IBHS) is an insurance industry-based effort that was founded to research and promote methods to reduce risk and vulnerability to natural hazards as well as social and economic effects from them. The group has an associate membership level for members who are not from insurance or reinsurance companies (www.disastersafety.org/). The IBHS supports preparedness of the public by promoting adequate quality in construction and maintenance of buildings.

National Incident Management Systems and Advanced Technologies (NIMSAT). This institute was founded in 2007 after Hurricanes Katrina and Rita. The NIMSAT institute is collation of 20-plus private and public organizations/companies whose objective is to increase and enhance the resilience of the United States to withstand natural and artificial hazards. NIMSAT is an entity that enhances the collaboration of public and private organizations concerned with mitigation of natural and human-made disasters, including terrorism. The institute is helping to lower loss of life and loss of property as well as strengthening the private-sector supply chains that drive the national economy, and protecting the nation's critical infrastructure and key resources that support our economy and our way of life. www.nimsat.org/AboutUs.asp

www.fema.gov/plan/prevent/bestpractices/index.shtm. This website contains examples of mitigation best practice activities.

www.oregonshowcase.org/downloads/pdf/resources/Grant%20Programs.pdf. This website contains examples of grant programs.

Chapter 5

The Growing Role of the Private Sector in Mitigation

Monica Farris and Alessandra Jerolleman

Contents

Learning Objectives

- Understand the importance of the private sector in hazard mitigation.
- Understand that the technical requirements of hazard mitigation planning and implementation can pose challenges to resource-strapped local officials.
- Understand the challenges in evaluating the work of contractors faced by local officials.
- Awareness of the potential pitfalls in dealing with the private sector in mitigation efforts.

Introduction

Hazard mitigation, from planning to project administration, is often undertaken with the assistance of the private sector. Some communities work in partnerships with local businesses through collaborative models, which embody the notion that all mitigation starts from the ground up. Others hire private sector contractors to manage what they do not feel they can or should manage themselves.

There is much that is unique about the hazard mitigation industry that influences the way in which the private sector is involved. Hazard mitigation, as a federally funded activity, had its genesis at a historical time of increasing privatization, a movement that had begun gaining strength in the United States in the 1980s and carried over through the 1990s and beyond (Henig, 1989–1990). An outcome of this timing is that hazard mitigation may perhaps be the only federally required activity that is publicly funded but designed for private sector implementation.

A 2006 report on government contracting revealed that procurement spending had reached $377.5 billion annually as of 2005 (U.S. House of Representatives Committee on Government Reform, 2006; Waxman, 2006). At the time, this meant that 40 cents of every discretionary dollar spent by the federal government was on contracts with private companies (U.S. House of Representatives Committee on Government Reform, 2006; Waxman, 2006). In addition to the staggering financial costs of these private contractors, the report found overwhelming mismanagement costs associated with these contracts that supported various federal programs including homeland security, the rebuilding of Iraq, and recovery from Hurricane Katrina.

This chapter addresses the importance of mitigation and the current role that the private sector is playing in it. Given the frequency with which the private sector is used for mitigation, it is important for local officials to learn how to best engage with the private sector while avoiding common pitfalls. The case studies found at the end of this chapter illustrate some of the challenges that can arise when contractors are utilized without sufficient accountability.

Types of privatization include contracting, vouchers, public–private partnerships, franchises, grants and subsidies, asset sales, volunteerism, and private donations (Auger, 1999).

Growing Disaster Losses

Across the globe, disaster losses continue to increase. In examining costs of weather-related disasters around the world, Bouwer et al. (2007) found an increase in annual average costs of $8.9 billion from 1977 to 1986 to an average of $45.1 billion from 1997 to 2006. Unfortunately, these costs are

projected to continue to rise and of course, the United States is confronting the same situation. In fact, disasters caused by natural hazards such as hurricanes, tornadoes, and earthquakes are some of the defining events of our nation's history. Significant and long-lasting impacts resulted from events such as the Northridge earthquake in 1994 that caused 72 deaths and an estimated $44 billion in losses (Iwan et al., 1999). Most recently, the United States experienced its costliest disaster to date when Hurricane Katrina devastated portions of the Gulf Coast of the United States. In 2005, Katrina made landfall in Louisiana and resulted in 1800 deaths and estimates of over $125 billion in losses across Louisiana, Mississippi, and Alabama.

Demonstrated increases in disaster losses are seemingly not the result of an increase in the occurrence of natural hazards (Iwan et al., 1999; Bouwer et al., 2007). Research demonstrates that factors such as population growth, composition, and distribution as well as socioeconomic inequality lead to increased vulnerability to disasters (Donner and Rodriguez, 2008; Wisner et al., 2004). Increases in population and the migration of populations toward coastal areas, as well as significant increases in the value of our possessions, have all led to increased risk (Donner and Rodriguez, 2008; Iwan et al., 1999).

Confronted with increased numbers exposed to the impacts of natural hazards, it becomes necessary to ask if federal investments in natural hazard mitigation are truly cost-beneficial and are having an impact on losses. One challenge is continued development in hazard-prone areas. Development itself does not have to be problematic and can be beneficial to the community, but it must take into account the natural environment and be constructed in such a way that people are not put in harm's way.

A few years ago, the Federal Emergency Management Agency (FEMA) commissioned a study with the objective of quantifying expected benefits and potential future savings related to three FEMA hazard mitigation programs. Overall, the study conducted by the Multihazard Mitigation Council of the National Institute of Building Sciences concluded that mitigation results "in significant net benefits to society as a whole" (p. 5). Among key findings, the researchers estimated a 4.0 benefit-cost ratio when examining total benefits of specified FEMA mitigation grants between mid-1993 and mid-2003. Hence, for every $1 spent on mitigation activities, there is an average savings of $4. Study results indicated that every dollar spent on mitigation grants could lead to an average savings of $3.65 to the federal treasury in terms of post-disaster relief spending and federal tax revenues. In addition to the direct monetary benefits of mitigation programs, the study revealed that FEMA mitigation grants led to other risk reduction projects, not funded by FEMA, in five of the eight communities studied.

As federal grant funds become less available, including potential impacts to disaster response and recovery dollars, due to economic constraints it will

become more important for communities to take action on the front end to reduce losses. Currently, one mechanism locals can rely on to better understand their risks and vulnerabilities, as well as the potential actions they can take, is mitigation planning. However, mitigation plans require a great deal of involvement and expertise to be useful to the community. Communities often choose to hire consultants for mitigation planning due to their own time and knowledge constraints. This makes them a good example of the challenges local governments face in accessing consultant expertise.

Complexity of Rules and Regulations

Hazard mitigation planning is governed by the Disaster Mitigation Act of 2000. Additionally, there are a few guidance documents, all prepared by the private sector under contract from FEMA and the actual language contained within the Code of Federal Regulations (CFR).

What is interesting about the guidance is the fact that it is purposefully subjective. There is a goal to allow local groups to have some flexibility, yet the room for interpretation can also result in very rigid and contradictory explanations from different FEMA and state officials. This puts local officials at a huge disadvantage given their typical lack of knowledge of the regulations. A private sector firm with experience among the various FEMA regions is more able to point out the misinterpretations or areas that are subjective and fight against the system. This results primarily from their experience with a wider range of interpretations of the guidance.

The Local Hazard Mitigation Planning Crosswalk, most recently updated in 2008, is the checklist for all local mitigation plans. This document contains language directly out of 44 CFR. Requirements include the need for a planning process:

> §201.6(b): An open public involvement process is essential to the development of an effective plan. In order to develop a more comprehensive approach to reducing the effects of natural disasters, the planning process shall include:
>
> 1. An opportunity for the public to comment on the plan during the drafting stage and prior to plan approval;
> 2. An opportunity for neighboring communities, local and regional agencies involved in hazard mitigation activities, and agencies that have the authority to regulate development, as well as businesses, academia, and other private and nonprofit interests to be involved in the planning process; and
> 3. Review and incorporation, if appropriate, of existing plans, studies, reports, and technical information.

However, once again, there is a range of possible interpretations as to what exactly is required by this language. To further complicate matters,

communities sometimes seek to meet the bare minimum due to funding or time constraints or simply because they do not value the process.

For example, the public comment can take place in many ways. Some communities chose to make a copy available via the Internet or by placing it at a public place. Others choose to hold meetings and present the findings to the public in that fashion. The language within 44 CFR does not specify how that comment should take place, and often the comment periods are formalities.

Another example of complex, but subjective regulation, is the risk assessment requirement:

> §201.6(c)(2): The plan shall include a risk assessment that provides the factual basis for activities proposed in the strategy to reduce losses from identified hazards. Local risk assessments must provide sufficient information to enable the jurisdiction to identify and prioritize appropriate mitigation actions to reduce losses from identified hazards.
>
> §201.6(c)(2)(ii): [The risk assessment shall include a] description of the jurisdiction's vulnerability to the hazards described in paragraph (c)(2)(i) of this section. This description shall include an overall summary of each hazard and its impact on the community.

The risk assessment portion of the hazard mitigation plan can be one of the most challenging for a community to undertake so much so that FEMA has created some tools such as HAZUS designed to be of assistance. However, these tools are only applicable to certain hazards and are limited by the availability of data. Communities often struggle to define the impacts of certain hazards, particularly those hazards which are infrequently experienced.

For example, determining potential losses from low probability events such as earthquakes in areas that do not experience frequent seismic activities and may not have appropriate construction codes can be quite challenging. The wide range of potential impacts from other hazards such as tornadoes, which can vary in magnitude as well as the area impacted, can also be difficult to quantify. Communities often turn to contractors who may have more experience in conducting such risk assessments.

Local officials, who do not often deal with hazard mitigation planning, do not necessarily have experience in the interpretation and application of the regulations. They may not be aware of national best practices or the various ways of making the best use of the limited data available. Using experienced contractors can have certain advantages in this situation.

The flexibility of the guidance not only poses challenges for the writing of the plans but also for their review. Consultants with experience in multiple communities are more able to successfully appeal reviewer decisions

based on previously acceptable determinations from other reviewers. This can be seen as an advantage of relying on outside consultants for mitigation planning.

Some potential disadvantages include missed opportunities for locals to fully engage and learn from the process as well as the difficulty of gauging contractor performance. In some cases, communities who do not significantly engage in the process are left with documents they do not fully understand and/or are unable to implement. The challenge for community officials is to find the best way to utilize contractor expertise while still maintaining ownership in the process.

Challenges Related to Local Capacity

In its capability assessment, the State of Louisiana acknowledges the limitations of its mitigation staff (State of Louisiana Hazard Mitigation Strategy—Volume I, State of Louisiana Hazard Mitigation Plan Update, April 14, 2008). Specifically, it is stated that the hazard mitigation staff of the Governor's Office of Homeland Security and Emergency Preparedness (GOHSEP) are "relatively new" to their positions and do not have the necessary expertise in "mitigation, floodplain management, GIS, or integrated land use planning." As a result, the staff must spend programmatic time on training. This is of course a cause for concern considering the fact the "largest number of the mitigation policies, programs, and activities undertaken by Louisiana State agencies occur within GOHSEP."

Practical Advice for Local Officials

Currently, there is not a great deal of guidance available to local officials regarding the selection and management of consultants beyond the federal procurement regulations. A few local and state statutes do address bidding and procurement regulations, but not service delivery or the management of contracts (Hansen, 2003). This is particularly problematic when local officials are purchasing technical services such as hazard mitigation planning or grants administration. In fact, several authors who have dealt with the concept of privatization have pointed out the challenges of having the private sector conduct service delivery (Chamberlin and Jackson, 1987).

The first decision that a local government or agency faces is the question of whether to contract at all, sometimes referred to as the make-or-buy decision (Cohen and Eimicke, 2008). This decision is affected by several factors including the type of good or service, local capacity, and the function of the agency doing the contracting. Chamberlin and Jackson observe that goods and services all vary in the amount of information that is required for decision making, the consequences of a poor decision,

and the costs of acquiring information. They add that services may be more difficult to evaluate than direct purchases, a factor which should always be a consideration in deciding whether or not to contract for hazard mitigation.

Cohen and Eimicke, in their recent book designed specifically to provide practical advice to local officials regarding contracts and contract management (the first of its kind), recommend that the make-or-buy decision begin with an analysis of an agency or department's core function. They then suggest that activities which do not fall under that umbrella are the most appropriate for contracting (2008). Hazard mitigation planning and grants administration can be managed by a wide range of agencies, from emergency management departments which may have mitigation as a core function to overworked county governments in smaller communities that do not have dedicated staff for mitigation or even necessarily emergency management.

Along these lines, Cohen and Eimicke also recommend beginning the process with an internal capacity inventory in order to have a clearer understanding of what can and cannot be done by existing personnel. An additional consideration is whether contracting might provide access to proprietary technologies, such as grants management software, or in some cases even reduce overall costs (2008). However, it is worth keeping in mind that contracting itself carries management and administration costs and that privatization has not proven to be cost-effective in all circumstances (Feigenbaum and Henig, 1994). As Foster and Plowden (1996) have pointed out, contract management costs should not exceed the savings from contracting.

Once the decision to use a contractor has been reached, a local government must pass through the procurement process. As mentioned previously, there is extensive federal guidance regarding legal procurement methods, which will not be discussed in detail within this chapter. However, the distinction between a request for proposals (RFP) and a request for qualifications (RFQ) is an important consideration.

Typically, hazard mitigation–related contracts are let out through the release of an RFP. Many states provide standardized language to counties and local governments, which can be used for hazard mitigation planning. These RFPs focus primarily on legal procurement requirements at the state level as well as on the overall scope of work. The scope of work is the basis for the resulting contract and is typically focused on meeting the minimum federal requirements for hazard mitigation planning. Unfortunately, these requirements focus entirely on the end product and its technical components, with little attention paid to the process or to the role played by the community and public officials within the process. These RFPs do not include any additional provisions for maintaining accountability and simply

require that a contractor state that they can complete the bare minimum by reiterating the scope of work already provided.

An alternative to the RFP is the RFQ, which typically would not include a scope of work as the RFP and instead requires bidders to showcase their particular abilities and craft their own scope of work. An RFQ allows communities to compare consultants in a very different way than an RFP allows for. For example, it is more valid to compare technical qualifications between firms when they have listed their particular processes instead of simply reiterating the scope of work within the RFP.

Following the selection of a contractor, local governments must sign a contract with the firm or individual selected. The contract is an important mechanism for maintaining accountability over the work of consultants. Too often it is the case that private firms have extensive legal departments which provide the contract language, while local governments may lack the resources or personnel to review these documents and ensure that their best interests are being met. A contract must both be specific enough to ensure quality services and flexible enough to allow for changing needs (Cohen and Eimicke, 2008) (Figure 5.1).

Within the literature, there are a few references to the need for maintaining control over contractors through specifications within the contracts (Ferris and Grady, 1986), but few examples of specific language or clauses which ought to be included.

One alternative to the selection of a contractor may be partnerships with local nonprofits or university research centers that have experience in hazard mitigation planning. Or, it may be possible to utilize contractors for expert

FIGURE 5.1 A contract for mitigation, or any service, must be flexible enough to allow for changing needs, but specific enough to protect the community, hold the contractor accountable, and ensure quality service.

advice while still maintaining control over the document and process. Private sector assistance can be sought on an hourly basis or only for certain portions of the process, such as the risk assessment, which include the greatest technical complexity.

Case Study: The "Blue Roof" Program

FEMA's "Operation Blue Roof" program exemplifies various problems related to managing government contracting and has been the subject of congressional hearings following Hurricanes Katrina and Rita. Problems related to this program demonstrate those resulting from lack of precontract planning, the contract award process, and lack of contract oversight.

The "Blue Roof" Program funded the provision of blue tarps for roofs damaged by wind during Hurricanes Katrina and Rita. The tarps were intended to temporarily protect damaged houses and to allow people to return to their homes thereby decreasing the need for temporary housing. FEMA purchased the tarps and tasked the U.S. Army Corps of Engineers with hiring the companies to conduct the installation. Three major companies were selected for most of the work in Louisiana and Mississippi. However, these companies subcontracted out the work (and in some cases those companies also hired subcontractors), which led to multiple layers of contracts. It was estimated that companies were charging $2,235 to $2,625 per job for a job that actually cost under $300 (Davis, 2005). In some cases, a new roof could have been installed for the same price of the temporary blue tarp (Davis, 2005).

Senator Tom Coburn, chair of the U.S. Subcommittee investigating federal relief spending stated "... I'm certain we paid too much for blue roofs ..." (Coburn, 2006). In the end the program cost $330 million for over 190,000 temporary roofs across Florida, Louisiana, Mississippi and Texas (Strock, 2006).

Recommendations for state and local officials: Officials could have reduced costs had they sought competitive bids in advance.

Case Study: The Road Home Program

Following Hurricanes Katrina and Rita, Congress provided federal funds in the amount of $16.7 billion to support the largest housing recovery program in U.S. history (HUD, 2007). These funds were issued through the U.S. Department of Housing and Urban Development's (HUD) Community Development Block Grant (CDBG) fund. In May 2006, HUD approved the State of Louisiana's long-term housing recovery

program called "The Road Home." This program provides funding to eligible homeowners and renters whose primary residences were destroyed or severely damaged due to Hurricanes Katrina and/or Rita (HUD, May 2006).

Lacking the capacity to handle a program of such size, ICF International (ICF) was contracted by the Louisiana Office of Community Development to administer and manage The Road Home Program (GAO, 2009). What began as a contract for $756 million eventually increased to $912 million as the number of estimated eligible homeowners increased from 100,000 to 160,000 (GAO, 2009). In order to implement The Road Home, ICF hired over 2000 employees and set up service centers throughout Louisiana and Texas (ICF International, 2007). In July 2006, the company began a pilot program to assist a small group of homeowners (The Road Home Program, 2006a). In August 2006, homeowners from across Louisiana began to apply for funds and initial disbursements were made to some homeowners from the pilot program (The Road Home Program, 2006b). Although The Road Home appeared to be a program that was off to a late but good start, it quickly became a target of criticism mostly due to the slow disbursements of funds following those initial payments.

The slow payout process not only affected the average applicant requesting funds to rebuild but especially impacted those requesting funds to mitigate while rebuilding. The Road Home Program offered various options to homeowners ranging from funds to allow individual mitigation measures such as raising a washer and dryer to funds to raise entire homes. Funds for home elevations were not disbursed until April 2008 as the elevation program was delayed due to potential shortfalls in The Road Home Program beginning in April of 2007 (New Orleans City Business, 2008). Concerns over the budget were also blamed for delays in funding individual mitigation measures originally offered in October 2006 but did not really become available until November 2009 (Hammer, 2009b). Checks were not issued to homeowners until November 2010 (State of Louisiana Office of Community Development, 2010).

From its inception, The Road Home Program along with ICF were viewed in an extremely negative light. Delays in the launching of the program, the lengthy and cumbersome payment process, and constantly changing rules and policies led to frustrated homeowners and contributed to the overall slow recovery of many Louisiana residents (Norcross and Skriba, 2008). Discontent with ICF and The Road Home was voiced from all levels including homeowners, the Louisiana state legislature, and the federal coordinator for rebuilding (Hammer, 2009a; Goldfarb, 2007; Gonzales, 2008). Calls were made by the Governor's Office for a legislative audit of ICF's contract and for an investigation of that contract by the Louisiana Inspector General (www.katrinaconnection.com).

While there were many accusations of mismanagement by the contractor, there was blame to be found at many levels (Norcross and Skriba, 2008). Officials with ICF claimed that its staff had to overcome politics and almost 150 program and policy changes directed by state and federal officials while implementing The Road Home Program (ICF International, 2007). Some argue that goals established for The Road Home Program were too extensive, which allowed too many homeowners to be potential applicants for funding (Norcross and Skriba, 2008). State officials maintained the need for HUD officials to be available on the ground to provide technical assistance regarding items such as federal regulations and environmental requirements that often led to considerable delays. Instead, the CDBG funds were managed in Washington, DC (GAO, 2009). Louisiana officials also complained of conflicting information regarding combining various streams of funding from various federal agencies (GAO, 2009).

As of June 27, 2011, The Road Home Program disbursed $8.80 billion related to 128,537 homeowner applications (http://www.road2la.org, retrieved January 7, 2011). Hence, nearly 6 years after the storms, 86% (128,537 of 148,887) of the homeowner applications that were considered eligible actually received some level of funding. As this chapter is being written, thousands of homeowners are still awaiting their funding.

Recommendations for state and local officials:

Performance measures including financial penalties for ICF were finally instituted in 2008, which arguably sped up the disbursement of funds to homeowners (www.katrinaconnection.com). These types of measures could have been instituted from the beginning.

Additionally, a report written by The University of New Orleans includes the recommendation that FEMA should partner with state officials to develop best practices for developing a state homeowner recovery program for catastrophes (Laska et al., 2010).

Summary

Hazard mitigation is becoming increasingly important as disaster losses continue to rise beyond the ability of government to cover under traditional disaster relief practices. As previously discussed, the private sector plays a key role in hazard mitigation at all levels of government. Given the frequency with which the private sector is used for mitigation, it is important for local officials to learn how to best engage with the private sector while avoiding common pitfalls. Government officials can work with private sector contractors in collaborative models that make best use of the expertise which consultants can bring to the table, while ensuring that capacity is built at the local level and that local knowledge is taken into account.

End-of-Chapter Questions

1. What are some of the challenges that local officials face in hazard mitigation planning?
2. Can you think of other examples, in addition to the case studies provided, which illustrate the role of the private sector in hazard mitigation?
3. What are some strategies that local officials could use to access private sector expertise while still building local capacity?

References

Auger, D. (1999). Privatization, contracting, and the states: Lessons from state government experience. *Public Productivity and Management Review, 22*(4), 435–454.

Bouwer, L. M., Crompton, R. P., Faust, E., Hoppe, P., & Pielke, R., Jr. (2007). Confronting disaster losses. *Science*, 318, 753.

Chamberlin, J. R., & Jackson, J. E. (1987). Privatization as institutional choice. *Journal of Policy Analysis and Management, 6*(4), 586–604.

Coburn, T. (2006, April 11). Senators grill corps, FEMA. In News. Retrieved from http://www.coburn.senate.gov/public/index.cfm/news?ContentRecord_id=b90cbf36-802a-23ad-4fec-b45ed882597e&ContentType_id=abb8889a-5962-4adb-abe8-617da340ab8e&Group_id=2b5f5ef9-5929-4863-9c07-277074394357&MonthDisplay=4&YearDisplay=2006.

Cohen, S., & Eimicke, W. (2008). *The Responsible Contract Manager: Protecting the Public Interest in an Outsourced World.* Washington, DC: Georgetown University Press.

Collins, B. K., & Gerber, B. J. (2006), Redistributive Policy and Devolution: Is state administration a road block (grant) to equitable access to federal funds? *Journal of Public Administration Research and Theory, 16*, 613–632.

Davis, A. C. (2005, September 30). U.S. Paying a Premium to Cover Storm-Damaged Roofs. *Knight Ridder*.

Donner, W., & Rodríguez, H. (2008). Population composition, migration, and inequality: The influence of demographic changes on disaster risk and vulnerability. *Social Forces, 87*(2), 1089–1114.

Feigenbaum, H. B., & Henig, J. R. (1994). The political underpinnings of privatization: A typology. *World Politics, 46*, 185–208.

Ferris, J., & Grady, E. (1986). Contracting out: For what? With whom? *Public Administration Review, 46*, 332–344.

Foster, C. D., & Plowden, F. J. (1996). *The State Under Stress.* Philadelphia, PA: Open University Press.

Goldfarb, Z. A. (2007, August 29). Va. firm grows fast, but Katrina aid lags. *The Washington Post*, p. D01. Retrieved March 1, 2011, from www.washingtonpost.com.

Gonzales, J. M. (2008, March 14). Katrina contractor ICF getting richer. *Associated Press.* Retrieved March 1, 2011, from www.theeagle.com.

Hammer, D. (2009a, June 11). ICF's oversight of Road Home Program comes to an end. *The Times Picayune*. Retrieved March 9, 2011, from www.nola.com.

Hammer, D. (2009b, 16 November). Road Home grants available up to $7,500 for storm shutters, roof tie-downs, other mitigation measures. *The Times Picayune*. Retrieved March 9, 2011, from www.nola.com.

Hansen, J. J. (2003). Limits of competition: Accountability in government contracting. *Yale Law Journal, 112*, 2465.

Henig, J. R. (1989–1990). Privatization in the United States: Theory and practice. *Political Science Quarterly, 104*(4), 649–670.

ICF International (2007). The Road Home Program. An overview of ICF's housing management services contract with the State of Louisiana. Retrieved March 9, 2011, from www.icfi.com/markets/community_development/road-home-faqs.asp.

Iwan, W. D., Cluff, L. S., Kimpel, J. F., Kunreuther, H., et al. (1999). Mitigation emerges as major strategy for reducing losses caused by natural disasters. *Science, 284*(5422), 1943.

Laska, S., Jenkins, P., Montjoy, R., Birkland, T., et al. (2010). *Achieving Successful Long-Term Recovery and Safety from a Catastrophe: The Federal Role*. New York, NY: Ford Foundation.

Multihazard Mitigation Council (2005). Natural Hazard Mitigation Saves: An independent study to assess the future savings from mitigation activities—Volume 1. Washington, DC: Multihazard Mitigation Council.

New Orleans City Business (2008, April 8). Road Home begins awarding elevation checks. Retrieved March 9, 2011 from http://neworleanscitybusiness.com/blog/2008/04/08/road-home-begins-awarding-elevation-checks/.

Norcross, E., & Skriba, A. (2008, May 25). The Road Home: Helping homeowners in the Gulf after Katrina. Mercatus Policy Series, Policy Comment No. 19, Arlington, VA: Mercatus Center at George Mason University. Retrieved from SSRN: http://ssrn.com/abstract=1350519 or http://dx.doi.org/10.2139/ssrn.1350519.

State of Louisiana Division of Administration, Office of Community Development (2010, November 18). Road Home Program Cuts First Individual Mitigation Measures Checks to Fund Storm Windows, Shutters and Other Safety Supplies. Retrieved from http://www.doa.louisiana.gov/cdbg/DR/News%20Items/IMMrelease11-10.htm.

Strock, C. A. (2006, April 10). Complete Statement of Lieutenant General Carl A. Strock, Chief of Engineers, U.S. Army Corps of Engineers, Before The Subcommittee On Financial Management, Government Information and International Security Committee On Homeland Security and Governmental Affairs, United States Senate. Department of the Army Management and Oversight of Federal Disaster Recovery: Debris Removal, Blue Roof Program, Haul and Install Case Studies. Retrieved from http://www.hsgac.senate.gov/download/041006strock.

The Road Home Program (2006a, July 12). The Road Home pilot opens in Baton Rouge, Retrieved August 6, 2012 from https://road2la.org/news_releases/pilot-opening-071206.htm.

The Road Home Program (2006b, August 22). The Road Home opens 10 housing assistance centers statewide; Louisiana Housing Recovery Program underway. Retrieved August 6, 2012 from https://road2la.org/news_releases/HACs-082206.htm.

U.S. Department of Housing and Urban Development (HUD) (2007, August 31). Fact Sheet: Rebuilding housing and improving lives after Katrina and Rita. Retrieved March 11, 2011, from http://www.hud.gov/katrina/factsheet.cfm.

U.S. Department of Housing and Urban Development (HUD) (2006, May 30). Jackson approves Louisiana's $4.6 billion "Road Home Program." Retrieved March 11, 2011, from http://archives.hud.gov/news/2006/pro06-058.cfm.

U.S. House of Representatives Committee on Government Reform—Minority Staff. "Dollars, Not Sense: Government Contracting Under the Bush Administration," June 2006, p. 15. Retrieved from http://democrats.reform.house.gov/Documents/20060620I40127-02294.pdf#search=%22blue%20tarps%20did%20not%20compete%20cost%20hurricane%20katrina%20site%3A.gov%22.

United States Government Accountability Office (GAO), Gulf Coast Disaster Recovery (2009, June 19). Community Development Grant Program guidance to states needs to be improved. GAO-09-541, Washington, DC: GAO.

Warrick, J. (2006, March 20). Multiple layers of contractors drive up cost of Katrina cleanup, *The Washington Post*.

Waxman, Henry A. (2006, May 8). Re: New Information About Katrina Contracts. Memorandum to the Democratic Members of the House Government Reform Committee, p. 8. Retrieved December 1, 2009 from http://democrats.reform.house.gov/Documents/20060508161101-77956.pdf.

Wisner, B., Blaikie, P., Cannon, T., & Davis, I. (2004). *At Risk: Natural Hazards, People's Vulnerability, and Disasters* (2nd ed). London: Routledge.

Chapter 6

The National Flood Insurance Program and the Community Rating System

French Wetmore

Contents

Learning Objectives

After reading this chapter, you should be able to

- Describe the major historical factors that shaped the National Flood Insurance Program (NFIP).

- List the roles of the federal, state, and local agencies and the private sector in the NFIP.
- Describe the NFIP's floodplain mapping program.
- Describe the NFIP's floodplain regulatory criteria.
- Summarize the insurance aspects of the NFIP.
- Explain how the Community Rating System works.
- List other NFIP mitigation activities.

Introduction

Created as a way to reduce disaster assistance costs, the National Flood Insurance Program (NFIP) has become the nation's largest mitigation program. Through a combination of floodplain maps, development regulation requirements, insurance rating tools, and mitigation grants, the NFIP has a major impact on how communities address flooding. The program is a model on how the various levels of government and the private sector can cooperate to reduce the nation's exposure to flood damage.

History

Before there was an NFIP, people could only hope for help from their neighbors and charitable organizations in the event of a flood. Government assistance was spotty and generally felt to be a state or local responsibility. It was not until the late 1920s that the federal government assumed a role in flood protection in the form of implementing flood control projects and periodically providing limited assistance to flood victims.

During this time, the primary flood protection approach at all levels of the government was to control floodwaters through structural measures such as levees and reservoirs. The shortcomings of flood control were identified in Dr. Gilbert White's seminal 1945 book, *Human Adjustment to Floods*, which noted that "floods are an act of God, but flood losses are largely an act of man." Instead of trying to control floodwaters, the government should be controlling human settlements built in the path of floodwaters.

Dr. White was an active participant in studies conducted for Congress during the 1960s that evaluated how the federal government approached flood protection. The findings of several studies and reports noted the following:

- The need for flood protection was increasing because people continued to build in floodplains.
- Levees, dams, reservoirs, and other flood protection structures were expensive, and the federal budget could not build enough to protect everyone.
- Federal disaster relief programs were expensive, and they could not cover all the costs of flood damage.
- Although federal flood protection projects were funded by all taxpayers, only residents of floodplains benefited.

- The private insurance industry could not sell flood insurance at affordable rates because only those at high risk were interested in buying it.

To rectify these deficiencies, Congress created the NFIP under the National Flood Insurance Act in 1968. The objectives of the program were to

- Use flood insurance premiums to transfer the costs of flood losses from the taxpayers to floodplain property owners
- Provide flood victims with financial aid after floods, especially smaller floods that do not warrant federal disaster aid
- Guide development away from flood hazard areas
- Require that insurable buildings be constructed in ways that will minimize flood damage

Responsibility for the program was given to the newly created Federal Insurance Administration in the Department of Housing and Urban Development. The NFIP was originally intended to be a voluntary program. If a community wanted federally supported flood insurance, it would need to enact regulations governing new development in the floodplain. By 1972, though, there were few communities participating in the program and fewer than 100,000 buildings covered by flood insurance policies.

In 1972, rain from Hurricane Agnes caused severe flooding in the Northeast, resulting in record levels of disaster assistance. Very few people in the affected areas had bothered to purchase a flood insurance policy. In response, Congress passed the Flood Disaster Protection Act of 1973. The Act created the mandatory purchase requirement.

The 1973 Act had an impact. By 1980, more than 15,000 communities participated and 2 million flood-prone homes and businesses were insured. Since the spurt of growth in the 1970s, participation has leveled off at over

THE MANDATORY PURCHASE REQUIREMENT

If a community is in the NFIP, buildings located in flood hazard areas must have flood insurance coverage as a condition of

- Federal aid (e.g., housing support, veterans' home loans, and EPA grants)
- Federal disaster assistance
- Loans from federally insured banks, credit unions, and other lenders

If a community is *not* in the NFIP

- The two types of federal assistance cannot be provided
- Federally insured private lenders can extend loans to flood-prone properties, provided that the recipient is informed of the flood hazard and told that there will be no disaster assistance after a flood

21,000—practically every community in the country that has a significant flood hazard has joined the NFIP.

In 1979, the Federal Insurance Administration and the NFIP were transferred to the newly created Federal Emergency Management Agency (FEMA). In the early 1980s, the Reagan Administration made changes, such as raising premium rates, to eliminate the taxpayer subsidy. Since 1986, the NFIP has been funded almost wholly by premium income. However, because Congress has set limits on rate increases, it brings in only enough money to pay claims during a normal loss year. When claim payments exceed revenue, the program borrows money from the Treasury and pays it back over time.

After the Midwestern floods of 1993, Congress looked at the NFIP to find out why so few residents had flood insurance. It was concluded that the primary reason people buy a policy is the mandatory purchase requirement. Accordingly, the National Flood Insurance Reform Act of 1994 tightened up the rules and penalties for the federal lending agencies, such as the FDIC and Fannie Mae. There was another boost concurrent with changes due to the Reform Act of 2004. As shown in Figure 6.1, the number of policies in force has increased since then, reaching 5.7 million by 2007.

As shown in Figure 6.2, the NFIP has written policies throughout the country. The largest numbers of participants are along the Gulf of Mexico and Atlantic coasts. Forty percent of the policies are in Florida.

Since 1978, the NFIP has paid out over $37 billion in flood insurance claim payments. Roughly half of that was paid out after Hurricane Katrina in 2005. The claims in 2005 were far beyond the average claims of $650 million in a normal loss year (see Figure 6.3). Hurricane Katrina resulted in more claim payments than all the claims paid during the years 1968–2004. As a result, the NFIP owes the Treasury around $17 billion. Congress has been reviewing new reform acts that would help reduce this deficit.

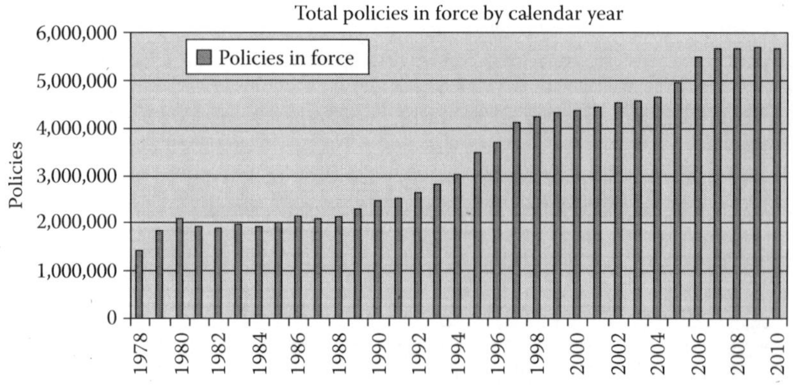

FIGURE 6.1 Total policies in force by calendar year. (Reproduced from http://www.fema.gov/business/nfip/statistics/cy2010_totpif.shtm.)

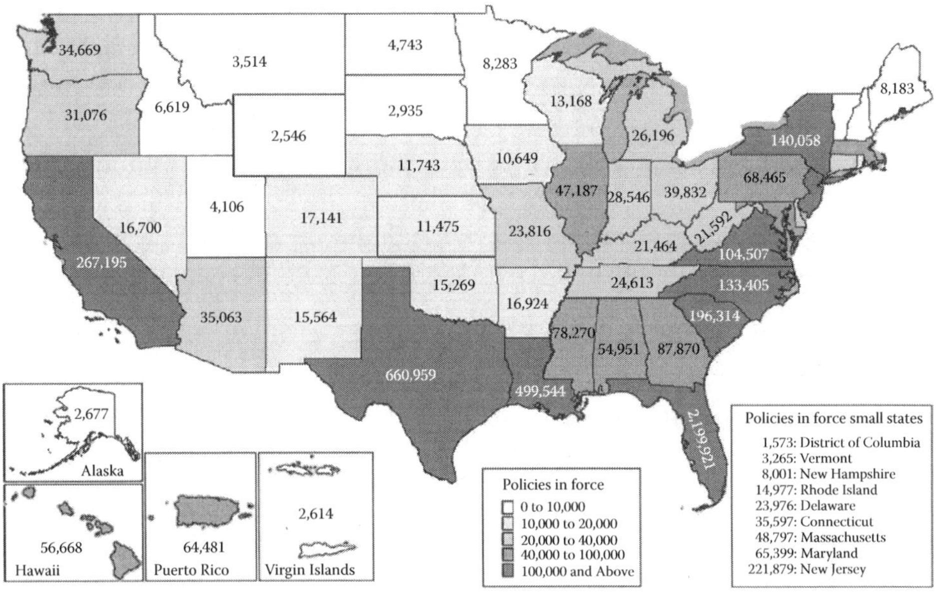

FIGURE 6.2 (See color insert.) NFIP flood insurance policies in force by state, as of 9/30/2007.

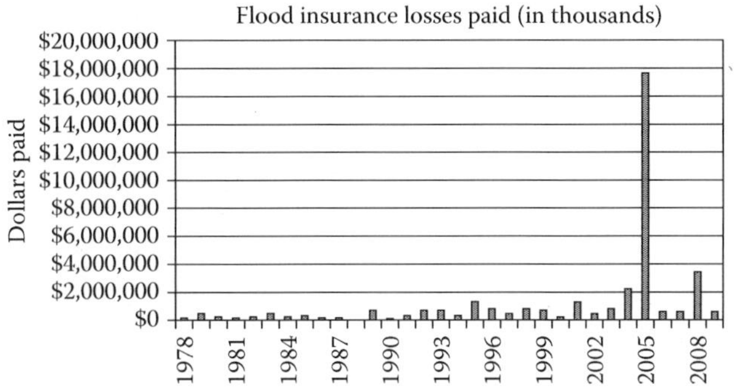

FIGURE 6.3 Flood insurance losses paid (in thousands).

The Players

There are four major players in the NFIP: local governments, state coordinating agencies, federal agencies, and private companies. From a mitigation perspective, the key player is the local government. The insurance and floodplain management benefits are realized only if local governments opt to join and fully implement their obligations.

Local Governments

The NFIP is fundamentally an agreement between FEMA and a community: FEMA will make flood insurance available if the community manages future floodplain development. A community is a local governmental

body with the statutory authority to enact and enforce development regulations. These are usually cities and counties. Other local governments, such as townships, school districts, and levee districts, do not have the statutory authority to qualify. Indian tribes can and do participate too.

To participate, a community must adopt and enforce the minimum NFIP floodplain regulations, which are spelled out in the Federal Register (44 CFR parts 59 and 60). These may be incorporated into the community's zoning or building codes or adopted as a separate ordinance. The regulatory standards are discussed in Chapter 15.

State Coordinating Agencies

Each state governor designates a state coordinating agency for the NFIP. These are often in the water resources or natural resources department, but some are in the emergency management agency, the local government affairs department, or the state planning office. The state coordinating agency provides technical assistance to communities and coordinates the activities of various state agencies that affect the NFIP. Most have a cooperative agreement with FEMA, whereby FEMA provides financial support for activities such as training and monitoring community regulations. States are also expected to enforce the NFIP regulations on state-owned properties, such as highways, state buildings, and state parks, or face the same sanctions that communities do.

State coordinating agencies should think beyond the NFIP. They can play a strong hazard mitigation role by ensuring that state and local agencies know about and comply with FEMA and state floodplain management criteria. They should also be active in state land-use planning and hazard mitigation planning and work closely with their state emergency management counterparts during and after floods and other disasters that affect floodplain properties.

Federal Agencies

Since 2003, FEMA has been a part of the Department of Homeland Security. Ten regional offices work with the states and communities. Each region has a mitigation division that handles community assistance, mapping, grants, and flood insurance.

FEMA headquarters includes a Federal Insurance and Mitigation Division with three branches for each of three parts of the program:

- Risk Analysis: mapping and planning
- Risk Reduction: grants, building science, and floodplain management
- Risk Insurance: underwriting, actuary, claims, and marketing

Private Sector

Most insurance applications and claims are processed by private insurance companies through an arrangement with FEMA called the Write-Your-Own (WYO) Program. Nearly 100 insurance companies participate, and together they manage 95% of the policies. FEMA's Risk Insurance branch sets the rates and coverage for flood insurance policies and monitors the WYO companies' performance and expenses. Other private companies provide training and assistance in cooperation with FEMA's regional offices.

A new industry was formed following the 1994 Reform Act, which increased the penalties for lenders that do not require flood insurance. There are now over 130 flood zone determination companies that contract with lenders and insurance companies to provide floodplain map information.

A third nongovernment actor is the various professional associations that represent aspects of the NFIP. The Association of State Floodplain Managers is the oldest. It has training and advocacy activities for state and local governments and manages the Certified Floodplain Manager program. The Institute for Business and Home Safety is an association of insurance companies interested in reducing losses from natural hazards. It has a flood committee that conveys industry concerns to FEMA. The National Flood Determination Association coordinates the concerns of the map information companies.

The Three-Legged Stool

The NFIP has been likened to a three-legged stool. There are three basic parts to it; if any one of them is missing, it does not work. The three legs are

1. ***Mapping:*** Flood hazard areas must be shown on a map. These are called flood insurance rate maps (FIRMs) (see Figure 6.4). They are used by all the actors in the program:
   - They are used by lenders and federal agencies to determine who has to purchase a flood insurance policy as a condition of a loan or federal assistance.
   - They are used by insurance agents to set premium rates.
   - They are used by communities to identify the minimum areas that are subject to their development regulations.
   - They are used by many local, state, and federal agencies that need to plan for or design facilities.

   Most communities in the country have been mapped. Since the 1990s, FEMA has produced countywide maps. In the early 2000s, FEMA's Map Modernization program produced new maps on digital

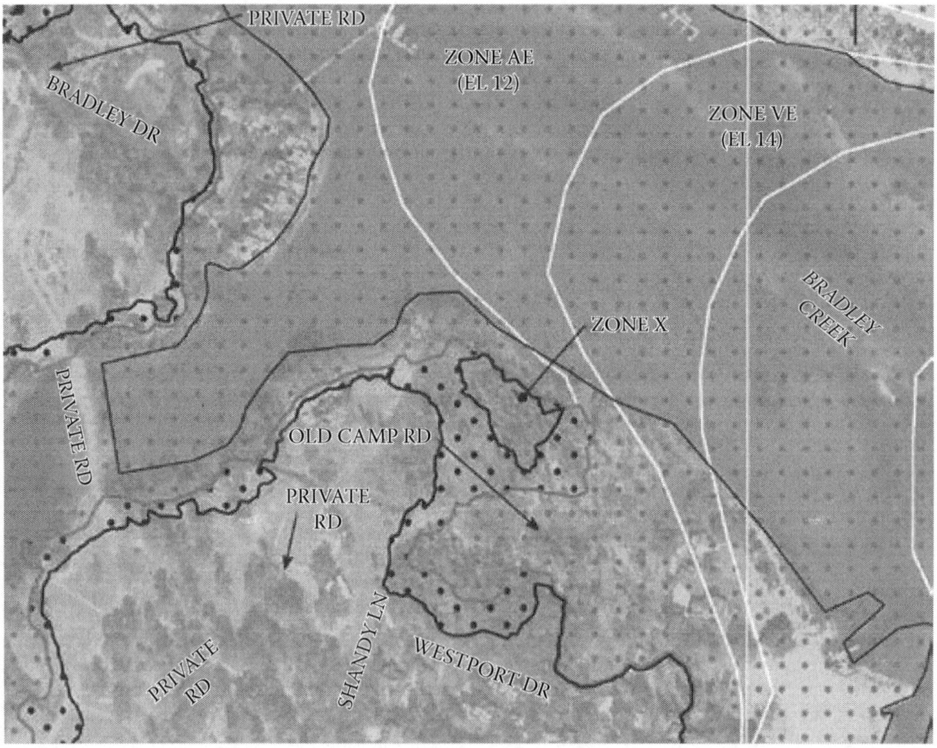

FIGURE 6.4 (See color insert.) Excerpt from a digital flood insurance rate map (DFIRM). Recent FIRMs have been produced on a digital platform and are called DFIRMs. Many are on aerial photo base maps. For copies of FIRMs, see FEMA's Map Service Center at http://msc.fema.gov.

bases, so communities can better incorporate them in their geographic information systems (GIS).

By 2010, the Map Modernization program had been folded into a new concept, Risk Mapping, Assessment, and Planning, or "Risk MAP." Flood studies are being done on a watershed basis, using better ground elevation data. Risk MAP products include more than just flood hazard data—they have risk assessments and information on other hazards in GIS layers and other formats that can dovetail into local hazard mitigation planning efforts.

2. ***Insurance:*** Flood insurance is available in every community that participates in the NFIP. Policies cover buildings, including those in and not in the mapped floodplain. The premiums are based on the level of flood protection, so they are generally lower for buildings not in the mapped floodplain. Buildings constructed after the community receives its FIRM are known as post-FIRM buildings and are subject to lower rates (because the community ensures that they are built protected to the flood level shown on the FIRM).

REPETITIVE LOSSES

In an effort to improve the NFIP, FEMA has identified repetitive loss properties. These are buildings that have incurred two or more claim payments of more than $1000 within a 10-year period since 1978. Repetitive loss properties account for less than 2% of the NFIP policies, but 33% of the NFIP claim payments.

The Flood Insurance Reform Act of 2004 created a new category of severe repetitive loss properties. These are 1–4 family residences that have had four or more claims of more than $5000, or two claims that cumulatively exceed the building's value. Severe repetitive loss policies are managed by a special direct facility, not by the WYO insurance companies.

Mitigating repetitive loss properties is a priority for Community Rating System (CRS) communities and certain grant programs.

Pre-FIRM buildings are not subject to actuarial rates, that is, rates based on the level of flood protection. They are grandfathered into the program with flat rates that are still higher than those of a properly constructed post-FIRM building. However, if they are substantially improved or substantially damaged, the community's floodplain regulations require that they are brought up to the flood protection level of a new building and the rates will be adjusted accordingly.

3. ***Regulations:*** The National Flood Insurance Act was based on the understanding that the federal government could afford to underwrite flood insurance on pre-FIRM buildings because new (post-FIRM) construction would be built that protected from the flood hazard delineated on the FIRMs. Over time, pre-FIRM buildings would be replaced by new buildings and the federal subsidy would eventually disappear.

The community regulations that make the NFIP a successful program are summarized in the Floodplain Regulations box on page 107, as well as in Chapter 15. FEMA stresses that these are minimum standards: "Any flood plain management regulations adopted by a State or a community which are more restrictive than the criteria set forth in this part are encouraged and shall take precedence" (44 CFR 60.1(d)).

Many floodplain property owners have never experienced a flood or feel that the flood they had experienced will never happen again in their lifetime. They want the freedom to build what they want near an attractive

body of water. In rural areas in particular, enforcing floodplain regulations can be difficult and counter the goals of the elected leaders.

Therefore, FEMA and the state NFIP coordinating agency periodically visit communities to evaluate how well they are upholding their part of the NFIP agreement. If it is found that the community is deficient and not willing to make corrections, FEMA has a series of tools to encourage compliance:

1. Removal from the Community Rating System (CRS) (see page 109).
2. Probation, whereby all flood insurance premiums in the community will be subject to an additional $50 surcharge.
3. Suspension from the program, which means that no new policies can be sold in the community and that existing policies cannot be renewed. Without flood insurance policies, there can be no new federally supported or insured mortgages or home improvement loans for floodplain properties and no disaster assistance for floodplain properties in the event of a flood.

These tools have proven effective in getting compliance. FEMA has only had to use the strongest sanction, suspension, less than 20 times for failure to comply with the NFIP's development regulations.

Of course, a community should want to avoid any of these compliance sanctions because it should want to do a good job managing floodplain development to protect its citizens. Various sources of assistance can help local officials to do this:

- FEMA and the state NFIP coordinating agencies conduct training programs. The key one is the weeklong course "Managing Floodplain Development through the NFIP," conducted at FEMA's Emergency Management Institute (E273) or field deployed to the states (L273).
- The Floodplain Management Desk Reference (FEMA 480) provides guidance, policies, and examples on how to meet the requirements of the NFIP.
- Every few years, FEMA and the state NFIP coordinating agencies conduct community assistance visits to see if communities need help.
- Most states have a floodplain management association that provides training and conferences that are excellent forums to discuss problems with fellow local officials.
- The Association of State Floodplain Managers has a program to certify local floodplain managers, giving their communities reassurance that their staff is qualified.

FLOODPLAIN REGULATIONS

Most communities with a flood problem participate in the NFIP. As a condition of making flood insurance available for their residents, these communities agree to regulate new construction in the area subject to inundation by the 100-year (base) flood. The floodplain subject to these requirements is shown as an A or V Zone on the FIRM.

The NFIP sets five major minimum floodplain regulatory requirements:

1. All development in the A and V Zones must have a permit from the community. The NFIP regulations define development as any human-made change to improved or unimproved real estate, including, but not limited to, buildings or other structures, mining, dredging, filling, grading, paving, excavation, or drilling operations or storage of equipment or materials.
2. Development along a river or other channel cannot obstruct flows, causing an increase in flooding on other properties. An analysis must be conducted to demonstrate that the proposed development will not adversely increase the water surface elevation of the base flood.
3. New buildings may be built in the A and V Zones, but they must be protected from damage by the base flood. In riverine floodplains, the lowest floor of residential buildings must be elevated to or above the base flood elevation. Nonresidential buildings must be either elevated or floodproofed.
4. Development in the coastal high-hazard area (shown as a V Zone on the FIRM) cannot obstruct the flow of waves, so the lower areas of an elevated building must remain open.
5. A substantially improved building is treated as a new building. The NFIP regulations define substantial improvement as any reconstruction, rehabilitation, addition, or other improvement of a structure, the cost of which equals or exceeds 50% of the market value of the structure before the start of construction of the improvement. This requirement also applies to buildings that are substantially damaged.

Communities are encouraged to adopt local ordinances that are more comprehensive or provide more protection than the federal criteria. The Community Rating System provides insurance premium credits to recognize the additional flood protection benefit of higher regulatory standards.

Other Mitigation Activities

The NFIP was designed to provide insurance for existing and new properties and to ensure that new development meet the minimum construction requirements. Its primary objective was to see that things do not get worse. It has been successful in this mitigation objective. Recent studies have found that post-FIRM buildings, constructed to NFIP standards, suffer 70% less

flood damage than pre-FIRM buildings. It has been estimated that the program saves over $1 billion per year in flood damage prevented.

The substantial improvement and substantial damage regulations have helped to reduce the flood exposure to some existing buildings. These regulations are hard to enforce, unless the building is obviously being replaced or has been demolished. In an effort to accelerate the replacement of pre-FIRM buildings with compliant ones, FEMA has instituted the following additional flood mitigation programs.

Postflood Assistance

After a flood, there are many opportunities to replace damaged buildings with compliant ones. However, if the community moves too slowly, people often rebuild quickly to their preflood condition. FEMA, as well as many states, send staff to the flooded communities to remind them of their regulatory obligations and help with inspections and other technical matters. To help with determining whether a building is substantially damaged, FEMA developed the Substantial Damage Estimator, a software tool that removes much of the subjectivity in determinations.

Increased Cost of Compliance

To help with the cost of meeting the substantial damage requirement (see item 5 in the Floodplain Regulations box on page 107), the NFIP has the Increased Cost of Compliance (ICC) provision. This is an additional flood insurance claim payment of up to $30,000 to help meet the code requirements. A community may also amend its codes to include repetitive flood losses in its substantial damage definition. To date, ICC has been used to elevate, demolish, or relocate thousands of flooded buildings.

Grants

Several grant programs have been designed to mitigate the damage posed to hazard-prone properties. Congress has created three specifically for flood hazards that are funded by the NFIP.

- Flood Mitigation Assistance (FMA)—each state receives a set amount each year, based on a formula that includes the number of flood insurance policies. Each interested community submits an application to the state.
- Severe Repetitive Loss (SRL)—communities apply through the state for funds that are reserved for severe repetitive loss properties.
- Repetitive Flood Claims (RFC)—a grant that FEMA administers for certain repetitive loss properties where there is no local government sponsor.

TABLE 6.1 NFIP Mitigation Funding Programs

	Grants			
Types of Projects Funded	**FMA**	**RFC**	**SRL**	**ICC**
Acquisition of the entire property by a government agency	X	X	X	
Relocation of the building to a flood-free site	X	X	X	X
Demolition of the structure	X	X	X	X
Elevation of the structure above flood levels	X		X	X
Replacing the old building with a new elevated one			X	X
Local drainage and small flood control projects			X	
Dry floodproofing (nonresidential buildings only)	X		X	X
Percent of project paid	75%	100%	75%	100%

Table 6.1 summarizes the eligible activities for the funds from these three programs and the NFIP's Increased Cost of Compliance (ICC) provision. In most cases, the non-FEMA share is funded by the owners, although some state and local governments may contribute. FEMA has other mitigation grant programs that are funded with general revenue funds, such as the Hazard Mitigation Grant Program.

States and communities set their own priorities for the use of the grant funds, but they are strongly encouraged to address their repetitive flood problems. In no case can a FEMA grant be used on a project without the voluntary agreement of the owner.

Community Rating System

In 1990, the CRS was initiated to give communities an incentive to go above and beyond the minimum requirements of the NFIP. A community can qualify for the CRS if it undertakes additional activities, such as providing flood protection information to residents, regulating areas not mapped by the NFIP, setting higher construction standards, helping insurance agents obtain flood data, and establishing a flood warning program.

To join, the community designates a CRS Coordinator to work with the FEMA CRS team. Each activity that the community implements is given points, as explained in the *CRS Coordinator's Manual*. Table 6.2 shows the relationship between the points, the CRS class, and the insurance premium reduction.

The CRS has proven very popular, especially with communities with large floodplains (and therefore, large numbers of benefiting flood insurance policy holders). Of the 21,000 ± communities in the NFIP, over 1,200 are in the CRS. Although less than 6% of the NFIP communities are in the CRS, they have 66% of the flood insurance policies.

TABLE 6.2 Community Rating System: Premium Reductions

		Premium Reduction	
Class	Points	In A and V Zones	Outside A and V Zones
1	4500+	45%	10%
2	4000–4499	40%	10%
3	3500–3999	35%	10%
4	3000–3499	30%	10%
5	2500–2999	25%	10%
6	2000–2499	20%	10%
7	1500–1999	15%	5%
8	1000–1499	10%	5%
9	500–999	5%	5%
10	0–499	0%	0%

SOUTH HOLLAND'S FLOOD ASSISTANCE PROGRAM: AN NFIP MITIGATION SUCCESS STORY

Following a flood in 1990, residents of South Holland, Illinois, were angry that the village had not done more to protect them. The Village initiated a three-pronged approach:

1. It created a Flood Liaison Committee, where residents and staff met and discussed options.
2. It commissioned a study of flood control alternatives. A major regional reservoir was planned, but no one knew when (and if) it would be built. The study concluded that the reservoir would be built in 15 years, but Village officials knew that there would still be drainage problems and spot flooding.
3. Staff was sent to a workshop on the CRS. The village joined the CRS and then reviewed the *CRS Coordinator's Manual* to see what other credits could be received. A floodplain management plan was prepared and adopted, following the CRS guidelines. The plan recommended a formal flood assistance program.

The flood assistance program has the following components:

- A Flood Assistance Coordinator (FAC) was appointed in 1994. The person was given a full-time job in the Building Department with part-time duties to help residents with their flooding problems.
- The FAC attended training on the NFIP and floodproofing at FEMA's Emergency Management Institute and workshops sponsored by Chicago-area associations.

- Backup technical assistance was provided by the village's engineering and floodplain management consultants.
- In 1996, the village published *Guide to Flood Protection* and *Guide to Protection from Basement Flooding*. These cover a variety of topics, including flood insurance and floodproofing.
- The village's monthly newsletter began regular articles on flood protection topics. Each issue reminds readers about the flood assistance program.
- In 1994, the village budgeted $100,000 for rebates and loan subsidies to help residents floodproof. The rebates provide a 25% cost share, up to $2500 for projects that protect property from sewer backup, basement flooding, or surface flooding.
- The rebates were expected to cover projects under $10,000, and a loan program would help with more expensive projects. The loan program was not initiated because there were no requests for expensive projects.
- The initial $100,000 was not used up in the first year, so it was carried over into later fiscal years. To date, the village has spent $250,000 to support 569 projects at a total cost of $1,000,000. The cost of the projects ranged from $133 to $10,000, with the average cost at $1750.
- The breakdown by type of project is as follows:

227 Drain tile system	195 Waterproofing/foundation crack repair
21 Sump pumps or power backup	100 Sewer backup prevention
15 Dry floodproofing	11 Other

U.S. Army Corps of Engineers, 2005

Studies by Texas A&M University have shown a direct correlation between a community's CRS class and historical flood losses. A 5% or 10% premium reduction for residents has been shown to be enough of an incentive to get communities to initiate less-expensive activities, such as public information projects and higher regulatory standards. It has also encouraged communities to better coordinate their flood protection activities among the different departments that have flood-related programs.

Summary

The NFIP grew from a small initiative to reduce federal disaster assistance payments into the largest mitigation program in the country. Over the years, new requirements and directions have been added by Congress to expand the program from an insurance carrot to encourage local development

regulations to a well-rounded mitigation program that involves over 21,000 local governments and covers nearly 6 million properties.

The NFIP depends on federal, state, and local agencies to map floodplains and manage new development in flood-prone areas. Local communities are responsible for ensuring that new buildings are protected from the base flood and that new construction will not increase flood hazards on other properties.

The NFIP depends on participating insurance companies to manage insurance policies and claim payments. Other private-sector participants ensure that recipients of mortgages, home improvement loans, and federal assistance to floodplain properties cover those properties with flood insurance policies, as required by law.

The NFIP has created several programs to accelerate the replacement of existing buildings with grandfathered premium rates and repetitive loss properties with open space or buildings that are protected from flood damage. These programs include increased assistance after a flood, the Increased Cost of Compliance funding tool, and grants. The CRS is an NFIP program that has been shown to encourage communities to become more active in flood hazard mitigation.

End-of-Chapter Questions

1. What were the original objectives of the NFIP?
2. What are the three main parts of the NFIP?
3. When does a person have to buy a flood insurance policy?
4. What happens to a community that does not participate in the NFIP?
5. Summarize the regulatory requirements of an NFIP community.
6. What is the difference between a pre-FIRM and a post-FIRM building?
7. Name the four NFIP sources of mitigation funds.
8. What does a community have to do to participate in the CRS?

Further Reading

FEMA's website on the NFIP: http://www.fema.gov/national-flood-insurance-program
FEMA's Map Service Center: http://msc.fema.gov
Flood Smart, FEMA's site on flood insurance policies: www.floodsmart.gov
Floodplain Management Desk Reference, FEMA publication no. 480: http://www.fema.gov/library/irlSearchFemaNumber.do
FEMA's Emergency Management Institute: http://training.fema.gov/EMI/
Association of State Floodplain Managers: www.floods.org/

Institute for Business and Home Safety: http://disastersafety.org/
National Flood Determination Association: www.nfdaflood.com/
Community Rating System: http://www.fema.gov/national-flood-insurance-program/community-rating-system
FEMA mitigation grants: http://www.fema.gov/hazard-mitigation-assistance
Flood Mitigation Assistance (FMA): www.fema.gov/government/grant/fma
Repetitive Flood Claims (RFC): www.fema.gov/government/grant/rfc
Severe Repetitive Loss (SRL): www.fema.gov/government/grant/srl

Reference

U.S. Army Corps of Engineers (2005). Local Flood Proofing Program. Available at http://www.usace.army.mil/Missions/CivilWorks/ProjectPlanning/nfpc.aspx.

Chapter 7

Risk Communications

Betty Hearn Morrow

Contents

Learning Objectives

After reading this chapter, you should be able to

- Describe several ways experts define risk and be able to defend one definition.
- Identify some common heuristics or rules of thumb that can bias risk perception.
- Identify factors that tend to make some risks more acceptable than others.
- Apply the factors.
- Design a public communication product such as a flyer or a radio script promoting mitigation.

- Understand why top-down approaches to risk management rarely work.
- Apply social marketing techniques to hazard mitigation promotion.

Introduction

When promoting hazard mitigation, knowing what actions are needed in order to reduce the risk is only a first step. The crux of risk communication is understanding how the specific risk is perceived and then knowing what it takes for people to be sufficiently concerned to take mitigating action. This is a complex task, but, fortunately, a sizable body of knowledge related to risk analysis and communication has evolved across several disciplines and has been applied to numerous risk-related issues, such as smoking, seat belt use, toxic waste, gambling, and, most recently, climate change. This chapter provides an overview of some findings that are particularly relevant to emergency managers and others responsible for promoting more resilient communities through effective hazard mitigation.

Defining Risk

The concept of risk is complex and difficult to explain in ways that are convincing and that subsequently lead to effective risk avoidance. Even in cases where the risk is well defined and consequences are high, some people do not take the recommended action. For example, emergency managers have a challenge convincing some people in areas threatened by hurricane surge to evacuate. Hurricane Katrina was predicted to make landfall on the Mississippi coast with over 20 feet of surge. A mandatory evacuation was ordered. Nevertheless, many residents refused to leave, and more than 200 died there. Four years later, about 15,000 Galvestonians did not heed the mandatory evacuation order for Hurricane Ike in spite of warnings of possible 20-foot surge in the bay (Jonsson 2008). These people accepted life-threatening risk for a variety of reasons, some no doubt associated with inadequate perception of the risk involved in staying.

Risk Perception

The scholarship related to risk perception and communication includes work done in a diverse range of fields, including cognitive psychology, social psychology, consumer behavior, marketing, advertising, economics, mass communications linguistics, anthropology, decision science, sociology, political science, health education, behavioral medicine, public health, environmental health, law, and philosophy (Covello, von Winterfeld, and Slovic 1986). Several scientific organizations, such as the National Research Council, have conducted national studies on risk communication (National

Research Council 1989), weather forecast uncertainty (National Research Council 2003, 2006a), natural hazards (National Research Council 2006b), and other risk-related topics. Obviously, this body of knowledge cannot be summarized here, but a few findings are particularly relevant.

At first glance, getting people to adequately evaluate their level of risk in a given circumstance appears to be an education problem with a straightforward solution—just provide adequate information in an understandable way. The simple definition of risk, Risk = Hazard × Exposure × Probability (National Research Council 1989), implies that if decision makers at all levels are provided with adequate information about the hazard itself (such as hurricanes), correct information on their level of exposure (such as whether they are located in a surge zone), and estimations of the probability of being impacted at that location (track probabilities and surge models), they can make a reasonable estimation of personal risk and behave accordingly. If that were all it took, then any two people given the same information and set of circumstances would make similar decisions regarding evacuation. We know that that is not the case. Human behavior is far more complex, and this is particularly true when choices are made under risky conditions (Plattner, Plapp, and Hebel 2006). Risk perception does not necessarily result in effective response (see Figure 7.1). For example, the extent to which homeowners perceive hurricane risk is important, but not sufficient to explain why they take protective actions, such as the purchase of shutters (Peacock, Brody, and Highfield 2004).

Providing reliable data is only part of the risk assessment and behavior process. Knowledge is important, but our experiential system also comes into play (Leiserowitz 2007). The feelings, emotions, and values we have

FIGURE 7.1 Risk means different things to different people. In addition, people's varied backgrounds, perceptions, and experiences can greatly influence people's perception of risk.

gained through experience, including the experiences of our social networks, have a major effect on our decisions. Recent experiences tend to exert the most influence, and the effects of experiences tend to decline over time. In the hazard context, hurricane research shows that people are much more likely to respond appropriately if they have experienced a hurricane recently (Morrow and Gladwin 2005). However, this effect dissipates with time.

People anticipate the outcomes from their decisions. Something associated with bad feelings tends to be avoided as a choice, even if the objective evidence supports it. For example, people may be told that flu shots are extremely unlikely to cause illness, but may avoid them anyway based on a bad experience they have had in the past, or have heard about from others. Going back to the case of people not evacuating for Hurricane Ike, in the interim since Hurricane Katrina, there had been a mass evacuation for Hurricane Rita that turned into a traffic nightmare for many people. Experiencing this, either in person or watching it in the media, may have influenced the decision not to leave for Hurricane Ike. Research conducted after Hurricane Georges indicates that the indirect experience of seeing reports on television showing evacuees having problems reentering the Florida Keys had a negative influence on people's statement of future evacuation intentions (Dash and Morrow 2001). In fact, those watching it on television were more likely to say that it would keep them from evacuating than those who actually experienced the delays. Mass media has tremendous influence over opinion, including opinion about hazards and hazard response.

People receive information from a variety of sources in addition to the experts: "Ordinary people bring more to their definitions and evaluations of risk than recognised in the reductionist framing of experts" (Wynne 1996). This does not imply irrationality, but different perspectives. Most people want to understand their level of risk and will use that understanding to guide their decisions. People are also influenced by those they care about. For example, the presence of children in the household has been found to be an important factor in motivating hurricane evacuation (Morrow and Gladwin 2005).

Risk assessments constructed by experts tend to differ from the risk perceptions of the general public. Experts are likely to consider their own perspective as being purely objective and to negate the average citizen's ability to understand it. It is true that when common sense and science conflict, people often reject the science (Sterman 2008). It is useful to recognize that each of these perspectives reflects unique experiences. Citizens' risk perceptions are affected by the norms of the groups with which they identify, just as the risk assessments of the experts reflect the norms of their associates. It is about competing social and subjective rationalities that involve values, emotions, and power rather than pure instrumental rationality (Horlick-Jones 2005; Zinn 2008). "Risk, it is widely argued[,] is a social construct, and the public's conception is every bit as valid as that of scientists, perhaps more so" (Perhac 1998, p. 236).

In essence, they are speaking two different languages. Lay risk perception is based on a wider framing of topics, considerations, and agendas. It reflects personal experiences and circumstances, and it is highly influenced by context, including interpersonal networks (Maibach 2008). Professional expertise may reflect the science, but often lacks local and practical knowledge. There is no neutral way to talk about risk because it is about what is important, so it is therefore hard to separate hard facts from soft values (Horlick-Jones, Sime, and Pidgeon 2003): "Citizens are well informed with regard to personal choices if they have enough understanding to identify those courses of action in their personal lives that provide the greatest protection for what they value at the least cost in terms of those values" (National Research Council 1989, p. 27). It is suggested that Probability + Values = Real Risk (Tinker and Galloway 2008).

Decisions made about risk are largely insensitive to changes in probability (Lowenstein, Hsee, Elke, and Welch 2001). For example, people often buy life insurance without asking about probabilities—they are seeking peace of mind. Lottery promoters highlight the pleasure associated with the anticipation of beating terrible odds. Thus, emotions tilt many decisions against the objective evidence available about the level of risk.

A common strategy is to try to scare people by talking about dire consequences, such as death. There is extensive evidence that when people are asked to compare the level of risk between various alternatives, their list looks different from what might be expected from mortality rates. For example, people tend to rate the risk from cancer higher than the risk from automobile accidents in spite of the fact that the latter results in far more annual deaths. As stated by one expert, "… the risks that kill you are not necessarily the risks that anger and frighten you" (Sandman 1987, p. 21). He suggests using two different terms: *hazards* to describe the part of risk perception that is based on objective data such as death rates, and *outrage* to describe risk perception based on other factors, such as emotions. Thus, Risk = Hazard + Outrage.

Numerous factors have been found to be associated with what does and does not elicit strong feelings or outrage related to risk. Some important factors include the following:

Voluntariness: A voluntary risk is much more acceptable than a coerced one.

Control: When people have some control over prevention and mitigation, the risk is evaluated as being lower.

Fairness: Those who have to endure more risk than others, without access to greater benefits, are naturally more outraged.

Process: This refers to how the risk is handled by authorities. If the process of communicating about the risk is open and those doing the communicating are considered trustworthy, less outrage is likely.

Morality: Some types of risk cause moral outrage beyond that expected by their incidence, such as child molestation.

Familiarity: Familiar risks tend to cause less outrage than more exotic ones do.

Memorability: A memorable event such as a tsunami makes the risk easier to imagine and thus it seems more risky.

Dread: The effects of some risk factors are far more dreaded than the effects of others. For example, people dread Alzheimer's more than most diseases.

Diffusion in time and space: A rare event that kills many people causes more outrage than an event that kills smaller numbers, but on a regular basis. A good example is nuclear power accidents versus car accidents (Amendola 2001).

Perhaps a useful way to look at risk perception is Hazard × Probability × Personal Factors (values, attitudes, context) = Risk Assessment.

It is important to accept emotional factors not as distortions, but as a normal part of risk perception. There is a tendency for the public to pay too much attention to the outrage factor, and for experts to pay too little attention to it. It can be useful to address the two separately when developing risk management strategies. Similarly, awareness of the context of people's lives is essential to understand the way they assess risk.

Making Decisions about Risk

Making decisions about anything is a complex cognitive process. This is particularly true when risk and uncertainty are involved, and the stakes are high. To simplify the decision process, we rely on intuition, heuristics, or rules of thumb that allow us to sift through data and decide where to direct our attention. These are usually effective, but they can lead to severe and systematic errors. One way to think of these heuristics is as cognitive illusions similar to optical illusions (Nicholls 1999).

Several types of heuristics in risk decision making have been described in the literature (Amendola 2001; Nicholls 1999; Tversky 1974). They include the following:

Framing effect: How an issue is described strongly affects how its associated risk is evaluated. For example, people react differently when faced with gains rather than losses. People tend to be conservative when offered gains and more adventurous when faced with losses (Nicholls 1999). This is a common source of error in citizen surveys where question wording sets up the frame of reference. For example, asking people how they feel about a 1-in-3 chance of winning versus

asking them how they feel about a 2-in-3 chance of losing will likely result in different answers even though the odds are the same.

Representativeness: When trying to understand a new idea, we look for something comparable in our experience.

Anchoring and adjustment: We tend to evaluate things from some starting point and that point can have a large effect on the results. An increase in numbers from 5 to 10, for example, will be looked at differently from an increase from 0 to 5.

Underweighting of base rates: The neglect of prior probabilities in judging the probability of events is common.

Overconfidence: People tend to be overconfident about their estimates.

Added information bias: Contrary to what we might expect, it turns out that more information is not always helpful and does not necessarily lead to the right actions (Moser 2007). It can confuse and detract from effective judgment.

Inconsistent intuition: People tend to put too much reliance on intuition, and it can be faulty (compared to more objective evidence) and inconsistent. For example, people tend to see themselves as facing less risk than the average person, and this can prompt greater risk taking (Fischhoff, Bostrom, and Quadrel 1993).

Hindsight and confirmation bias: People tend to overestimate the degree to which they would have predicted an outcome. A good example is when a hurricane changes course and the Monday-morning quarterbacks claim that they knew it would.

Belief persistence: People tend to weigh more heavily evidence that is presented first (primacy). Furthermore, once a belief is established, it is very difficult to change. Inertia may lead people to ignore evidence that contradicts this held belief.

Recognizing these common heuristics or cognitive illusions is an important first step in developing risk management strategies. Of course, it is essential that the experts assess the extent to which their own decisions are being affected by the same heuristics.

It is false to think of risk choices as being between two mutually exclusive options in which a person chooses one level of risk over another (Green, Tunstall, and Fordham 1991). There are often several alternate paths that must be weighed. How they are weighed will differ. "Decision-makers don't choose among risks but among alternatives, each with many attributes, only some of which concern risk" (National Research Council 1989, p. 50). Once the information is obtained, people will decide whether the degree of risk is acceptable.

To be precise, one does not accept risks—one accepts options that entail some level of risk among consequences. Whenever the decision-making

process has considered benefits or other (nonrisk) costs, the most acceptable option need not be the one with the least risk (Fischhoff 1989).

To complicate matters further, risk decisions are usually made under conditions of uncertainty. An example of this is when an elderly woman decides to ignore an evacuation order because she is more afraid of the known health risks of evacuating to a shelter than the uncertain possibility of being hurt or killed.

Getting people to protect themselves and their property, that is, to do what officials suggest or mandate, is particularly difficult in a democratic, individualistic society where people depend heavily on their personal assessment of situations, including levels of risk. They have differing values and priorities, circumstances, and experiences on which to base their decisions.

Risk Acceptance and Response

Attitudes toward risk can range from extreme risk aversion to risk seeking. Some people are more conservative when it comes to taking chances. Gambling provides a good example of this; some people love it, and even become obsessed with it, whereas others cannot stand to lose, and thus avoid taking chances. Differences can be linked to culture, experience, and perhaps even to physiology (Ripley 2008). In general, males tend to be more risk seeking (explained by culture, perhaps some biological link) and older people tend to be more risk averse (perhaps because of experience and/or perceived vulnerability).

Table 7.1 summarizes some conditions found to influence the degree to which risk is acceptable.

TABLE 7.1 Effects of Risk Characteristics on Risk Acceptance

Greater Acceptance of Risk	Less Acceptance of Risk
Voluntary	Coerced or imposed
Has clear benefits to individual	Has little or no benefit
Under the individual's control	Controlled by others
Fairly distributed	Unfairly distributed
Open, transparent, and responsive risk management process	Secretive, unresponsive process
Natural hazard	Human-made or technological hazard
Diffused over time and space	Catastrophic
Message generated by trustworthy, honest, and concerned risk managers	Message generated by untrustworthy, dishonest, or unconcerned managers
Affects adults only	Affects children
Familiar	Unfamiliar or exotic

Source: Adapted from Covello, V. T. (2008). Risk communication: Principles, tools, and techniques. *Global Health Technical Briefs*. Washington, DC: United States Agency for International Development.

These echo many of the factors that differentiate hazard from outrage in the earlier discussion of risk perception. They help explain why risk assessments, such as flood risk, made from authorities or from outside the community without understanding the local context are frequently contested or rejected.

This section ends on a rather negative note. In the context of hazard warnings, even when people understand the hazard risk and understand their choices, they may not mitigate for a number of reasons, including the following:

- A personal tendency to be less risk averse.
- Other priorities may take precedent.
- Other signals may contradict the warning.
- An aversion to following authority.
- Lack of the economic, physical, or mental capacity to respond.
- Tendency to not be worried until they experience a negative outcome.

On a positive note, there is evidence that the greater the perceived risk, the more likely people are to support proactive government management of hazards (Gerber and Neeley 2005). Therefore, reality can make a difference!

Communicating Risk

The goal of most risk communication is action. Figure 7.2, adapted from Earle and Cvetkovich (1990), illustrates how risk message evaluation leads to effects, including the capacity to act.

A combination of the ability to understand and personal relevance leads to interest and involvement, which in turn lead to a desire for information. Then, if options are available to the receiver, the result is likely to be the intention to do something to reduce the risk. In the hazard mitigation context, messages about the level of risk have to be clear and understandable and

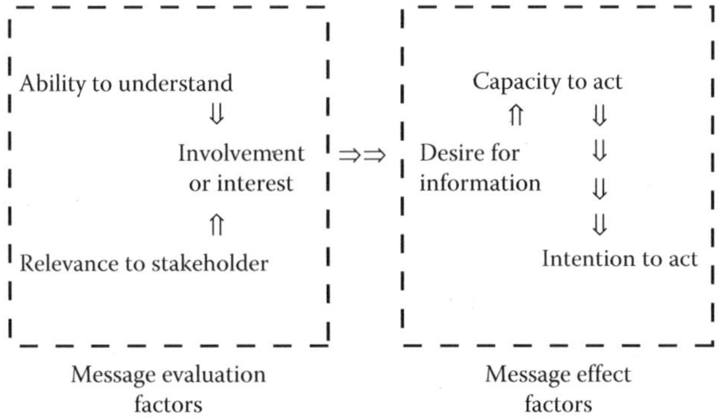

FIGURE 7.2 Risk communication model.

of personal relevance to the intended receivers. This should promote their interest and desire for information. However, they must also understand whatever mitigation options are within their means and ability to adopt. For example, if the goal is to promote protection from hurricane winds, homeowners need to understand how their homes could be affected. If they internalize this risk, there will likely be a readiness to receive specific information about how to protect the windows and doors of their homes. Last, but very important, they must have the economic and/or physical resources to purchase or build the shutters. In other words, Risk assessment × Motivation × Resources = Mitigation.

The simple logic of this paradigm belies the complexity of the actual process.

Knowing the Community

Regardless of the objective or goal, messages need to be developed according to the socioeconomic and cultural contexts in which they will be received. Thus, the first step in risk communication is getting to know the targeted population (Mileti and Peek 2002). This cannot be overemphasized. It is important to know how they understand and feel about the hazard in question (Plattner 2005). There are numerous examples where risk assessments, such as flood risk, made by authorities or by individuals outside the community who do not understand the local context are frequently contested or rejected. Top-down campaigns that use a heavy-handed approach to try to convince people that they or their property are at risk are not likely to succeed, and may be resented: "Rather than viewing publics as passive receivers of expert knowledge, they might better be depicted as active citizens who evaluate the multiple sources of knowledge to which they are exposed and who often have valid and useful lay knowledge" (Burningham, Fielding, and Thrush 2008). If included in the risk assessment process, citizens are more likely to accept the results, and to perceive their risk effectively.

The risk communication process should begin with an in-depth assessment of the stakeholders who may be affected by the hazard. What are the daily circumstances of their lives? What is important to them? How does the risk associated with this hazard compare to other risks they face? Whose opinions do they value? What resources do they have? What risk-reducing options are available to them? What mitigation expectations are realistic? Who are the leaders or influential people in their lives? There is no simple way to gather this information. Quantitative surveys (closed questions such as multiple choice and true or false) are an effective way to gather certain kinds of data. However, they are heavily influenced by the way questions are worded, the base rate given, terms with different meanings to different cultures, and so on (Fischhoff, Bostrom, and Quadrel 1993). Ethnography,

that is, an in-depth study of the local culture, is needed to adequately evaluate what people are thinking and to understand the daily circumstances of their lives. For this reason, qualitative data collection through field observations, in-depth interviewing, and focus groups is an essential first step in risk communication.

Although emergency managers and public officials are not likely to have the resources to do in-depth community studies, there are ways they can begin to know their targeted stakeholders. Community leaders, such as ministers and priests; teachers and school principals; social workers engaged in the community; and even local business leaders can serve as key informants. However, nothing takes the place of personal contacts though public meetings, working with local organizations, and spending time in neighborhoods. A community-based approach is more likely to be successful in changing risk-related behavior. Risks are shared and experienced collectively. People look to their social networks for information and guidance, particularly their trusted sources. An effective way to change risk behavior is by facilitating community interaction to address the issue.

Developing the Message

Public disaster preparedness and mitigation campaigns present a special set of challenges. It is important to recognize that they encompass far more than distributing a brochure or designing a website. In a recent book, *Communicating Emergency Preparedness*, the authors emphasize the importance of a step-by-step, carefully crafted process: "While it may be possible to hastily design, produce and release individual risk information products and messages, these poorly aimed 'hip shots' rarely achieve any measurable change in public behavior in the absence of a greater strategy" (Coppola and Maloney 2009, p. 13).

Guidelines for developing warning messages and other risk communication materials are abundant. One example is the edited book *Designing Health Messages* (Maibach and Parrott 1995). The guidelines consistently stress being short and brief. One interesting suggestion is the 27/9/3 template: limit a flyer or warning notice to 27 words, 9 seconds, and 3 messages (Covello 2007). Apparently, under low stress, the brain processes information in linear order, at average grade level, and can hold 7 messages at a time. Under high stress, however, it processes information based on primacy or recency, processes information at average grade level minus 4, and can only hold 3 messages on average. Therefore, it is important to choose a few messages with the highest potential impact.

Educational materials for the public have been developed for many natural, environmental, and technological hazards, as well as health

issues. They can be found on a multitude of federal agency websites. It is important that materials be carefully matched with the audience related to reading level, values, and knowledge. This is often not the case. For example, the materials on county emergency management websites in one state were found to be unsuitable for use with low-income minorities (James, Hawkins, and Rowel 2007). It is recommended that materials be written at no higher than a 5th-grade reading level if they are to reach vulnerable groups. However, many of the current resources on federal websites are written at much higher levels (Morrow 2008). One excellent suggestion is that materials be packaged not by hazards, but by users—a public-specific view (Mileti 2006). Developing separate materials and methods in order to reach different segments of the population, such as children, mothers, the elderly, persons with disabilities, various minorities, and tourists is time-consuming, but could improve the results significantly.

It is also important that messages be tested before widespread application and evaluated regularly to see if they are accomplishing the objectives. Materials and ideas for communicating with the public are available from most of the major government agencies, such as the Environmental Protection Agency (EPA), the Association of State Flood Plain Managers, and the U.S. Department of Health and Human Services. EPA (1988) has published the following list of rules to follow when communicating with the public:

Seven Cardinal Rules of Communication

1. Accept and involve the public as a legitimate partner.
2. Listen to the audience.
3. Be honest, frank, and open.
4. Coordinate and collaborate with other credible sources.
5. Meet the needs of the media.
6. Speak clearly and with compassion.
7. Plan carefully ahead of time and evaluate the process as well as the results.

An interesting book, *Communicating Science* (Laszlo 2006), provides other advice on how to communicate science orally to the lay public.

Suggestions for Oral Presentations

1. Start with a real-life situation.
2. Build a story.
3. Use illustrations.
4. Use a personal tone as though talking to a family member.
5. Carefully choose a few points to drive home.
6. Plan your talk—and then throw away most of your material!

Social Marketing

The social marketing movement that applies commercial marketing practices to the public sector holds promise for promoting coastal risk management goals. In social marketing, the objectives promote social good rather than financial gain. Typically, this methodology is used to accomplish specific behavioral goals with targeted audiences in relation to a specific topic. It is more than just the general use of business techniques in a public project, but refers to a focused approach toward tangible results. Effective social marketing is more than just advertising and promotion. A quote from a book by Kotler and Lee designed to teach government employees to use a social marketing approach describes its scope:

> It involves a customer (citizen-centered) approach, one that will help address citizen complaints, alter their perceptions, and improve your performance. It is a disciplined approach, requiring you to develop a formal plan by conducting a situational analysis, setting goals, segmenting the market, conducting marketing research, positioning your brand, choosing a strategic blend of marketing tools, and establishing an evaluation, budget, and implementation plan. (Kotler and Lee 2006, p. 13)

Community-based social marketing (CBSM) focuses on collective involvement and is particularly suitable for promoting social change. This approach has been used by government agencies to promote a variety of goals, including healthier school cafeteria diets, energy-saving appliances, seat belt use, organ donation, reduction in water use, and weight reduction. In California, the LEAN Project is a major CBSM initiative directed at improving the diets of low-income families (www.CaliforniaProjectLean.org). Since it is especially effective in areas where there are barriers to be reduced, CBSM fits the natural hazards situation well (McKenzie-Mohr N.D.). A CBSM initiative has been successful in promoting wildfire mitigation in California (Steinberg 2008). The program enlists neighborhoods, provides education from credible sources, provides explicit directions and guidance on what to do, and has rewards and incentives. Social marketing was used by the Virginia Coastal Management program to promote water quality (Coastal Services Center 2007). In particular, the campaign's goal was to keep people from using spring fertilizer that pollutes the bay. The promoted benefit was crabs, and the theme was "Save the Crabs—Then Eat Them." It was a perfect example of using a positive instead of a negative (guilt) incentive.

The risk manager who wishes to adopt a social marketing approach will have no difficulty getting assistance. Many related educational programs and materials are available on the Internet, including a national training website at the University of Florida. Many social marketing consultants offer their services to agencies, and there are advertising agencies that specialize in

using social marketing techniques to promote beneficial health and safety. Several books are available (Kotler and Lee 2006; McKenzie-Mohr 1999) that provide examples and guidelines such as the following 12 principles for those planning a social marketing program in the public sector:

> Take advantage of prior and existing successful campaigns.
> Start with the target groups that are most ready for action. In other words start with the easiest group and let them lead the way.
> Promote single, simple, doable behaviors—one at a time.
> Identify and remove barriers to behavior change.
> Bring real benefits into the present.
> Highlight costs of competing behaviors.
> Promote a tangible object or service to help target audiences perform the desired behavior.
> Consider non-monetary incentives in the form of recognition and appreciation.
> Have a little fun with messages.
> Use media channels at the point of decision making.
> Get commitments and pledges.
> Use prompts for sustainability.
>
> (Kotler and Lee 2006, pp. 187–213)

It is easy to perceive how these principles could be used to accomplish goals such as responsible land-use practices and hazard mitigation. However, the importance of the process cannot be overemphasized—the process of working with targeted communities as partners, where possible, in evaluating the issues, identifying the possible solutions, and working together toward more resilient communities.

Case Study: Communicating Hurricane Storm Surge Risk

Most coastal residents are well aware of hurricanes, either through personal experience or from the extensive media coverage given land-falling hurricanes. As part of their hurricane evacuation planning efforts, the Federal Emergency Management Agency (FEMA) and the U.S. Army Corps of Engineers (USACE) often contract with social scientists to conduct behavioral studies directed toward understanding the attitudes, knowledge, and intentions of coastal residents should they be threatened with a hurricane. When asked what concerns them most about hurricanes, the most common answer is the wind (e.g., Morrow and Gladwin 2011). This is in spite of the fact that water, particularly storm surge, poses the greatest danger. It should be expected that the drowning deaths from Hurricane Katrina in Mississippi and Louisiana would have had more effect. Thousands of coastal

residents living in storm surge zones still report that they do not intend to leave for a major hurricane (Morrow and Gladwin 2011).

Therefore, the first problem faced by emergency managers and public safety officials is that citizens may not understand the hazard, particularly, that a violent surge of water rushes in and in many coastal areas can be 20 feet or higher. Even 2 feet of surge can be life threatening. Many attempts have been made to explain storm surge. The National Weather Service (NWS) has developed resources including videos and schematics to explain how surge occurs and to explain the factors that affect its depth and power (e.g., www.nhc.noaa.gov/ssurge/ssurge_overview.shtml). While essential, as discussed in this chapter, knowledge is only a first step.

People need to feel the risk the hazard poses. They have to fear what would happen if they or their loved ones were at its mercy. To that end, "Run from the Water, Hide from the Wind," a short video developed by the NWS, not only explains storm surge, but also provides dramatic footage showing its violence (www.nhc.noaa.gov/ssurge/ssurge_resources.shtml). This is an excellent tool for educational and outreach activities. Sometimes people do not grasp the scale of the danger. Pinellas County, Florida, could be impacted by up to 24 feet of storm surge, and local officials have a 24-foot banner that is hoisted by a fire truck ladder during presentations. Residents are asked to stand in front of it or, better yet, to have their children do so. This personalizes the risk. The low probability of being impacted by a hurricane and by storm surge at any one place and time makes it especially imperative to dramatize the level of danger, should it occur.

Next, people need to understand the extent to which they are personally at risk. Surge and/or evacuation zones are established in coastal communities based on surge modeling. Research indicates that many, often most, living in a high-risk zone are unaware of their status (Morrow and Gladwin 2011). Some officials are using new technologies to inform residents about their hurricane risk. Lee County, Florida, has a smartphone application where people can enter their addresses or tap on a map to learn if they are located in an active evacuation area (www.leeeoc.com/admin/Breaking%20News/LeeEvac%20description.pdf). Social media is becoming a standard risk communication method used by meteorologists and public officials to portray hazards.

A lower-tech method used by many jurisdictions is to install poles in at-risk neighborhoods that indicate the potential or historical water depth from flooding or surge. In areas expected to evacuate for certain hurricanes, many methods are used to depict evacuation zones. Each zone is typically represented on maps by a different color. In Charlotte County, Florida, the emergency management director developed colored vinyl collars that are installed on stop signs (http://charlottecountyfl.com/Emergency/). This clever idea became much more powerful due to community involvement in

their installation. The emergency management director gives talks at all the elementary schools, involving children in the process. At last count, 9000 collars had been put on stop signs by local scouts, students, churches, and other organizations. By assisting in this effort, these citizens are buying into the issue and are the word in their families and neighborhoods. However, efforts to depict flooding or surge risk are often met with resistance from local economic interests who fear that this knowledge will lower property values or impede real estate sales. This is where a community-based approach that builds local interest and participation can make a difference.

Summary

At first glance, it might seem that effective risk communication is a simple matter of clearly explaining the hazard: Develop a good brochure, distribute it widely, and the job is done. In this chapter, you have learned that it is a far more complicated process. The goal is protective action, and for that to occur, people have to believe that the risk is real—that there is a chance they could be impacted and that the consequences could be serious. Further, they need to understand how to minimize the danger, and that it is within their power to do so. The various gleanings from the risk communication literature discussed here can best be summed up with this formula: Hazard × Probability × Personal Factors (values, attitudes, context) = Risk Assessment × Motivation × Resources = Protective Action.

End-of-Chapter Questions

1. Why do you think so many people refused to leave Galveston Island in spite of a mandatory evacuation order for Hurricane Ike? What are some ways emergency managers could find to answer that question?
2. Explain the relationship between values and risk perception.
3. Why do you think citizens' assessment of risk often does not reflect the actual risk, such as mortality rates?
4. Describe the outrage factor and things that influence it. Can you think of a better word to use for this factor?
5. What do you think is the best equation for describing risk?
6. What are some heuristics that can influence how citizens view their risk? What are some heuristics that can influence how emergency managers view risk?
7. How can a risk communicator learn more about the targeted community?
8. Give examples for each of the listed factors that make people either accept or not accept risk.

Resources

Risk communication materials can be found on the websites of

American Red Cross
Association of Floodplain Managers
Centers for Disease Control and Prevention
Environmental Protection Agency
Federal Emergency Management Agency
National Weather Service
United States Health and Human Services Agency
University of Florida's Social Marketing Training website

References

Amendola, A. (2001). Recent paradigms for risk informed decision making. *Safety Science, 40*, 17–30.

Burningham, K., Fielding, J., & Thrush, D. (2008). "It'll never happen to me": Understanding public awareness of local flood risk. *Disasters, 32*, 216–238.

Coastal Services Center. (2007). *Social marketing: Selling behavior change around the Chesapeake Bay* (pp. 1–3 in Coastal Services). Charleston, SC: National Oceanic and Atmospheric Administration.

Coppola, D. P., & Maloney, E. K. (2009). *Communicating Emergency Preparedness: Strategies for Creating a Disaster Resilient Public.* Boca Raton, FL: CRC Press.

Covello, V. T. (2007). Core slides: Risk communication. Retrieved October 21, 2010, from www.docstoc.com/docs/952454/Risk-Communication-Core-Slides-Center-for-Risk-Communication.

Covello, V. T. (2008). Risk communication: Principles, tools, and techniques. *Global Health Technical Briefs*. Retrieved July 17, 2012 from http://www.au.af.mil/pace/handbooks/risk_comm_usaid.pdf. Washington, DC: United States Agency for International Development.

Covello, V. T., von Winterfeld, D., & Slovic, P. (1986). Risk communication: A review of the literature. *Risk Abstracts, 3*, 171–182.

Dash, N., & Morrow, B. H. (2001). Return delays and evacuation order compliance: The case of Hurricane Georges and the Florida Keys. *Environmental Hazards, 2*(3), 119–128.

EPA, Environmental Protection Agency (1988, April). *Seven cardinal rules of communication.* Pamphlet drafted by Vincent T. Covello and Frederick Allen. OPA-87-020.

Earle, T. C., & Cvetkovich, G. (1990). The effects of involvement, relevance and ability on risk communication effectiveness. In K. Borcherding, O. I. Larichev, & D. M. Messick (Eds.), *Contemporary Issues in Decision Making* (pp. 271–289). North Holland: Elsevier Science Publishers B.V.

Fischhoff, B. (1989). Risk: a guide to controversy. In *Improving Risk Communication* (211–319). Washington, DC: National Academy Press.

Fischhoff, B., Bostrom, A., & Quadrel, M. J. (1993). Risk perception and communication. *Annual Review of Public Health, 14*, 183–203.

Gerber, B. J., & Neeley, G. W. (2005). Perceived risk and citizen preference for governmental management of routine hazards. *The Policy Studies Journal, 33*, 395–411.

Green, C. H., Tunstall, S. M., & Fordham, M. (1991). The risks from flooding: Which risks and whose perception? *Disasters, 15*, 227–236.

Horlick-Jones, T. (2005). Informal logics of risk: contingency and modes of practical reasoning. *Journal of Risk Research, 8*, 253–272.

Horlick-Jones, T., Sime, J. & Pidgeon, N. (2003). The social dynamics of environmental risk perception: implications of risk communication research and practice. In *The social amplification of risk* (262–285). Cambridge, UK: Cambridge University Press.

James, X., Hawkins, A., & Rowel, R. (2007). An assessment of the cultural appropriateness of emergency preparedness communication for low income minorities. *Journal of Homeland Security and Emergency Management, 4*(3).

Jonsson, P. (2008). Defying Ike: Why 140,000 stayed behind. In *Christian Science Monitor*. Retrieved October 21, 2010, from www.csmonitor.com/USA/2008/0919/p04s04-usgn.html.

Kotler, P., & Lee, N. (2006). *Marketing in the Public Sector: A Roadmap for Improved Performance*. Upper Saddle River, NJ: Wharton School Publishing.

Laszlo, P. (2006). *Communicating Science: A Practical Guide*. Berlin: Springer.

Leiserowitz, A. (2007). Communication climate change: Episode one. In J. Cone (Producer), *Communicating climate change series*. Retrieved October 21, 2010, from http://seagrant.oregonstate.edu/blogs/communicatingclimate/transcripts/Episode_1_Leiserowitz.html.

Lowenstein, G. F., Hsee, C. K., Elke, U. W., & Welch, N. (2001). Risk as feelings. *Psychological Bulletin, 127*, 267–286.

Maibach, E. (2008). Communicating climate change: Episode six. In J. Cone (Producer), *Communicating climate change series*. Retrieved October 21, 2010, from http://blogs.oregonstate.edu/communicatingclimatechange/2008/04/10/episode-6-ed-maibach/.

Maibach, E. C., & Parrott, R. L. (Eds.) (1995). *Designing health messages: Approaches from communication theory and public health practice*. Thousand Oaks, CA: Sage Publications.

McKenzie-Mohr, D. (1999). *Fostering Sustainable Behavior: An Introduction to Community-Based Social Marketing*. Gabriola Island, BC: New Society Publishers.

McKenzie-Mohr, D. (n.d.). *Quick Reference: Community-Based Social Marketing*. Charleston, SC: NOAA Coastal Services Center. Retrieved July 17, 2012 from http://www.csc.noaa.gov/digitalcoast/_/pdf/social_marketing.pdf.

Mileti, D. (2006). Promoting risk wise behavior. *Presentation at Natural Hazards Workshop*, Boulder, CO, July 11.

Mileti, D., & Peek, L. (2002). Understanding individual and social characteristics in the promotion of household disaster preparedness. In T. Deitz & P. Stern (Eds.), *New tools for environmental protection: Education, information and voluntary measures* (125–139). Washington, DC: National Academy Press.

Morrow, B. H. (2008). Language and literacy. In B. D. Phillips (Ed.), *Social Vulnerability in Disasters*. London: Taylor and Francis Group.

Morrow, B. H. (2009). Risk behavior and risk communication: Synthesis and expert interviews. Final Report for the NOAA Coastal Services Center. Retrieved October 20, 2010, from www.csc.noaa.gov/Risk_Behavior_&_Communication_Report.pdf.

Morrow, B. H., & Gladwin, H. (2005, August). *Final report. Hurricane Ivan behavioral analysis* (with Hugh Gladwin). Submitted through Dewberry to U.S. Corps and FEMA. Retrieved October 20, 2010, from http://chps.sam.usace.army.mil/USHESDATA/Assessments/2004Storms/PDFfiles/Ivan%20Final%20Behave%20download

.pdfhttp://chps.sam.usace.army.mil/USHESDATA/Assessments/2004Storms/PDFfiles/Ivan%20Final%20Behave%20download.pdf.

Morrow, B. H., & Gladwin, H. (2011). *Final report: Behavioral analysis for the Alabama Hurricane evacuation study*. Dewberry & Davis for USACE, FEMA, and Alabama Emergency Management Agency.

Moser, S. (2007). Communicating climate change: Episode two. In J. Cone (Producer), *Communicating climate change series*. Retrieved October 21, 2010, from http://blogs.oregonstate.edu/communicatingclimatechange/2008/01/23/episode-2-susanne-moser/.

National Research Council (1989). *Improving Risk Communication*. Washington, DC: National Acadamies Press.

National Research Council (2003). *Communicating uncertainties in weather and climate information: A workshop summary*. Washington, DC: National Academies Press.

National Research Council (2006a). *Completing the forecast: Characterizing and communicating uncertainty for better decisions using weather and climate forecasts*. Washington, DC : National Academies Press.

National Research Council (2006b). *Facing Hazards and Disasters: Understanding Human Dimensions*. Washington, DC: National Academies Press.

Nicholls, N. (1999). Cognitive illusions, heuristics, and climate prediction. *Bulletin of the American Meteorological Society, 80*, 1385–1397.

Peacock, W. G., Brody, S. D., & Highfield, W. (2004). Hurricane risk perceptions among Florida's single family homeowners. *Landscape and Urban Planning, 32*, 434–448.

Perhac, R. M., Jr. (1998). Comparative risk assessment: Where does the public fit in? *Science, Technology, & Human Values, 23*, 221–241.

Plattner, Th. (2005). Modelling public risk evaluation of natural hazards: A conceptual approach. *Natural Hazards and Earth System Sciences, 5*, 357–366.

Plattner, Th., Plapp, T., & Hebel, B. (2006). Integrating public risk perception into formal natural hazard risk assessment. *Natural Hazards Earth System Science, 6*, 471–483.

Ripley, A. (2008). *The Unthinkable: Who Survives When Disaster Strikes and Why*. New York: Three Rivers Press.

Sandman, P. M. (1987). Risk communication: Facing public outrage. *EPA Journal, 13*, 21–22.

Sandman, P. M. (2003). Stakeholders. Retrieved October 21, 2010, from www.psandman.com/col/stakeh.htm.

Steinberg, M. (2008). Becoming firewise: A neighborhood approach. *Natural Hazards Observer, XXXII*, 1–3.

Sterman, J. D. (2008). Risk communication on climate: Mental models and mass balance. *Science, 322*, 532–533.

Tinker, T., & Galloway, G. E. (2008). How do you effectively communicate flood risks? Booz Allen Hamilton. Retrieved October 21, 2010, from www.emforum.org/vforum/BAH/How%20Do%20You%20Effectively%20Communicate%20Flood%20Risks.pdf.

Tversky, A. (1974). Assessing uncertainty. *Journal of the Royal Statistical Society, 36*, 148–159.

Wynne, B. (1996). May the sheep safely graze? A reflexive view of the expert-lay knowledge divide. In S. Lash, B. Szerszynski, & B. Wynne (Eds.), *Risk, environment and modernity* (pp. 44–83). London: Sage.

Zinn, J. O. (2008). Introduction: The contribution of sociology to the discourse on risk and uncertainty. In J. O. Zinn (Ed.), *Social theories of risk and uncertainty: An introduction* (pp. 1–17). Malden, MA: Blackwell.

Chapter 8

Natural Hazards and the Law

Edward A. Thomas

Contents

Learning Objectives

- Understand the key role that our human decisions can play in reducing future disaster losses and floodplain management.
- Understand the fundamental legal concept of not harming others through your use of property and the importance of this concept to building a safer future.
- Understand the key legal issues surrounding hazard mitigation and floodplain management.

Introduction

The globe is plagued with reports of "natural" disasters such as wildfires, flooding, earthquakes, tsunamis, and more recently, the horrific, cascading, tsunami-induced damages from a catastrophe at a nuclear power plant. Each disaster appears to be more horrendous and cause much more damage and loss than the last one.

Many people say that Mother Nature causes all these disasters all over our world—it is Mother Nature doing this to us. Mother Nature has thus been accused of monstrous and hideous crimes, murder, mayhem, and deaths of thousands, and yet, she has never been given a chance to confront her accusers.

I suggest a different perspective. Are natural disasters really "natural"? I think Gilbert White said it best: "Floods are acts of nature, but flood losses are largely acts of man." The great American cartoonist, Walt Kelly, through his character Pogo, famously observed the spoiled landscape after an Earth Day celebration—litter, garbage, wrecked park benches, just a mess. Pogo looked at it and said, **"We have met the enemy and he is us."**

This chapter concentrates on legal issues relating to *floods*: one of the most foreseeable, yet the most costly natural hazard challenges, faced by the United States and the world. The chapter then suggests ways to reduce risk of harm from floods and, by extension of legal concepts, all foreseeable natural hazards through wise use and safe development, within the constraints of morality, ethics, and legal principles.

The Water's Edge

For centuries, towns and cities grew up around rivers as sources for moving goods and supplying much needed water for industry. Over time, while supplying those same historical benefits, our rivers became a source of scenic vistas and numerous recreation activities.

Today, the "place to be" is at the river's edge, and we, as less than stellar stewards of our environment, have filled in vast amounts of floodplain lands to develop our precious river valleys in order to "urbanize" our landscape. All the while, we, as the American public, believed we were so much cleverer than nature and, most importantly, we ignored or fought back against natural processes without due consideration of rare, large, and foreseeable natural events. When nature acted through usually foreseeable processes such as floods, wildfire high winds, tsunamis, hurricanes, we all too often tried to fight against those natural processes with ill-conceived quick fixes, which all too often had disastrous consequences. As a society, we launched a counteroffensive of squeezing water between levees, constructing hurricane barriers and sea walls, channeling water into concrete culverts and long spaces of underground pipes, and otherwise attempting to control natural

forces. Yet, all too often as we constructed these attempts to control natural processes without due regard to the fundamental principle of emergency management: hope for the best but plan for the worst. Nature always has the last word. Sometimes that last word seems to us as a punishing fury, such that millions everywhere across the globe are speaking of nature's devastation, nature's misery, and the "natural disaster" loss of life and property. In utter submission, at least for some, the world's people are finally coming to the realization that we must do something quite different from what we are doing and we must do it now.

Safe and Sustainable Development

I suggest that our choice is not between development and no development. Demographic pressures clearly indicate that we will have development. Our choice is rather between safe and sustainable development that creates jobs and a better society and our current development practices that inevitably lead to misery and suffering, as well as tremendous waste and abuse of taxpayers. This concept is based on ancient legal principles, which are in fact best expressed by the maxim of Roman property law: use your property so that you do not harm others. A maxim of law is, by definition, universally accepted and inarguable. No one has the right to use their property in a way that harms other people. The Association of State Floodplain Managers (ASFPM) has developed this ancient concept into a modern expression quote "No Adverse Impact" (NAI). No adverse impact is a concept/policy/strategy that changes one's focus from building within the environment to "do no harm." NAI is an approach that ensures that the action of any community or property owner, public or private, does not adversely impact the property and rights of others. The true strength of the NAI approach is that it encourages local decision making to ensure that future development impacts will be identified, considered on a watershed-wide basis, and mitigated. It is a truly comprehensive strategy for reducing the losses, costs, and human suffering caused by flooding. The Natural Hazard Mitigation Association (NHMA) has expanded and restated the concept of NAI to be "safe and sustainable development" where one looks at all foreseeable hazards before undertaking development or redevelopment.

The pluses to the safe and sustainable view of development are eye-catching:

- Will reduce future disaster damages
- Changes the dynamics of development from a view where one side wins and one side loses to look at opportunities for mutual gain
- Will reduce future suffering
- Will protect the community's natural resources and amenities

- Will improve the quality of life
- Will provide for more sustainable growth within the community
- Will reduce the community's liability for litigation due to harm caused by ill-thought-out development and redevelopment

Other potential benefits to the community of using the Safe and Sustainable or NAI approach can include the following:

- Improved water quality and reductions in nonpoint pollution impacts
- Green corridors that also serve as additional areas for floodwater storage
- Improved groundwater recharge
- Better bank stabilization and better erosion control
- Possible increased property values near these "green" areas

Communities can begin now to explore the positive results of safe and sustainable development. They can start by defining the foreseeable threats due to their community's unique conditions. (This is not a one-size-fits-all philosophy.) "Foreseeable hazards" can be defined by evaluating their community's hazards and also their community's programs for addressing those potential hazards. Most importantly, communities can require all adverse impacts to be mitigated at the time that development or redevelopment occurs.

The principles associated with the NHMA concept of Safe and Sustainable Development and the ASFPM's NAI concept should serve as the basis for a proper and safe future for our nation and the world. Local communities can emphasize that they are saying yes to good, well-planned development and ready to use the Safe and Sustainable Development concepts to say "Yes!" to good development that will not cause harm, over time and on a cumulative basis, to the community or nation. Such comprehensive safe and sustainable considerations would include development of comprehensive plans that include watershed-based considerations. Such comprehensive plans must recognize existing natural hazards, such as wildfire and earthquake; use environmentally sensitive zoning ordinances; promote development and redevelopment that will protect existing and future generations; expand resource mapping so that developers, officials, business and industry, and homeowners better understand risk; and include disaster-resistant building codes.

Safe Development and the Law

It is important to note that courts have broadly and consistently upheld performance-oriented regulations, building codes, and requirements for safe construction including those that exceed minimum standards set

forth in state law or by federal regulation at 44 CFR 60.3 for participation in the National Flood Insurance Program. Regulations that require additional freeboard, establish setbacks, impose tighter floodway restrictions, or very tightly regulate high-risk areas have consistently been upheld by the courts.

The question of the rights, duties, and prerogatives attendant to the ownership of land has bedeviled attorneys, philosophers, and governments since ancient times. Some philosophers, such as John Locke, advocate an expansive view of property rights that would very much minimize governmental restriction. This philosophy is expressed wonderfully in books such as *Property Rights in 21st Century America* (by Timothy Sandefur, The Cato Institute, 2006). Other philosophers such as Benjamin Franklin advocate a view of property rights that emphasize the primacy of the needs of the society of a whole at the expense of an individual landowner. Books such as *The Land We Share* (by Eric T. Freyfogle, Island Press 2003) beautifully express the philosophy of the primacy of societal needs in evaluating property rights.

The founding fathers of this nation seemed to advocate a somewhat middle course between the philosophies of Locke and Franklin. The debate over the point at which private property rights become subordinate to the overall needs of the society rages on today in courts, articles, and daily interaction between property owners and governments. This chapter need not attempt to reconcile these differing philosophies. One thing upon which virtually all moral, ethical, and legal philosophers agree is that nobody possesses a right to use their land to harm others (Thomas 2008).

It is widely held that governments have a fundamental duty to protect the present and preserve a community's future. Far too many of them shirk their responsibility, however, especially in the regulations arena, for fear of and concerns about "takings," as found in a recent NOAA research report (NOAA 2010).

Taking Issues

Since the late 1980s, there have been a series of cases from the United States Supreme Court that have confused many people about the point at which land-use regulation so restricts the rights of a landowner that a compensable taking of property has occurred under the Fifth Amendment to the Constitution. These cases are usually referred to as "taking issue" cases. This has led to serious concern and uncertainty on the part of planners and other regulators as to just what extent property can be fairly, properly, and legally regulated.

In 2005, the Unites States Supreme Court unanimously issued an important ruling, *Lingle v. Chevron*, 544 US 528, 125 S. Ct 2074 (2005), that

significantly clarifies "takings" jurisprudence. In *Lingle*, the court held that there is a four-part test to determine if a regulation is a taking: (1) physical intrusion; (2) denial of "all economically beneficial use"; (3) a significant, but not complete denial of beneficial use; and (4) a land use exaction that has little or no relationship between the exaction and the articulated government interest; (5) in addition, Justice Kennedy noted in concurring with the unanimous court that the decision did not foreclose the possibility of litigating a regulation that was "so arbitrary or irrational as to violate due process" (Kusler and Thomas 2007; Thomas and Medlock 2008).

There has been a huge increase in taking issues cases and related controversies involving development. Jon Kusler and Ed Thomas reviewed thousands of cases for ASFPM and found one common thread: Courts have modified Common Law to require an increased standard of care as the state of the art of hazard management has improved. The Kusler–Thomas research found that regulations that were clearly based on hazard prevention and fairly applied to all were, in almost all cases, found NOT to be a taking. Further, they found many, many cases where communities and landowners were held liable for causing harm to others. That is right—increasingly states are allowing lawsuits against communities for alleged "goofs" in permitting construction or in conducting (or lack of conducting) inspections. That is not to say that there have not been cases where communities were on the losing end of litigation taken against them for attempting to prevent building in a hazardous area. In almost every losing case, however, the community has refused the requested permit based on nebulous environmental or aesthetic concerns. Had the community clearly related the permit refusal to harm prevention, the outcome, very likely, would have had a different result. *Gove v. Zoning Bd of Appeals*, 444 Mass. 754 (Mass. 2005) alleged that the town took their property without compensation in violation of the Fifth and Fourteenth Amendments for refusing to issue a building permit. The courts found in favor of the town. "It is undisputed that (lot 93) falls within a floodplain, and that its potential flooding would adversely affect the surrounding areas if the property were developed with a house. Reasonable government actions mitigating such harm … typically do not require compensation."

In fact, state and local governments are vastly more likely to be successfully sued for permitting development resulting in problems such as roads, stormwater systems, and bridges than they are for prohibiting such development.

In a review of these cases, there is a common theme that clarifies what communities failed to do:

1. Do NAI planning.
2. Identify the impacts of the development activity.

3. Notify the soon-to-be-afflicted members of the community.
4. Redesign or reconsider the project.
5. Require appropriate and necessary mitigation measures.

Governments have been held liable in the following situations:

- Construction of a road that blocks drainage.
- Stormwater system increases flows.
- Structure blocks watercourse.
- Bridge built without adequate opening.
- Grading land increases runoff.
- Flood control structure causes damage.
- Filling wetland causes damage.
- Issuing permits for development that causes harm to a third-party pact (Thomas 2008).

In deciding whether regulations "take," courts examine the impact of the regulations on private-property owners:

- Does the owner actually "own" the property in question?
- Is the area subject to public trust?
- Are the proposed activities nuisance-like?
- Is there diminution in value?
- Is there denial of all economic use?
- Does the regulation impact on the whole property?
- Does the regulation impact on reasonable investment-backed expectations?

The courts also investigate the nature of the government actions:

- Is the government action factually supported?
- Is it nondiscriminatory?

Simply put, to avoid taking issues, the community must avoid interfering with the owner's right to exclude others (*Loretto*), avoid denial of all economic use (*Lucas*), in highly regulated areas, consider transferable development rights or a similar residual right so that the land has appropriate value (*Penn Central*), clearly relate the regulation(s) to preventing a hazard (*Gove; Annicelli v. Town of Kingston; Lopes v. Peabody*), and establish a fair variance procedure.

The *Lingle* decision by the nation's highest court enormously supports the principles of both the National Flood Insurance Program (NFIP) and NAI floodplain and stormwater management. Both NFIP and NAI seek to require the safe and proper development of land subject to a hazard. Neither NFIP nor NAI floodplain and stormwater management requires or supports government regulations that oust people from their property.

The court summed up its reasoning by stating that the tests articulated in *Lingle* all aim at identifying regulatory actions that are functionally equivalent to a direct appropriation of or ouster from private property. This clear statement by the nation's highest court tremendously supports the concept of Safe and Sustainable development. Both the NFIP and NAI seek to require the safe and proper development of land subject to a hazard.

Other Relevant U.S. Supreme Court Cases

Other relevant cases decided by the U.S. Supreme Court include the following:

Kelo v. New London, 126 S. Ct. 326 (2005).

Kelo involved condemnation, a "paid taking" of residences. The case concerned whether economic development in a community was considered a "public use" for purposes of a taking as described in the constitution. The five-to-four decision that, yes, economic development can be considered a public use, shows how much deference the majority of the justices are willing to give to local decision makers who, in this case, had decided to condemn private land so that commercial redevelopment could take place. Progovernment and planning associations cheered the decision. However, the announcement of the decision was also greeted by widespread public concern, outrage, and proposed legislative correction of the decision from property rights advocates and groups concerned about the rights of minorities. This widespread concern illustrates the extreme sensitivity of issues involving property rights. For floodplain and stormwater managers, the primary lesson of this case is that the court was willing to give enormous deference to local decisions about what is best for a community, thus supporting the concepts and principles of the Flood Insurance Program and NAI floodplain and stormwater management.

San Remo Hotel v. City and County of San Francisco, 125 S. Ct. 2491 (2005).

This unanimous decision in a case involving fees charged to permit the change of use of a hotel does not directly relate to hazard regulation. Nevertheless, it is important to all concerned with managing natural hazards because it indicates that takings claimants who have already litigated an alleged taking in a state court do not necessarily get another "bite at the apple" in a federal court.

Legal Summary

Stormwater and floodplain managers can be heartened by the decisions and opinions in three Supreme Court cases and three state cases, all of which support the concept of government management of areas prone to flooding, as summarized below

1. Four tests for a taking have been clearly delineated by the Supreme Court, all of which tend to restrict takings to fairly narrow circumstances.
2. The court indicated that deference will be given to local decisions in matters of land use and community development—a stance helpful to stormwater and floodplain management because it underscores the responsibility for and prerogatives of localities for management of land within their jurisdictions.
3. When NAI planning is practiced and the community's plans and regulations seem that they may meet resistance from landowners and developers, here are some hints to help frame the regulation to avoid a taking ruling:
   a. Avoid interfering with the owner's right to exclude others. See, for example, *Loretto v. Teleprompter Manhattan*, 458 US 419 (1982).
   b. Avoid denial of all or nearly all reasonable economic uses. A nuisance-like use that hurts other people is not a reasonable use. See, for example, *Lucas v. South Carolina Coastal Council*, 505 US 1003 (1992).
   c. In highly regulated areas, consider transferable development rights or a similar residual right so that the land has appropriate value. See *Penn Central Transportation Company v. City of New York*, 438 US 104 (1978).
   d. Clearly relate regulation to preventing a hazard, if and only if the regulation is in fact designed to prevent harm. See the very favorable court rulings in *Gove v. Zoning Board of Appeals of Chatham, Massachusetts*, 444 Mass. 754 (2005), and *Smith v. Town of Mendon*, 822 N.E.2d 1214 (2004); in contrast see the unfortunate cases of *Annicelli v. Town of South Kingston*, 463 A.2d 133 (1983); and *Lopes v. Peabody*, 417 Mass. 299 (1994).
   e. Improve your odds by the following:
      i. Establishing a fair variance system to deal with true hardships for situations that will not cause harm to others
      ii. Providing flexibility in the regulation
      iii. Applying the principle to the local government's own activities
   f. See also the American Planning Association's (APA) *Policy Guide on Takings* adopted in 1995.

When one considers its basic concept of developing and redeveloping property safely, NAI has broad support. For example, the Cato Institute is a conservative think tank considered by many as closely associated with the "Constitution in Exile," the "Property Rights Movement," and other similar causes. The institute stated that *compensation is not due when*, "… the government acts to secure rights—when it stops someone from polluting his neighbor … it is acting under its police power … because the use prohibited … was wrong to begin with." The institute also testified before Congress about legislation requiring government to pay landowners for regulations limiting what a property owner can do. The Institute testified that there should be provided a "… nuisance exception to the compensation requirement …. *When regulation prohibits wrongful uses, no compensation is required*" (emphasis added).

Local officials should understand that (1) hazard-based regulations are generally sustained against constitutional challenges; and (2) the goal of protecting the public is afforded enormous deference by the courts. Therefore, local officials should (1) be confident; (2) be assertive protecting the public and the landowner; and (3) partner with other hazard regulators, such as wetlands programs. One can follow a safe development approach and set the regulatory standards needed to protect the property rights of all in the community, including developers (other cites too).

Once you get past the taking issue, you have to start grappling with the adaptation issue and whether it is in the community's best interest to consider higher standards. Once you consider the uncertainties with flood elevations (and the current and often outdated flood insurance rate maps), flood height increases, the analysis that there is a 50% chance that the 1% flood will be exceeded in 70 years, the analysis that there is a 26% chance of flooding during the life of a 30-year mortgage (compared to a 9% chance of fire), the fact that 25% of all flood insurance claims are outside the mapped special flood hazard area (SFHA), the fact of sea level rise and the possibility of climate change, higher regulatory standards appear to be a wise choice for a community. Sea level rise is a very well-documented fact. It has been going on from 12 to 18,000 years. We may not be certain of its continued rate of rise, but in terms of emergency management, we ALWAYS hope for the best and plan for the worst. That basic principle, for example, leads to a need for freeboard, stronger building design, and improved emergency management, to name a few.

Higher standards are not an issue that the American public has not already dealt with in the past. Reduction in the incidence of airplane disasters found enormous success in the 20th century due to higher regulatory standards. Basically, we reduced airplane disaster by learning from experience and from adopting the idea that airplane disasters were not natural disasters. As a nation, we achieved success in reducing airplane disasters even as the numbers of flights per day increased tremendously.

Fire loss in the United States was another issue tackled and severely reduced due to higher regulatory standards. "One hundred years ago, American cities faced a devastating challenge from the threat of urban fires. Whole cities had become the victims of these events. Entire neighborhoods lived with the very real threat that an ignited fire would take everything, including their lives." "Today, the threat of fires is still with us. But we have done a lot to address the risk, minimize the incidence and severity of losses, and prevent fires from spreading. Our states and localities have an improving system of codes and standards; most of us are aware of the risks; we have accomplished a lot, but we have much more to do." "... [T]he success of America's fire services over the past 100 years is instructive for the strength and sustainability of America's communities for the next 100 years as well." "Today, we must not only continue and reinvigorate our successes, but also expand them to include the natural and man-made threats that each of our counties, cities, towns and villages face every day—floods, earthquakes, hurricanes, hazardous material spills, highway accidents, acts of terrorism, and so much more" (FEMA 2002, p.1).

In many communities, current approaches to land use and development are creating future disasters. Those disasters are, in many cases, predictable, foreseeable, calculable, and measureable with today's advanced engineering practices. Even if the climate stabilized, and no further climate change were to take place, we would still have millions of people at risk and that risk will be growing on a daily basis, as we ignore the nature of our watersheds and continue to flush water off as though it is garbage. We are flushing water off of our landscape with such a speed, and at such an enormous intensity, that not only are we dynamically increasing the flood risk, but we are also creating a life safety issue. In short, we are turning docile streams into savage killers.

We, as a society, therefore, need to design conservatively, safely, and properly and with a clear, convincing, and accepted motive of harm prevention, even if we do not, in any manner, way, shape, or form, hold with the climate change theory. In short, we must adapt. It's all a matter of collaboration, coordination and a lot of planning. The change is not going to be quick, painless, or easy.

Hope

While the debate about climate change drones on and on, the new battle cry of the floodplain managers, the hazard mitigation specialists, and emergency managers everywhere must become, "we must find a way to create a safe, sustainable future using less public funding."

The future is looking brighter in regard to creating a safe and sustainable nation. New and exciting APA and American Bar Association (ABA)

awareness and initiatives are taking place. APA's Hazards Planning Research Center has currently released a FEMA-funded project, *Hazard Mitigation: Integrating Best Practices into Planning* brilliantly authored by APA's Jim Schwab, showing how hazard mitigation and adaptation plans can be integrated into comprehensive planning efforts at all scales—from the neighborhood to the region. ABA has adopted a series of resolutions that address hazard mitigation. FEMA has entered into the Risk MAP phase of their mapping efforts and is looking at reforming the NFIP to make the program more effective. The National Hazard Mitigation Collaborative Alliance and the Natural Floodplain Function Alliance (NFFA) have recently organized and look to chart a new course in floodplain and natural hazards management. Organizations like ASFPM and NHMA continue to grow and flourish and have an enormous impact on policy and policy makers. The USACE Silver Jackets Program is taking hold in many states. NAI floodplain management promises a new direction in floodplain management policy. Finally, and probably most importantly, the media and other national leaders are "catching on" to the real reasons flooding and other natural disasters are occurring and increasing in consequence. We, as the public, have the ability and the opportunity to change legislation over the next few years—legislation that will dictate our future and our own susceptibility to risk.

New Management Options

What can we do to reduce the toll of disasters on our world?

First, we must adapt. For example, when dealing with floods, we must learn how to better manage the high volumes of surface water we have created by years of irresponsible land use and by virtually paving over our landscape. The traditional approach to managing stormwater is gradually being recognized as unsustainable and often quite costly.

Our cities and towns must explore the use of innovative and sustainable urban drainage schemes to protect freshwater ecosystems, mitigate the effects of climate change, and help reduce the impacts of flooding; and we must break down the social, cultural, and political barriers to do it. Examples of these innovative and sustainable urban drainage schemes include (but are not limited to) green roofs and green buildings, grass filter strips and other porous surfaces, rain gardens, wetlands restoration, infiltration basins, bio-retention ponds, and urban river restoration. Many of these will not only help with water quantity, but also improve water quality, boost biodiversity, and provide more aesthetically pleasing landscapes and added amenity value, as well. Permeable paving allows surface water to be absorbed, filtered, and cleaned before recharging the groundwater in our aquifers (Timlett and Gordon-Walker 2011). Parks, preserved open

spaces, and conservation green spaces not only serve as natural buffers but also provide permeable areas for stormwater, aid in groundwater recharge, and can contribute to the character and identity of a community. Rain barrels and underground cisterns can store rain water for future reuse. Meandering rivers and wetlands are valuable for wildlife and have added value to society as they slow and store floodwater, provide recreation and tourism opportunities, improve water quality, and act as the focus for raising awareness of flooding issues in local communities (Timlett and Gordon-Walker 2011). All these sustainable urban drainage schemes can work together to lessen the demand on built drainage structures, reduce stormwater runoff, provide natural habitat creation or rejuvenation, improve water quality, and potentially attenuate flows, especially flash flood flows, during rainfall events.

Water quality is an important issue in its own right, but one we will not discuss within the context of this chapter.

Second, we must deal with stormwater at its source. Stormwater is not a commodity to be handled with kid gloves on a particular site, only to be discharged with little regard to adjacent and downstream property owners and thus to have those discharges from that site increase flood risks downstream and potentially impact river corridor habitat. That is to say, stormwater is not something to be collected and then moved quickly away from valuable urban areas to natural water courses (Timlett and Gordon-Walker 2011) and eventually on to the sea, with little regard for what happens in between. Whether we like it or not, and whether we are ready to accept it or not, there is a direct link between humans and the river. Water is not garbage. Therefore, the focus of any truly sustainable program for managing surface water must start with changing the behavior of Joe Q. Citizen, the property owner.

Third, we must educate community officials and the public if we want to be truly successful. The end result of an ineffective stormwater management system is a shared risk for each member of a community. Education and public awareness are the keys to a community that is more responsive and more ecologically sensitive. Wise use of water and wise disposal of water are but a few of the behavioral changes that must be made, and government entities must lead by example to reinforce a sustainable approach to surface water management. In many cases, it means that community leaders must increase their skill sets on issues such as ecosystem functions, low-impact development, green infrastructure, interrelationships among comprehensive land-use planning, zoning, hazard mitigation planning and emergency management, hazard analysis, strategic thinking skills, and wise use of incentives and disincentives. Community engagement is a key component to success, and the community must become invested in taking the appropriate measures to reduce their stormwater footprint. Again, strong

community leadership is key, and the local government must champion the cause of encouraging the community to support sustainable stormwater solutions. Partnerships with other communities are vital since floodplains, rivers, creeks, and streams generally do not stop at the jurisdiction line of the community. This is where watershed planning and regional land use planning come into play and where coordination between up- and downstream communities is imperative. Regulations can also play a significant role in changing or modifying community behavior and in developing a sustainable framework for stormwater management. Of course, at the end of the day, nothing worth doing can be done well without planning. Communities have to take a long, hard look at the interrelationship between all local planning processes and their hazard mitigation planning, their long-range planning, including their capital improvement projects (water, sewer, storm sewer), and their local land-use planning. A good jumping off point is APA's *Hazard Mitigation: Integrating Best Practices into Planning* (PAS 560). Edited and authored in part by APA's Jim Schwab, *Hazard Mitigation: Integrating Best Practices into Planning* seeks to close the gap that often exists between hazard mitigation planning and other local planning and regulatory land-use processes. It introduces hazard mitigation as a vital area of practice for planners; provides guidance on how to integrate hazard mitigation strategies into comprehensive, area, and functional plans; and shows where hazard mitigation can fit into zoning and subdivision codes.

Finally, we must work tirelessly at link safe development to sustainable development. The truly excellent book *Design for Flooding*, by Watson and Adams, John Wiley and Sons, 2011 brilliantly describes the linkage between climate adaptation, climate change, safe development, and sustainablity.

Conclusion

All one has to do is to look at the devastating video and news footage of Sendai, in eastern Japan, as the town is literally washed off of the map, to understand the emotion behind the mantra of the hazard mitigation and emergency management specialists. President Barack Obama described his feelings very succinctly after viewing images of the devastation in Japan following the 8,9 earthquake and subsequent tsunami: "I am heartbroken," Obama said. "When you see what's happening in Japan, you are reminded that for all our differences in culture or language or religion, that ultimately humanity is one."

After working several disasters a little closer to home, FEMA Administrator Craig Fugate has applied a sense of urgency to dealing with disasters in the United States. Administrator Fugate recently had this to say, "I've got three simple rules in a disaster: Meet the needs of survivors, take care of your team, and rule three is to see rule one." Fugate summed up the feelings

of many disaster specialists with this: "Our immediate priority is the safety of the people and communities." With that in mind, it is the closing thought of this author that we still "have miles to go before we sleep."

End-of-Chapter Questions

1. What are some ways in which local land-use policies can be improved to minimize disaster risk and losses?
2. Describe the legal precedent that supports the NAI approach.
3. How can governments be held liable for failing to take hazard mitigation into account?

Resources

Recent Hazard Mitigation and Floodplain Management Legal Publications

G. Galloway, E.A. Thomas, et al. (2008). A California Challenge Flooding in the Central Valley: A Report from an Independent Review Panel to the Department of Water Resources, State of California. Available at http://www.water.ca.gov/news/newsreleases/2008/101507challenge.pdf.

J. Kusler and E.A. Thomas. (2007, November). No Adverse Impact and the Courts: Protecting the Property Rights of All. Special Edition. Available at http://www.floods.org/PDF/ASFPM_NAI_Legal_Paper_1107.pdf.

J. Kusler, P. Parenteau, and E.A. Thomas. (2007, March). "Significant Nexus" and Clean Water Act Jurisdiction. Discussion paper for the Association of State Wetland Managers. Available at http://www.aswm.org/pdf_lib/significant_nexus_paper_030507.pdf.

NOAA. (2010, April 26). Hazard Resiliency Planning: Perceived Benefits and Barriers among Land Use Planners. Financial research report. Retrieved from http://www.csc.noaa.gov/digitalcoast/_/pdf/hazard-and-resiliency-planning.pdf.

W. Shaw, E.A. Thomas, et al. (2007). Brochure Titled: Property Rights and Community Development: A Legal Framework for Managing Watershed Development. ASFPM staff-developed document based on materials developed for the Massachusetts Coastal Zone Management Agency's StormSmart Coasts Program. Available at http://www.floods.org/NoAdverseImpact/NAI_Legal_Framework_Watershed_Development_2007.pdf.

W. Shaw, E.A. Thomas, et al. (2008a). Massachusetts Coastal Zone Management Agency StormSmart Coasts Materials [brochure]—StormSmart Coasts Fact Sheet 1, *Introduction to No Adverse Impact (NAI) Land Management in the Coastal Zone*. Available at http://www.mass.gov/czm/stormsmart/resources/stormsmart_nai.pdf.

W. Shaw, E.A. Thomas, et al. (2008b). Massachusetts Coastal Zone Management Agency StormSmart Coasts Materials [brochure]—StormSmart Coasts Fact Sheet 2, *No Adverse Impact and the Legal Framework of Coastal Management*. Available at http://www.mass.gov/czm/stormsmart/resources/stormsmart_legal.pdf.

W. Shaw, E.A. Thomas, et al. (2008c). Massachusetts Coastal Zone Management Agency StormSmart Coasts Materials [brochure]—StormSmart Coasts Fact Sheet 3, *A Cape Cod Community Prevents New Residences in Floodplains*. Available at http://www.mass.gov/czm/stormsmart/resources/stormsmart_chatham.pdf.

E.A. Thomas. (2006). Liability for Water Control Structure Failure due to Flooding. Association of State Floodplain Managers. Available at http://www.floods.org/PDF/NAI_Liability_Failure_Facilities_0906.pdf.

E.A. Thomas. (2007, May). Failed Dams and Levees: Examining Engineering Liability. PowerPoint for a webcast for the American Council of Engineering Companies. Available at http://www.acec.org/advocacy/pdf/may07_thomas_presentation.pdf.

E.A. Thomas. (2008). Protecting the Property Rights of All: No Adverse Impact Floodplain and Stormwater Management. The Rocky Mountain Land Use Institute. Retrieved from http://www.law.du.edu/images/uploads/rmlui/rmlui-sustainable-floodplainMgmt.pdf.

E.A. Thomas. (2008, April). A Perfect Storm of Opportunities to Establish and Fund a Program to Reduce Misery and Protect Water Resources. *Louisiana Coastal Law*, Vol. 89. Available at http://www.lsu.edu/sglegal/pdfs/lcl_89.pdf.

E.A Thomas and S. Bowen. (2009, November). Preventing Human Caused Disasters. *Natural Hazards Observer*, Vol. XXXIV, No. 2, Available at http://www.colorado.edu/hazards/o/archives/2009/nov_observerweb.pdf.

E.A. Thomas, A. Jerolleman, T. Turner, D. Punchard, and S. Bowen/Natural Hazard Mitigation Association. (2011). Planning and Building Livable, Safe & Sustainable Communities: The Patchwork Quilt Approach. National Floodproofing Conference, New Orleans, November 2008. Available at http://www.floods.org/PDF/Patchwork_Quilt/Patchwork_Quilt_Floodproofing_Conference_10908.pdf.

E.A. Thomas and S.R. Medlock. (2008). Mitigating Misery: Land Use and Protection of Property Rights Before the Next Big Flood. *Vermont Journal of Environmental Law*, Vol. 9. Available at http://www.floods.org/PDF/Mitigation/ASFPM_Thomas&Medlock_FINAL.pdf.

E.A. Thomas and T. Turner/American Bar Association. (2011, Spring). *Climate Change and Emergency Management: Adaptation Planning*, Vol. 34, No. 3. Available at http://www.americanbar.org/content/dam/aba/publications/state_and_local_law_news/sl_34_3_thomas_turner.authcheckdam.pdf.

FEMA, Federal Emergency Management Agency. (2002). America at Risk: America Burning Recommissioned II. FEMA Publication FA-223. Available at http://www.usfa.fema.gov/downloads/pdf/publications/fa-223-508.pdf.

R. Timlett and S. Gordon-Walker. (2011). *Dealing with the Deluge—Urban Water Management in a Changing Climate*. World Wide Fund for Nature and RSA Insurance Group. Available at http://www.wwfrsapartners.com/static/uploads/page_files/WWFRSA_SuDsReportFINAL.pdf.

D. Watson and M. Adams. (2011). *Design for Flooding: Architecture, Landscape and Urban Design for Resilience to Flooding and Climate Change*. John Wiley & Sons. Hoboken, NJ.

Chapter 9

Involving the Community in Mitigation and Outreach

Richard L. Krajeski and Kristina J. Peterson

Contents

Learning Objectives

- Understand the complexities of the concept "community."
- Be able to explain the different ways of describing community and how these different perspectives influence mitigation.
- Be able to explain "social resource mapping."

"Reaching out and involving your community in hazard mitigation can magnify your effectiveness manyfold. Each diverse constituent and partner brings his or her unique gifts to you, in terms of fresh insights, energy, constituencies, resources, and innovations." (Ann Patton)

Introduction

James Lee Witt, the former director of the Federal Emergency Management Agency (FEMA), is quoted as saying, "All mitigation is local." Director Witt believed that legislation and policies are important and even critical, but he also understood that individuals, families, households, businesses, institutions, agencies, governments, associations, private and public sectors, and whatever else makes up communities are the ones who do mitigation. While he was the director, Witt started Project Impact, a community-based mitigation program that tried to involve as many stakeholders as possible. At the natural hazards meeting in Boulder, Colorado, Director Witt announced what he called a national "community-based" mitigation initiative. He said that he was sponsoring a series of "town hall" meetings around the country and listed the kinds of stakeholders he was inviting. The list was lengthy and included many of the well-known nongovernmental organizations (NGOs) that are active in disaster response, but he left out many of what are known as community-based organizations (CBOs) and faith-based organizations (FBOs). When we brought this to his attention along with our concern that any mitigation program should not negatively impact poor and marginal citizens like much of the national "urban renewal" programs did in the decades proceeding, Witt was quick to make arrangements to include CBOs and FBOs. The CBOs and FBOs were not in his field of vision. He did see our point and involved the religious community in mitigation planning, and this enabled us to work with FEMA. In this chapter, we hope to enable you to see the complex nature of community, hear from the voiceless, and feel what it means to be part of a community-of-place (see Figure 9.1).

FIGURE 9.1 Town meetings as one way to get feedback, present information, or otherwise interact with a community: Here, Douglas Glowacki, Emergency Management Program specialist, Connecticut, talks about different mitigation programs and grants that may be available to residents impacted by a recent storm. (Courtesy of Jocelyn Augustino/FEMA, Plainville, Connecticut, October 1, 2011.)

Using "Plain" Language

True Story

Many years ago, we overheard the following: One local said to another, "They wanted me to go to some all-day meeting on mitigation. I told them I did not want to spend a day hearing about all that legal stuff." The local person was not familiar with the word "mitigation" and mistook it for the word "litigation."

Rule-1A

The meaning of a message is ALWAYS determined by the hearer.

Rule-1B

The meaning of a message is the response you get.

It is critical that all discourse involving dialogical intersubjectivity be executed at a concentration of linguistic standards that increase the probability of maximizing reciprocated comprehension. Is this CLEAR? It is not likely. We begin by urging you to use clear, easily understood language and to check regularly to make sure that what is being said is clear to everyone and what is being heard has a direct relationship to what is being said. (This is often harder than it sounds.) Academic, governmental, and professional disciplines often have their own "language" and set of terms that may be well understood in the profession but are meaningless, confusing, and often misleading to others. It is important to remember when doing interdisciplinary, interdepartmental, or intercommunity/interethnic work with different groups of citizens that the same word can be used in VERY different ways. Using the language of a discipline or profession may be important and even necessary (we are not sure that it is as necessary as some think) in some cases, but when the language of a discipline or profession is used to communicate with people outside that discipline or profession, the "professional talk" is experienced by the outsiders as confusing, mystifying, elitist, nonsensical, oppressing, excluding, and disingenuous. The use of such professional language does not help learning or understanding.

Listening: The Important Part of Talking

We all think we know how to listen, but often our listening is hearing ourselves (what we think a person is saying, what we want them to say, and what we are going to say to them) rather than giving our full attention to the person speaking. We set up listening sessions, focus groups, and town hall meetings, all to listen—listen to stakeholders, listen to citizens. These ways of listening are not bad, but they are almost always limited. Not everyone in a community can or will come to these meetings. Some people do not talk

in groups. Listening to all of the stakeholder voices takes the creative design of listening places, times, and styles. In a democracy, listening to all of the voices is a requirement.

Rules for Listening

1. If you are not sure what a person means, ASK.
2. If you are sure you KNOW what a person means, ASK if you are right.
3. Ask yourself, "Who should be speaking but is not?" Call on them.
4. Ask yourself, "Who is not here who should be?" Seek them out.

Community, community—everybody loves community. But what is community? Who is community?

Definitions of Community

1. Political
2. Social
3. Geographical
4. Psychological
5. Spiritual/normative
6. Stakeholders

People "picture," think about, and "spell" community in many different ways. The definitions that people and agencies carry around in their heads and sometimes in their formal and official documents indicate how they conceptualize community, who they see (and do NOT see) as leaders of a community, who and what they believe is important, and how they interact with communities. Some people and agencies seem to spell community as g-o-v-e-r-n–m-e-n-t and they, therefore, functionally understand community as elected officials and bureaucrats. Others spell community as b-u-s-i-n-e-s-s and, therefore, businesses become their benchmark for understanding community. People and agencies that think this way center their activities on these official leaders and institutions and are likely to disregard other people, groups, and institutions that make up and have interests and power in communities. Some people spell community as p-l-a-c-e. Others spell community as u-s—n-o-t—t-h-e-m.

Exercise

List as many parts and types of communities as you can think of. Do NOT limit your thinking to just things. Include concepts such as community history and spirit. Think of positive and negative things and concepts. (How did you decide to label some things positive or negative?) Ask WHO is in this community? WHAT is in this community? WHERE is this community?

WHAT communities are in this community? WHO thinks they are in but are not in? Is an Internet chat group a community? Why? Why not? How do our definitions of community enhance and limit our abilities to mitigate?

Definitions serve at least two very important functions beyond naming something. Definitions limit a subject or expand a subject. Definitions close and open doors to the ways we think about things. Textbooks, professors, governmental officials, and dictionaries like short and concise definitions. Somehow the idea that the shortest definition is the best has become part of our scientific mindset. The problem is that it is not scientific.

True Story

A few years ago, we were involved in a research/policy/action project with several other institutions involving RESILIENCY (in some ways resiliency is the new name of mitigation, or at least we mitigate to help create resiliency). The three institutions involved in the project had three different ways of going about things, talked about resiliency in somewhat different ways, and had different ways of looking for indicators of resiliency. About halfway through the meeting, perhaps because of the continuous arguing about the term "resiliency," a member of the sponsoring organization suggested that we come up with a working definition. A member of our group spoke against the idea pointing out that we needed to keep the definition open and to keep pushing the definition as far as we could because we did not want to leave out important ideas or concepts. We lost and, from our perspective, so did the groups in terms of their chances to discover new meanings and examples of resilience.

Questions

1. What are some of the advantages of short definitions?
2. What are some of the dangers of short definitions?
3. How can you be sure your definitions are helpful and not dangerous?

So, we want to EXPAND the thinking about the meaning and experience of community.

But first, a digression…

Digression

Maps and mitigation go together like hands and gloves; the questions are which hands and what gloves?

Geographers (Harvey 1990, 1996, 2006; Relph 1976) remind us that maps are always distortions of reality. Southern Hemisphere activists remind us that our maps that show North America, Europe, and Asia as up disclose not-so-well hidden cultural biases. Bandler and Grinder (1979) remind us

that we all have "internal maps that guide our behavior" and that "the map is not the territory." So, maps are not unbiased representations of objective reality, but tools or "frames" (Schon 1994) or lenses that help us manipulate and gain perspective on what is out there.

There are many ways to map a community and the kind of map you "draw" or have drawn for you determines what you see and thus what you know and can use. Hazard risk is one thing that can be effectively mapped. Traditional mapping is good at showing physical features and political boundaries, but it may not be so good at showing cultural, psychological, social, and informal political boundaries. It is much harder to map vulnerability (which is not the same as hazard), capacity, resilience, networks, and values. But as a "mitigator" all of these should be on your map.

A geographic information system (GIS) is a wonderful tool, but similar to most good tools, folks try to use it in inappropriate ways. Sometimes tools determine a project (this is happening with GIS), whereas the correct process is for the project to determine the tools.

When it comes to mitigation, maps are important and the maps that are in the minds of local people are very important.

Some questions to ask your maps are as follows:

- What do you tell me?
- What do you not tell me?
- Whose interests do you represent?
- Whose interests do you hide?
- Whose interests are denied?
- If I follow you, where will you lead me?
- How do I get back from there?

Community can be viewed in some critical ways, which are discussed in the following subsections.

Community as Physical Geography

Some (maybe most) communities exist in a limited, definable, and mappable space. The features of natural geography (rivers, valleys, hills) and human-made geography (buildings, highways, industrial parks) help to form, define, limit, and change communities. Rivers, valleys, hills, buildings, highways, and industrial parks can increase and decrease a community at the same time.

Exercise

Get a detailed copy of the map of your city or area. Mark on the map where you think the boundaries of different communities exist. List the criteria you used to make the determination. Where are the cultural boundaries? Where are the social boundaries? Where are the economic boundaries? Can you see

the social and political networks in the map? List the things the map will not tell you about where the communities are. Does the map give you any ideas about where some mitigation might be needed? Does it tell you who is vulnerable and why? How can physical geography be used to promote mitigation?

Psychological Community

Sometimes, a community is better understood by its "feeling" or feelings of the people who call it a community than by the most detailed map. Sometimes, there are feelings in a community (safety, fear) (Bachelard 1964) or "about" feelings in a community that run very deep, are very old, are never spoken of publicly, and exercise great control on its people (Tuan 1979). People move to or reject a community because of how it feels. There is growing evidence that successful mitigation efforts may be impacted MORE by how people feel—their sense of safety or beauty, their feeling of commitment and belonging to a place—than by economic incentives.

Exercise

How can people's feelings about their community be used to foster mitigation? How do you really find out how people feel about their community?

Spiritual/Normative Community

People talk about "community spirit," the "spirit of a place," the "inspiration of a place," and the "depression of a place." Many native people and traditional people have what they call a very deep spiritual relationship with the place to which they belong; it is a relationship so important to them that they will sacrifice almost everything to remain there. Some people say that their personal identity and the meaning of their life are tied to a particular concrete place. When they say that they cannot live anywhere else, they mean it.

Exercise

Is there a place where you find fulfillment, peace, and meaning? How would you feel if that place was threatened? Where are your "safe" places? How can a person's or a group's spiritual attachment to a place help or hinder mitigation? How can people's spiritual and normative ties to communities-of-place be used to promote mitigation?

Community as a Stakeholder

It might be fair to say that without stakeholders, mitigation is a piece of cake. Most mitigators would say that stakeholder conflicts are one of the major problems in mitigation. Stakeholders not only have different

opinions about what should be mitigated when but also disagree on who should pay, when the payment should be done, and who should have to move. More and more in the business of mitigation, community is defined by stakeholders and as stakeholders. Stakeholders can be defined as individuals, households, institutions, and groups who have a stake in something. We now have stakeholders meetings where once we had community meetings. This is more than just a change in terminology; it is a basic value change. It is a change from understanding the collective/cooperative nature of responsibility to each other in a community, to an individualistic self-interest view.

Exercise: My Favorite Stakeholder

List as many stakeholders as you can think of for a mitigation project in your community. Rank them in terms of (1) political power, (2) social mobility, (3) physical mobility, (4) economic need, (5) social support, and (6) ties to their community-of-place. Should they all have the same amount of power to determine the project? Should people who live in the area have more or less say in the project than a developer who lives miles away? Develop a list of criteria to assess the categories and degrees of power that stakeholders should have.

How can stakeholders be encouraged to support mitigation?

Community as Geopolitical

Communities are located in some geography (even cyberspace) and are political (formally or informally) to some degree because they are human. Geography and power relations contribute to or detract from well-being and success.

Exercise

List and rank those who have power in your community. How do you know?

What kinds of power do they have? How do you know?

Who is powerless in your community? What kind of power do they need? How do you know?

Try to map the power structures of your community.

How can power be used to promote mitigation? How can power be used to stop mitigation?

Some scholars and community organizers do a POWER ANALYSIS of the communities they are working in.

Community as Concrete Interpersonal Networks

Bowles and Gintis say, "By a community, we mean a group of people who interact directly, frequently, and in multifaceted ways. ... the list suggests that connection, not affection, is the defining characteristic of a community." They continue,

> "Our analysis is predicated on the fact that the individual motivations supporting peer monitoring and other aspects of community governance are not captured by either the conventional self-interested preferences of Homo economicus or by unconditional altruism towards one's fellow community members. Rather, it is predicated on strong reciprocity, which is a predisposition to cooperate in a collective enterprise, and a predisposition to punish those who violate cooperative norms, both of which are individually costly but conducive to strong social capital" (Gintis et al. 2005, pp. 381, 382).

Bowles and Gintis stress the direct, frequent, and multifaceted nature of these relationships. They are not necessarily related in or through organizations. Bowles and Gintis, who are economists by training, reject the traditional ideologies of Homo economicus and unconditional altruism, which they trace back to sixteenth- to nineteenth-century philosophy of the likes of Hobbs, Locke, and Marx. They suggest that a more empirical biological model of reciprocity is needed. Measures must include more than organization counting and organization contacts but must include informal, often unnoticed, and perhaps "invisible" cooperation.

Exercise

Look through the Yellow Pages of your phonebook and count the number of clubs, organizations, religious institutions, and gathering places. These are often considered sources of social capital. Try to map them. What do you discover? What mysteries do you discover? Are you aware of sources of support that are not reflected in the Yellow Pages? If so, what are they? How do you discover them? How can interpersonal relations be used to promote mitigation?

Community as Networks-of-Networks

Communities are more than individuals. To understand communities is to see networks, which may be formal, like an organization, or informal, like four wheelers, the local pub, and the barbershop. I do not see these kinds of informal measures in the social capital assessment tools in the material of the World Bank and other institutions. We consider the term social capital to be dangerous and misleading unless it is carefully defined. Some experts define and measure a community's resilience or mitigation ability by the number of formal organizations and social services it has. Our research has

shown that many communities that have few organizations or institutions and are understood by some scholars as deprived of social capital are, in fact, rich in informal networks and contacts. You have to know where to look.

Exercise

Construct a personal or class network map. Put one class member's name or your name in the middle of a large piece of paper. Around the name put the groups, organizations, institutions, gathering places, and any other connection places you can think of. What have you learned? How can networks be used to promote mitigation?

Community as Place-World, Body-World, and In-Placement

Sociologists like Alfred Schutz (1970); geographers like Anne Buttimer (2001), E. Relph (1997), David Seamon (1979, 1989, 1993), David Harvey (2006), and Yi-Fu Tuan (1974, 1977); landscape architects like Robert Thayer (2003); environmentalists like David Abram (1996); and phenomenologists like Martin Heidegger (1971), Maurice Merleau-Ponty (1964), and Edward Casey (1993, 1997, 2002) hold place, place-world, in-placement to be a fundamental human reality that determines who, how, where, and what we are. This human attachment to a place and a place's attachment to human beings is particularly significant for native peoples and traditional "historied" (storied) communities, for example, West Virginians, the Grand Bayou (Louisiana), many people in southern Louisiana, and many others. We do know that displacement is traumatic for many people, even when it is voluntary. Some people and communities seem to be little bothered by displacement, whereas others suffer greatly from it. Finding measures for this attachment to place will be critical.

Exercise

Are there places where you really feel like yourself? Are there places where you do not feel like yourself? What makes the difference? What would it be like to dwell in a place where you never felt like yourself? How can the feeling for a place be used to promote mitigation?

Community as Memory and Re-membering

Casey (1987) claims that place is the basic stuff of memory and that Re-membering is an important psychosocial activity. Reunions and going back to one's roots are important activities for many people. These are more than get-togethers or trips into the past. They have power, normative (shared) value, and psychological and social meaning. These may be

measures on the importance of places for some people and communities. People "invest" much on protecting their memories and the place where those memories live. Stories abound of people who will not leave their memoried place. Others cannot wait to get away from a place. Some will say that "this place is full of memories," whereas others will say, "this place has no memories for me."

Exercise

List your memoried places. What makes them important? How did they form you? How would being separated from them change you? How can memoried places be used to promote mitigation?

Community as a Knowledge Source

Anthropologists and geographers often speak about indigenous and traditional knowledge of individuals but communities and places themselves have a kind of knowledge that gives their residents (and perhaps some outsiders) what Habermas and Peter Park would call relational and reflexive knowledge. Casey talks about "body knowledge," and anyone who has spent any time with the Grand Bayou fishers (or the like) know that their bodies and their senses have a kind of knowledge that cannot be articulated. For some, place and community knowledge tell them who they are, how they are to live, where they are to be, and how they are to act. When this kind of knowledge, which comes with place and community, is taken away, some people are literally lost, directionless, and out of place. This kind of knowledge is of great value to mitigators, but it is often overlooked.

Example

In southern Louisiana, we have disappearing marsh grass and an invasive critter known as nutria. A nutria is (1) a big rat that eats grass, (2) a hat worn by George in *Seinfeld*, or (3) all of the above. The answer is all of the above. Some experts from a university devised a plan to replant an area in southern Louisiana with grass. The research was done and the grass planted ignoring the local people and their knowledge. Finally, the nutria, who loves young grass, entered the field. A multithousand-dollar mitigation project was destroyed overnight because not one person talked to the locals, who would have told the experts that the nutria must be removed first.

Community as Meaning

Community and place are critical sources of meaning for many people. This meaning can be contained in common and private historical sites and in stories, narratives, and conversation.

Community as Norm

Communities have historically set and enforced norms. It seems clear that the disruption and displacement of some communities have serious consequences on the communities' ability to construct, teach, and enforce norms.

Community as Story

Stories say as much about the future as they do about the past. Stories show community members what is important, how to relate to the world, and what the future should and could look like. Stories tell people how to relate to each other and the world, who can be trusted and who cannot be trusted (Ricoeur 1991).

Community as Well-Being

There is a sense of well-being among the people of a community, even if that well-being is unhealthy.

Discovering Communities

Social Resources Discovery

Taylor and Kent in *Pre-Crisis Management* (1984) use what they call social resource mapping when they work with communities. They describe the geographic area of communities—how the human ecosystem is structured and performs various functions.

Publics and their interests: A public is a segment of the population or a group of people having common characteristics, interests, or some recognizable demographic features. Publics are groups like farmers, neighborhoods, parents, small business people, and minorities. By identifying the publics and characterizing each public's interests, a change agent can determine how various segments of a population are affected differently by project or program decision making.

Networks: A network is a structured arrangement of individuals who support each other in predictable ways because of their commitment to a common purpose, shared activities, shared beliefs, or similar attitudes. There are two types of networks: (1) networks that are informal arrangements of individuals who join together to express their interests, values, or beliefs, and (2) networks that are formal arrangements of individuals who belong to formalized organizations to represent and communicate their interests. Knowledge of networks formed by people to express their interests is essential for identifying public issues relating to project or program development and monitoring the effectiveness of decisions.

Settlement patterns: A settlement pattern is the distribution of a population in a geographic area, including the historical cycles of settlement—how, where, for how long, and who settles in an area.

Work routines: Work routines comprise the ways in which people earn their livelihood and make a living, including where and how they do it. They include skills needed, sources of livelihood, pay and income, opportunities of advancement, business ownership, and stability of livelihood and employment. Where, when, and how people work or do not work is specified. Knowledge of work routines is used to evaluate how changes caused by programs will alter the way people make a living.

Supportive services: A supportive service is any arrangement that people use for taking care of each other; such services include the institutions serving a community and informal caretaking activities of individuals. Examples of informal caretaking activities include the ways in which people manage on a day-to-day basis using family, neighborhoods, and friendships.

Recreational patterns: A recreational pattern is the way in which people spend their nonwork time and where. How and where do people spend their nonwork time? This includes places for recreation and street corners, porches, and bars.

Geographic boundaries: A geographic boundary is any unique physical feature that defines the extent of a population's routine activities. Physical features generally separate the cultural identity and daily activities of a population from other populations living in other areas. These physical features include both natural and human-made boundaries, such as rivers and highways.

Asset Analysis

All communities, even communities that are extremely poor in resources, have assets and liabilities. Some of the first things we need to learn about assets and liabilities are that they are often hard to detect (sometimes they are invisible to both residents and outsiders) and that they change regularly (to such an extent that assets become liabilities and liabilities become assets). Thus, assets and liabilities are contextual; change over time; and vary in terms of class, race, age, and gender.

Types of Assets

Formal and Informal Assets

Included in community are formal structures (like government, government agencies) and formal agencies and organizations (like the United Way, the Chamber of Commerce, the American Red Cross, and religious

organizations). Also included in community are the informal community or citizen based organizations and publics (which are defined as interest groups like hunters, ATV riders, and soccer moms and are closely related to stakeholders, networks [formal and informal], structures, systems, and local citizens). Building trust and cooperation must be encouraged throughout the recovery, preparedness, and mitigation process. This is particularly true for the informal groups and networks of a community.

Most of the people who write about and work with communities stress strongly that building trust is critical for all program development (Fischer 2000, 2003, 2009; Forester 1988, 1989). Early identification of existing structures (formal and informal) is vital. Helping these structures—households, groups, agencies, organizations, businesses, formal and informal networks, and publics—to effectively increase their capacity; cooperate with each other; and actively participate in planning, decision making, and follow-through is a most important and necessary step in successful disaster preparedness, disaster recovery, vulnerability reduction, and future sustainable development. It is the people of a community that make it resilient. The involvement of citizens and their formal and informal organizations, networks, and systems is important because this involvement reflects the nature of our democracy. It is also important because it is the best way to have a successful and sustainable program on the one hand and reduce conflict and litigation on the other.

The Nature of the Informal

The groups and informal systems of citizens take many forms, but some groups are almost FORMLESS. These groups include ministerial associations; community organizations like Heart and Hand houses; Catholic Community Services; community action; the Cooperative Extension Service; and neighborhoods and neighborhood associations, groups, gangs, and so on. Informal systems are much less structured and much less visible than the aforementioned informal groups, but they often exercise great influence in the community and involve elaborate networks. Informal systems often exist within formal organizations, for example, the group that gathers at the water fountain. These informal systems and networks often take the form of folks around the lunch table and people that meet at the local restaurants, bars, barbershops, and beauty shops. These informal entities are the guys who meet at the garage, the families that meet at the game, the "men in the smoke-filled room," the women at the gym or at the well, and the people who gather after religious services or at work. These organizations and systems are usually apolitical in the formal sense, but they may have considerable political influence. They can represent significant parts of a community, may have great formal and informal connections and

influence, and will have varying degrees of access to all parts of the community including the formal decision-making systems. They often have the trust and respect of both the citizens and the establishment. They are for many people and many neighborhoods the basic media of information and opinion exchange.

Beyond Needs Assessments: Community Assets, Identities, and Convictions

Traditional disaster preparedness, response, and mitigation and traditional community organizing and development programs have focused on the needs, vulnerabilities, and problems of a community. This, of course, is necessary for the development of any program. However, discovering and documenting needs, vulnerabilities, and problems is not enough, because communities are more than their needs, vulnerabilities, and problems, even communities recovering from devastating disasters. Communities, even communities that have experienced a "natural" disaster or a catastrophic economic event, have assets, identities, and convictions (values).

The identification and assessment of a community's assets, identities, and convictions (values) is necessary for any successful and sustainable program of disaster preparedness, recovery, mitigation, development, and resiliency building. This identification and assessment of a community's assets includes assessing the individuals, household groups, institutions, and networks for assets, identities, and convictions. Communities and the parts of communities have formal assets such as land; industry; schools; religious, civil, and caregiving groups; financial resources; government; and so on. All of them are important. But a community has more than these formal assets.

A community also has informal assets. Informal assets include informal groups and networks that often have access to other significant assets. Assets are not just "things." Assets include human skills, abilities of organizations, relationships, connections, history and historical artifacts, culture, and anything else that someone considers valuable. These are now being called things like human capital and cultural capital. It is a sad commentary on human nature that communities and organizations that have experienced overwhelming devastation may be forced to market their destruction (make their disaster an asset) in order to bring in valuable resources. In this sense, even needs can be an asset.

It is normal for most groups and communities to view themselves as asset deprived in ordinary times, and almost all groups and communities will feel even more deprived of assets in times of disaster. Helping communities

and groups to discover their assets will provide a material, emotional, and organizational boost to such communities and groups.

Identity and Convictions

It may seem strange to list identity and conviction as assets. Identities and convictions can be great assets or great liabilities. ALL communities, organizations, groups, families, households, and networks have some kind of identity and convictions about the nature and meaning of themselves, others, and life in general. They will value these ideas and often defend them strongly, usually uncritically, and often unconsciously. These valued identities and convictions give meaning and direction to people's lives and define what is valuable, possible, worth working for, and even worth fighting and dying for. These convictions and identities are powerful forces and can determine directions, attitudes, involvement, commitment, and resistance to any project or program. Identities and convictions vary greatly from community to community. Some communities have little "corporate" identity or conviction about themselves as a geographic, historic, or "relational" community and the members of the community can move in and out with little sense of loss and with little disruption to their daily lives and core values. Other communities have strong identities and convictional, relational (as well as strong livelihood-specific), geographic, and historical ties to their community. For example, many suburban homeowners think about their homes in economic terms. A major concern for them seems to be the resale value of their homes. People who have strong convictions about a place and strongly identify with that place are not concerned with resale value but with the preservation and "passing on" of the place. People with strong convictions about a place and strong identity with the place want to "preserve the place for its people and preserve its people for the place." There is a kind of dual ownership: People own a place and the place "owns" the people. The place holds values that cannot be transported to another place.

These identities and attitudes are, sometimes, considered to be irrational by those who do not share the identity or conviction. In fact, identity and conviction are suprarational, that is, they are above reason and are the foundation of reason. These identities and convictions are often held with great fervor, pathos, and emotion, and are often well thought out and beautifully articulated, particularly by indigenous and local peoples. In our experience, these people use the powerful language of poetry to express their values instead of the limiting language of economics. People, groups, and even communities hold strong convictions about fate, personal responsibility, government, human limits and possibilities, giving and receiving aid, race, gender, and class; the list is endless. These convictions move people into

fellowship and a resilient future or keep them in an isolated and repetitive past. It is a mistake of great proportions to think of or treat these strongly held convictions as irrational, superficial, primitive, unsophisticated, or unimportant.

Because these identities and convictions can be so strong, it is important that program developers and change agents identify them and understand their importance and place in the lives of people and communities. Failing to take the time to discover and understand these identities and convictions and the people who hold them will prove to be a costly mistake.

Identifying informal assets, identities, and convictions not only provides more tools to accomplish a program or project but also can have a positive impact on the attitudes and energy of individuals, groups, and communities.

We have found that helping individuals, groups, and communities to document their assets, embrace their identities, accept their differences, honor their history, and celebrate their convictions empowers them and builds their capacity. We find that after these kinds of assessments, people, groups, and communities have increased energy, are more hopeful, feel closer, are more trustful, and begin to explore new possibilities.

In our experience, when a needs or vulnerability assessment is the first item on the agenda, people in attendance feel depressed, estranged, overwhelmed, mistrustful, and not very hopeful. Whenever possible, we begin our work with an "asset, identity, and conviction assessment," even if it must be a very brief assessment. We realize that at times a need or issue is so much in the minds and hearts of people that they can think of little else and are overwhelmed by the concern. In such cases, it is important to go with the flow, to listen sympathetically to the people, and honor their concerns. For example, in one recovery project, we worked with an elderly woman whose home needed a fair amount of work so that she could be comfortable and safe in the coming winter. But all she could talk about was the mud where her lawn used to be. So we planted grass seeds in the area knowing that they had NO chance of growing. Once that was done and she could see her new lawn in her mind's eye, we could plan for her home repairs. In another situation, the survivors of a hurricane were much more committed to restoring the environment than rebuilding their homes.

We try to avoid starting our work with a needs assessment. Beginning with a needs assessment is often demoralizing to people, particularly to people and communities who have been through some kind of trauma. Even if we can take only a few minutes of asking people to share a few things, such as the value of their community or group and what their strengths have been, we take the time. Establishing assets and strengths is much more important than listing needs. Individuals, households, groups, and communities seem to be much more aware of their needs and vulnerabilities than they are of their assets and capacities.

It is our belief that in the context of asset, identity, and conviction assessments, preparedness, mitigation, resiliency, and sustainable development become more than just abstract ideas about the possible future. Preparedness, mitigation, and development, in this context, become urgent activities to protect, preserve, and enhance what people value most. Taking people through an asset, identity, and, conviction assessment before doing a needs, hazard, or vulnerability assessment seems to us to be a very good use of even limited time. An asset, identity, and conviction analysis will often "lift up" needs and vulnerabilities that will not be discovered in ordinary needs, hazard, or vulnerabilities assessments.

Marlene Wilson, in her book *Survival Skills for Managers*, explains why change is resisted. We summarize her findings here. A change is resisted when it

1. Is perceived as lowering status
2. Causes fear
3. Affects jobs, livelihoods, and lifestyles
4. Reduces authority or freedom
5. Disrupts established routines
6. Rearranges formal and informal relationships
7. Is forced on people without explanation or participation
8. Comes at times of system overload

Some barriers to change are as follows:

1. Failing to be specific
2. Failing to show why
3. Failing to provide the affected people with a say
4. Using personal appeal or pressure
5. Disregarding a community's habit patterns
6. Failing to keep people informed
7. Failing to allay fears about failure
8. Creating excess pressure
9. Failure to deal with anxieties

In order to minimize resistance to change, it is important to carefully consider

1. The change itself
2. Those affected by the change
3. Ways in which the change is introduced

People are more likely to accept change when they are

1. Involved in the process
2. Asked to contribute

3. Told the reasons and advantages of the change
4. Provided honest communication
5. Respected for their feelings (Fischer 2009, chapter 10)
6. Asked what help they need
7. Given recognition

Some questions to ask yourself when you are planning a change are as follows:

1. Who will be affected?
2. How will they be affected?
3. Which reasons for resistance might affect each group?
4. What methods could be used to introduce the change that might minimize resistance?

Characteristics of relationships that lead to conflict and can serve as early warnings of trouble are as follows:

1. Ambiguous or disputed jurisdictions
2. Conflict of interest
3. Communication barriers
4. Overdependency of one group
5. Differentiation in organization
6. Association of the groups
7. Need for consensus
8. Behavior regulations
9. Unresolved prior conflicts

Levels of conflict are as follows:

1. Facts or data: remember that feelings ARE facts.
2. Processes and methods.
3. Goals and purposes.
4. Values.

Defining the Problem

Thomas Gordon, family and organizational psychologist and consultant, says that people often argue about COMPETING solutions when they do NOT share the same definition of a PROBLEM. He suggests the following:

1. Define problems in terms of needs and not in terms of competing solutions.
2. Generate possible solutions (NO evaluation at this step).
3. Evaluate various solutions.
4. Decide on a mutually acceptable solution.

5. Implement the solution (who, when, where, how).
6. Evaluate the solution.

Consensus Building

Consensus building is not just about technics but more importantly about the attitude of those trying to bring about change. Helpful attitudes emphasize

1. Cooperation
2. Emphasis on mutual trust
3. Common ownership of ideas
4. Valuing feelings (FEELINGS ARE FACTS)
5. Valuing differences
6. Valuing the contributions of all

Keys to help a group function are as follows:

1. Guiding the agenda
2. Keeping the discussions on topic
3. Clarifying and reshaping
4. Equalizing participation
5. Pacing (aiming to keep moving and giving time to think)
6. Reformulating
7. Identifying interpersonal problems
8. Summarizing
9. Aiding a group's emotional climate (FEELINGS ARE FACTS)
10. Identifying individual emotions as they arise
11. Conflict management
12. Testing the agreement
13. Soliciting feedback
14. Decision identification and implementation (what, when, who, how)

Lydia Alexander, in the book *Wearing Purple*, says that there are six categories of loss:

1. Attachments
2. Turf
3. Structure
4. Future
5. Meaning
6. Control

Most of these categories of loss have little to do with the price of things. Survivors and caregivers experience loss in all six areas. Some examples of the losses experienced by survivors are discussed in the following subsections.

Attachments

"I loved that old chair so much." "I am sorry but we could not find your kitty." "I just will never feel the same about this place." "We can never rebuild a house with all of those memories." "My dolly is all dirty and broken." "I have lost the sense of safety I always had before." "I can never believe in a loving God again."

Turf

"This piece of ground will never be the same for me." "We are going to have to sell the farm and move to the city." "They say that we cannot build back here." "Right here was the porch where I rocked all my babies." "My tree house is gone." "They are trying to take my rights to build where I want from me."

Structure

"I don't know what to do or where to turn." "It is so hard to get out of bed and do anything." "I just wander from this to that." "I feel like the whole world is in chaos."

Future

"What are we going to do?" "We're too old to start over." "How can we take out a mortgage at our age?" "I was hoping to leave all of this to the kids." "How can we start over?"

Meaning

"My whole life was wrapped up in this place." "My God, WHY?" "I don't feel like I am anybody anymore." "How can you make sense out of all of this?" "Can there be any meaning to this?" "Who am I now?" "Does life mean anything?" "My kitty was my best friend."

Control

"Everything is out of control." "My nerves are shot." "This form, that form—I think I'm going crazy." "I just do not feel safe anymore, anywhere." "Oh, to be able to know what tomorrow will bring." "I used to feel so in control."

Exercise

List an example of each of the following:

1. ATTACHMENT mitigation
2. TURF mitigation
3. STRUCTURE mitigation
4. FUTURE mitigation
5. MEANING mitigation
6. CONTROL mitigation

["knowledge is not enough."—E. Rogers]

Part of a conversation that can be heard over and over again at any meeting of hazard risk and disaster scholars, emergency-preparedness professionals, and emergency-policy makers is "THOSE PEOPLE ...." Those people are the people who do not listen to the messages and warnings and who do not have a 72-hour emergency kit (after a lot of research, the experts now say 3-day emergency kit). Those people are the people who do not elevate, who build in 100- and 400-year floodplains, who like living among the pine trees, and who love the view of the ocean from their beach house.

The preparedness plans were well conceived and well produced, but no one listened. The hazard-mapping program went well, and people continued to build in dangerous areas. The display on mitigation and retrofitting won awards, but no one came to see it. "What is it with THOSE people?" There may be a great distance between a great plan and program design and a successful outcome. One of the reasons for this, according to Rogers, is that we often fail to plan for successful outcomes. It is not uncommon to hear the following from researchers: "I do description NOT prescription" or "I document, I don't implement." The point is that often, the implementation and evaluation of a program that might have been expertly planned is done in haste with little knowledge of what Rogers calls the "adoption process." It is the contention in this chapter that a holistic hazard reduction, disaster resilience planning process must include planning on implementation and evaluation. To get a successful outcome from a planned program, a complex process that demands care and attention must be followed.

Typical of hazard risk, or preparedness, or mitigation programs are media campaigns and little else and they are generally not very successful (Mileti 1999).

Rogers has identified a five-step process that people go through when adopting a technology, simple or complex:

1. *Knowledge*: People must receive information about new ideas, methods, or technology. This information and the media used must be compatible with the community's communication systems, beliefs, and values. Information must be internalized to the extent that people have knowledge of the new technology and can conceptualize the advantages of adoption. One of the many problems faced by promotion planners is that people exhibit patterns of selective exposure, that is, the tendency to attend to communication messages that are consistent with one's existing attitudes and beliefs. The three types discussed by Park (2001), representational, reflective, and relational, all come to bear on how people take in and process information. There may be some gender differences in knowledge acquisition. Consider three individuals, Jordan, Garry, and Giligan. Giligan, for example, might suggest that women are more likely to trust the

information they receive from other trusted people and process the information in terms of their concrete relationship with particular people.

2. *Persuasion*: Information and knowledge generally are not enough for people to adopt new ideas or a new technology. Persuasion is almost always necessary. There is a real sense today in which persuasion falls into the category of politically incorrect behavior. Persuasion usually involves informal communications networks, a community's value systems, and inputs of trusted change agents and community opinion leaders.
3. *Decision*: People must make a decision to adopt a new technology. The decision-making process is a complex process and involves much more than knowledge and "cost/benefit analyses" of the new technology. Values, culture, emotions, time and timing, and political and economic realities play major roles in the decision-making process. Rogers points out that there is "active" and "passive" rejection. Change agencies (planners and others), according to Rogers, often do not look carefully at the reasons why a program or technology is rejected. When they do investigate the reasons for the rejection, they tend to look only at the knowledge stage and the information given.
4. *Implementation*: Implementation is also a complex enterprise involving time and timing, skills, resources, and support. The easier the implementation is, and the closer it fits with existing technology, methods, and values, the more likely the adoption of the technology is to occur. Reinvention is the process by which a technology, idea, or program is modified by the users, sometimes in rather extreme ways.
5. *Confirmation*: In order for adoption to take place, practical and visible confirmation of a new technology's value is required. This is of course difficult in hazard and disaster planning. The local adopters of an innovation must be able to continue with the innovation even after all outside aid has left.

These five elements of the decision-making process run in sequence, but one part will not necessarily lead to or generate another. Knowledge does not necessarily lead to persuasion, persuasion does not necessarily lead to decision, and so on. Because the adoption of a technology is a process with a number of steps, planning is needed throughout the whole five-stage sequence. Most existing preparedness and mitigation projects are limited to "information giving"/knowledge and occasionally persuasion; therefore, the likelihood of adoption of the desired preparedness or mitigation activities is small. It is important to note that information giving and knowledge are not the same. Information given does not equal information received, understood, and owned.

Rogers identifies five categories of adopters in terms of the speed with which they adopt a change: (1) innovators, (2) early adopters, (3) early majority, (4) late majority, and (5) laggards. He makes the following generalizations about the adoption of new ideas or technologies: To choose to work with later adopters and laggards is to choose a very long and difficult road. This journey requires much commitment, time, energy, and preparedness and many resources. However, the late adaptors and laggards are in most cases the ones who are most at risk and vulnerable and have the least capacity and resilience.

Successful innovations (planning strategies), according to Rogers, have the following attributes:

1. They have a "relative advantage." They fit well within the social, economic, and value systems.
2. They have "compatibility" with the beliefs, values, previous ideas, and needs of the people and their community.
3. They are "not complex." The more complex an innovation, the less likely its adoption is to occur.
4. The innovations are "trialable." The community can have trials of the new technology without a big commitment or cost and see quickly that they work.

As one plans for the adoption of a program, the planner needs to plan for what Rogers calls change agents. Change agents are project managers, educators, field staff, consultants, local leaders, and what Rogers calls opinion leaders. All of these change agents provide a communication link between a resource system of some kind and a client system. Change agents help develop the need for change. They establish an information exchange relationship with a community and enable the diagnosis of the community's problems. Change agents help create the intent for chance in the clients and help foster intent into action. Change agents also help to stabilize adoption and prevent discontinuance of the innovation. Finally, a change agent achieves a terminal relationship and enables the clients to continue on their own.

Change agents need to be sensitive to the realities of the communities in which they operate. One basic reality, among others, is that communities define themselves and are not defined from the outside. Change agents are successful to the degree that they contact many clients and client systems, are client oriented and not agency centered, and develop programs to meet the needs felt by their clients. Empathy, relationships, social participation, being seen as credible, and working with and through local opinion leaders are all part of the process according to Rogers, and they must be part of any planned change strategy. It becomes apparent that participation in a community and the community's participation in the planning and implementation of a program are critical to success. It also shows how much successful planning depends on community.

Summary

As we have illustrated in this chapter, involving the community in outreach is vital to comprehensive, holistic, and functional mitigation strategies. In this chapter, we look at some of the various and unspoken definitions of community and what it means to involve the community in planning. Individuals, families, households, businesses, institutions, agencies, governments, associations, and private and public sectors are what make up communities and together are what also make the community "go." Scheduling listening sessions, focus groups, and town hall meetings to listen to the stakeholders and citizens of a community is a good start, but it is important that overtures are made to all demographics and all voices within the community. We discussed the notion that sometimes community is better understood by its feeling or the feelings of the people who collectively call it their community. Bowles and Gintis stress the direct, frequent, and multifaceted nature of community relationships and add that they are not necessarily in direct relation through traditional organization, but more often through informal, often unnoticed, and perhaps invisible cooperation. All communities, even communities that are extremely poor in resources, have assets and liabilities. These assets and liabilities are contextual; can change over time; and vary in terms of class, race, age, and gender. Identifying informal assets, identities, and convictions not only provides emergency managers and planners more tools to accomplish a program or project but can also have a positive impact on the attitudes and energy of individuals, groups, and communities. Finally, according to Rogers, empathy, relationships, social participation, being seen as credible, and working through local opinion leaders are all part of the engagement process and must be part of any planned change strategy.

End-of-Chapter Questions

1. Explain the importance of using plain language when dealing with community organizations.
2. Explain the concept of community as it relates to natural hazards.
3. Identify and describe the two principal types of community assets.

References

Abram, David (1996). *The Spell of the Sensuous: Perception and Language in a More-Than-Human World*. NY; Pantheon Books.

Bachelard, Gaston (1964). *The Poetics of Space*. Boston: Beacon Press.

Bandler, Richard and Grinder, John (1979). *Frogs into Princes*. NY: Real People Press.

Buttimer, Anne (ed.) (2001). *Sustainable Landscapes and Lifeways: Scale and Appropriateness*. Dublin: Cork University Press.

Casey, Edward S. (1987). *Remembering: A Phenomenological Study*. Bloomington: Indiana University Press.

Casey, Edward S. (1993). *Getting Back into Place: Toward a Renewed Understanding of the Place-World*. Bloomington: Indiana University Press.

Casey, Edward S. (1997). *The Fate of Place: A Philosophical History*. Berkeley: Univ. of Cal Press.

Casey, Edward S. (2002). *Representing Place: Landscape Painting & Maps*. Minneapolis: University of Minnesota Press.

Fischer, Frank (2000). *Citizens, Experts, and the Environment: The Politics of Local Knowledge*. Durham: Duke U Press.

Fischer, Frank. (2003). *Reframing Public Policy: Discursive Politics Deliberative Practices*. Oxford: Oxford Press.

Fischer, Frank. (2009). *Democracy and Expertise: Reorienting Policy Inquiry*. Oxford: Oxford University Press.

Forester, John (1988). *Critical Theory and Public Life*. Cambridge: MIT Press.

Forester, John. (1989). *Planning in the Face of Power*. Berkeley: University of California Press.

Gintis, Herbert, Bowles, Samuel, Boyd, Robert, and Fehr, Ernst, eds. (2005). *Moral Sentiments and Material Interests*. Cambridge: MIT Press.

Harvey, David (1990). *The Condition of Postmodernity: An Enquiry into the Origins of Cultural Change*. Oxford: Blackwell.

Harvey, David (1996). *Justice, Nature and the Geography of Difference*. Oxford: Blackwell.

Harvey, David. (2006). *Spaces of Global Capitalism: Towards a Theory of Uneven Geographical Development*. London: Verso Press.

Heidegger, Martin (1971). *Poetry, Language, and Thought*. NY: Harper.

Merleau-Ponty, Maurice (1964). *The Primacy of Perception and Other Essays*. Evanston: Northwestern University Press.

Mileti, Dennis (1999). *Disaster by Design: A Reassessment of Natural Hazards in the United States*. Washington, DC: Joseph Henry Press.

Relph, Edward (1976). *Place and Placelessness*. London: Pion Limited.

Ricoeur, Paul (1991). *From Texts to Action*. London: Continuum.

Schon, Donald M. (1994). *Frame Reflection: Toward the Resolution of Intractable Policy Controversies*. NY: Basic Books.

Schutz, Alfred (1970). *On Phenomenology and Social Relations: Selected Writings*. Chicago: University of Chicago.

Seamon, David (1979). *A Geography of the Lifeworld: Movement, Rest, and Encounter*. London: Croom Helm.

Seamon, David (1993). *Dwelling, Seeing, and Design: Toward a Phenomenological Ecology*. Albany: State University of New York.

Seamon, David and Mugerauer, Robert (1989). *Dwelling, Place, & Environment: Towards a Phenomenology of Person and World*. NY: Columbia University Press.

Taylor, Donald and Kent, James (1984). *Pre-Crisis Management*. Denver: SRM Corporation.

Thayer, Robert (2003). *LifePlace: Bioregional Thought and Practice*. Berkeley: University of California Press.

Tuan, Yi-Fu (1974). *Topophilia: A Study of Environmental Perception, Attitudes, and Values*. Englewood Cliffs: Prentice Hall.

Tuan, Yi-Fu (1977). *Space and Place: The Perspective of Experience*. Minneapolis: University of Minnesota Press.

Tuan, Yi-Fu (1979). *Landscapes of Fear*. NY: Pantheon.

Chapter 10

Persuasion and Policy

Tammy Barnett Esteves

Contents

Learning Objectives

- Learn the importance of becoming aware of the social, economic, and political forces operating in your community.
- Learn how to BE; the importance of credibility to overcome resistance and attitudes.
- Learn how to KNOW; the importance of preparation and knowledge to effectively deliver a persuasive message.
- Learn how to DO; take your message to the community with power, conviction, and confidence.

Introduction

In 1986, the whole world watched as the first teacher, Christa McAuliffe, was being sent into space on board the Space Shuttle *Challenger.* The whole world watched as the crew took their walk to the shuttle, and the whole world then watched as disaster struck when the shuttle exploded only 73 seconds into flight. Later discussions would focus on a couple of engineers who had tried to stop the launch by raising concerns about the potential for O-ring failure in cold weather conditions, but the launch had already been delayed twice and there was considerable pressure to proceed with the launch as scheduled, for both financial and public relations reasons.

The problem with mitigation is that for many types of disasters, we never know when we have been successful. We cannot know in advance of a hurricane if it might change its path and head in a different direction. We will never know that a terrorist attack was averted or that another shuttle may have exploded because we mitigated the circumstances. So, if the engineer had been successful in convincing NASA not to launch, costing NASA and the taxpayers additional money and rearranging the schedules of all the schools participating in the launch festivities, we would have never known that he saved the lives of the *Challenger* crew. Instead, we now ask questions about "why?" Why were they not more insistent? Why did the supervisors ignore the engineers?

Manipulation. Motivation. Persuasion. Leadership is getting people to work together for a common goal, while manipulation is getting people to work together for your goal. With hazard mitigation, we need to help individuals see that our goal needs to also be their goal, making sure our critical messages get through to all concerned from John Q. Citizen to Jane Q. Senator. The stakes are high; if we are unsuccessful, an inability to persuade relevant audiences to take action not only invites failure and frustration, but also could be dangerous and life-threatening in disaster-related circumstances. Our task is to promote mitigation and convince all relevant stakeholders to take action prior to an event, even (and especially) when disasters are not on their minds or agendas. Our attention spans can be short-lived and short-activated. It is difficult to encourage action when the last time a hurricane evacuation was issued John Q. Citizen sat in traffic for 8 hours only to have the hurricane take a different route; the next time around, he is less likely to leave, at least not until he is sure of the hurricane's path, which may be too late.

Blanchard (2008) calls for emergency management professionals "who can articulate a persuasive and defendable case for disaster prevention and emergency management to top elected and appointed officials," as this issue is "primarily about capacity building within individuals and within systems" (Britton and Lindsay 2005). Furthermore, public involvement can enhance the capacity-building process when they are involved in the decision-making process (King and Stivers 1998). We must be able to overcome resistance and

attitudes through our intentions, power, and credibility, and this chapter will help you develop the tools you need to be successful as a catalyst and leader (Dickie 1979).

> Speech is power: speech is to persuade, to convert, to compel.
>
> **Ralph Waldo Emerson**

Persuasion

In many circles, persuasion is a negative concept that equates to arm-twisting, manipulation, and backroom deals. Mills (2000) states, "25 percent, pollsters tell us[,] believe that persuasion is sorcery, a mysterious black art practiced by wizards who masquerade as politicians, advertisers, and spin doctors." However, persuasion is simply rhetoric or the skillful use of words to get things done. Persuasion can be defined as "human communication that is designed to influence others" (Dainton and Zelley 2010), which includes "the process of changing or reinforcing attitudes, beliefs, or behavior" (Mills 2000). The Athenians were so impressed with this extraordinary power of language that they made annual sacrifices to the goddess of persuasion, Peitho (Majone 1989). In rhetoric, the message and the messenger are both critical components of the persuasion process. In fact, the message is only as good as the messenger.

Dangers of Persuasion

There is the potential public perception of persuasion as manipulation. This is a definite danger and one that needs to be examined. There is indeed a subtle interaction between force and diplomacy, and power and service. Most of us are familiar with the 1963 Milgram experiments where study participants were instructed to administer shocks to individuals whenever they gave the wrong answers to questions. Of course, the shocks were not real but the person administering them did not know that, and they continued to administer stronger and stronger shocks even though they had been informed at the beginning that shocks at that level could potentially cause great harm and possibly death. Why would they do that? Milgram stated (in Mills 2000), "It has to do with a deep-seated sense of duty to authority within us all." Unfortunately, that "deep-seated sense of duty to authority" is often forgotten when we require individuals to take certain actions that may seem counterintuitive to them. This was also the situation in the 1971 Stanford prison experiment where students were recruited and isolated in a prison scenario. Some students were assigned to be guards and others to be prisoners. They ultimately ended the experiment early because the experiment became much too real as power and control issues took over.

Ensuring Success

There are four universal barriers between us and our goal of getting our message across—ignorance, apathy, disciplinary boundaries, and lack of political will (Hays 2009). These four barriers exist regardless of the sender, message, or receiver. Do any of these following scenarios sound familiar to you?

- You are the city planning official in Nags Head, North Carolina, trying to pass new regulations that will limit the rebuilding of homes that are in an area historically prone to hurricanes.
- You are the mayor of Galveston, Texas, trying to convince the public of the need to evacuate when the weather is gorgeous and the last time they evacuated, they sat in traffic for 4–6 hours, only to finally get out of town just to have the hurricane shift course and miss your area altogether.
- Alternatively, in the previous scenario, you are the emergency services director trying to convince the mayor of the need to issue the evacuation order, potentially costing the city millions of dollars in lost tourist revenue if you evacuate and then the hurricane changes course.

Regardless of the sender, message, or receiver, persuading individuals to listen to your message involves three stages—BE, KNOW, DO. We will now examine each of those three steps to effective persuasion.

Level 1: Be

> To be persuasive, we must be believable; to be believable, we must be credible; to be credible, we must be truthful.
>
> **Edward Murrow (n.d.)**

In preparation for this chapter, over a period of 6 months, I asked every police officer, firefighter, EMT, and so on who crossed my path one basic question—"How do you get people to listen to your message?"—and 9 times out of 10 the response has been a chuckle and then the comment, "good luck with that one." In other words, the person on the receiving end of our message has to make the choice to listen or not, which is not something we can do for them. Even if they choose to listen, they will also have to decide whether to act or not. Much of the initial impetus for them to listen and act upon your message will depend on a congruence of four issues—influence, integrity, passion, and vision.

Influence

The purpose of leadership is for the leader to influence others to reach a common goal. While power is often used interchangeably with influence, it is important to differentiate between them. Power is the ability to produce

results; influence is the result of the use of power (Daft 2005). There is both position and personal power. Based on that delineation, the French and Raven model of power (presented in Daft 2005) gives us five types of formal powers—legitimate, reward, coercive (position power), expert, and referent (personal power):

- Legitimate power is the authority granted from a formal position in an organization. Weber (1946) refers to this as legal power. This authority gives them certain rights, responsibilities, and prerogatives, and followers are willing to accept the rights of leaders to set goals, make decisions, and direct activities.
- Reward power is the authority to bestow rewards on other people. Through the use of rewards, leaders control resources and their distributions, and in return, this reward power influences the behavior of the subordinates.
- Coercive power is the negative side of legitimate and reward power—the authority to punish or recommend punishment. Punishment can include various things such as firing, demotion, or criticism.
- Expert power is a leader's special knowledge or skill regarding tasks performed by followers. Expert power can be a two-edged sword in leadership—individuals are often promoted based on technical skill or experience but are lacking in leadership training or ability, and then, as they move up further in the organization, leaders generally lack expert power because their subordinates now have greater technical skills than they do. It is important for leaders to surround themselves with individuals they trust to provide them with this information.
- Referent power is sometimes drawn from charismatic leadership (Weber 1946) and is based on personality characteristics that command attention, respect, and admiration. Leaders can use referent power for both positive and negative outcomes and purposes.

Depending on the use of power, Daft (2005) identifies three possible outcomes—compliance, resistance, or commitment. When there is a successful use of position power (legitimate, reward, or coercive), the result is usually compliance, where individuals will simply follow the directions of the person with power, whether or not they actually agree with those directions. Unfortunately, if the reward or coercive power is used to an extreme, then it will lead to resistance where individuals will deliberately try to avoid carrying out instruction, even to the point of attempting to disobey orders. Personal power, however, generates commitment as individuals will both adopt the leader's viewpoint and enthusiastically follow the instructions. This is especially critical for successful mitigation efforts.

True influence is difficult to define, but you know when somebody has it or when they do not. In general, there are two motives that direct the need for power (Daft 2005):

- Personalized power, which is power for one's own self-centered needs, not for the good of the group or the organization
- Socialized power, which is service of higher goals to others; it often involves self-sacrifice toward those ends, and is usually empowering rather than autocratic in style

Influential power tactics become unethical when used to jeopardize organizational or community best interests, manipulate or deceive, injure others, and/or encourage illegal or immoral activities. This use, or rather, misuse, of power stems from a lack of integrity. What is the ultimate goal of our actions? Just as power is driven by a need for personalized or socialized power, ethical reasoning is grounded in common sense and two broad philosophical perspectives, one centered on duty or principle and the other on results, or as Northouse (2001) describes it, between conduct and character (integrity).

Integrity

Albert Schweitzer states, "Example is not the main thing in influencing others, it is the only thing." This is integrity. Personal integrity is a normative ideal of personal responsibility for which "individuals should and almost always do strive to obtain. It provides an understanding of how individuals can simultaneously hold several commitments and balance among them in a morally defensible manner" (Dobel 1990). Integrity arises out of our sense of ethics, which Josephson has defined as "a system or code of conduct based on universal moral duties and obligations which indicate how one should behave; it deals with the ability to distinguish good from evil, right from wrong and propriety from impropriety." In any case, integrity is pure ethics or how you are when no one is watching—authentic. Byrnes (2005) says that integrity is "a matter of being genuine, being motivated by your deeply held values to make your organization and your coworkers better off. This is where the passion comes from … [W]ithout integrity, you're simply promoting yourself, and people will not follow your lead."

There is a difference between "leader" and "leadership." Just having the title "leader" does not mean you exhibit good leadership. Leadership begins and ends with authenticity, not traits, or styles, but character and integrity (George 2003).

Passion

Passion is driven by a sense of purpose. It empowers us and motivates us to action. It is driven by our vision that we have a reason for being, that

there is a destiny waiting for us to fulfill. Byrnes (2005) lists passion as the most important of eight essential characteristics for leading paradigmatic change—"First and foremost, you need a burning drive to make things better. Change management is a grueling process, and passion will see you through it. Some managers just seem to have 'fire in the belly.'" There is a Chinese proverb that states, "If your vision is for a year, plant wheat. If your vision is for ten years, plant trees. If your vision is for a lifetime, plant people." Passion is such an important part of leadership that it is how Byrnes (2005) defines leaders—as "people who leave their footprints in their areas of passion." Passion-driven people want their lives to make a difference. They have a vision that is driven by a higher goal, rather than selfish power.

Vision

Stanley (1999) says that vision is a preferred future, "born in the soul of a man or woman who is consumed with the tension between what is and what could be." Vision always stands in contrast to the world as it is. Stanley's coined phrase, "visioneering," is "a clear mental picture of what could be, fueled by the conviction that it should be." This conviction will feel like a moral imperative for action. Benjamin Zander, the Conductor of the Boston Philharmonic Orchestra, states it this way: "Goals can be energizing—when you win. But a vision is more powerful than a goal. A vision is enlivening, it's spirit-giving; it's the guiding force behind all great human endeavors. Vision is about shared energy, a sense of awe, a sense of possibility." Vision is always accompanied by a sense of responsibility and often requires sacrifice and risk, and courage and confidence.

The Four in Action

It is the influence of the visionary that serves as the "platform and podium ... visionaries must be influencers ... you must be able to move people from where they are to where you believe they could and should be" (Stanley 1999). Often, the passion that accompanies that vision is all that it takes to elevate a visionary's influence. People who influence us do not necessarily have authority and power in the traditional sense, but it is something about their lives that gives them authority that translates into influence. We are drawn to them and want to go where they are leading. Colin Powell states it this way: "You know you're a leader when your men will follow you if only out of curiosity." It is the alignment between an individual's convictions and behavior that makes their life persuasive; the phrase that best captures this dynamic is moral authority (Stanley 1999). Persons with moral authority "walk the walk and talk the talk." Moral authority positions you

to influence people at the deepest level—heart, mind, and conscience—and will enable you to maintain your influence with those who feel called to follow you.

This differentiation is even more important in the public arena where there is a sense of public duty and responsibility, where each citizen willingly accepts the responsibility to maintain honesty and courage while assuming responsibility for the safety and well-being of their fellow citizens. The ultimate goal of civic duty, as expressed in the last line of the Athenian oath, is to leave society a better place: "We will strive unceasingly to quicken the public sense of public duty. That thus, in all these ways, we will transmit this city not less, but greater, better, and more beautiful than it was transmitted to us." This charge represents an active, not passive, sense of duty and responsibility. Unless we accept the risks of being involved and active, the Athenians would say we have vacated the ethical arena (Chandler 1999). Once that occurs, we will have lost our window of opportunity to connect with our audience and get our message accepted. It can be extremely difficult to gain someone's trust initially, but it can be even more difficult to maintain and nearly impossible to regain when lost. Thus, it is critical that we KNOW our facts and can present them realistically and confidently.

Level 2: Know

Knowledge is power.

Sir Francis Bacon (1561–1626)

It is all about preparation. Know your information. Know your facts. Know your audience. Mills (2000) says there are three areas and three critical questions you need to consider when preparing to present your message—knowledge, interest, and support. How much do they already know about your topic and are they interested and/or supportive? There are six types of audiences you are addressing, and it is likely that there will be some of each type within your audience—hostile, neutral, uninterested, uninformed, supportive, and mixed (Mills 2000). Different approaches will be required based on the type of audience you will be facing. The hostile audience is against your message before you even state it, so you will need to get them to feel comfortable with you before you even think about giving your message. Earn their trust and respect; if they do not know you at all, you should consider bringing someone they do know, trust, and respect with you when you present your message. The neutral audience neither supports you nor opposes you, so you need to reach out to them where they are and help them see why your message should be important to them as

well. Help them to see all sides of the issue and their options and the possible benefits of heeding your message versus ignoring it. The uninterested audience does not really care, so it is up to you to show them why they should. The uninformed audience does not have all the information they need to belong to one of the other groups. As with the others, you will present your message after establishing your credibility to do so. The supportive audience is already in your corner; you need to get their commitment for action. Finally, the mixed audience is most difficult because you first have to ascertain who is hostile, neutral, uninterested, uninformed, or supportive and then reach out to all of them. Perhaps, you will find that some of those in the audience who are supportive can help you with others in the audience who are not there.

Based on your analysis of the audience, anticipate possible concerns and questions and be ready to counter with arguments that are well structured and organized. Make sure you have relevant data available and in a visual format that will get their attention. Use current technology, like a geographic information system (GIS), to emphasize your points. In fact, I will confess my own example to illustrate this point. I grew up in Virginia and I admit I had become quite complacent about hurricane threats (I proudly wore my "I survived Hurricane Isabel" T-shirt even though Hurricane Isabel was not even a Category 1 when it made landfall and caused considerable downed tree limbs and a loss of power for 11 days). I heard all the messages, I heard all the warnings, but nothing affected me as much as seeing a GIS-produced map showing the Hampton Roads area of Virginia and identifying where the tidal surge would be based on the various categories of hurricanes. At that time, we were actually living in a location that according to the map would still be above water even with a Category 5 storm although every gas station, grocery store, and so on would be under water.

As you can tell from Figure 10.1, there are very few white spaces that would avoid even the Category 4 storm surges. A visual such as this may be just what it takes to get someone's attention. I finally started heeding warnings more closely (and then we relocated to the West Coast where I am now faced with listening to messages on earthquakes, which unfortunately do not provide the kind of advanced warning I had grown to expect from hurricanes!).

Using social scientific theory and research such as this GIS example, or even research reports, surveys, and polls, can be effective in helping to persuade the public to accept you and your message or your organization's point of view. Be visual, be consistent, and partner with other organizations so that the message is being heard from multiple venues. This will greatly enhance your chances of success as you move toward the third and final leg of the model, DO.

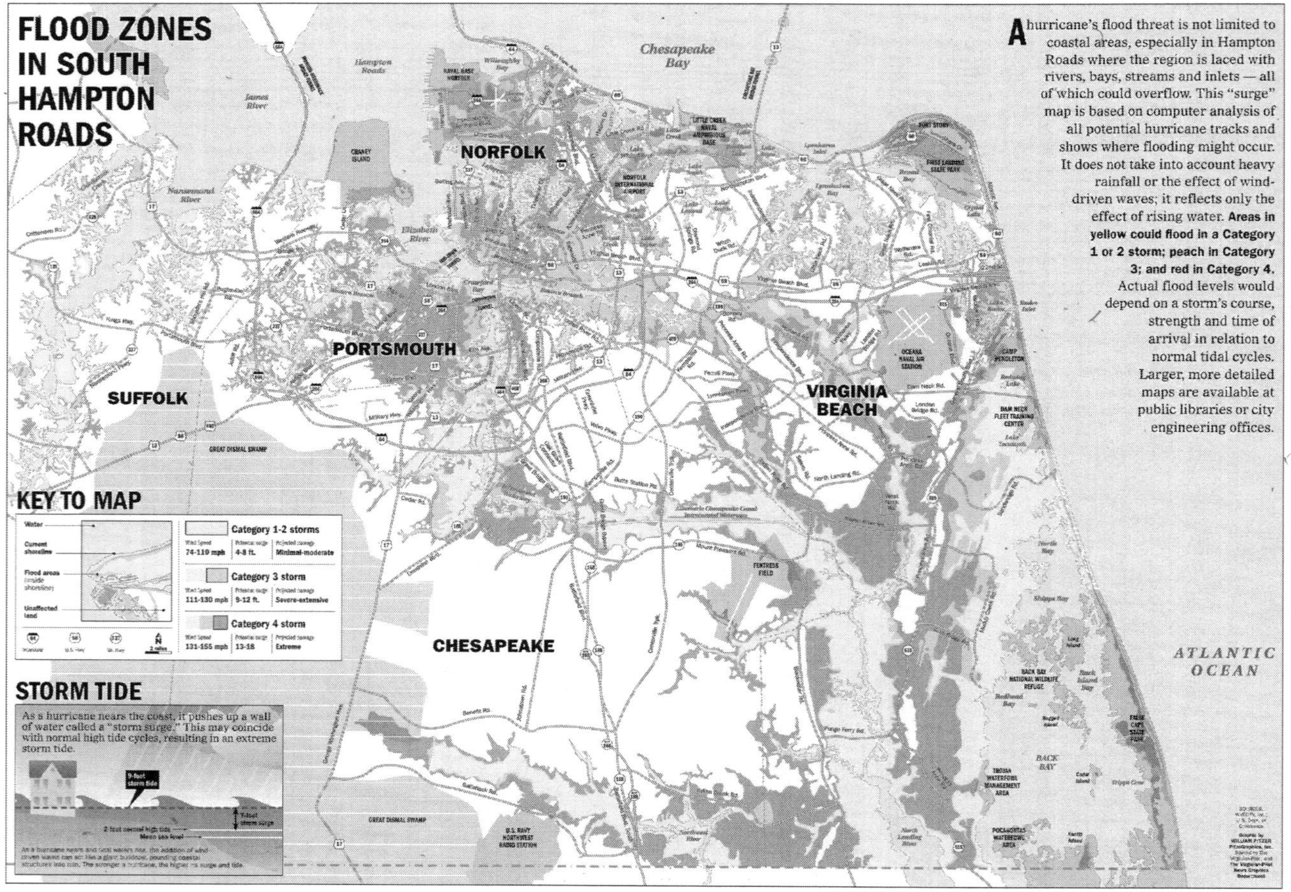

FIGURE 10.1 Flood zones in South Hampton roads.

Level 3: Do

> It's not enough that we do our best; sometimes we have to do what's required.
>
> **Sir Winston Churchill (1874–1965)**

So, it's not enough to be, it's not enough to know … we must do. To change human behavior, Hays (2009) suggests four steps:

Step 1: Provide clear information about the goal and the barriers that prevent people, institutions, and communities from reaching it.
Step 2: Visualize solutions that will overcome human, institutional, and community inertia.
Step 3: Promote conformity of thinking and acting because people, institutions, and communities will do what they think others are doing.
Step 4: Mandate the implementation of a strategy that has a higher power than the one you are using now (an integrating strategy).

You will be successful in presenting your message if you are consistent, persistent, confident, and understand some key "rules of the game."

- *There is power in numbers.* If the same message is being delivered and supported by several individuals and/or organizations, as well as through various types of media, your message will be perceived more strongly. The "power in numbers" also applies to the number of times a message is delivered—consistency and persistency is important.
- *Perception can be influenced by culture.* Know your individual and organizational culture and understand how it may potentially conflict with the individual and organizational culture of the person hearing your message. It is a fact of human nature that generally, people listen to individuals similar to themselves. Additionally, "preemptive strikes" can be powerful. If you can anticipate when cultures might clash, you can be prepared. For example, in the City of Oakland, there is a lot of tension between the general public and the Oakland Police Department. Unless the message is very persuasive, they are not going to listen.
- *Look the part.* Individuals have a preconceived idea of what a person in leadership and authority should look like, so be sure to wear uniforms and business suits where appropriate and use titles and credentials!
- *Timing is everything.* The best time to score points for mitigation is just after a disaster as disasters create "policy windows" of sensitizing the public and its elected leaders to the need to act and to prepare for

future events; unfortunately, these "windows" may close just as rapidly as they opened as the memory of disaster fades (Waugh 2000).

- *Make them think it is their idea.* Give them enough information that they reach the same conclusion for action.
- *Make your case personal.* If they will not listen for themselves, appeal to the concern they have for their family, friends, or neighbors.

An individual who exemplified the philosophy of "be, know, do" was Rick Rescorla, an unsung hero of the September 11 terrorist attacks. Rescorla was the head of security with Morgan Stanley and he spent years preparing Morgan Stanley for what he believed to be an inevitable terrorist attack. Based on consultations with Dan Hill and Fred McBee and others on his formed "Team Rescorla," at one point in 1990, he tried to convince key organizational leaders that being in one of the New York City twin towers was putting them out there as a "sitting duck"; unfortunately, he was told their lease was not up for several more years, so moving to New Jersey was not an option. A few years after the first attack on the garage of the World Trade Center (1993), Rescorla took advantage of the momentum created by that disaster and was able to get the leadership to buy into regular evacuation drills where all employees (top leadership included) would participate. This preparation would prove invaluable on September 11, 2001. Although the Port Authority was telling individuals in Tower 2 not to evacuate, Rescorla insisted that the employees of Morgan Stanley evacuate, and because of his efforts, all but 6 of the 2700 Morgan Stanley employees survived. Unfortunately, he was one of those who did not survive as he kept going back to the floors to make sure everyone had gotten out of the building.

The Political Reality of Persuasion

Unfortunately, you can do all the right things, follow the "be, know, do" guidelines, and still not have success in persuading individuals to respond to your message: "Even good ideas can be subverted by economic and political factors … for mitigation to be effective it has to be based on the intrinsic values that the public embraces" (Craig Fugate, quoted in Edwards and Goodrich [2007]).

Mitigation programs depend on public policy formulation. Whether it comes from a top-down approach of legislative leadership or a bottom-up approach of street-level bureaucrats envisioning change, mitigation policy needs two elements. First, it must "transmit clear and consistent objectives," and second, it must "understand what will cause the desired outcomes." Once these primary issues are addressed, funding for implementation, identifying the implementers, and coordination and control among the

implementers—power allocation—are needed for success (Smith and Larimer, in Edwards and Goodrich [2007]).

Management no longer survives long in a strict "command-and-control" environment but rather now emphasizes collaboration, participation, and capacity-building approaches. While formal environments such as incident and unified command structures are still critical during times of disaster, they are not the models of choice during disaster mitigation planning and decision making. Waugh (2000) focuses on a political model of emergency management, a model that epitomizes the "be, know, do" persuasion structure emphasized in this chapter, understanding the wide variability among various emergency response agencies and organizations and their organizational structures, cultures, and even value systems to provide a "forum that encourages open communication, sharing of resources, preserving the autonomy of the agencies, and involving all in strategic and operational decision making as much as possible."

Persuasion is not accidental, nor is it coercive; rather, it is inherently communicational (Dainton and Zelley 2010) and requires three criteria to be met:

- First, persuasion involves a goal and the intent to achieve that goal on the part of the message sender.
- Second, communication is the means to that goal.
- Third, the message recipient must have free will (otherwise, it is force, not persuasion).

There are four theories that are helpful to us as we seek to develop and enhance persuasive measures (Dainton and Zelley 2010)—social judgment theory, the elaboration likelihood model, the theory of planned behavior, and inoculation theory.

Social judgment theory: Knowing a person's attitudes on subjects can provide you with clues about how to approach a persuasive effort.

Elaboration likelihood model: Persuasion is a cognitive event where a person uses mental processes of motivation and reasoning (or a lack thereof) to accept or reject persuasive messages.

Theory of planned behavior: This theory moves us beyond persuading someone to think or feel, to action.

Inoculation theory: Knowing how to resist persuasion.

All four theories emphasize the fact that we will deliver a better message when we know our audience. Dale Carnegie (1936), well known for his book *How to Win Friends and Influence People* reminds us that we can "make more friends in two months by becoming more interested in other people than you can in two years by trying to get people interested in you." Individuals are actively comparing the message they are receiving to their own attitudes,

and there must be some incentive provided if we are to be effective in getting individuals to not only change their attitude or opinion but also to move them to action.

Summary

At the beginning of this chapter, I discussed Hays's (2009) premise that there are four universal barriers between us and our goal of getting our message across—ignorance, apathy, disciplinary boundaries, and lack of political will. Persuasion policy and the model of "be, know, do" can provide the structure for overcoming these universal barriers. If the recipient of our message is ignorant, we can overcome this with our knowledge and by presenting the information in a way that the individual can understand. If the recipient is apathetic, we need to capture their attention and show them why they need to care about the scenario and action being presented and proposed to them. Disciplinary boundaries can be overcome by developing a network of relevant organizations and working together toward mutual goals through collaboration. Finally, if there is a lack of political will, it is time for a champion, someone who believes in your cause and has the connections to make things happen. Risk management and mitigation is all about analyzing the threat, determining the vulnerability, and assessing potential consequences. As we approach these issues proactively, we will greatly reduce the level of reactive measures that need to be taken, and we increase the level of resiliency in our communities.

Communications during times of crisis are different from communications at other times, as "emotions are on edge, brains are not fully functioning, and events are occurring so rapidly that drafting a plan during a crisis is unthinkable. Simply following one is difficult" (Fearn-Banks 2002). Dale Carnegie (1936) reminds us that "when dealing with people, remember you are not dealing with creatures of logic, but with creatures of emotion, creatures bristling with prejudice and motivated by pride and vanity." Ultimately, we all want the same thing. We want strong and safe communities. We want sustainable communities that are prepared for disasters and then recover quickly. The last thing we want is to fall victim to turf battles or resource wars. Successful hazard mitigation will enhance the resiliency of our organizations and our communities.

End-of-Chapter Questions

1. The text presents Rick Rescorla as an example of someone whose leadership and actions epitomized the practice of "be, know, do." What sets Rescorla apart? Are there other individuals you would identify who also meet these standards?

2. As discussed at the beginning of the chapter, Hays (2009) states there are four main boundaries between us and our audience—ignorance, apathy, disciplinary boundaries, and lack of political will. Which is the most difficult in your organization/community?
3. Why is it so difficult to be an authentic leader? How can we strengthen relationships and build trust to develop stronger organizations and community relations?
4. In addition to GIS, what are other ways that technology can be utilized to demonstrate the "know" standard?

References

Blanchard, B. W. (2008, July 1). *Higher education project.* A conference presentation to the Emergency Management Institute.

Britton, N., & Lindsay, J. (2005, May). Designing educational opportunities for the (EM) professional of the 21st century. Retrieved from http://training.fema.gov/emiweb/edu/docs/emfuture/Future%20of%20EM%20-%20Designing%20Educational%20Opportunities%20EM%20Profes.doc.

Byrnes, J. (2005, September 6). *The essence of leadership.* Harvard Business School Working Knowledge. Retrieved from http://hbswk.hbs.edu/archive/4983.html.

Carnegie, D. (1936). *How to Win Friends and Influence People.* New York, NY: Simon and Schuster.

Chandler, R. C. (1999, Winter). Deontological dimensions of administrative ethics, revisited. *Public Personnel Management, 28*(4), 505.

Daft, R. L. (2005). *The Leadership Experience.* Mason, OH: Thomson/South-Western.

Dainton, M., & Zelley, E. D. (2010). *Applying Communication Theory for Professional Life* (2nd ed.). Thousand Oaks, CA: Sage.

Dickie, L. (1979, April). A conceptual framework for developing a persuasion policy model. *NASSP Bulletin*, 18–25.

Dobel, J. P. (1990, May–June). Integrity in the public service. *Public Administration Review, 50*(3), 354–366.

Edwards, F. L., & Goodrich, D. C. (2007). Organizing for emergency management. In W. L. Waugh, Jr., & K. Tierney (Eds.), *Emergency management: Principles and practice for local government* (2nd ed.). Washington, DC: ICMA Press, 39–55.

Fearn-Banks, K. (2002). *Crisis Communications: A Casebook Approach* (4th ed.). Mahwah, NJ: Lawrence Erlbaum Associates, Inc.

George, B. (2003). *Authentic Leadership: Rediscovering the Secrets to Creating Lasting Value.* San Francisco, CA: Wiley and Sons.

Hays, W. (2009, June 1). Incorporating a new body of disaster knowledge in EM Hi-Ed courses: A major challenge. Presentation to the FEMA/EMI Higher Education conference.

The History Channel. *Man who Predicted* 9/11. September 11, 2005.

King, C. S., & Stivers, C. (1998). *Government is Us: Public Administration in an Anti-government Era.* Thousand Oaks, CA: Sage Publications, Inc.

Majone, G. 1989. *Evidence, Argument, and Persuasion in the Policy Process.* New Haven, CT: Yale University.

Mills, H. 2000. *Artful persuasion: How to command attention, change minds, and influence people*. New York, NY: AMACOM.

Murrow, E. (n.d.). The Murrow project. Retrieved from http://www.murrowproject.com/.

Northouse, P. (2001). *Leadership Theory and Practice* (2nd ed.). Thousand Oaks, CA: Sage Publications.

Stanley, A. (1999). *Visioneering*. Sisters, OR: Multnomah Publishers, Inc.

Waugh, W. (2000). *Living with Hazards, Dealing with Disasters*. New York, NY: M.E. Sharpe, Inc.

Weber, M. (1946). Bureaucracy. In J. M. Shafritz and A. C. Hyde (Eds.), *Classics of Public Administration* (6th ed.). Boston, MA: Thomson-Wadsworth.

Chapter **11**

Non-FEMA Mitigation

Local Government Actions

Frances L. Edwards and Daniel C. Goodrich

Contents

Learning Objectives

- Understand the role of the preexisting environment, including projects, policies, and plans, on local government mitigation decisions.
- Understand the role of politics in local mitigation programs.
- Understand the impact of intergovernmental relations on local government–sponsored mitigation.

- Understand the importance of historical data for risk assessment.
- Understand the role of land-use regulations in local mitigation decisions.

Introduction

Chapter 10 described the theoretical framework in which disaster mitigation occurs at the nonfederal levels of government. It also described the role that the state and its agencies play in developing and implementing mitigation measures within its borders. However, regardless of where a mitigation policy is developed and funded, mitigation always happens in some (and sometimes several) local governments' jurisdiction.

As of June 30, 2007, the Census Bureau reported that there were 89,527 governmental units within the United States. One is the federal government, and 50 units are state governments. The other 89,476 are local governments. Of these, there are 3,033 county; 19,492 municipal; and 16,519 town or township governments, accounting for 39,044 government units. The remaining 50,432 units are special purpose, comprising special districts (37,381) and public school systems (14,561). The special districts include fire districts and utility districts, such as water, sewer, airports, hospitals, libraries, open space, port facilities, transit, solid waste, and lighting (Census Bureau, 2007).

Mitigation may take place in any of these local governments, and mitigation may require the cooperation of various groupings of local governments because hazards and their mitigation often overlap jurisdictional boundaries. For example, riverine flooding occurs along a watercourse as it travels through counties and municipalities. Add the other stakeholders such as residents, businesses, and nonprofit organizations, and the challenge of developing and implementing mitigation measures becomes clear.

On the other hand, most citizens do not differentiate among government entities when they seek services or interaction. They try to pay taxes at the city hall and get building permits from the county. When they are told that rats are a county problem and loud parties are a city problem, they sigh and mutter about slothful bureaucracy and "passing the buck." Similarly, when confronted with natural hazards they do not consider which elements of government are responsible for what services. They just want the problem solved. Thus, the multiple units of local government must be prepared to cooperate and collaborate for successful mitigation.

As James Lee Witt frequently said, "All disasters are local." But who is responsible for what?

The Preexisting Environment of Local Government Mitigation

Invisible Infrastructure

In his article for *The Annals of the American Academy of Political and Social Science's* edition on Hurricane Katrina, Raymond Burby noted, "Few local governments are willing to reduce natural hazards by managing development since they see it as a minor problem compared to unemployment, crime ... and other problems" (Waugh, 2006, p. 114). He also notes that term limits and the fact that mitigation is taken for granted are other challenges to effective local government hazard mitigation. "Also, the costs of mitigation are immediate while the benefits are uncertain, may not occur during their tenure, and are not visible" (Waugh, 2006, p. 114).

Modern cities and suburbs already have significant infrastructures in place that serve as mitigation measures. For example, curbs, gutters, and storm drains mitigate the impact of flooding in two ways: (1) During heavy storms, properly functioning storm drains carry away urban and small stream runoff to prevent localized flooding in intersections and neighborhoods. (2) During catastrophic flooding with river overflows—or even levee failures—storm drains facilitate the rapid drainage of floodwater out of the community.

Residents take curbs and gutters for granted, most seeing them as decorative parts of the urban landscape or as a way to prevent erosion of the parking strip between the curb and the sidewalk. Because years ago most cities had combined storm and sanitary sewers that had water in them all through the year, many people think of the storm drain as a trash disposal system and push the trash, especially fallen leaves, into the gutter or even into the culvert. When they are needed for their real function of water drainage, the trash and leaves become impediments to good drainage, often causing localized neighborhood and intersection flooding.

Natural waterways in urban areas are frequently surrounded by parks and open space. In some communities, these become magnets for unwanted household items, old tires, and stolen market carts. When it rains, the watercourse is blocked with debris, which slows down the flow of water out of the community. In some cases, debris may pile up at bends or low spots, allowing water levels to rise significantly behind these "debris dams." However, when enough water runs off the urban hardscape, the debris dams may suddenly fail releasing a tall wall of water into the watercourse, which causes flooding in low-lying neighborhoods.

Levees were created in the last century for agricultural irrigation, but with urbanization, these levees assumed the role of *de facto* flood protection. These levees were placed to facilitate the delivery of water to fields and

were generally not designed by engineers. Most were built of local materials, generally local soil, and are subject to loss of integrity through burrowing by small rodents and to erosion by runoff.

Public health departments provide mitigation against diseases. Many of the systems in place today were developed in the days before antibiotics and inoculations were widely available. Isolation and quarantine laws are carryovers from the early 1900s. Infant inoculations, school vaccination laws, and public education are the principal methods used to protect public health. The public health department runs prenatal care, well-baby programs, and inoculation clinics and inspects restaurants and food stores to prevent food-borne diseases. They inspect hospitals to prevent hospital-based infections and spread of diseases. They also run special programs for lead paint abatement, AIDS prevention, and tuberculosis mitigation.

As long as these mitigation measures function as designed, they are "invisible infrastructure." However, when leaves block a storm drain or a decrease in the number of food inspectors results in the outbreak of listeriosis, the public becomes aware of the mitigation measures that have failed.

Local Politics and Mitigation

Mitigation takes different forms such as land-use regulation, capital projects, and inspection and enforcement. All mitigation requires funding, usually at least some of which must come from the local government. Even federal buyout programs come at long-term local government expense. For example, when the Federal Emergency Management Agency (FEMA) buys out an owner of a low-lying piece of land, the land is turned over to the local government as perpetual parkland. The local government then becomes responsible for its maintenance and liable for future runoff that may damage other properties adjacent or downstream to this land. Thus, even "free" mitigation measures may have long-term cost implications and have to be included in the local government's budget; these activities are placed in direct competition with other desirable services like police and fire services, library hours, or sports teams. The competition for scarce local funds leads to political stresses among elected officials, local government staff, and the community.

Another impediment to mitigation that embodies politics is the tension between land-use regulation for mitigation of future hazards, and landowners and developers. City staff from the emergency services and planning departments may concur on the need to prevent development in floodplains or coastal areas. However, the owners of that land may feel entitled to the financial windfall inherent in the development of the property for residential or recreational uses (San Jose, 2008b), creating a political motivation for city

council action.* For example, in San Jose, California, a mayor proposed the development of a pristine floodplain area to accommodate housing for high-technology companies to attract them to build in the area (San Jose, 2002).† Staff noted that the area was flood-prone, had a water table at 6 ft, was a wildlife transit area from one mountain range to another, and was part of the flyway for migratory birds (San Jose, 2008a).

Only when the cost of flood mitigation was described in terms of single family home elevations and loss of first-floor occupancy for commercial buildings did the prime developer withdraw from the project. The landowners at the time then pressured the city council to change the floodplain development ordinance to allow them to make the same profits from the sale of their agricultural land as farmers in north San Jose had made when their area was developed. They couched their demands in terms of entitlement for having paid taxes on the land for years.

The high-tech company demanded walking-distance or short-commute housing for potential workers, including significant numbers of low-income and affordable housing. Only when the public safety departments provided budgets detailing the annual costs of providing police, fire, and emergency medical response services to that distant area did the city council finally reject the proposal. The ultimate mitigation was to have California's Midpeninsula Regional Open Space District acquire the land, ending all development proposals for the prime center area of the valley (Gonzales, 2009).

The political impetus toward development forces staff members concerned about mitigation to approach the challenge from an incremental perspective. They must get public acceptance of one step, get the funding in place for that step, and then take the next step toward mitigation. For example, the Santa Clara Valley Water District (SCVWD) is the flood control agency for San Jose. The SCVWD board of directors knew that the whole Guadalupe River needed channel work and a bypass to end the flooding of downtown San Jose. The federal government provided funds matched by the city's redevelopment agency to create a bypass and improved channel from the downtown to the bay, but this left residential areas to the south at risk of continued flooding. Only after the downtown reaches were improved could flood protection for the residential areas be undertaken (Santa Clara Valley Water District, 2008), as the city council acting as the redevelopment board had to find matching funds from the redevelopment agency's budget and this could be done only when more high-profile and political Strong Neighborhood Initiative improvement projects for poor areas of the city were funded.

* Note the lack of reference to hazard mitigation or public safety in the elements outlined in #7. Regardless of its designation as a floodplain by FEMA, the mayor's staff report contains no mention of this impediment to development, nor of the need to mitigate potential flooding.

† These notes provide some insight into the issues raised by owners after the prime developer withdrew.

Even after a focusing event, mitigation projects are still in political competition for funding and implementation with other projects and programs. In the 1994 Northridge, California, earthquake, 17 people were killed in the soft-story Northridge Meadows apartment building collapse; yet only a handful of local governments in California have passed ordinances requiring a public inventory of such dangerous buildings, and no agency has a mandatory retrofit program in place for soft-stories like San Jose and Long Beach, California have for unreinforced masonry (URM) buildings (Selna, 2009). Few members of the public understand the risk of soft-story buildings; so building a coalition to provide political support for mitigation measures is a challenge.

Similarly, even though the flooding of New Orleans, Louisiana, following Hurricane Katrina in 2005 demonstrated the danger of living in low-lying areas of the city, the political pressure to rebuild the Lower Ninth Ward overcame the expert advice to rezone the flooded area for nonresidential uses. *The Annals of the American Academy of Political and Social Science* states in its recommendations, "To mitigate the potential for natural disasters, we need to change the way we control new construction in hazardous areas. The ideal would be to stop construction in hazardous areas, and not to rebuild in high-risk flood-prone areas and coastal areas. Where construction is allowed, special construction codes must be required and enforced by local governments. Banks need to restrict construction loans and mortgages to those structures that meet the new codes" (Waugh, 2006, p. 330). Yet local activists and movie stars like Brad Pitt have pressed for reconstruction even where the FEMA flood maps require an elevation of 25 ft to get flood insurance (Pogrebin, 2007).

Yet another political challenge is the creation of a budget to fund mitigation projects. Local government may not run a deficit. Raising extra revenue for capital projects through bonds requires a vote of the public in most states and a supermajority in some, like California. The budget process in most states runs from 18 months to develop a 1-year budget to 24 months for a 2-year budget. Although enthusiasm for funding mitigation may be high immediately after a focusing event, the passage of time, while the budget is developed and the bond election is held, can permit a cooling of interest and a redirection of political support to a new project. Tom Tobin, who was the executive director of the California Seismic Safety Commission during the Northridge earthquake, told the commission members that legislation embodying change is likely to be passed only if it is introduced and passed within a few weeks of the focusing event. He noted that the California URM legislation was passed within weeks of the URM-caused deaths in the Loma Prieta earthquake (Tobin, 1995). Yet, as has been noted, no soft-story legislation was passed as a result of the Northridge deaths, mainly because there was no immediate consensus on the appropriate mitigation measures, and by the time the engineering studies were completed the focus had shifted to the economy and other political concerns.

Finally, developing a staff report on a mitigation issue makes the political actors aware of it and at the same time it may cause them to accrue some liability if they fail to act. Depending on state law and the specific circumstances of a mitigation project, the knowledge of a threat to public safety and a failure to act to mitigate or end it may constitute misfeasance in office or accrue personal liability for those who are informed if they fail to act and injury actually occurs. For example, a city manager was told that the city should consider a soft-story building retrofit project. The city manager responded, "It is projects like this that get city managers fired," because she feared the anger of the building owners who would be publicly identified as having dangerous buildings. Failure to act to mitigate the danger to tenants could constitute negligence on their part. Failure to take action to protect the tenants could constitute a legally culpable failure on the city's part. The city attorney, who was present at the interview, deemed the whole communication to be covered by attorney–client privilege and forbade the staff member from mentioning the project again. So, although a known danger existed that could have been mitigated, no action was taken.

Intergovernmental Relations: Downstream Impacts

Mitigation projects need to be carefully designed to consider possible downstream impacts involving neighboring communities. The design of mitigation measures for one local government should take into account their consequences in the larger ecosystem. The role of the Mississippi River Gulf Outlet (MR-GO) canal in the passage of Hurricane Katrina's storm surge into New Orleans is one example of the kind of unintended consequence that a capital project can have (Cooper and Block, 2006, pp. 26–28). Mitigation measures taken to channelize watercourses or divert water may create new problems for downstream communities.

Management of the possibility of downstream consequences must be addressed with neighboring communities during the design phase of a mitigation measure to prevent political fallout when the mitigation measure is in place. However, communities frequently fail to consider worst-case scenarios for impacts on neighboring communities until they are presented with the results during a disaster. For example, in March 1995, San Jose, California experienced severe flash flooding as a result of saturated soil and full reservoirs. The flap gates at the end of storm drains were closed by the rise in the river water level, resulting in stormwater backing up into the community. The stormwater and the river overflow at several upstream low spots combined to flood a number of below-grade parking garages in the relatively new high-tech industrial park, resulting in a loss of access to buildings, as well as the destruction of cars, trucks, and other equipment parked in the below-grade garages. The light rail line, operated by another

government, the Santa Clara Valley Transportation Agency (VTA), was also closed due to flooding on the tracks. The VTA not only had to bear the expense of repairing the flooded tracks but also had to provide a bus bridge around the flood-damaged area until the repairs were completed. The VTA and affected businesses demanded a mitigation project from the city council to protect their properties in the future. The city bore some liability for the damage because the water came from their backed-up storm drains.

Because federal funds were not available for hazard mitigation capital projects in 1995, the city designed and built a new pumping station for $20 million using local funds. It was designed for the pumps to come on automatically when the storm drain flap gate closed, move the water out of the storm drains and into the river channel over the banks, and take advantage of the unused channel capacity above the storm drain outfall level. The plan called for the city to manually override the pump operation if the water level rose to 1 ft of freeboard on the levee.

When flooding next threatened the area in 1997, the pump operation went smoothly; but in 1998 when the storm season came and flooding was again threatened, the pump was turned on as soon as the flap gates blocked the storm drains, and the river channel was filled down to the delta of the river in the neighborhood of Alviso, San Jose, California,. This neighborhood is home to one of the members of the SCVWD Board who was alarmed by the high river level passing by his community, and at the next SCVWD meeting he demanded action to control the operation of the San Jose pumps.

The SCVWD is the flood control agency for the county. As preparations for the next storm season began, there was a three-way dispute among the parties involved with the previous year's pumping. The SCVWD demanded control of the pumps during storms in their role as the flood control district. The city of San Jose intended to retain control of the pumps, as they had been built with city money to meet the needs of resident businesses and the VTA and were located within the city's jurisdiction. The SCVWD wanted to be consulted before the pumps were turned on so that they could participate in the discussion about the timing of the operation of the pumps, giving them a chance to notify Alviso neighbors of potential areas of induced flooding.

The staff members of the SCVWD and city entities met for months during the succeeding summer in an attempt to create an emergency response plan and a memorandum of understanding (MOU) to memorialize it. The plan was developed in draft, but no MOU wording was agreed on.

In 2003, the issue was raised again (Santa Clara Valley Water District, 2003). The result of the dispute was 2 years of meetings and negotiations among the parties at the end of which no agreement was reached (Edwards, 2005). The city raised its rights as a sovereign government, and a charter city, noting that the operational plan for the pumps called for them to be monitored and to be turned off when the water in the river channel reached 1 ft of

freeboard. The contribution of water to the river from upstream communities with new development was noted. The city added that the city council of the upstream community had not required the developer to create retention basins because river capacity had been measured only within that community. The SCVWD had not required the developers to take into account the contribution to the river's capacity downstream. The SCVWD argued that the excess water being pumped over the banks into the river worsened the potential downstream-flooding problem, as water from upstream communities continued to be added to the river through runoff and ultimately arrived at the pumping area, raising the surface level of water above the level observed at the site of the pumping station. The downstream community agreed that the damage from the first use of the pumps was minimal. The SCVWD questioned the city's right to place flood protection of its residents above flood protection of residents of other communities.

The next rainy season came; it was a drought year, so the pumps never turned on. Few of the staff members who participated in the pump discussion are still with any of the entities involved, so when the pumps go on automatically during the next winter with high rainfall and the downstream community is at risk of flooding, will anyone remember? When the next developer asks for development permission from the upstream community, will its staff understand why the development needs a retention basin? Will the mitigation measure work for San Jose, the light rail, and the high-tech community, or will the flooding just come directly from the overfilled river instead of from the blocked storm drains? Have the downstream river improvements added adequate capacity to carry away the pumped water without incident?

Intergovernmental Relations: Whose Responsibility? Whose Regulation?

Mitigation projects may seem obvious and yet still be difficult to implement. Getting debris out of the waterway seems like a simple mitigation for localized flooding, yet conflicting jurisdictions and laws may make such a cleanup difficult to achieve. Appropriate management of underbrush seems like a simple mitigation for wildland urban interface (WUI) fire, yet conflicting environmental and property rights may be barriers to it.

In California, the property owner whose land borders a creek owns the creek to its centerline. Access to the water was an important property right in the days before municipal water systems when farming and ranching dominated the economy. The owner of the land is responsible for the maintenance of the creek channel in a clean condition. In modern cities, access to a creek may be impossible due to grade separations and lack of adjacent access ways. Owners frequently are unaware of their responsibilities. The SCVWD started a program of creek cleanups in its role as the Santa Clara County flood control agency.

The SCVWD offered owners the opportunity to give the district an easement over their land for access to the creek in exchange for having the district clean the creek at no cost to the owner. Many owners did not agree to the easement, either because they were reluctant to have the SCVWD's heavy equipment roll across their lawns twice a year or because they had no access from their property to the water. In some places, homes are 20 ft or more above the creek.

The buildup of debris in creeks is exacerbated by the dumping of household goods and unwanted materials in such areas. Especially in the poorer parts of a city where people cannot afford to pay dump fees or the extra charges for trash-haulers, appliances, furniture, and broken bicycles are left along the creek banks, where the accumulation of trash slides into the creek during the summer and is washed into the creek when the winter storms come. Since the creek's owners do not have access to the creek and the SCVWD does not have an easement of access to the creek, the debris becomes part of the natural ecology of the streambed, sometimes providing homes for wildlife. Such dumping is, of course, illegal, but cities have few code enforcement officers, and as they focus first on life safety hazards like illegal house conversions and overcrowding there is little time left for surveillance of creek dumping.

The SCVWD decided to sponsor an annual creek cleanup day and invited community members to volunteer their services in removing debris. The SCVWD had to get Environmental Protection Agency (EPA) and U.S. Fish and Wildlife Service permits to do any work in the channels because they are natural habitats. The permits took over a year to get and, when finally issued, they had strict regulations about what could be removed. Only human-generated debris that had not become naturalized was permitted to be removed, greatly decreasing the flood control value of the creek cleanup program as large branches and dead trees blocked narrow sections of urban creeks.

In 1996 the creek cleanup day drew hundreds of volunteers in boots and waders. Bicycles, motor bikes, and supermarket carts were commonly removed debris, along with a queen-sized mattress from the bank and a car-sized chamois cloth that was fully submerged and lying over a dam. The submerged tires had to be left *in situ*, however, because the fish and wildlife agency permit defined them as "habitat for tadpoles and small fish." So the community's debris became naturalized and protected.

The winter of 1997 was a very wet one, and the Anderson Dam in Morgan Hill, California was filled to overflowing. The uncontrollable flow of water over the spillway created a Niagara Falls–like condition with colorful rainbows visible for a mile downstream. The next storm that came through caused the creek to turn into a torrent, moving natural branches and downed trees, storm debris, and freshly deposited trash downstream together. At a bend in the creek, the debris created a debris dam that was 6 ft high as new debris caught on old debris. The stream gauges through San Jose showed water at a level well below flooding, until the debris dam finally broke

from the pressure of a queen-sized sleeper sofa floating into it. The resulting release of pent-up water created a wall over 6 ft high that raced downstream and overflowed the creek's banks into a neighborhood on January 27, 1997, severely damaging 25 apartment buildings, with water 4–5 ft deep (Army Corps of Engineers, 2000). It overflowed into Happy Hollow Zoo, San Jose, and inundated the ornamental carp pond.

The evacuation of over 2000 people could have been avoided with better creek maintenance, which is a fact known to all parties. The city's zoo was inundated and its beautiful Japanese Friendship Garden and historic carp pond were severely damaged with carp being found miles downstream. Half of the evacuees were non-English-speaking Cambodians, illiterate in any language, and the other half were Spanish speakers, mostly undocumented workers. Almost all were renters and dependent on their landlords for the repair of their homes. First-floor dwellers were out of their homes for months.

The WUI areas pose another threat to human life that is easily mitigated but requires multilayer cooperation. People move into the WUI because they like proximity to trees, distance from neighbors, and narrow roads that discourage traffic. Each of these perceived assets may become a detriment in hot, dry periods. Residents are warned to clear "defensible space" around their homes, install "wet landscaping" like irrigated lawns or naturally wet plants like succulents, such as ice plants, and cut back trees. Dead natural materials should be removed from the property. However, seasonal fires throughout the American West demonstrate the refusal of WUI residents to consistently undertake good brush management. The modern fire code requires fire-resistant roofs and building materials in WUI areas, but existing buildings are not subject to enforcement of the new building codes unless a building is 50% (of value) renovated or destroyed. The result is that once started, a fire has ample fuel in shake roofs and cedar shingle siding. The Oakland Hills, California, firestorm in 1991; the San Diego, California, fires of 2003 and 2007; and Colorado's frequent WUI fires all prove the value of the simple mitigations that could be performed by property owners, yet the devastation in the wake of these events proves how infrequently these relatively inexpensive mitigation steps are taken.

Another challenge is the tension between the "green lobby" and the fire protection sector. Climate change has demonstrated the value of large old trees that process greenhouse gases and provide shade to adjacent properties, cutting down on household energy consumption. However, such trees can also be fire hazards in WUI areas and wind hazards in built-up areas. Many cities have tree ordinances that require an owner to get a permit to remove trees from his or her property that are over a certain size or age, which may be called "heritage trees." Owners applying for tree removal permits for fire safety in suburban areas are routinely denied permits on the basis of the heritage tree ordinances. Proponents of "urban forests" for "green" purposes encourage residents to plant

trees without consideration for the size, type, and fire-resistant characteristics of the species residents might select. Second owners find themselves in possession of "living Christmas trees" planted years ago by previous owners that are now 40 ft tall, full of dead branches, pose a wind damage and fire threat to neighboring properties, and are considered irremovable heritage trees.

Failure to mitigate tree-based hazards may not lie with the owners being denied a tree removal permit. Will the local government bear the cost when a tree falls onto a neighbor's roof in a storm? Will the local government be liable when a tree catches fire in a wildland fire–generated event that has burned into the suburban neighborhood? Will the owner be liable for maintaining an unsafe condition on his or her property?

One successful method of flood mitigation is to change channel conditions so that water may flow unimpeded through a community during heavy rains. As mentioned earlier in this section, to do any work in a waterway, a city or other local government agency must get permits from the EPA and federal fish and wildlife agencies, a process that may take multiple years. Depending on the size of the project, there may also be a requirement for state or federal environmental impact reports, which adds both time and cost to the project.

San Jose is subject to flash flooding from rapid runoff into its creeks. It is located at the bottom of a valley and was formerly an agricultural community full of orchards and fields. Since the advent of the silicon chip, it has become Silicon Valley with acres of formerly productive land paved and roofed with impervious materials, thereby increasing the storm runoff. After the significant downtown flooding in 1995, the SCVWD as the flood control agency proposed an aggressive waterway restoration program to ensure that water would move out of the community. In order to start the project, it proposed to remove a thick growth of freshwater plants that had developed in the riparian reaches of the river at its delta with San Francisco Bay. This area had historically been a marine environment, but the incursion of reeds had blocked the tidal flow from the bay, creating a freshwater ecosystem that choked the mouth of the river. For 2 years following the 1995 floods, the SCVWD worked to get permits to perform reed removal, experiencing significant resistance from the permitting agencies. The project was proposed to be performed in the summer months when water levels are low; days are long, providing good light for working; and bids could be received to guarantee the best price.

On Super Bowl Sunday of 1997, a strong storm arrived after a wet December. Water levels rose in the river, and water began to collect at the delta where the former natural outlet was blocked with mud and reeds. As an emergency measure to protect the low-lying neighborhood of Alviso (sunken to 6 ft below sea level), the SCVWD obtained an emergency contract for reed and mud removal. The work began at sunset in January in the midst of torrential rain and high water levels. Work was performed in slippery mud, which limited the areas of reeds that the workers could excavate

for removal. Working through the night they managed to create enough of an outlet to relieve the unsafe condition adjacent to Alviso, but this was at a cost estimated to be many times higher than a competitively bid contract in the safer summer months. The emergency removed the requirement for the permits, which were not granted until 2009, but at a high cost for a small project that had no long-term benefits.

Factors That Engender Mitigation Actions

Regardless of the roadblocks that are often experienced, mitigation projects are still completed by local governments across the nation. One motivation is residents' and businesses' desire to live in safety. Just as residents press local governments for economic development projects to create jobs and antigang programs to enhance safety from crime, they demand activities to protect their community against geological and weather-related perils. When a major high-tech company was contemplating whether to move from Texas to San Jose, a community prone to both flooding and earthquakes, its executive vice president and risk manager visited the San Jose Emergency Operations Center and interviewed the director of emergency preparedness to determine if the community's disaster preparedness plans met its standards.

City councils take mitigation actions in response to the political pressure from constituents, which as noted earlier is typically high only immediately after a disaster event. For example, after the 1989 Loma Prieta earthquake, the San Jose City Council passed in 1990 ordinances requiring that all URM buildings be either retrofitted or demolished within 10 years. It encouraged compliance by establishing a funding mechanism for the retrofits through formation of a special assessment district and providing grants for the cost of the initial engineering (Edwards-Winslow, 2003). After the 1991 Oakland Hills firestorm, the people of Oakland voted for a bond measure proposed by the city council to install new gravity-flow cisterns at the top of hills to provide firefighting water for future major fire events that would damage the existing water piping and pumping system.

Land-use ordinances can also become mitigations in communities. Subdivision, zoning, and site-planning ordinances are adopted by city councils or similar local government governing bodies, albeit under the limitations of state law. Land in flood zones is zoned for low-intensity uses and usually requires significant mitigation steps, such as building elevation above the floodline. These steps also enable owners to purchase national flood protection insurance, which some have characterized as a "license to dare" since it shares the risk of building in floodplains between the owner (with a deductible) and the taxpayers who back the National Flood Insurance Program (NFIP) (Haddow and Bullock, 2003, p. 40). Beachfront property may be zoned to forbid future construction, such as the North Carolina

coastal setback ordinance that is locally enforced (Haddow and Bullock, 2003, p. 40), although, as will be discussed further in Chapter 12, the *Lucas v. South Carolina Coastal Commission* decision makes it difficult to prevent rebuilding of existing homes. The San Jose City Council created a hillside development limitation in the general plan to prevent the construction of housing and commercial developments in areas with slopes above 15% as mitigation against damage from future landslides or earthquakes (San Jose, 2008c, p. 80). Most zoning ordinances that follow the Euclidean model of single use zones (Philadelphia Zoning Code Commission, 2010) forbid mixing hazardous materials uses with residential uses as mitigation against hazardous materials accidents impacting vulnerable human receptors.

Local governments also adopt and enforce building codes to enhance the safety of communities. States adopt the basic building code, but local governments then adopt their own versions of the code that may include stricter building regulations that respond to the specific hazards in a community. For example, the chief building official for Irvine, California, had been in the San Fernando, California earthquake of 1971 where he saw split-level homes separate into two segments and water heaters fall over, rupturing natural gas lines that subsequently fed fires. He drafted amendments to the building code for Irvine, which were adopted by the city council, requiring stronger connections between the walls and roof of a house and more robust strapping for water heaters. Irvine is 8 mi from the Newport–Inglewood Fault and 25 mi from the San Andreas Fault. These mitigation measures were designed to lessen the damage to homes in the event of an earthquake.

Local governments also enforce all the building-related codes through their inspection programs. City councils signal their commitment to building safety by setting high standards of training and experience for building inspectors and other code inspectors and appointing an experienced and knowledgeable chief building official, who in California is recognized as a public safety official. Mitigation expert Dennis Mileti has noted "Any code is only as good as the enforcement that goes along with it" (Mileti, 1999, p. 165). Mileti also notes that although Florida's building code was considered strict, "Hurricane Andrew proved that even a rigorous code is ineffective if it is not properly enforced" (Mileti, 1999, p. 165). The tragic loss of life in schools in China's 2008 earthquake (Areddy et al., 2009) is just the latest example of the cost of poor enforcement of building codes.

Practical Applications

Mitigation for Wildland Urban Interface Fires

Land-use regulations are a critical part of the WUI mitigation process. Limiting construction in WUI areas, requiring roads wide enough for fire vehicle access, and requiring a water system that can deliver adequate

supplies of water are crucial planning steps for WUI mitigation. In addition, building codes can dictate construction materials that are forbidden in the WUI, such as shake roof and cedar shingles. They can require internal fire sprinkler systems and vegetation clearance areas.

Landscaping regulations can also be part of the scheme of land-use regulations in a community. The National Fire Protection Association has created *Safer from the Start: A Guide to Firewise-Friendly Developments* that includes guidance for "firewise" landscaping principles (NFPA, 2009, pp. 34, 35). Homeowners can follow the zone concept of clearances around structures to minimize the chance of ignition for their houses.

California also has local fire safe councils that organize neighbors in fire hazard areas to undertake joint mitigation measures. Newsletters and websites enable the leading fire agency to share seasonal guidance on fire prevention and property protection. A good example may be found at the Santa Clara County Fire Safe Council's educational website, http://www.sccfiresafe.org/.

The value of fire safety principles has been proved in WUI fires in California's major cities. San Diego, the second largest city in the state and the seventh largest in the nation, had a series of damaging fires in 2003. Residents learned that the fire safety principles made a difference in the survival of their homes.

Before evacuating their home in 2007, one family living in a canyon area cleared the brush down the hill as far as they could safely stand. They "watered" the concrete tile roof and then moved all flammable decorations and furnishings into the garage, all the while running the sprinklers on the lawn that covers their 30 ft clearance to saturate it. They left their garden hose laid out in the backyard in case the firefighters needed extra water supply. When they returned home to an undamaged neighborhood, thanks to neighbors who were equally vigilant, they found that indeed, the firefighter assigned to protect their block had draped garden hoses over the side of the canyon to irrigate the area while the fire burned, thereby preventing embers from finding any dry material to spread to.

Weed abatement is another critical fire prevention action. The Santa Clara County Board of Supervisors has adopted weed abatement program standards that require all vegetation to be 6 in or lower within 10 ft of highways, driveways, and fence lines and clearance of all nonornamental vegetation within 30 ft of any structure (Santa Clara County, 2010b). Although the goal is voluntary compliance, any properties not meeting the standards are abated by a contractor and the cost, plus a fee, are added to the owner's tax bill (Santa Clara County, 2010b).

It is noted that WUI residents need to be assured of rapid fire response if a wildfire starts on or near their property. However, many WUI residents do not have standard street addresses but rather get their mail through a rural route

post office box or may even have a box at the post office. They often live on private roads that can extend miles from the main highway and offer no visibility from the public roadway (Pleasant Unity Volunteer Fire Department, 2010). After over 100 years without a wildland fire, in 2008, the Telegraph Fire burned on the west side of Yosemite National Park, California, along Highway 140. About 17 homes were destroyed in the 25 mi^2 blaze, as firefighters were unable to find the houses reported to be on fire (CBS News, 2008).

This loss was the incentive for the local fire company to join the nationwide emergency response campaign, "If we can't find you, we can't help you." Fire departments all over the country are sponsoring this mitigation program that sells both bright green reflectorized house number signs and new "lane name" markers that allow residents to identify their location out on the main road. The WUI dwellers find or select a name for the lane or private road on which they live. The post office then assigns a house number based on the number range on the main road. This allows a fire or police vehicle or ambulance to drive rapidly to the correct lane and find the house buried back in the woods. Inspired by the challenges faced by dispatchers when voice-over-IP telephones did not trigger reverse 9-1-1 directory listings (APCO, n.d.), the "If we can't find you" program was adopted by police (Mount Olive Police Department, n.d.) and fire departments across the nation to encourage residents to ensure that they can be found in an emergency. When riding down Route 140 in Mariposa, California, one can see the bright green reflective signs that are proof of the successful implementation of this mitigation program.

Mitigation for Disease

Vector control is a service provided by local governments to lessen the likelihood of disease outbreaks in urban settings. Long known for fighting the urban rat population, spraying for mosquitoes, and picking up dead animals from the road, vector control gained new importance with the onset of West Nile virus in New York, which spread across the country. County vector control agencies launched aggressive campaigns to get people to maintain their swimming pools, drain all standing water from ornamental items and wading pools, and use DEET at dawn and dusk to "fight the bite" (Mercury News, 2007). The Centers for Disease Control and Prevention launched an aggressive campaign to support local efforts to prevent the spread of West Nile virus (CDC, 2007). Picking up and counting dead birds became a new focus for the local vector control organizations, along with fogging, holding intensive public education campaigns, and distributing mosquito fish to owners of birdbaths and ornamental ponds (Santa Clara County, 2009).

Other vector-borne illnesses remain objects of concern and require mitigation measures. Mosquitoes carry encephalitis, fleas carry plague, rodents

carry hantavirus, and deer carry ticks that cause Lyme disease. Even the backyard raccoon can be a vector for roundworm. Mitigation of zoonoses such as West Nile virus and plague require wild animal population surveillance as well as prevention education for the human population.

Hazardous Materials Mitigation

The U.S. Department of Transportation maintains the Emergency Response Guidebook that identifies hazardous materials in transit (U.S. DOT, 2008). The book contains a list of such hazardous materials and emergency response to accidents, including first aid, personal protective equipment, and standoff distance guidance. There is also a depiction of all the placards that are used to identify hazardous materials and hazardous waste in transit, whether by road or rail. This book serves as a guide for local first responders called to the scene of a hazardous materials accident, mitigating the likelihood of injury to first responders by making clear the dangers of and precautions for interacting with the materials and providing guidance for medical personnel for the care of exposed patients.

The National Fire Protection Association has created a placard, called the "NFPA diamond" for its shape, for fixed locations with hazardous materials in reportable quantities, such as warehouses and manufacturing facilities (NFPA, 2010). The placard is designed to warn first responders and the public of the presence of hazardous materials in a building. The four segments of the diamond are color-coded and numbered to represent levels of fire danger, health danger, and explosive tendencies of the materials housed there. The fourth quadrant is used for special notices, such as the presence of oxidizers. Any location that keeps 55 gal, 500 lbs, or 200 ft^3 (a reportable quantity) of a hazardous material for 30 days must display a placard.

However, if the materials are packaged in consumer packaging, such as quarts of motor oil or quarts of pesticide, placarding is not required. Likewise, terminals that house such materials only as they are transferred from one mode of transportation to another and wholesalers who decant and repackage the products are also not required to placard their facilities unless the materials remain there for over 30 days. Enforcement of placards and safe handling of hazardous materials is generally done by the local fire department.

Depending on the number and type of hazardous materials in a community, the city council may decide to invest in a hazardous materials team within the community's fire department to respond to and mitigate any accident involving hazardous materials use and protect the community from offsite consequences of a release of the materials. The hazardous materials team may be an on-call or on-contract group external to the city's full-time staff or may include up to four on-duty personnel trained to the specialist or technician level.

During a hazardous materials–related event, such as a plating shop fire or an industrial spill, the hazardous materials team may be supported by fire personnel who assist in abating the event, emergency medical service personnel who care for victims, and even the city transportation department personnel who supply sandbags to block storm drains if runoff has occurred. If the event occurs outdoors, mitigation may require the use of bulldozer operators to create berms or dams to stop the flow of material into the environment.

Hazardous materials personnel conduct regular inspections of all hazardous materials users with reportable quantities of materials on site for more than 30 days to ensure that they are following safe handling procedures. Each organization with reportable quantities is required to provide the local fire department with a hazardous materials management plan that details its operations, providing information on how the materials are "handled, stored, and monitored" (San Jose, 2005, p. B-1). The reports include a list of all the chemicals on site, together with the materials safety data sheet for each chemical, and a site map showing where each material is stored.

Some hazardous materials are particularly dangerous to human beings or the environment and are categorized by state and federal agencies as "extremely hazardous materials" or "acutely hazardous materials." These include arsenic, cyanide, and similar inhalation and ingestion hazards. Users of such materials must also provide a risk management and prevention program report that includes a more detailed plan for the manufacturing processes and their plan to prevent releases or accidents involving the hazardous materials.

Flood Mitigation

Flood mitigation is typically a community project. Storm drain maintenance and creek and river management require local communities to undertake public works and seasonal projects, such as those discussed earlier in this chapter. Individuals may create flood damage mitigation in their homes by avoiding construction in a floodplain or raising the structure above the flood level. One typical sight in the suburban areas around New Orleans after Hurricane Katrina was homes elevated 10 ft or more on sturdy pilings designed to allow future storm surges to pass through. Some homes even had their air conditioners elevated and provided long ramps for easier access to the living spaces.

Homes unavoidably located in flood-prone areas or subject to water damage from hurricanes can also be built to make recovery easier. For example, wallboard can be hung horizontally instead of vertically to lessen the amount of wallboard that has to be removed after limited interior flooding. Flooring can be tile or stone that can be completely washed and sanitized

after a flood instead of carpeting and padding or hardwood that has to be discarded. The breaker box and other utility connections can be located on the second floor of the house, provided the climate is not extreme.

Maintenance of swales and drainage is crucial to mitigate against flooding even for homes not in the floodplain. Runoff from higher ground can accumulate around the foundation of a house if drainage elements are not maintained. Even irrigation water can lead to basement flooding or the development of mold in a crawl space if the drainage has been compromised for aesthetic reasons. Regrading should never be undertaken without an engineered plan.

People as Mitigation

In addition to specially trained, professional public safety personnel, members of the community may also be part of a community's mitigation programs. Community Emergency Response Team (CERT) members not only learn how to respond to the threats to their communities but also learn how to take pre-disaster steps to mitigate the effects of natural hazards on the community. The CERT is a national program sponsored by the Department of Homeland Security, with training being given through FEMA to enable community residents and business people to act appropriately in all four phases of emergency management in all three periods: (1) pre-event, (2) response, and (3) post-event. The program requires 24 hours of training for certification. Members are typically organized at the neighborhood level, and then the community level, usually under the sponsorship of the Office of Emergency Services or the fire department, although nonprofits, schools, and law enforcement agencies also sponsor CERTs (CERT, n.d.b.). The CERT is now part of the Citizen Corps Council, and its goal is to organize neighbors for all four phases of emergency management, with an emphasis on pre-disaster mitigation. The first CERT class is on classic mitigation and the steps a person can take personally and within the home to lessen the impact of a disaster on the person and his or her household and community. Techniques like strapping large furniture against wind- or earthquake-related shaking, clearing defensible space in WUI areas, and making disaster kits for cars and homes are typical CERT mitigation programs. The CERT defines its mission to include giving neighbors the "message about preparedness and mitigation" for the time when first responders will be overwhelmed by a disaster (CERT, n.d.a.).

Mitigation may lessen the need for public safety and medical responders in a disaster. The Northridge earthquake, which happened at 4:45 a.m. on January 15, 1994, is a good example of how a simple mitigation step could have prevented thousands of hospital visits. The number one most frequent injury in this earthquake was glass in the feet. The second-most frequent

injuries were lacerations and contusions requiring medical attention that came from falling over objects. For example, the parking lot attendant at Tarzana Medical Center in Tarzana, California reported that in the dark he fell over a new piece of furniture that had toppled in the earthquake, resulting in a gash on his arm that required 25 stitches to close. The CERT teaches the simple mitigation technique of keeping jogging shoes and a flashlight under the bed. If an emergency occurs in the dark and the electricity has failed, a person can put on the shoes, light the flashlight, and thereby avoid walking on broken household goods or tripping over furnishings, thus lessening the number of injured people requiring medical care.

Personal actions can be part of larger community mitigation. Purchasing appropriate insurance policies can mitigate disaster-related financial losses, helping to mitigate the economic losses inherent in damaged and unoccupied homes that generate no real estate tax income for the community to use for recovery. Installation of smoke and carbon monoxide detectors can mitigate fire- and CO-related death. The creation of a family emergency plan can mitigate injury and loss of life to household residents. Washing hands and getting a seasonal flu shot can help mitigate an epidemic.

Summary

Local governments in the United States bear most of the responsibility for the implementation of mitigation. Local buildings officials, police, and fire personnel enforce the codes that implement mitigation requirements. Local city councils, boards of supervisors, and special district boards make the investment of scarce resources in mitigation measures. Local residents work together to clean up creeks and create CERT teams. Effective mitigation requires that community members play an active role in informing their elected officials that mitigation is the community's priority. All disasters really are local, and the solution to most vulnerability lies with the local community and its priorities.

End-of-Chapter Questions

1. Select one local natural hazard, define the mitigation steps that should be taken for it, and prioritize them.
2. Discuss which of the mitigation steps in question 1 have been taken in your community and by which government or private entity.
3. Discuss which of the mitigation steps in question 1 have not been taken, and list which entities should be responsible for implementing those mitigation steps.

References

APCO (n.d.). If we can't find you, we can't help you. Retrieved January 12, 2010, from http://www.apcointl.org/new/commcenter911/downloads/If%20We%20Cant%20Find%20You.pdf.

Areddy, J. T., Chao, L., Leow, J., Oster, S., Zhang, K., & Zhu, E. (2009). Rescue effort overwhelms China. *Wall Street Journal-Eastern Edition, 251*(114), A1–A12.

Army Corps of Engineers (2000). Notice of intent to prepare a Draft Environmental Impact Statement (DEIS)/Draft Environmental Impact Report (DEIR)/Feasibility Study for Coyote Creek at Rock Springs Flood Damage Reduction Study, City of San Jose, Santa Clara County, CA.

CBS News (2008, July 27). Homes destroyed by big fire near Yosemite. Retrieved January 12, 2010, from http://cbs5.com/local/yosemite.california.wildfires.2.781090.html.

CDC (2007). Fight the Bite! Retrieved January 12, 2010, from http://www.cdc.gov/ncidod/dvbid/westnile/prevention_info.htm.

Census Bureau (2007). Local governments by type and state, 2007. Retrieved January 10, 2010, from www.census.gov/govs/cog/govorgtab03ss.html.

CERT (n.d.a.). About CERT. Retrieved January 12, 2010, from https://www.citizencorps.gov/cert/about.shtm.

CERT (n.d.b.). Community emergency response teams. Retrieved January 12, 2010, from https://www.citizencorps.gov/cert/.

Cooper, C., & Block, R. (2006). *Disaster! Hurricane Katrina and the failure of homeland security*. New York, NY: Times Books.

Edwards, F. (2005, April 26). Emergency Operation of Guadalupe River Pumps. Memo to Del Borgsdorf, City Manager, City of San Jose, CA.

Edwards-Winslow, F. (2003). *Keeping our architectural heritage: The unreinforced masonry retrofit program in San Jose, California*. Paper presented at Disaster Resistant California III, San Jose, CA.

Gonzales, S. (2009, October 30). Santa Clara County takes ownership of historic Rancho San Vicente. *Mercury News*, p. B-1.

Haddow, G., & Bullock, J. (2003). *Introduction to Emergency Management*. New York, NY: Butterworth Heineman.

Mercury News. (2007, April 18). West Nile facts. p. B4.

Mileti, D. (1999). *Disasters by Design*. Washington, DC: Joseph Henry Press.

Mount Olive Police Department. (n.d.). If we can't find you, we can't help you. Retrieved January 12, 2010, from http://www.mopd.org/signs.pdf.

NFPA (2009). *Safer From The Start: A Guide To Firewise-Friendly Developments*. Quincy, MA: NFPA.

NFPA (2010). Codes and Standards, 704. Retrieved January 12, 2010, from http://www.nfpa.org/faq.asp?categoryID = 928&cookie_test = 1.

Philadelphia Zoning Code Commission (2010). Zoning matters: types of zoning codes. Retrieved January 12, 2010, from http://www.zoningmatters.org/facts/trends.

Pleasant Unity Volunteer Fire Department (2010). The Officers and Members of PUVFD Explain the Importance of Displaying Your Address. Retrieved January 12, 2010, from http://www.puvfd.org/news.htm.

Pogrebin, R. (2007, December 3). Brad Pitt commissions designs for New Orleans. *New York Times*. Retrieved December 4, 2007 from http://www.nytimes.com/2007/12/03/arts/design/03pitt.html?ex = 1354338000&en = e1582 aa45b627ab2&ei = 5088&partner = rssnyt&emc = rss.

San Jose (2002). Coyote Valley Specific Plan Staff Report. Retrieved January 10, 2010, from http://www.sccgov.org/SCC/docs/SCC%20Public%20Portal/attachments/keyboard/5275 35TMPKeyboard200361000.pdf.

San Jose (2005). Audit Report: Hazardous Incident Team, Glossary. Retrieved January 12, 2010, from http://www.sanjoseca.gov/auditor/auditreports/9304/9304appdxb.pdf.

San Jose (2008a). Coyote Valley Plan. Retrieved January 10, 2010, from http://www.sanjoseca.gov/coyotevalley/CVP_text/cvp-coverintro.pdf.

San Jose (2008b). Coyote Valley Task Force Meeting: Summary of North and Mid-Coyote Property Owners Meeting, January 31, 2008. Retrieved January 10, 2010, from http://sanjoseca.gov/coyotevalley/agendas/minutes/01_31_08_NorthMid_Summary.pdf.

San Jose (2008c). San Jose 2020 (San Jose General Plan). Hillside Development Policy, p. 80–82.

Santa Clara County (2009). Vector Control District. Retrieved January 12, 2010, from http://www.sccgov.org/portal/site/vector/.

Santa Clara County (2010a). Weed Abatement Program General Information. Retrieved from http://www.sccgov.org/portal/site/ag/agencychp?path=%2Fv7%2FAgriculture%2C%20Division%20of%20%28DIV%29%2FWeed%20Abatement%20Program%2FGeneral%20Information.

Santa Clara County (2010b). Weed Abatement Program Standards. Retrieved January 12, 2010, from http://www.sccvote.org/portal/site/ag/agencychp?path=%2Fv7%2FAgriculture%2C %20Division%20of %20(DIV)%2FWeed%20Abatement%20Program%2FWeed%20Abatement% 20Program%20Standards.

Santa Clara Valley Water District (2003). Lower Guadalupe river levee overtopping emergency action plan draft.

Santa Clara Valley Water District (2008, May). Guadalupe River (upper) flood protection project.

Selna, R. (2009, October 12). Bay Area cities lag in making housing quake-safe. *San Francisco Chronicle*. p. B-1.

Tobin, T. (1995, July). Personal communication.

U.S. DOT (2008) Emergency Response Guidebook. Retrieved January 12, 2010, from http://www.phmsa.dot.gov/hazmat/library/erg.

Waugh, W. L., Jr. (2006, March). Shelter from the storm: Repairing the national emergency management system after hurricane Katrina. *The Annals of the American Academy of Political and Social Science. 604*. p. 288–332.

Chapter 12

State Initiatives

Frances L. Edwards and Daniel C. Goodrich

Contents

Learning Objectives

- Describe how a state can incorporate mitigation in all phases of the comprehensive emergency management cycle.
- Describe the state's specific role in mitigation within the comprehensive emergency management cycle.
- Explain how mitigation policy is created, including the limitations and incentives for state action.

- Describe how mitigation and prevention differ and where each is best applied.
- Describe practical applications of mitigation policy and programs at the state level.
- Explain the cost/benefit of mitigation programs.

Introduction

In August 2005, Hurricane Katrina struck the Gulf Coast of the United States, wrecking havoc in coastal Louisiana, Mississippi, and Alabama and causing the flooding of New Orleans due to levee breaks. While the federally owned and operated levees along the Mississippi River withstood the hurricane's forces, the locally owned and managed levees along Lake Ponchartrain failed. The Industrial Canal, 17th Street Canal, and London Canal were all breached. The funds that were raised through taxation to maintain these levees were redirected toward the creation of a marina and an airport, while the levees deteriorated (Cooper and Block, 2006). Although mitigation is often considered a federal activity, with a frequent focus on large post-disaster public works projects built with federal matching funds, the most critical mitigation work is done at the state and the local government levels, by special districts and by private businesses and residents.

In 1979, the National Governors Association defined emergency management as having "four phases": mitigation, preparedness, response, and recovery (National Governors Association, 1979). Known as the Comprehensive Emergency Management Program (Davis Logic, 2005), the cycle moves from the response to a disaster to recovery work, which incorporates aspects of mitigation and engenders an interest in other mitigation activities in the community, with very fluid boundaries between the "phases." Mitigation then leads to preparedness and planning work, setting the stage for a successful response to the next disaster.

Local government emergency managers have used these four phases to plan for, develop, and manage community capability to withstand emergencies and disasters. The programmatic work has evolved since World War II through a civil defense emphasis, to an all-hazards focus, to a terrorism prevention emphasis following the 9/11 attacks, and now, after Katrina, to a time when all-hazards mitigation planning is again taking center stage.

In 2009, Craig Fugate, formerly Florida's emergency management director, was appointed the new head of the Federal Emergency Management Agency (FEMA). At the 2009 Annual Natural Hazards Workshop in Colorado, he stated his belief in mitigation as FEMA's central mission, while acknowledging that "disasters are best managed locally." FEMA needs to focus on its

desire to change the outcomes of events by supporting local initiatives like building codes: "Fix it so we don't come back again" (Fugate, 2009).

Why Does Mitigation Matter?

Mitigation at the state level matters because the loss of life and property is large and growing yearly, as populations cluster along coasts and rivers, increase in density along earthquake fault lines, and spread into forested areas. The Canadian Institute for Catastrophic Loss Reduction noted, "Worldwide, natural disasters killed more than 650,000 people during the 1990s, and caused more than $1 trillion (Canadian) in damage. Disaster damage payments by insurance companies, governments and international aid organizations have been doubling every five to seven years since the 1950s" (Institute for Catastrophic Loss Reduction, 2009).

States may decide to invest money and time to take steps to lessen the impact of a disaster before it occurs. Since resources are scarce, a risk assessment is essential to provide the basis for an allocation of mitigation resources for the greatest benefit to the community.

Risk Assessment

The decision to allocate scarce financial and time resources to specific types of mitigation activity has to be based on a comprehensive risk assessment for the state community. FEMA has provided a website to assist local mitigation planners (http://www.fema.gov/plan/mitplanning/risk.shtm) with information about the most frequent or devastating natural disasters. The planner collects data on disaster events that have actually occurred in the community or state, in surrounding communities or states, and that have a reasonable scientific likelihood of occurring in the community or state. Data is then collected on the likelihood of these hazards occurring. Some are cyclical or seasonal, while others occur with no warning. Investments in mitigation are usually undertaken only for those with a relatively high likelihood of occurrence or high consequences.

The next question is what the consequence of the hazard will be if it occurs. Loss of life, endangering human populations, damage to the environment, and property damage are all considered. FEMA has a management tool called "HAZUS" (http://www.fema.gov/plan/prevent/hazus/index.shtm) that uses maps and overlays to estimate what the losses would be in a given area if certain natural hazards, such as earthquakes, hurricane winds, wildland fires, or floods, occurred. The HAZUS data considers "physical damage, economic loss and social impacts" (FEMA, 2009). However, HAZUS is only a tool and is only as good as the data that is input into the program.

The last factor to consider for mitigation planning is the vulnerability to the hazards. Communities and states located along fault rupture zones, along warm water coastal areas, with large rivers and wildland urban interface areas—places where homes are built in forested areas—are more vulnerable to the effects of the hazards, so mitigation projects can provide a high level of cost/benefit to a community. For example, John Holmes, the United Nations' emergency relief coordinator, states that "every dollar spent on disaster risk reduction [mitigation] will save $7 on future emergency response costs" (Padden, 2009). A cost/benefit ratio of 7:1 creates an incentive for an organization to invest in a variety of mitigation activities.

Focusing Events

Catastrophic disasters become "focusing events" that change national policy (Birkland, 1997). The focusing event of 2001, the terrorist attacks on the World Trade Center and the Pentagon, changed national emergency management policy from focusing on natural hazards mitigation to focusing on terrorism "prevention" (Roberts, 2006, p. 75). It changed the locus of emergency management from an "all-hazards" approach that included criminal acts to a single-minded focus on terrorism "prevention," supplanting federal grant support for natural hazards mitigation. In 2005, Hurricane Katrina changed the focus of emergency management back to a recognition of the need for a balance between natural and human-caused events planning and mitigation implementation. The creation of the National Response Framework and the passage of the Post-Katrina Emergency Management Reform Act of 2006 (Title VI of P.L. 109-295) and related legislation demonstrated the changes in Congressional mandates for FEMA and its organizational structure (Bea, 2006). While the law gives the FEMA director direct access to the president during a presidentially declared major disaster, FEMA's loss of independence as an agency is clearly demonstrated in its place on the Department of Homeland Security's organization chart: four rungs down from the director, but on par with the Coast Guard and Immigration and Customs Enforcement (McCarter, 2009, p. 34).

The current challenge for state government emergency managers is to balance the need for terrorism prevention with the demand for maintaining capability for natural hazard mitigation and response. As shown in Table 12.1, in the past 35 years, there have been three terrorist attacks of note within the borders of the United States (1993 World Trade Center, 1995 Murrah Building, and 9/11/01 attacks), yet there have been hundreds of damaging floods, dozens of significant hurricanes, and eight major earthquakes within the United States in that same time period.

TABLE 12.1 U.S. Disaster Experience: 1971–2008

Type	Name	Year	Loss Estimate
Terror attacks			
Inside United States	World Trade Center Bombing	1993	$510 million
	Oklahoma City Bombing	1995	$80 million
	World Trade Center Bombing	2001	$40 billion
Hurricanes			
10 highest losses	Hugo	1989	$7 billion
	Andrew	1992	$26.5 billion
	Allison	2001	$5 billion
	Charley	2004	$15 billion
	Frances	2004	$9 billion
	Ivan	2004	$14 billion
	Katrina	2005	$80 billion
	Rita	2005	$9 billion
	Wilma	2005	$14 billion
	Ike	2008	$21 billion
Earthquakes (in 2000 dollars)			
Last 41 years	San Fernando	1971	$2.2 billion
	Imperial Valley	1979	$70 million
	Coalinga	1983	$18 million
	Whittier Narrows	1987	$522 million
	Loma Prieta	1989	$10 billion
	Petrolia	1992	$80 million
	Landers	1992	$120 million
	Northridge	1994	$46 billion
	Nisqually	2001	$2 billion
Flooding			
Costliest	Midwest Floods	1993	$20 billion
	Tropical Storm Alberto	1994	$544 million
	Red River Valley	1997	$731 million
	Midwest Floods	2008	$15 billion

(Continued)

TABLE 12.1 U.S. Disaster Experience: 1971–2008 (*Continued*)

Type	Name	Year	Loss Estimate
Over $100 million	Northeast Coastal Storms	1992	$100 million+
	Arizona Floods	1993	$100 million+
	California	1993	$100 million+
	Houston Floods	1994	$100 million+
	California	1995	$100 million+
	Mid-Atlantic	1996	$100 million+
	Pacific Northwest	1996	$100 million+
	Ohio River Valley	1997	$100 million+
	California	1998	$100 million+
	Texas	1998	$100 million+

Sources:

Terror Attacks: http://www.cnn.com/2003/US/Northeast/02/26/wtc.bombing/, http://news.bbc.co.uk/1/hi/world/americas/1319772.stm, and http://www.significancemagazine.org/details/webexclusive/1340691/World-Trade-Centre-anniversary-What-did-911-really-cost.html.

Hurricanes: http://www.factmonster.com.ipka/A0778285.html and http://www.rms.com/NewsPress/PR_102408_Revised_Ike.asp.

Earthquakes: http://www.consrv.ca.gov/cgs/rghm/loss/ and http://www.amre.com/content/home/news/quake_compare.htm.

Flooding: http://www.fema.gov/library/df_7.shtm, http://www.wunderground.com/hurricane/damage1980.asp, and http://pubs.usgs.gov/fs/2006/3026/2006-3026.pdf.

Mitigation and State Implementation

Mitigation is the link between recovery and preparedness. Since 1979, when the National Governors Association issued the first analytical report on American response to disasters, emergency management has been understood as a cycle of activities with very fluid boundaries (National Governors Association, 1979).

Examples of mitigation actions could include the use of engineering, construction, urban planning, and even population training to lessen the impacts of future disasters on a community. Actions taken could include the construction of flood control structures, the prohibition of construction in a floodplain, the requirement for using specified building codes in the construction of homes, and commercial and industrial buildings that include special strengthening for earthquakes or wind, as well as the development of a community emergency response training (CERT) program for all residents and businesses in the community.

Dennis Mileti (1999, p. 23), former director of the Natural Hazards Center in Colorado, defines mitigation as "policies and activities that will reduce an

area's vulnerability to damage from future disasters ... mitigation activities can be characterized as structural, infrastructural and non-structural."

Mitigation applies to all hazards, whether natural, technological, or human-caused. Modification of the built environment can be multipurpose, such as when seismic resistance also achieves a level of blast resistance (Baumann, 2004; Hamburger and Whitaker, 2004). Winter-proofing a home makes it a more secure location for sheltering against a chemical accident or terrorist attack using a chemical weapon, because double-paned windows and weather stripping limit the amount of exterior air that can enter a home. Other successful mitigation steps include raising homes within a floodplain, securing the foundation and reinforcing cripple walls in earthquake-prone areas, brush clearance and installing tile roofs in wildland urban interface fire areas, and creating a safe room in tornado-prone areas.

What Is Mitigation About?

Mitigation is an active effort to prevent future damage through actions taken before another disaster event. Mitigation has been the subject of considerable study. Roberts (2009, p. 763) states that "the consequences of disaster are a combination of natural events and social factors." Beverly Cigler (2009, p. 754) has noted that natural hazards only "become disasters when we place people and property in harm's way." Fugate (2009) states, "We build and live in areas that create disasters." Jim Schwab (2009) of the American Planning Association notes the importance of integrating hazard mitigation into local planning, and the disincentive that is contained in federally subsidized flood insurance.

The landmark work on mitigation is Mileti's *Disasters by Design*, which challenged local government planners and implementers to have a vision of mitigation that includes sustainability. Reflecting on decades of flood mitigation through building levees, paving creeks to create storm channels, and building dams, Mileti noted that while damage was averted from the natural flooding, the mitigation measures themselves led to new problems: "(M)any efforts at disaster mitigation and many disasters result in short-term or cumulative environmental degradation and ecological imbalance, which, besides being detrimental to society, also contributes to the occurrence and severity of the next disaster" (Mileti, 1999, p. 24). For example, the loss of wetlands along the Louisiana Gulf Coast and the construction of the Mississippi River Gulf Outlet (MR-GO) canal are both blamed for the severity of the storm surge related to Hurricane Katrina that swamped coastal areas (Cooper and Block, 2006, p. 27). David H. Moreau (2006, p. 12) notes, "Flooding disasters in New Orleans follow a repetitious cycle of urban development, followed by construction of protective barriers, followed by hurricanes and floods that have overwhelmed the barriers."

While federal mitigation measures have generally been associated with large public works projects, state governments have engaged in mitigation measures that involve the private sector and individual owners as partners. Most state mitigation programs are related to property management, building construction, and personal response to risk. Mary Comerio (1998) studied the Loma Prieta earthquake's impacts on communities. She recognized the importance of building mitigation into recovery planning after a disaster. She notes that "A good disaster recovery program starts with a serious commitment to reducing future damage through…mitigation … Improved mitigation benefits insurance companies through lower payouts, taxpayers through lower program costs, and renters and home owners through reduced damage" (Comerio, 1998, p. 27).

Comerio (1998, p. 244) goes on to note that while earthquake mitigation for single family homes is relatively inexpensive—about \$3000–\$5000 per home—the lack of incentives and financing for the work makes owners unlikely to invest in mitigation. She notes that insurance companies should change their underwriting policies to incorporate more accurate risk categories for pricing insurance and rewarding private mitigation efforts (Comerio, 1998, p. 245).

The economic consequences of failure to mitigate damage are especially notable on affordable shelter in large urban areas. For example, Eugenie L. Birch (2006, p. 141) notes that the Loma Prieta earthquake did disproportionate damage to "low-cost multifamily rental and single room occupancy units—San Francisco lost 4500 rentals and Oakland 1300 SROs. Most were in buildings whose low rent reflected their overcrowded and substandard conditions." Pre-disaster mitigation steps like unreinforced masonry (URM) building retrofits and soft-story building retrofits can change the profile of damaged buildings. For example, Los Angeles, California's 1981 URM building retrofit ordinance was credited with preventing URM building collapses in the 1994 Northridge earthquake. However, the California Seismic Safety Commission notes that housing mitigation programs will require additional government intervention, beyond city-based retrofit programs, including "incentives that encourage cost saving mitigation measures" (California Seismic, 1997, p. 39).

Given that the home is generally the family's largest investment, self-preservation would seem to dictate that homeowners would take mitigation measures. However, Howard Kunreuther (2006) points to the disincentives to individual action inherent in current federal disaster relief policy. If a family "expects to receive government assistance after a loss, it will have less economic incentive to invest in mitigation …." (p. 210). Many cities, including New Orleans, do not enforce building codes designed to mitigate damage to structures and do not enact land use ordinances designed to prevent construction in high hazard areas (Kunreuther, 2006, March, p. 209).

These two actions result in loss of shelter, community recovery delays, individual financial losses, and even deaths. Yet, sound public policy for disaster mitigation at the state levels is difficult to implement.

Mitigation and Public Policy

Public policy formulation may actually be or become a barrier to mitigation programs. All of the public policy programs that require the "sustained actions" that lead to effective mitigation also require public policy formulation at the local and state levels. Reflecting on the impacts of Hurricane Katrina on New Orleans, Kraft and Furlong (2007) state, "One lesson from Hurricane Katrina is that governments might have avoided the enormous human and economic toll had they made smarter decisions over the previous decade" (p. 60). Different land use regulations and enforced building codes might have changed the outcome for thousands of residents and businesses. "How much more should state and local governments do to try to anticipate the risks of natural hazards? … (W)hat obligation do various levels of government have to protect their citizens?" (p. 171).

Fugate has noted that even good public policy may be subverted by economic and political factors at the state level. Florida has a planning law designed to discourage building near the coast, "but it does no good." The plans were modified by communities "based on the public demand for waterside high rises in cost-effective developments. For mitigation to be effective it has to be based on the intrinsic values that the public embraces" (Fugate, 2009).

Regardless of the answer to "how much more" the government should do to protect its citizens, state governments do not have an unfettered ability to make public policy to create disaster mitigation. The property rights of the owners of land in risky areas and the police power of the government exist in tension. *Lucas v. South Carolina Coastal Council* (SCCC) suggests that state governments have limited policy making power to prevent poor choices by property owners. The SCCC passed the Beachfront Management Act in 1988 to prevent further residential construction in harm's way, but in 1992, the Supreme Court determined that the act constituted a taking under the 5th and 14th Amendments and thus required the state to buy the land in order to enforce the SCCC's building ban (*Lucas v. South Carolina Coastal Council*, 1992). Most states lack the financial ability to buy back all the nonriparian coastal property in harm's way from storm surge or beach erosion, for example, so mitigation by land-use regulation becomes impossible in highly desirable coastal and waterfront areas with high land values. Testimony by the Building Owners and Managers Association to the California Seismic Safety Commission

in 1992 prevented the commission from recommending mandatory retrofit for URM buildings in Seismic Zone 4, a proven mitigation measure (Winslow, 1992).

Birkland (2006, p. 106) states that research on mitigation has shown a preference for "policies that employ land use controls, improved building codes, or actuarially sound insurance programs … as long term solutions." This preference places effective mitigation in the state realm, where such regulations are made. Referring to California's earthquake experience, Birkland (2006, p. 130) notes that the "state government is a national leader in [earthquake] hazard mitigation measures because it has the longest experience with the hazard. State leadership is less obvious in hurricane policy, where several states are equally at risk from hurricanes." Regardless of the "hurricane lobby's" less unified front, the State of Florida enacted legislative policy changes that resulted from Hurricane Andrew. The Governor's Disaster Planning and Response Review Committee of 1993 made 94 recommendations, including a surcharge on homeowners' insurance policies to give emergency management a steady stream of funding, leading to improvements in evacuation planning, shelter planning, intergovernmental coordination, and training (Birkland, 2006, p. 142). In 1995, the focus of the effort shifted from response to mitigation through a comprehensive planning process and the building code. Every community must have a natural disaster element in its plan (Birkland, 2006, p. 143). In addition, attention was focused on the need to enforce the building code, even in the face of opposition from the building industry representatives who were concerned about costs. The legislation included a trade-off of stringent building codes for lowered homeowners' insurance rates on the wind damage premium (Birkland, 2006, p. 145).

Birkland (2006, p. 132) has produced a table showing the progression of California earthquake mitigation policies from the Field Act following the Long Beach earthquake to protect schools, through the Hospital Seismic Retrofit Program following the 1994 Northridge earthquake, demonstrating the impact of focusing events and showing that timely introduction of legislation may overcome stakeholder resistance to action. However, it should be noted that the Hospital Seismic Retrofit and Replacement Program was shepherded through the state legislature by an assembly member with both name recognition and a personal stake in the law. Tom Hayden, married to Jane Fonda and a close associate of former Governor Jerry Brown, rescued his mother from St. John's Hospital when it was severely damaged by the Northridge earthquake on January 17, 1994. She was awaiting hip replacement surgery scheduled for later that day. His passion in describing the earthquake risk to hospitalized people made hospital seismic safety a salient item on the legislature's agenda. SB 1953 was introduced on February 25, 1994, and

signed into law by Governor Pete Wilson on September 21, 1994. However, while initial compliance deadlines were 2002, 2008, and 2013, with closure of unretrofitted hospitals by 2030, later, hospital industry pressure on the legislature resulted in 5-year extensions to the retrofit dates through SB 1661.

Mitigation programs depend on public policy formulation. Whether it comes from a top-down approach of legislative leadership or a bottom-up approach of street-level bureaucrats envisioning change, mitigation policy needs two elements. First, it must "transmit clear and consistent objectives," and second, it must "understand what will cause the desired outcomes." Once these primary issues are addressed, funding for implementation, identifying the implementers, and coordination and control among the implementers—power allocation—are needed for success (Smith and Larimer, 2009, pp. 166ff). Gall and Cutter (2007) note the importance of local government mitigation action in Hurricane Katrina. "(K)ey factors that contributed to the losses from Hurricane Katrina...were a direct result of local governments' ineffective and/or non-existent hurricane mitigation" (p. 195). In contrast to Florida's effective emergency planning and policies, the Louisiana transportation department failed to provide evacuation resources for New Orleans' indigent population because they had "no plans in place to do any of this" (Cooper and Block, 2006, p. 239).

Mitigation, then, depends on the creation of good public policy and the successful implementation of that policy. Support from state officials and participation by stakeholders are both essential elements of successful state disaster mitigation.

Practical Applications

All-hazards emergency management posits that preparing for any disaster that has significant community consequences provides a platform for response to any other major disaster. Thus, in California, most communities prepare for earthquakes, while in Florida, communities prepare for hurricanes, but in both cases, a response to an explosion can be managed from the same emergency operations plan and the same emergency operations center.

Likewise, in some ways, mitigation has multiple benefits that are cumulative across the disaster spectrum. For example, community disaster preparedness education creates a population base that is self-supporting for the first hours of a disaster event, regardless of its cause. Creation of a thorough risk analysis for the community provides first responders with pre-disaster knowledge of vulnerabilities, such as slopes, poor soil, or fault areas, which may inform their response decisions in all hazards.

The Community: Mitigation and Prevention

While prevention is situation-specific, such as preventing crime or preventing floods, mitigation crosses situations, benefiting response regardless of the hazard. For example, the mitigation embodied in the development of communications interoperability or geographic information system (GIS) maps will serve first responders in any disaster. Many federal grant programs have retained an emphasis on prevention, especially those related to the Department of Homeland Security. However, this creates the investment limitations of a single disaster focus, usually terrorism, while a return to the mitigation philosophy provides a broader-based use of funding for community protection. The 2008 National Response Framework incorporates both concepts in its discussion of the role of the annexes "to ensure a seamless integration of and transitions between preparedness, prevention, response, recovery and mitigation activities" (FEMA, 2008).

State-Based Mitigation

State government provides leadership in programs with a statewide impact. As noted earlier, California and Florida both have active state-based efforts to engender mitigation programs throughout the state. The State Hazard Mitigation Plan (SHMP) embodies the breadth of state goals for mitigation programs at all government levels. A threat assessment for the state provides the basis for its mitigation programs. For example, California has no hurricane mitigation plans because its coastal water is cooled by the Humboldt Current below a temperature level that would support hurricanes. Conversely, Florida has no earthquake mitigation program because it is one of only two states without the potential for earthquakes.

When the Disaster Mitigation Act of 2000 was passed, it contained a requirement for each state to create a SHMP to be eligible for future federal funds for disaster recovery, mitigation, and fire suppression (California SHMP, 2007, Statement). California's plan emphasizes the risks to the state, such as earthquakes, floods, wildfire, climate change, levee failure, and tsunamis (California SHMP, 2007, Executive Summary).

Governor Pete Wilson called California "America's Disaster Theme Park" when he addressed state leaders following the Northridge earthquake. During his time as governor from 1990 to 1998, he declared states of emergency for earthquakes, wildland fires, floods, drought, and agricultural pests. In half a century, the California population tripled, while deaths held constant at about 100 people per decade, with the current population now over 37 million. The low death toll of 193 people from 12 major earthquakes during that time has been attributed to the strong building codes and strict

enforcement (California SHMP, 2007, pp. 59–60). While it is difficult to evaluate the losses avoided, comparison of deaths in urban earthquakes of similar magnitude such as those in Kobe, Japan (6,000) (Comerio, 1998, p. 10), and Bam, Iran (26,000) (International Federation, 2004), seems to bear out the assertion that enforced building codes save lives.

Wildland fires continue to plague California, even with state's mitigation efforts. The California Division of Forestry and Fire Protection (CalFire) has remapped the high hazard vulnerability areas within its area of responsibility and is providing updated maps for Very High Fire Hazard Severity zones to local fire agencies. Strict building codes to mitigate against residential losses in wildland fires are further described later in the Building Code section of this chapter (California State Hazard, 2007, p. 394). The California Building Commission has adopted the Wildland Urban Interface Code for ignition-resistant construction in the wildland interface (California State Hazard, 2007, p. 395).

Flooding is the nation's most frequent and costly disaster. In the same 50-year period with 193 earthquake-related deaths, there were 292 deaths from flooding and 45 presidential disaster declarations for floods in California. California's FloodSAFE programs are aimed at stormwater management that is sustainable. State funding for studies and engineering work for levees is also a priority (California State Hazard, 2007, p. 230).

State leaders recognize other substantial threats to safety in California, notably, the potential for failure of the agricultural levees that protect the state's freshwater supply. These nonengineered structures are, for the most part, over 100 years old, and a future earthquake could lead to levee failure, flooding of the state's capital, loss of a major freshwater supply, and even deaths. Despite these known risks, it is still a challenge for the state to pay for mitigation for potential levee failure. Although Governor Schwarzenegger took President George W. Bush to see the area in a helicopter, and to ask for federal assistance, the lack of a nexus with terrorism has, to date, denied California any federal aid to implement mitigation for this hazard.

In the absence of federal funding, the state voters passed a $4.1 billion bond in the fall of 2006 to provide funding for repairs to the levees that the state controls. However, the federally owned levees are still deteriorating. In addition, federal agencies like the Fish and Wildlife Service and Environmental Protection Agency must provide permits for state agencies to work in the navigable waterways and flood control channels that the levees protect. A historic memorandum of understanding between the state and the federal agencies resulted in a streamlined permitting process to ensure that repairs were made in advance of anticipated seasonal flooding in 2006, but the permitting process for the major repairs to be funded by the bonds will be more complex and time consuming (Office of the Governor, 2006).

State legislation governs land-use laws, building and other construction-related codes, insurance regulations, real estate transaction regulations, and environmental regulations. It creates agencies to oversee safety in general and elements of mitigation specifically. As seen in Chapter 11, local governments and special districts may enact additional legislation to further regulate these same issues within their jurisdictional boundaries.

Land-Use Regulation

Land-use regulation is one means of mitigation that is used throughout the United States. The police power enables government to regulate the use of land to ensure that it is not injurious to neighbors, does not detract from their property values, and does no general harm to the larger community. Most zoning occurs at the local government level, but overarching state land-use laws can mandate specific elements within a jurisdiction's land-use regulations. California, for example, mandates that every jurisdiction have a general plan, which includes a safety element that includes a map of all geological and fire hazard areas. The zoning for the jurisdiction must then take into account the hazards in selecting the "highest and best use" of each part of the jurisdiction. Florida has a similar requirement for a community plan with a hazard element and the development of concomitant zoning.

Following the Sylmar earthquake, when numerous homes and other structures were damaged by surface fault rupture, the California legislature enacted the Alquist-Priolo Special Studies Zones Act of 1972. It gave all local governments in the state the right to modify their General Plans "to prohibit the location of developments and structures for human occupancy across the trace of active faults …" as identified by the State Geologist (Alquist-Priolo, 1972). Maps of the quarter-mile-wide special study zones are given to each affected jurisdiction for incorporation into its general plan. When the mapped land is to be developed, a licensed geologist has to prepare an evaluation of the property to ensure that it contains no active faults. If it does, a setback from the fault trace is required for any buildings, usually at least 50 feet (California Geological, 2007).

California also has the California Environmental Quality Act. While originally envisioned as a means to prevent noxious activities from proliferating within the state, some of its provisions are also bulwarks for hazard mitigation. For example, any development of more than four dwellings must file an environmental impact report, which explains any geologic features of the site and describes how that portion of the site will be used. Construction is forbidden on specified types of material, such as ancient landslides or steep slopes.

Building Codes

The state can create its own building code or adopt a national model code, with or without local modifications. The International Code Council creates model codes for building regulation, historic and preexisting building retrofits, and related plans. The National Fire Protection Association creates a model fire code. Electrical and mechanical codes are also produced by code agencies. Once the state adopts these codes, they take effect throughout the state, although in California, local jurisdictions may adopt more restrictive code provisions to meet community needs. The California Code of Regulations contains the adopted versions of California Building Standards Administrative Code, California Building Code, California Electrical Code, California Mechanical Code, California Plumbing Code, California Energy Code, California Elevator Safety Construction Code, California Historical Building Code, California Green Building Standards Code, and California Reference Standards Code (California Division of the State Architect, 2009). The building codes are modified to include seismic strengthening requirements for all types of buildings in California.

The California Division of Forestry and Fire Protection works with local governments to ensure that the International Fire Code is also used for building construction management. Tile roofs and fire-resistant stucco siding are among the precautions against wildland fire embodied in the code (California State Hazard, 2007, p. 395). Public Resources Code Section 4291 contains the requirements for clearance of 30 feet around structures and up to 100 feet in high fire areas (California State Hazard, 2007, p. 254).

In Florida, the building code addresses building design and strengthening for wind damage. After Hurricane Andrew, the state recognized that standard construction practices did not provide mitigation against hurricane winds. The new code is designed to help homes resist the explosive forces of the wind and to cut down on the generation of wind-driven debris that damages other structures. "The things that really have improved are enforcement and implementation of the code. You could write the strongest code in the country and if you don't inspect properly, it wouldn't matter" (Stark, 2002). While the code upgrade and stricter enforcement are adding \$4000–\$6000 to the cost of a typical single family home in Florida, about a 3–4% increase, the savings in damage for homeowners and communities are expected to be substantial. The Institute for Business and Home Safety, an insurance industry organization, estimates that if these codes had been in place during Hurricane Andrew, there would have been "\$10-billion less damage, about one third less" (Stark, 2002).

Similarly, the value of strengthened codes and their enforcement was experienced in the U.S. Virgin Islands. The damage to the islands from

Hurricane Hugo's 125-mile-per-hour winds was great. Eighty percent of the homes were destroyed, and the power grid and telephone service were wiped out (York, 1989). Working with the U.S. Department of the Interior, the Virgin Islands adopted and enforced new building codes. In 1998, when Hurricane Georges struck the same area, less than 2% of the homes had severe damage, and the power grid and other infrastructure remained intact (FEMA, n.d.).

The state may also enact special purpose codes for specified building types. For example, California has the Field Act that requires all public schools to be built with extra seismic strengthening. After the 1906 San Francisco earthquake, California schools were built of brick to be fire resistant. These were built as URM structures, and in the 1933 Long Beach earthquake, they collapsed. Fortunately, the event occurred at 5:55 P.M., so no children were in school, but the damaged buildings gave mute testimony to the deaths and injuries that would have befallen children inside during the earthquake. The Field Act has proven effective in creating schools that withstand earthquake shaking, and no child has ever died in an earthquake in a California school.

The Field Act adds costs above typical construction costs of a business building, but the cost/benefit ratio is high. The four strengthened elements are seismic design standards requiring a licensed structural engineer and architect, plan review by the Division of State Architect (DSA), construction inspectors provided by the DSA, and special tests on any unique materials or designs (California Seismic, 2007b, p. 8). These steps have been proven effective in successive earthquakes. The Marina Middle School, located in San Francisco's badly damaged Marina District, withstood the Loma Prieta earthquake shaking and served as a community shelter for days after the earthquake. While the Landers Elementary School sustained only minor damage in the 1992 earthquake, the nearby residential development had significant damage. It should be noted that the school was less than 1 mile from the fault that generated the 7.3 magnitude earthquake that resulted in 12 feet of horizontal surface rupture that continued for 45 miles (California Seismic, 2007b, p. 9).

An even more outstanding example of Field Act performance comes from the 1994 Northridge earthquake in Los Angeles. While two community colleges that were built according to Field Act standards in the highest shaking area had about $5 million worth of damage between them, the nearby California State University at Northridge, which is not covered by the Field Act, suffered complete collapses of structures and significant damage to structures, resulting in losses exceeding $400 million and requiring months of rebuilding time (California Seismic, 2007b, p. 9). While complying with the Field Act adds about 4% to the cost of a school building as compared with a commercial building, there are benefits that accrue even if there is no earthquake.

The buildings are much safer and sturdier, requiring fewer routine repairs and experiencing a longer usable life (California Seismic, 2007b, p. 12).

Similarly, California has the Alquist Hospital Building Code, created after the collapse of two hospitals in the 1971 Sylmar earthquake, one of which was the new county hospital, and the other was the Federal Veterans Administration Hospital. The 1972 legislation, known as the Alquist Hospital Seismic Safety Act, requires hospitals to use stricter building code provisions for structural and nonstructural elements. The building design and construction is overseen by the Hospital Building Safety Board of the Office of Statewide Healthcare Planning and Development (OSHPD). For example, hospitals must have generators and water supplies on site and make provision for medical gases. After the Northridge earthquake, the regulations were strengthened through SB 1953 (mentioned earlier) to include go-slow elevators and stricter requirements for hospitals to remain operational following an earthquake to meet the needs of disaster-generated patients as well as existing hospital inpatients (California Seismic, 1995b, pp. 67–68).

Again, the cost/benefit of the extra strengthening is significant. In 1971, 17 of the 23 hospitals in the earthquake area were damaged or destroyed, while in 1994, only 928 patients had to be relocated due to damage to hospitals (California Seismic, 1995b, p. 68). Ironically, the newly rebuilt county hospital that had been destroyed in the 1971 earthquake had to be completely evacuated because the fire sprinkler system was activated by the shaking and flooded the building. The hospital was closed while operating rooms were sanitized and hospital surfaces were dried out (California Seismic, 1995a).

Mitigation Oversight

The California Seismic Safety Commission was created by the Seismic Safety Act of 1975. Its first charge was the creation of an earthquake mitigation plan for the state, originally called "California at Risk." This plan listed specific legislation and policy measures that could improve the safety of the built environment within the state. By 1997, its name was changed to the "California Earthquake Loss Reduction Plan," and the most recent version for 2007–2011 contains 11 elements that the Commission has designated as critical to the overall earthquake mitigation program within California. The plan serves as "the state's strategic plan guiding the Executive Branch agencies in their overall implementation strategies and priorities for seismic safety" (California Seismic, 2007a, p. 9). The three basic goals of the commission for this period are "learning about earthquakes, building to resist earthquakes, and living with earthquakes" (California Seismic, 2007a, p. 9). The plan offers a model for other states to use in mitigation planning.

Insurance Regulations

Insurance regulations are also a state obligation. The insurance department determines what types of policies may be sold in the state as well as the underwriting standards and claims adjustment expectations. When Hurricane Andrew caused insurers to pay out over 20 years of premium for one event, there was a move for insurers to leave the state of Florida. In 1993, the legislature created the Florida Hurricane (2002) Catastrophe Fund to "provide reimbursements to insurers for a portion of their catastrophic hurricane losses." This reinsurance is available to all insurers in Florida.

Florida also has a Citizens Property Insurance Corporation that provides insurance of last resort for property owners. It was created in 2002 and has property and casualty insurance policies. Coverage is available for privately owned and occupied residential property, commercial residential property, and commercial nonresidential property. They cover multiperil and wind-only exposures. By 2009, they had over 1 million policy holders whose needs cannot be met by the private insurance industry (Citizens Property, 2009).

The Northridge earthquake gave California insurance companies a similar loss experience, paying out 20 years of earthquake policy premiums, $12 billion, for one event. Over 50% of the losses were for damage to residential property (California Seismic, 1997, p. 38). Before this earthquake, California required all homeowners and fire insurance companies to offer earthquake insurance to their policy holders. This was called "bundling" and for many years proved profitable for insurers, as there were no major earthquakes between the 1971 Sylmar event and 1983's Coalinga earthquake, which impacted a small town in a mostly rural area of central California. In 1986, the Whittier Narrows earthquake impacted densely populated Orange County, in 1989, the Loma Prieta earthquake affected the Bay Area from Monterey County to San Francisco, and in 1994, the most expensive earthquake in history—Northridge—struck the San Fernando Valley area of Los Angeles. After this string of losses, many insurance companies stopped writing policies in California, since they could not sell homeowners or fire policies without also offering earthquake policies.

The result was an immediate impact on the local economy. Real estate transactions based on mortgages stopped, as mortgage holders require at least a full coverage fire insurance policy for the property, and 93% of the companies writing residential property coverage in California restricted their business (California Earthquake Authority, 2007). Then-Congressman Norman Y. Mineta held a media conference at a new home development to highlight the serious situation and call for a national all-hazards insurance policy program similar to the existing National Flood Insurance Program. In 1995, the state legislature changed state law to permit insurance companies

to sell "mini policies" that only covered the principal dwelling, not contents or ancillary structures like swimming pools.

Meanwhile, California Insurance Commissioner John Garamendi led the development of a state-sponsored earthquake insurance policy that would meet the basic requirement of housing replacement after an earthquake. In 1996, the legislature created the California Earthquake Authority (CEA). Insurers were able to "join" the CEA, and their payments into the program provided the initial capital. CEA members could then offer the CEA earthquake insurance policies to meet the "bundling" requirement. Over 60% of companies that sell residential insurance policies are members of the CEA.

California residents have not bought the limited CEA policy in large numbers. After the Sylmar earthquake, the sale of earthquake insurance rose and was estimated at about 35% of homeowners' policy holders by 1996, before the post-Northridge earthquake insurance changes (Lindlaw, 2006). By 2011, only about 12% of residential insurance policies included earthquake insurance (California Department of Insurance, 2012). The CEA policy offers very restricted coverage at a premium that appropriately underwrites risk but does not seem like a reasonable investment to most homeowners. The CEA coverage is only for the primary house structure, and it carries a 15% deductible, based on the fire insurance replacement value of the house. For example, a $300,000 house in Seismic Zone 4 (the coastal area of California where most active fault zones lie) has a deductible of $46,000, with an annual premium of almost $1,500, while a $500,000 house has a $75,000 deductible, with an annual premium of $2500 (Lindlaw, 2006).

Given California's strict building codes, most homeowners believe that the damage to their homes is unlikely to reach the deductible amount. Replacement living expenses and other coverage only becomes active once the deductible is exceeded. However, for those in older homes on poor soil, the policy may be a good investment.

Real Estate Transactions

One way to get existing buildings up to current code standards is to require that the seller disclose all seismic-related code compliance conditions to the buyer. In 1990, the California legislature passed AB 2959, which requires the owner to complete a disclosure form that describes any known construction defects for any home built before 1960 and provide it to the buyer at the time of sale. Licensed real estate agents are responsible for ensuring that the seller accurately completes the form and provides it to the buyer as part of the transaction.

The California Seismic Safety Commission created an educational booklet called Homeowners Guide to Earthquake Safety (California Seismic, 2005).

Originally, it was intended to explain the questions on the disclosure form so that people could give accurate answers. For example, many homeowners did not know what a cripple wall was or where to look for seismic bracing on the water heater. By the 2005 edition, the commission had added earthquake preparedness information and offered the booklet in English and Spanish. The booklet is shared by the seller and the buyer, so both homeowners become better informed about appropriate mitigation steps that can be taken to strengthen homes to resist earthquake shaking. Eight specific mitigation actions are highlighted, including bracing the water heater and bolting the house to the foundation.

The Seismic Safety Commission also created a Commercial Property Owners Guide to Earthquake Safety (California Seismic, 2006). The state's Business and Professions Code Section 10147 also requires commercial property owners to complete a disclosure form at time of sale. This disclosure includes the presence of tilt-up construction, concrete columns, and soft-first-story construction. Like the Homeowners Guide, the Commercial Owners Guide includes information on mitigation steps and other earthquake education.

Unreinforced Masonry and Soft-Story Regulations

URM buildings failed in the Coalinga earthquake of 1983. These are built with "unbraced parapets, walls and roofs that are not well attached to each other. When earthquakes occur, inadequate connections in these buildings can allow masonry to fall. Floors and roofs will collapse leaving occupants and passers-by in harm's way" (California Seismic, 2003, p. 2). In 1986, the California legislature passed the Unreinforced Masonry Building Law, Government Code 8875 et seq., mandating that the 286 local building officials in Seismic Zone 4 inventory all URMs in their communities. The inventory includes 24,400 buildings statewide, many of which have been retrofitted to correct the deficiencies in the original construction. While these buildings are only a fraction of the 12 million buildings in California, they include many culturally significant and historic structures (California Seismic, 2003, p. 3).

The law required the building official to notify the owner. The owner was required to post a sign on the exterior of the building to notify passersby and occupants of the building's unsafe status as the minimum response to the notification. Local governments were then encouraged to create a local program for mitigating the danger posed by the URMs, and actions included mandatory retrofits, demolitions, or abandonment of use. Retrofitting is controlled by the 1997 Uniform Code for Building Conservation Appendix Chapter 1 or the California Historical Building Code. Programs adopted include mandatory retrofit/abandonment or

demolition programs, voluntary retrofit/abandonment or demolition programs, notification-only programs, or some type of posting requirement (California Seismic, 2003, p. 4). By 2003, 70% of communities had a mandatory retrofit program designed to meet local economic and political needs (California Seismic, 2003, p. 6).

The California state legislature approved a prohibition of unfunded mandates on local governments in 1992. This effectively stopped the legislature from being able to mandate programs unless they were willing to pay the costs, so future local government mitigation programs had to be completely voluntary unless the state was willing to pay the costs (Shaffer, 1996). Therefore, when the danger of soft-story construction was emphasized by the deaths of 17 people in the Northridge Meadows Apartments as a result of the Northridge earthquake, there was not the same opportunity for a soft-story retrofit program.

Although the Seismic Safety Commission and structural engineers encouraged the state to take some action on retrofitting existing soft-story buildings, a mandatory state program would have been prohibitively expensive for the state. On October 5, 2005, the governor signed AB 304, amending the Health and Safety Code to recognize the need for a soft-story retrofit program, stating, "it is the intent of the Legislature to encourage cities and counties … to initiate efforts to reduce risks." Implementation is left to local government.

Conclusion: Mitigation Includes Prevention

While prevention and mitigation are each useful tools in preparing communities for specific disaster resistance across all hazards, natural hazards cannot be prevented, although through mitigation actions, the impacts on the population and the built environment may be lessened or eliminated. Terrorism may be preventable, but the rest of the threats—natural and technological—will come in cycles, with the seasons, or as a result of poorly understood natural phenomena. As Table 12.1 shows, the toll taken by all the other hazards far outweighs the toll taken by terrorism to date. While researchers speculate about "worst case terrorism," such as smallpox or a nuclear bomb, community emergency planners are facing the natural and technological threats that have no season and give no warning.

Mitigation includes prevention where possible. Federal and state governments build protective public works to prevent flooding and install complex valves to prevent hazardous materials releases. But what cannot be prevented must be mitigated through building codes, land-use regulation, public education, and public agency strategies like emergency plans and emergency operations centers.

Likewise, "all hazards" includes terrorism as one of many disasters that might befall a community. A terrorist chemical attack is the worst kind of hazardous materials event. A terrorist biological attack is the worst kind of medical epidemic.

The 2004 hurricane season provided four major disasters, followed by the tsunami in South Asia, the earthquake in Pakistan, and the Katrina/Rita/Wilma storms of 2005. The death and destruction was on a grand, multinational scale. The economic impact on each damaged community was almost irreparable. In each case, it was a failure to take mitigation seriously that caused large-scale loss of life, catastrophic environmental damage, and economic disaster. No amount of prevention would have worked.

The two terrorism events in Europe during that same time frame did not lend themselves to prevention either. The bombing of the train in Madrid, Spain in March 2004 occurred in a nation where domestic terrorism has been going on for generations, with the Basque separatists against the government. The London, England subway bombing occurred in a city that has weathered Irish Republican Army terrors for over 50 years and has sophisticated camera systems on its subways and a well-trained public with a "stiff upper lip." The Israelis have one of the most thoroughly antiterrorism indoctrinated populations in the world, and yet, terrorist acts continue to be a part of the community, occurring in cafes and markets and on buses. One could conclude from these examples that prevention does not work very well, even in societies with a community knowledge base and a long history of coping.

The disaster events of the past few years have taught one lesson. The worst "credible" terrorist attack cannot rival the instant havoc generated by an earthquake, hurricane, or tsunami in an urban area. Federal programs must be realigned to all-hazards and mitigation to best protect the nation against the most credible threats.

Summary

The state is the principal author of mitigation policy within its boundaries. A focusing event may be necessary to get legislative action on statewide mitigation. Based on its SHMP, a program of appropriate activities should be created, leading to improvements in the ability of businesses and residents to lessen the impact of hazards on their lives and economic well-being. These activities include the administration of land-use regulation, legislation for the adoption and enforcement of various building codes, oversight of insurance policy content and adjustment, and mandating of disclosures of property hazard during real estate transactions.

Mitigation has a high cost/benefit and can be undertaken for all hazards. Prevention is possible for human-caused events, but only the consequences of natural disasters can be prevented, and often, they can only be lessened

or mitigated. Mitigation can be incorporated into all four phases of emergency management, as planning and recovery offer many opportunities to mitigate, and even response can embody mitigation actions that lessen the community impacts of a disaster.

End-of-Chapter Questions

1. What are the principal risks to your state? What kind of mitigation steps should your state sponsor, encourage, or undertake?
2. How would you develop support for mitigation policy in your state? Has there been a focusing event that could be used to educate legislators and the public?
3. Where could your state get funding for critical mitigation projects? Would federal agencies have to be involved in permitting, in upgrading their owned facilities, or in funding state-controlled projects?
4. Considering the principal threat to your state, should your state create a body like California's Seismic Safety Commission? What kinds of programs would such a body sponsor to improve disaster mitigation measures? What role would public education play?

References

Baumann, H. U. (2004). *Recent advancement in tall earthquake resistant structures.* Retrieved March 18, 2006, from http://www.brdcorp.com/papers/iabse2k4fullfinalwithheader.pdf#search = 'earthquake %20resistance%20and%20blast%20resistance'.

Bea, K. (2006, November 15). Federal emergency management policy changes after hurricane Katrina: A summary of statutory provisions. Congressional Research Service. Retrieved from http://training.fema.gov/EMIWeb/edu/docs/Federal%20EM%20Policy%20Changes%20After%20Katrina.pdf.

Birch, E. L. (2006). Learning from past disasters. In E. L. Birch & S. M. Wachter (Eds.), *Rebuilding urban places after disasters.* Philadelphia, PA: University of Pennsylvania Press.

Birkland, T. A. (1997). *After Disaster: Agenda Setting, Public Policy and Focusing Events.* Washington, DC: Georgetown University Press.

Birkland, T. A. (2006). *Lessons of Disaster: Policy Change After Catastrophic Events.* Washington, DC: Georgetown University Press.

California Department of Conservation (1972). Alquist-Priolo Special Studies Zones Act. Retrieved August 23, 2009, from http://www.johnmartin.com/earthquakes/eqpapers/00000082.htm.

California Department of Insurance. (2012, July 27). Earthquake Premium and Policy Count Data Call Summary of 2011 Residential & Commercial Market Totals. http://www.insurance.ca.gov/0400-news/0200-studies-reports/0300-earthquake-study/upload/EQ2011_Summary_Revised.pdf.

California Division of the State Architect (2009). Retrieved November 20, 2009 from http://www.dsa.dgs.ca .gov/default.htm.

California Earthquake Authority (2007). *History*. Retrieved November 20, 2009 from http://www .earthquakeauthority . com/index.aspx?id = 7&pid = 1.

California Geological Survey (2007). *Alquist Priolo earthquake fault zones*. Retrieved August 23, 2009 from http://www.consrv.ca.gov/CGS/rghm/ap/Pages/index.aspx.

California Seismic Safety Commission (1995a, July). *Northridge earthquake: Hearings on the Governor's Executive Order*. Los Angeles, CA: CSSC.

California Seismic Safety Commission (1995b). *Northridge earthquake: Turning loss into gain*. Sacramento, CA: CSSC.

California Seismic Safety Commission (1997). *California earthquake loss reduction plan, 1997–2001*. Sacramento, CA: CSSC.

California Seismic Safety Commission (2003). *Status of the unreinforced masonry building law*. Retrieved August 23, 2009 from http://www.seismic.ca.gov/pub/URM_Report_June26_2003.pdf.

California Seismic Safety Commission (2005). *Homeowners guide to earthquake safety*. Retrieved from http://www.seismic.ca.gov/pub/CSSC_2005-01_HOG.pdf.

California Seismic Safety Commission (2006). *Commercial owners guide to earthquake safety*. Retrieved August 23, 2009 from http://www.seismic.ca.gov/pub/CSSC_2006-02_COG.pdf.

California Seismic Safety Commission (2007a). *California earthquake loss reduction plan, 2002–2011*. Sacramento, CA: CSSC. Retrieved November 20, 2009 from http://www .seismic.ca.gov/pub/CSSC_2007-02_CELRP.pdf.

California Seismic Safety Commission (2007b). *Field Act and public school construction: A 2007 perspective*. Retrieved August 23, 2009 from http://www.seismic.ca.gov/pub/CSSC_2007-03_Field_Act_Report.pdf.

California Emergency Management Agency (2007). *California State Hazard Mitigation Plan*. Retrieved November 29, 2009 from http://hazardmitigation.calema.ca.gov/docs/SHMP_Final_2007.pdf.

Cigler, B. A. (2009). Response to Ian Birdsall's "Looking for the FEMA Guy, Part 1". *Administration & Society*, *41*(6): 754–757.

Citizens Property Insurance Corporation (2009). *Frequently Asked Questions*. Retrieved November 20, 2009, from http://www.citizensfla.com/utilitybar/policyholderfaqs .cfm?CFID=940518&CFTOKEN=93122863.

Comerio, M. C. (1998). *Disaster Hits Home*. Berkeley, CA: University of California Press.

Cooper, C., & Block, R. (2006). *Disaster! Hurricane Katrina and the Failure of Homeland Security*. New York, NY: Times Books.

Davis Logic (2005). *Comprehensive Emergency Management Programs*. Retrieved from http://www.davislogic.com/CEMP.htm#Definition.

Federal Emergency Management Agency (FEMA), Mitigation Directorate (n.d.). *Building better: New building code & power upgrade, US Virgin Islands*. Retrieved September 1, 2009 from http://www .fema.gov/mitigation/brief.do?mitssId = 950.

Federal Emergency Management Agency (FEMA), Mitigation Directorate (2008, January). *National response framework*. Retrieved September 30, 2009 from http://www.fema.gov/pdf/emergency/nrf/nrf-core.pdf.

Federal Emergency Management Agency (FEMA), Mitigation Directorate (2009). *Hazard mitigation planning risk assessment*. Retrieved September 30, 2009 from http://www .fema.gov/plan/mitplanning/risk.shtm.

Florida Hurricane Catastrophe Fund (2002). Retrieved November 20, 2009 from http://www.sbafla.com/fhcf/AbouttheFHCF/tabid/278/Default.aspx.

Fugate, C. (2009, July 16). Keynote Address. 2009 Annual Hazards Workshop, Natural Hazards Center, Broomfield, CO.

Gall, M., & Cutter, S. (2007). 2005 Events and outcomes: Hurricane Katrina and beyond. In C. Rubin (Ed.), *Emergency management: The American experience 1900–2005*. Fairfax, VA: Public Entity Risk Institute.

Hamburger, R., & Whittaker, A. (2004). *Design of steel structures for blast-related progressive collapse resistance*. Retrieved August 2, 2012, from http://www.scribd.com/doc/57876471/Design-of-Steel-Structures-for-Blast-related-Progressive-Collapse-Resistance-by-Dr-Whittaker.

Institute for Catastrophic Loss Reduction (2009). Building resilient communities. ICLR.

International Federation of Red Cross and Red Crescent Societies (n.d.). *Red Cross Red Crescent Remains to Help Bam's Long Term Needs*. Retrieved September 24, 2004, from http://www.ifrc.org/en/news-and-media/press-releases/middle-east-and-north-africa/iran/red-cross-red-crescent-remains-to-meet-bams-long-term-needs/.

Kraft, M. E., & Furlong, S. R. (2007). *Public Policy: Politics, Analysis and Alternatives*. Washington, DC: CQ Press.

Kunreuther, H. (2006, March). Disaster mitigation and insurance: Learning from Katrina. *The Annals of the American Academy of Political and Social Science, 604*: 208–227.

Lindlaw, S. (2006, March 22). More Californians forgoing quake insurance. *The Boston Globe*. Retrieved November 20, 2009 from http://www.boston.com/news/nation/articles/2006/03/22/more_ californians_forgoing_quake_insurance/.

Lucas v. South Carolina Coastal Council (1992). 505 U.S. 1003.

McCarter, M. (2009, May). Napolitano's DHS: A vision and a focus. *Homeland Security Today*, *6*(5): 9–12.

Mileti, D. (1999). *Disasters by Design*. Washington, DC: John Henry Press.

Moreau, D. H. (2006). Levees and land use: The making of a disaster in New Orleans. In *Learning from Catastrophe: Quick Response Research in the Wake of Hurricane Katrina* (Special Publication #40). Boulder, CO: Institute of Behavioral Science, University of Colorado at Boulder, Natural Hazards Center.

National Governors Association (1979). *Emergency preparedness project final report*. Washington, DC: Government Printing Office.

Office of the Governor (California) (2006, October 10). *Gov. Schwarzenegger highlights completed levee repairs, presses federal government for reimbursement for work on federal levees*. Retrieved January 9, 2009 from http://gov.ca.gov/index.php?/press-release/4509/.

Padden, B. (2009, October 21). Earthquake-prone nations can reduce casualties. *Voice of America News*. Retrieved August 3, 2012, from http://www.51voa.com/VOA_Standard_English/VOA_Standard_English_34213.html.

Roberts, P. S. (2006, Spring). FEMA and the prospects for reputation-based autonomy. *Studies in American Political Development*, *20*, 75.

Roberts, P. S. (2009, October). An unnatural disaster. *Administration and Society*, *41*(6): 763–769.

Schwab, J. (2009, July 16). *Response to Craig Fugate*. 2009 Annual Hazards Workshop, Natural Hazards Center, Broomfield, CO.

Shaffer, R. M. (1996, Spring). Unfunded state mandates and local governments. University of Cincinnati Law Review, LexisNexis Academic. Retrieved November 20, 2009.

Smith, K. B., & Larimer, C. W. (2009). *The Public Policy Theory Primer*. Philadelphia, PA: Westview Press.

Stark, J. (2002, August 19). New building codes bring cost, confusion. *St. Petersburg Times*. Retrieved November 20, 2009 from http://www.sptimes.com/2002/webspecials02/andrew/day2/story1.shtml.

Winslow, F. E. (1992, February 18). Memo to Tom Tobin, Executive Director, California Seismic Safety Commission on the "Right to Know" report.

York, M. (1989, September 19). Deadly Hugo slams Puerto Rico, Virgin Islands. *Washington Post*, p. A01.

Chapter **13**

Leveraging Nonprofit Organizations and Volunteers in Hazard Mitigation

Dorothy Norris-Tirrell

Contents

Learning Objectives

- Identify common sources for mitigation volunteers.
- Describe the steps for developing an effective volunteer program.
- Identify the challenges of using hazard mitigation volunteers.
- Describe the characteristics of a collaborative model for community-wide hazard mitigation.
- Identify the factors important to successful hazard mitigation collaboration.
- Describe three models of community collaboration for hazard mitigation.

Introduction

While each locality brings a unique set of geographic, political, and socio-economic characteristics, strengthening community-wide disaster preparedness is an ongoing and critical need. Although more recently the emergency management field has been dominated by professionals, in earlier times volunteers played essential roles both formally (e.g., volunteer fire departments) and informally (e.g., neighbors helping each other). Historians and others have commented on the evidence of voluntary roles throughout U.S. history. Alexis De Tocqueville (1840/1945, p. 106) observed "Americans of all ages, all conditions, and all dispositions constantly form associations." From colonial times when citizens pitched in for public tasks, including building roads, constructing meeting houses, and fighting with militias (McKinney, 1995), volunteerism has flourished in the United States.

In addition, private nonprofit organizations have long served important roles in community-based disaster recovery. For example, the American Red Cross and the Salvation Army both have extensive histories of community response and recovery work. Much of their work is done through

the efforts of trained volunteers. However, the effective use of volunteers does not happen accidently; rather, it requires deliberate attention to the creation and ongoing development of volunteer programs designed to meet identified needs and clearly specified objectives. With this approach, volunteers can be an important resource in building prepared and resilient communities.

This chapter focuses on the nonprofit sector, including volunteers, as important but often underutilized actors in the emergency management cycle. The chapter begins with a description of the common sources for emergency management volunteers including faith-based institutions and professional associations. The next section discusses how to effectively plan, implement, and manage a volunteer program and the issues of particular concern for volunteers in disaster mitigation. Building on the assumptions that (1) precrisis preparation leads to more effective response and recovery and (2) precrisis community capacity (e.g., training, preparedness, communication channels, and working relationships) leads to more effective response and recovery, the next section provides strategic and tactical information for generating community collaboration across public, nonprofit, and private sector organizations that are charged with emergency management and mobilize many of the volunteers needed for comprehensive preparedness and mitigation. As a result, the many efforts organized by nonprofit agencies, faith-based groups, and professional associations can effectively and efficiently realize broader community mitigation goals.

Finding Volunteers for Disaster Mitigation

The productive labor of millions of individuals each year is harnessed to meet public need, without the costs of paying them, through volunteerism. According to the Corporation for National and Community Service, in 2009, about 61.8 million Americans volunteered through organizations, giving 8.1 billion hours of service worth approximately $162 billion to America's communities (CNCS, 2009). While most volunteers serve in their home communities, some individuals travel distances to volunteer for "voluntourism," a newer concept particularly attractive to young people that links vacation travel with the desire to help or to respond to natural disasters or crisis. The latter can be seen in the hundreds of thousands of volunteers who have traveled to Louisiana, Mississippi, Alabama, and Texas in the years following Hurricanes Katrina and Rita.

Charitable nonprofit organizations are a common host for volunteers; however, many government agencies, religious institutions, civic groups, and professional associations offer fertile ground for recruiting, training, and mobilizing volunteers for disaster mitigation and preparedness.

Nonprofit Organizations

According to the National Center for Charitable Statistics, 8840 charitable organizations (those with 501(c)(3) recognition in 2005 were identified in the category of "Public Safety, Disaster Preparedness & Relief)" (NTEE Category M) (see Figure 13.1). The involvement of nonprofits in this policy area is extensive, incorporating a wide range of organizational missions and functions. High-profile nonprofits such as the American Red Cross, the only congressionally mandated organization to provide aid to disaster victims, and the Salvation Army both have long histories of community response and recovery work following emergencies of all sizes and types, but are very different in mission and volunteer operations. Many of the nonprofit organizations in the following list have specific volunteer programs related to emergency management and offer training to develop the necessary knowledge, skills, and abilities to be effective in a volunteer role:

- American Radio Relay League
- American Red Cross
- Feeding America
- Feed the Children
- Habitat for Humanity International
- Humane Society of the United States
- International Relief and Development
- Points of Light Foundation/HandsOn Network
- Save the Children
- Salvation Army
- Society of St. Vincent de Paul
- United Way of America

In addition, other nonprofit organizations exist for the sole purpose of collecting and distributing money for disaster recovery. Some of these are

M01	Alliances & Advocacy
M02	Management & Technical Assistance
M03	Professional Societies & Associations
M05	Research Institutes & Public Policy Analysis
M11	Single Organization Support
M12	Fund Raising & Fund Distribution
M19	Support NEC
M20	Disaster Preparedness & Relief Services
M23	Search & Rescue Squads
M24	Fire Prevention
M40	Safety Education
M41	First Aid
M42	Automotive Safety
M60	Public Safety Benevolent Associations
M99	Public Safety, Disaster Preparedness & Relief NEC

FIGURE 13.1 National Taxonomy of Exempt Entities—Code M; Public Safety, Disaster Preparedness & Relief. (Rev. May 2005. See http://nccs.urban.org/classification/NTEE.cfm for more information.)

long-standing organizations while others are more temporary, created in response to a specific event such as 9/11 World Trade Center attacks or the 2004 Sumatra tsunami.

Faith-Based Organizations and Religious Institutions

Although often overlooked when building community capacity, religious and faith-based institutions also have a long history of emergency response and recovery activity. From collecting and distributing clothing, food, furniture, and money, to providing hands-on services ranging from childcare and transportation to debris cleanup and home repair, members of religious institutions are often the first on the scene, well before Federal Emergency Management Agency (FEMA) workers, and the last to leave. For example, after Hurricane Katrina, numerous faith-based groups provided essential services, including the Amish and Mennonites, who rebuilt homes, Lutheran and Islamic groups, who provided medical care, and Southern Baptists, who cooked over 14 million meals in the hard-hit Gulf Coast communities (Kunzelman, 2006).

In addition to the work of local congregations, synagogues, mosques, temples, and other religious institutions, many national faith-based and religious institutions have volunteer programs to support large disasters and to prepare local members for disaster-related volunteer work. These include the following:

- Adventist Community Services
- American Baptist Men USA
- Catholic Charities USA
- Christian Disaster Response
- Christian Reformed World Relief Committee
- Church World Service
- Episcopal Relief & Development
- Friends Disaster Service, Inc.
- Lutheran Disaster Response
- Mennonite Disaster Service
- Nazarene Disaster Response
- Presbyterian Disaster Response
- Southern Baptist Convention
- Unitarian Universalist Service Committee
- United Church of Christ—Wider Church Ministries
- United Jewish Communities
- United Methodist Committee on Relief

Relatedly, religious leaders in volunteer roles often take a lead in addressing the spiritual and emotional needs of victims (Koenig, 2006).

Government-Sponsored Groups

Government agencies, such as the U.S. Department of Homeland Security and the U.S. Department of Justice, also recruit, train, and assign volunteers through a variety of specific programs. Although the training and structure is provided by the sponsoring federal agency, these programs are locally based and operated:

- *Community Emergency Response Team (CERT) volunteers*: Over 2000 CERT programs across the country offer 20 hours of hands-on instruction for citizens in emergency preparedness, disaster medical operations, fire safety, and basic search and rescue. CERT is administered by the U.S. Department of Homeland Security.
- *Fire Corps*: Started in December 2004, nearly 400 programs across the United States are now registered. Fire Corps is a collaborative effort of the U.S. Department of Homeland Security, U.S. Fire Administration, the National Volunteer Fire Council, The International Association of Fire Fighters, and the International Association of Fire Chiefs.
- *Medical Reserve Corps*: With 350 units around the country, the Medical Reserve Corps engages citizen volunteer physicians, nurses, pharmacists, and others with an interest in a broad range of skills in medicine, public health, and other support fields.
- *Neighborhood Watch*: Funded by the U.S. Department of Justice and administered by the National Sheriffs' Association, over 14,000 Watch Programs exist, many with a revitalized mission that includes neighborhood emergency preparedness.
- *Volunteers in Police Service (VIP)*: More than 1000 programs are registered, representing all 50 states, the District of Columbia, and Puerto Rico. The International Association of Chiefs of Police administers VIPs with funding from the U.S. Department of Justice.

Professional Societies and Trade Associations

Another source of potential volunteers for disaster mitigation and preparedness efforts are trade associations and professional societies. Although organized around job function and professions, these groups are composed of volunteers with specific expertise and experience that may prove useful to emergency management. The following is a list of examples of national associations that are specific to disaster occupations:

- American Association of Avalanche Professionals
- Association of Contingency Planners
- Association of State Floodplain Managers
- Association of Civil Engineers Volunteer Disaster Assistance Program

- Central United States Earthquake Consortium
- International Association of Emergency Managers
- National Emergency Management Association
- National Association of Disaster Response Teams

Many of these have state- and local-based chapters. In addition, many other professional or trade associations exist that have ongoing programs or committees with a disaster preparedness/response focus. For example, the American Psychological Association has a Disaster Response Network, the American Bar Association has a Disaster Law Resources section on its website, and American Association of Civil Engineers has a Volunteer Disaster Assistance Program. A focused web search can result in an association for almost any specialty field that may be an outlet for volunteers.

Civic and Fraternal Organizations

Civic organizations are also a fruitful source for community volunteers. This set of organizations includes Lions Club, Rotary, Chambers of Commerce, Kiwanis, Optimists, Veterans of Foreign Wars, Friends of the Library, Masonic and Eastern Star chapters, fraternities and sororities, as well as various "leadership" training programs and groups. While many of these have national organization structures or alliances, the groups are community-based and often offer a pool of community-minded individuals easily accessible for training and assignment.

Emergent Volunteers

At the time of a disaster or emergency, volunteers spontaneously materialize to provide supplies and help. Such emergent volunteers are common and can provide much-needed assistance. This ad hoc assistance "can infuse vitality (and labor) ... and alert officials to the possibilities of volunteerism" (Brudney, 2005, p. 318). However, if not anticipated and planned for, emergent volunteers can overload the system and cause stress to a tenuous operation. Local volunteer centers often serve as a clearinghouse, providing a "matchmaking" service for emergent volunteers and community needs during a disaster and for the recovery period, thus allowing other nonprofit and government organizations to effectively fulfill their mandated roles.

Strategies for the Effective Use of Volunteers

The optimal use of volunteers requires pertinent knowledge, skills, and abilities for planning and managing a successful program. Many consider volunteers to simply be a source of unpaid labor. More importantly, when

used intentionally and appropriately, volunteers are a valuable human resource, providing an increased labor pool for covering needed tasks, access to desired expertise, improved contact with the community at large, and the ability to change a community's perspective. The roles that volunteers can play in disaster mitigation are varied and can include the following:

- Needs assessment and planning
- Feedback and observation on past disaster response and recovery
- Collection and distribution of preparedness items
- Assessment of temporary housing facilities
- Mock disaster scenario participation
- Damage assessment
- Language interpretation
- Data entry
- Answering phone calls and e-mails
- Transportation and delivery
- Community outreach through speakers bureau, fundraising, and marketing
- Volunteer management
    - Recruiting volunteers
    - Orienting and training volunteers
    - Assigning, referring, and redirecting emergent volunteers
    - Supervising volunteers
    - Planning/implementing appreciation events
- Lobbying and advocacy with officials and politicians

However, volunteers can be a potential public relations nightmare when the crucial steps of preparation, recruitment, orientation, management, and recognition are overlooked. In addition, possible disadvantages of using volunteers include a lack of control, uncertain reliability, time demands for volunteer supervision, and difficulties in recruiting enough qualified volunteers (McCurley, 2005). These disadvantages can be minimized with adequate preparation before inviting volunteer participation, and careful attention to volunteer recruitment, management, and recognition.

Preparation for a Volunteer Program

Before enlisting a single individual to serve, the purpose of utilizing volunteers and the roles they will play must be assessed to assure that a volunteer program is an appropriate strategy to meet or enhance the human resources needs of the disaster mitigation effort.

Purpose of Volunteers

The development of position descriptions that list the tasks and responsibilities needed begins the preparation. What needs to be done? What are the skills and expertise required? How much time will it take? Just like for a salaried job, a volunteer position description articulates assignments and expected accomplishments. Too often, volunteers are recruited to complete the tasks that paid staff does not want. While one person's "challenging" is another person's "frustrating," the key is to create volunteer assignments that clearly provide value to the overall effort.

Assessing the Volunteer Market

Examine the range of nonprofit organizations, faith-based institutions, and government volunteer programs and associations that exist in a given locale. Consider whether a program supported by these established organizations can provide the human resources, expertise, and capacity needed. Partnering and collaborating to build a prepared community offers advantages for recruitment and management, while strengthening community capacity, increasing knowledge about the challenges and needs related to hazard mitigation, and expanding the network of trained volunteers committed to assist (see the section "Building Community-Wide Knowledge and Capacity for Disaster Mitigation: The Importance of a Collaborative Model" in this chapter).

Understanding Volunteer Motivation and Availability

Individuals volunteer for many different reasons ranging from the desire to learn something new, meeting social affiliation needs, or giving back to the community. The time they have to spend volunteering also varies. Many volunteer programs provide a range of opportunities for potential volunteers, including regular weekly or monthly assignments as well as one time or short-term projects. Potential volunteers may work full time and require that programs schedule opportunities in the evenings or on the weekends. Some volunteers can travel distances to participate while others may need an assignment that can be completed in their home. Knowing the volunteer pool allows for the creation of a meaningful and successful volunteer program.

Recruitment and Orientation of Volunteers

Once the roles of volunteers are determined, strategies must be developed for recruiting individuals or groups to participate. The goal of a recruiter is not typically to elicit thousands of inquiries from unknown potential

volunteers; rather, successful volunteer recruiters target individuals and groups who are likely to be interested in the volunteer role and have the necessary competencies.

Recruitment

Many tactics can be used for recruiting including websites, announcements at meetings and schools, organization and association newsletters, e-mail lists, flyers, and mass media, including television, radio, and newspapers. Sometimes, "warm body" recruiting (i.e., generating a large supply of volunteers for easily taught tasks for a short time frame) is all that is needed (McCurley, 2005). Other times, targeted recruitment—seeking individuals or groups with a particular set of skills or expertise—will be required. For example, if the competences related to civil engineering are needed for a volunteer project, contacting and working with a local group of the American Association of Civil Engineers may be a good strategy. Many areas have volunteer centers that can also assist with targeted recruitment. Designing the request to reach the appropriate target group of volunteers is crucial so that individuals can screen themselves out (Ellis, 2001). Importantly, the most effective way to reach volunteers is to ask; a personal invitation is the most proven strategy for recruitment.

Matching

Once volunteer prospects have been identified, they must be screened and matched with the task that best suits their experience, abilities, and skills. Whether it is "warm bodies" needed to play a part in a disaster scenario, or individuals with trucks to deliver emergency preparedness kits and cots to local churches, potential volunteers must have the capacity and the willingness to perform the needed tasks. An application form or an interview will aid in matching qualifications and temperament to the volunteer opportunities. If the tasks require confidentiality or working with children, additional screening measurements, such as background checks and training sessions, should be required.

Orientation

To set the stage for a positive and rewarding experience, volunteers need information about their role and expected tasks. An orientation session is one mechanism to communicate with volunteers and have them begin to form relationships with other volunteers. Depending on the volunteer duties, the orientation may be held as a part of the recruitment process. If the volunteer experience is short term or one time, the orientation may be held on the day of the event. At minimum, the orientation should cover the purpose of the volunteers, duties (e.g., how they fit into accomplishing larger goals), the specific expectations for a particular volunteer, and the

rules and procedures (e.g., sign-in sheets and record-keeping tools) important to the fulfillment of the assignment. The orientation process should provide the context for the volunteer and make them feel a part of the team effort.

Managing the Volunteer Experience

To ensure that the experience is positive, volunteers must be supervised and managed. Management may seem less important when volunteers are donating their time and may be selective in the assignments they accept and the hours they work. However, without proper support and guidance, even well-intentioned volunteers can be ineffective (Grossman & Furano, 2002) and may leave if they are not treated properly. Smart management practices for both paid and volunteer staff remain centered on building trust, cooperation, and teamwork while emphasizing achievement, values, and commitment (Brudney, 2005).

Providing Needed Resources

Volunteers need access to the supplies required to complete the assignment. If volunteers are expected to bring the supplies themselves, the orientation process should clearly explain the requirements. In addition, volunteers must have a satisfactory work environment with access to basic amenities such as restrooms, seating, and water.

Management and Feedback

Ongoing positive supervision, communication, and useful feedback assure that the volunteer's time is not wasted but used efficaciously. No one wants to contribute their time to a misdirected effort or make mistakes that require someone else to remedy. Thus, clear and ongoing communication of assigned tasks and responsibilities includes establishing performance expectations and success criteria, a plan of work, and the opportunity for corrective action. In addition, feedback opportunities should incorporate self-assessment and supervisor comments for the volunteer's growth in the role and explicitly solicit the volunteer's suggestions about improving the volunteer experience (such as the need for more specific job duties, schedule changes, or additional training needs).

Continued Training and Development

Since one common motivation for volunteering is to develop new skills, further training can be an important tool for effective performance and

retention. Essential to an effective training program is the identification of the knowledge, skills, and abilities critical to good performance (McCurley, 2005). The training should be useful to the effort's effectiveness and to the volunteer, emphasizing practical and experiential methods. Mock disasters are a particularly useful training tool to increase value in the time of an emergency.

Recognition for Volunteer Service

Although volunteers do not serve solely for recognition, opportunities for positive reinforcement are an important component of volunteer management. Recognition strategies show appreciation for a volunteer's contribution and clearly communicate the value of their work.

Showing Appreciation

Showing appreciation to volunteers is vital to an ongoing volunteer effort. A sincere "thank you" at the time of service is important and may be all that some volunteers need. Others require more formal acknowledgment through activities such as award ceremonies, special events, certificates, plaques, or media attention. In addition to recognizing the effort of individuals and groups, these strategies also raise the visibility of the effort, bringing more volunteers and resources.

Valuing the Volunteer's Work

The most important recognition comes from leaders who articulate the volunteer assignments as meaningful to the overall effort. Volunteers want the results of their work to be worthwhile and clearly connected to positive results.

Volunteers in Disaster Mitigation

A few challenges are of particular importance when exploring the use of volunteers in disaster mitigation. Deploying volunteers to assume key responsibilities brings a certain amount of risk. However, working with nonprofit organizations, faith-based institutions, and professional associations for which volunteer liability is a common issue reduces the risk. At minimum, volunteer program designers should consider what will happen if a volunteer is injured during their participation (e.g., making sure sufficient liability insurance is in place) and create policies and procedures to reduce the likelihood of a legal claim by volunteers.

The relationship between paid staff and volunteers can also produce challenges. Ideally, these two categories of human resources should work hand in hand as a team—each fulfilling important roles for the accomplishment of projects or goals. To set the stage for coproduction, paid staff should be involved in the creation of position descriptions for volunteers, in orientation and training processes, and in ongoing assessment and evaluation.

Reliability of the volunteer commitment, particularly in the time of an emergency, is another challenge. Volunteers will naturally take care of themselves, their families, and friends first before responding to their volunteer assignment. In addition, logical issues related to communication (e.g., the phones are down and the electricity is out) and transportation (e.g., the roads are blocked with trees or the bridges have collapsed) can make predicting who will and can respond difficult. To anticipate these obstacles, it is essential that more volunteers than will be needed in the time of emergency be trained and assigned.

The time between volunteer training and the opportunity to put new skills into practice can also be challenging. Keeping volunteers engaged when there is no disaster requires ongoing opportunities for interaction, further training, and participation in useful activities such as mitigation assessment, tabletop exercises, and mock disaster scenarios.

While this section has focused on developing a program for the effective use of volunteers, in the time of emergency, leaders must be prepared for the intentional management of spontaneous or emergent volunteers. It is harder to gauge the motivations of this volunteer group. If planning for emergent volunteers has not occurred, they may negatively impact the determined priorities. An important pre-disaster planning activity is the identification of the group, such as a volunteer center, that will process, train, and assign emergent volunteers.

Building an effective disaster mitigation strategy that uses volunteers requires assessing volunteer need in a community, recruiting disaster volunteers, maintaining active volunteers, and managing emergent volunteers.

Building Community-Wide Knowledge and Capacity for Disaster Mitigation: The Importance of a Collaborative Model

Whether watching for enemy ships or responding to tornado damage, emergency management activities often require technical expertise and collaboration within local communities. In the 1970s, emergency management became the domain of professionals and administered through a public sector–controlled command and control model (Agranoff & McGuire, 2001;

Stephens & Grant, 2001; Ward, Wamsley, Schroeder, & Robins, 2000; Wise, 2002). Hierarchical organizations and decision-making processes continue in the emergency management context even as research suggests that a network or collaborative approach is a good predictor for readiness and response effectiveness (Carley & Harrald, 1997; Gillespie, 1993; Schroeder, Wamsley, & Ward, 2001). Today, the roles that each sector plays in disaster management are more recognized, but the value and importance of developing and sustaining broad-based collaborative planning processes and the relationships necessary to create community capacity are often underappreciated (Norris-Tirrell & Clay, 2006). Many of the key actors involved with emergency management are technical experts (such as firefighters, rescue, and police) with very specific functions in the emergency context and typically have had limited prior interaction with the other nongovernmental emergency actors. Since chaos is the common first reaction to any disaster (Comerio, 1998), to be effective, interagency collaboration crossing public, private, and nonprofit sector organizations must be developed and nurtured before the occurrence of a disaster. Building emergency management capacity is an evolutionary process and requires leadership, vision, resources, and relationships (Norris-Tirrell & Clay, 2010).

Schroeder, Wamsley, and Ward (2001) suggest that while everyone acknowledges the need for coordination in an emergency, nobody wants to be "coordinated," nor is it clear just what the term means in practice. Statutory authority is not easily transformed into legitimate political authority, and emergency management agencies are very seldom given anything but statutory authority to "coordinate" in the event of an emergency or disaster (p. 360).

The time before the emergency event is clearly the more effective time to create formal and informal collaborative relationships that strengthen the capacity of a community for disaster resilience. Every community has not only a distinctive and dynamic set of geographic, political, and socioeconomic characteristics, but also a unique history of disaster management and cross-sector collaboration. However, Norris-Tirrell and Clay suggest a common set of important characteristics that defines a mature, integrative emergency management collaboration:

1. Basic understanding that the command and control structure will take over in the time of emergency requiring all actors to be trained to play their role within the "official response" structure. The National Incident Management System (NIMS) is one example of a structure that has been widely tested and utilized.
2. General understanding of the roles that various public, nonprofit, voluntary, faith-based, and private organizations as well as private citizens play in all stages of emergency management including whether (a) technical knowledge needs are covered; (b) technical

equipment is available; (c) infrastructure is in place (i.e., alternate communication systems, power grids, and flood controls); (d) formalized mutual aid agreements are in place; and (e) sufficient numbers of trained volunteers are identified.
3. Fundamental understanding of the socioeconomic conditions of the locality and geographic distribution of these conditions, including identification of language and other access issues.
4. Building of a comprehensive planning, response and recovery vision, and an implementation plan that includes citizen and organization-level preparedness, short-term response (first responders), and long-term response and recovery (24 hours and beyond the disaster).
5. Rehearsal of possible disaster scenarios to test response capacity using various strategies and participants. Strategies range from interactive, computer-generated case studies and tabletop exercises to real-time simulations.
6. Inclusion of multiple feedback opportunities to identify problems and generate solutions through changes in policy, communications, and behavior.
7. Develop (and widely market) a central source for local information and referral during the time of an emergency that is in place before the incident.
8. Recognize the variables that are often not directly controlled by emergency management leaders and develop strategies to address them. These variables include the role of the media, the role of elected and appointed officials, the public perception of preparedness, and the public perception of past and current response efforts (Norris-Tirrell and Clay, 2006, p. 14).

One of the first tasks for a disaster mitigation collaboration is the development of community knowledge regarding the capacity of local, state, and federal government; nonprofit agencies; and faith-based institutions with mandates or missions focused on management. This inventory of existing assets should include expertise, facilities, tools, transportation machinery, and gear. The list may be very long and should have contact information and as much detail as possible. Once completed, the initial inventory provides important baseline information that can help avoid unnecessary duplication of capacity while identifying gaps, and serve as a mechanism for coordination and sharing. Because key players change constantly, maintenance of the inventory can be cumbersome. Developing a format that is accessible to many and easy to update can create a valuable resource for the community. In some localities, the telephone-based information and referral line 2-1-1 functions as a clearinghouse for disaster-related data and can be appropriate to coordinate a large and robust inventory.

The next task is to begin the process of strengthening current capacity. Ranging from public safety personnel to nonprofit staff and community volunteers, the participants in disaster mitigation collaborations may have great variation in background, experience, and knowledge about disaster mitigation and preparedness. Planners will need to develop flexible strategies that create concrete skills for this diverse audience while building a collaborative team.

Building Effective Disaster Mitigation Collaborations

Whether the collaboration is mandated by funders or other authorities or is created as a voluntary network, the keys to success remain the same: build consensus over priorities; focus on complementary rather than competitive relationships; and create strategies to communicate with participants, elected and appointed officials, other interested parties, and the general public. Once they are functioning effectively, collaborations are well positioned for creative thinking and innovative action. Critical to collaboration effectiveness is the use of consensus decision-making processes. These inclusive processes are often difficult when the professionals at the table are more used to authority-based decision making and represent known expertise (e.g., public safety officers and American Red Cross leaders and staff). However, allowing all participants to engage in information gathering and decision making lays the groundwork for working together more effectively in the face of a disaster. It is not about who is "right" but how information can be shared and coordinated to result in a better prepared and more responsive community.

One factor that increases the complexity of disaster mitigation collaboration is the need for cooperation and coordination across county and state borders, sometimes requiring multiple governments (e.g., cities, counties, and states), multiple nonprofit chapters (e.g., American Red Cross and Salvation Army), and community/civic groups (e.g., Rotary and Lions Club). However, making sure that everyone is at the table with access to the same information is an essential ingredient for success.

Creating effective cross-sector collaboration is not an easy task. Several models exist as a starting point for planning disaster mitigation collaborations.

Citizen Corps

Nearly 2000 communities have established Citizen Corps councils to strengthen collaboration between local governments, emergency service providers, and the public (www.citizencorps.gov). With the mission of "uniting

communities, preparing the nation," these local councils engage citizens in local emergency planning and training and also coordinate opportunities for citizen volunteers. Citizen Corps is coordinated by the U.S. Department of Homeland Security.

Volunteer/Hands-On Centers

Local volunteer centers or hands-on organizations play an active role in disaster mitigation as well as community preparedness and response. Volunteer centers can assist in the recruitment and placement of volunteers on an ongoing basis and at the time of a disaster when emergent volunteers appear. After a brief interview regarding their skills, experience, and availability, volunteers can be linked to an appropriate task or organization. Businesses, service clubs, and congregations can be enlisted to meet immediate and long-term recovery needs. Pre-disaster contact with a local volunteer center can speed the connection of these groups to volunteers with appropriate competencies. Disaster-related volunteer work may include tasks such as damage assessment, food preparation, language interpretation, and message delivery. Other tasks run the gamut from cleaning up to entering data, transporting people, and answering phones.

Voluntary Organizations Active in Disasters

Another model for community collaboration around disaster preparedness and mitigation is the Voluntary Organizations Active in Disasters (VOAD). The National Voluntary Organizations Active in Disasters (NVOAD) was formed after Hurricane Camille in 1969 as a strategy for coordinating, cooperating, communicating, and collaboration in the aftermath of a disaster. Today, the NVOAD lists 38 national member agencies on its website (www.nvoad.org). VOADs exist in all 50 states, as well as the District of Columbia, Puerto Rico, American Samoa, and the Commonwealth of the Northern Marianas Islands. The Tennessee VOAD (TNVOAD), for example, is a statewide consortium of nongovernmental organizations active in disaster relief. Its mission is to foster, through cooperation in mitigation and response, more effective service to people impacted by disaster. TN VOAD utilizes the resources and expertise of local volunteer centers to develop best practices tool kits. In recent years, community VOADS (cVOAD) have been formed with the same mission and a focus on building expertise, advocating policy change, improving communication patterns at the local level, and serving as a venue for important feedback and evaluation of community disaster preparedness and response.

CASE STUDY: IS MEMPHIS READY FOR "HURRICANE ELVIS"? MEMPHIS, TENNESSEEE, AND CVOAD

In late 2002, the local volunteer center in Memphis, Tennessee, received funding from the new U.S. Department of Homeland Security to form a community VOAD (Voluntary Organizations Active in Disasters). Memphis, Tennessee, has various geographic and economic features that make emergency planning important in assessing its vulnerability and assuring its viability. Located near the New Madrid fault and serving as an important distribution hub for the nation, the Memphis/Mid-South Region is vulnerable to natural and technological disasters as well as terrorist incidents. Two of the three bridges across the Mississippi River within the state of Tennessee are located within the Memphis city limits. City, county, state, and federal government offices are found within a few short blocks of the Mississippi River. The nation's largest inland naval base is found directly north of the city in Millington, Tennessee. The U.S. Coast Guard has the responsibility for monitoring all river traffic, and the U.S. Army Corps of Engineers maintains authority for management of the locks along the Mississippi River along more northerly stretches of the river before it reaches Memphis. Interstate Highway 40 traverses the city from east to west, while Interstate 55 carries traffic north and south. Barge, motor, and railroad shipping is a significant component of the city's business endeavors and important to the economic viability of the region and nation. Approximately 1 million people live in the Memphis/Shelby County metropolitan area. Many more live in surrounding counties in Tennessee, Arkansas, Mississippi, and Missouri. The predicted loss of life and damage to property and the regional economy from a major earthquake would be devastating (Charlier, 2005).

The creation of a VOAD as a community collaboration of nonprofit and faith-based organizations with missions on disaster management moved very quickly through the classic stages of collaborative development to play an important role in information sharing and problem solving. The membership of the collaborative was far reaching, including traditional disaster response agencies such as the American Red Cross and the Salvation Army; a broad group of faith-based initiatives including the Episcopal Diocese of West Tennessee, Southern Baptist Disaster Relief, and the United Methodist Committee on Relief; and other nonprofits including Senior Services, HandsOn Memphis, Search Dog South, and United Way of the Mid-South. As the group with the funding, Volunteer Memphis served in the role of facilitator and communication manager.

The first test for Memphis cVOAD came with a weather-related catastrophe on July 22, 2003. A windstorm, locally labeled "Hurricane Elvis," crossed the Mississippi River with winds clocked at 120 miles per hour, sending trees to the ground and everything not secured up in the air. Major roads were blocked and 306,000 homes and businesses lost power. The local emergency management agency (EMA) did not declare the event a

disaster until July 24, at 12:01 a.m. Until this time, first responders acted without support and many nonprofits provided services prior to official activation. Complicating the confusion was that local elected officials established multiple information hotlines. In the meantime, the cVOAD agencies jumped to action, brainstorming and communicating as much as possible without access to computers.

Less than a month after the windstorm, the cVOAD agencies met to critique the response, making a series of recommendations to the local EMA, city and county mayors, and the Department of Homeland Security:

- A central source for information and referral was needed. (Response: The Memphis Library System now serves in this role in the official Emergency Management Plan).
- There was a need to assist every organization and individual home to have its own disaster plan. (Response: Local EMA has emphasized CERT training throughout Shelby County. A local foundation has funded a baseline survey on resident preparedness and facilitated media collaboration to fund/implement preparedness campaign.)
- There was a need to train more than the estimated number of volunteers. Volunteers must first take care of their own families and homes before they are available to play their volunteer role. (Response: Ongoing role for cVOAD to coordinate training opportunities.)

For the next few years, the cVOAD had a strong volunteer structure and met regularly for communication and continued capacity building. However, once the volunteer center's grant expired and they no longer provided management support, the volunteer leadership was unable to maintain momentum. Following Hurricanes Katrina and Rita in August 2005, many of the cVOAD agencies were called in to action. For the past few years, ongoing efforts to broaden and reinvigorate the cVOAD membership, formalize the organization by clarifying bylaws, and continue regular programming to build emergency management capacity have struggled.

Farazmand (2001, p. 3) notes that "a central feature of all crises is a sense of urgency.... Situations change so dramatically and so rapidly that no one seems to be able to predict the chain of events or the possible outcomes." Thus, the ultimate goal of creating and maintaining local disaster management collaborations is to create the capacity for a locality to avoid local crises or disasters when possible and to manage them effectively when they do occur. Citizen Corps councils, local volunteer centers, and community VOADs offer models for community collaboration around disaster mitigation and preparedness. Collaboration can be a useful tool for increasing community-wide understanding and increasing organization and individual-level planning and action.

Summary

In the past decade, smart practice research related to volunteers and the need for collaboration in disaster management has grown significantly and is ongoing. Yet, communities are still learning the basics—the who, what, when, and how—of collaboration in this important policy area. The good news is that many of the players with solid expertise and proven capacity are in place, including local, state, and federal emergency management; traditional nonprofits like the American Red Cross and the Salvation Army; and a diverse set of religious institutions, civic groups, and professional associations. In addition, we know that individuals are generous with their time and donations, particularly in times of crisis. The task, then, is to build a strong collaborative team that includes all of these actors in a given community to advance public safety, disaster mitigation, and preparedness. In a nutshell, this requires the following:

- Creation of a vision for dynamic, comprehensive, community-wide mitigation, and preparedness. Planning of this magnitude requires ongoing processes and regular reinventions through workshops and conferences to create an evolving vision for operations planning and action.
- Inclusive approach to involving participants, identifying problems, and generating solutions at policy, organization, and individual levels. All types of organizations should be involved, including agencies typically charged with mitigation and post-disaster responsibilities as well as nontraditional participants such as private companies, religious institutions, civic groups, professional associations, and the media. Bringing these diverse groups together mobilizes the greatest number of needed volunteers across socioeconomic and culture lines.
- Continued development of volunteers through training opportunities, active utilization in mitigation activities, and testing of preparedness and response through tabletop scenarios and full-blown mock disaster exercises. With a continuous improvement perspective, all of these tactics increase the capacity of the volunteers, thereby increasing their value to nonprofit organizations and communities. At the same time, continued involvement increases volunteer retention by building commitment to the goal of a resilient community.

Communities are made up of systems (e.g., medical, transportation, education, communications, and economic) that are inextricably linked together. During a time of emergency when any one of these systems breaks down, it adversely affects the whole community—even systems that were properly prepared (Gallis, 2009). As such, strengthening the capacity of communities

for disaster mitigation and preparedness, particularly through the use of volunteers, is crucial. Building collaborations around these important functions is one strategy for increasing capacity while accomplishing important tasks. An important positive consequence of "thinking big" about the use of volunteers is that each volunteer becomes an advocate for mitigation and preparedness, taking the message to their family, friends, neighbors, colleagues, and elected officials. The goal of a prepared community is ambitious, but well within the reach if volunteers are effectively used.

End-of-Chapter Questions

1. Describe some sources for recruiting volunteers for a community-wide hazard mitigation effort.
2. Discuss the key steps for designing and implementing an effective volunteer program for emergency management.
3. Discuss the challenges of using volunteers in disaster mitigation and the strategies for overcoming these challenges.
4. Describe the important tasks for building community-wide disaster mitigation collaboration.
5. The case study tells the story of the Memphis cVOAD. Although the cVOAD initially played an important and useful role, it is now struggling. What happened that changed the status of the organization? What suggestions do you have for increasing its effectiveness?

References

Agranoff, R., & McGuire, M. (2001). After the network is formed: Process, power, and performance. In M. P. Mandell (Ed.), *Getting results through collaboration: Networks and network structures for public policy and management* (pp. 11–29). Westport, CT: Quorum Books.

Brudney, J. (2005). Designing and managing volunteer programs. In R. Herman et al. (Eds.), *The Jossey Bass handbook of nonprofit leadership and management* (pp. 310–343). San Francisco, CA: Jossey Bass Publishers.

Carley, K. M., & Harrald, J. R. (1997). Organizational learning under fire: Theory and practice. *American Behavioral Scientist, 40,* 310–332.

Charlier, T. (2005, December 13). Quake safety lost in layers. *The Commercial Appeal,* pp. A1, A7.

Comerio, M. C. (1998). *Disaster Hits Home: New Policy for Urban Housing Recovery.* Berkeley, CA: University of California Press.

Corporation for National and Community Service (CNCS) (2009). *Volunteering in American research highlights.* Retrieved from http://www.volunteeringinamerica.gov/assets/resources/VolunteeringInAmericaResearchHighlights.pdf.

Ellis, S. J. (2001). *The Volunteer Recruitment and Membership Development Book.* Philadelphia, PA: Energize, Inc.

Farazmand, A. (2001). Introduction: Crisis and emergency management. In A. Farazmand (Ed.), *Handbook of crisis and emergency management* (pp. 1–10). New York, NY: Marcel Dekker.

Gallis, M. (2009). Regional frameworks for resiliency and effective response. In *Controlling our own destinies: Proactive steps for resilient communities* (pp. 10–12). Washington, DC: Business Civic Leadership Center, U.S. Chamber of Commerce. Retrieved from http://bclc.uschamber.com/sites/default/files/documents/files/2009%20Disaster%20report%20PDF.pdf

Gillespie, D. (1993). *Partnerships for Community Preparedness.* Boulder, CO: Institute of Behavioral Science, University of Colorado.

Grossman, J. B., & Furano, K. (2002, July). Making the most of volunteers. P/PV Briefs.

Koenig, H. G. (2006). *In The Wake of Disaster: Religious Responses to Terrorism and Catastrophe.* West Conshohocken, PA: Templeton Foundation Press.

Kunzelman, M. (2006, February 17). On coast, faith-based groups carry the load—From Amish to Islam: 'It's God's work.' Commerical Appeal, A5.

McCurley, S. (2005). Keeping the community involved: Recruiting and retaining volunteers. In R. Herman et al. (Eds.), *The Jossey Bass handbook of nonprofit leadership and management* (pp. 587–622). San Francisco, CA: Jossey Bass Publishers.

McKinney, H. J. (1995). *The Development of Local Public Services, 1650–1860: Lessons from Middletown, Connecticut.* Westport, CT: Greenwood Press.

Norris-Tirrell, D., & Clay, J. (2006). Collaborative planning as a tool for strengthening local emergency management. *Journal of Public Management and Social Policy, 12*(1), 25–36.

Norris-Tirrell, D., & Clay, J. (2010). *Strategic Collaboration in Public and Nonprofit Administration: A Practice-Based Approach to Solving Shared Problems.* New York, NY: Taylor and Francis Publishers.

Schroeder, A. D., Wamsley, G. L., & Ward, R. (2000). The evolution of emergency management in America. In A. Farazmand (Ed.), *Handbook of crisis and emergency management* (pp. 283–292). New York, NY: Marcel Dekker.

Stephens, H. W., & Grant, G. O. (2001). A new use for an old model: Continuity of government as a framework for local emergency managers. In A. Farazmand (Ed.), *Handbook of crisis and emergency management* (pp. 283–292). New York, NY: Marcel Dekker.

Tocqueville, A. de. (1945, originally published in 1840). *Democracy in America* (Vol. 2, H. Reeve, Trans.). New York, NY: Random House.

Ward, R., Wamsley, G., Schroeder, A., & Robins, D. (2000). Network organizational development in the public sector: A case study of the Federal Emergency Management Administration (FEMA). *Journal of the American Society for Information Science, 51*(11), 1018–1032.

Wise, C. R. (2002). Organizing for homeland security. *Public Administration Review, 62*(2), 131–144.

Chapter 14

Area Analyses

Erin Patton Merrick and Maggie Olivier

Contents

Learning Objectives

- Understand what a repetitive loss area analysis (RLAA) is.
- Understand the ways in which RLAAs promote mitigation.
- Understand the different approaches to completing an RLAA.

Introduction

This chapter focuses on RLAA as a mitigation tool for both local officials and residents. The RLAA explores areas that have concentrations of repetitive loss (RL) properties to determine the causes of flooding, and examines a wide variety of mitigation measures to reduce such repetitive flood losses, including those not funded by a grant program.

The RLAA assists communities not only in understanding the flooding issues surrounding their RL areas but also in examining alternative mitigation measures to reduce flood claims. The National Flood Insurance Program (NFIP) imposes floodplain development regulations on all communities that wish to participate in its flood insurance program, in an effort to keep flood insurance premiums for everyone lower than the market rate. The stricter the development regulations the lower the likelihood of a flood insurance claim and the more affordable the insurance premium.

An RL property can be defined as any NFIP-insured property for which two or more flood insurance claims of $1000 or more have been paid within any rolling 10-year period since 1978. This means that a claim filed for a property in 1982 for $1000 and one filed in 1990 for $1500 would cause that property to be identified by Federal Emergency Management Agency (FEMA) as an RL property.

There is another segment of RL properties that is considered to be at greater risk of loss than others. These are called severe RL (SRL) properties. An SRL property can be defined as a single- or multiple-family residence that has had four or more claims of $5000 or more, or two claims that cumulatively exceed the building's fair market value. Under either qualification, two of the claims must be within a rolling 10-year period and at least 10 days apart.

Jefferson and Orleans parishes in Louisiana are the top two areas in the country as far as the number of RL properties is concerned. According to the "Strategic Plan Evaluation Repetitive Loss Strategy" draft report released by the Community Rating System's (CRS) Repetitive Loss Committee, these two parishes house 11,866 (43.54%) of the 27,250 RL properties in the country. It is critical that local governments address these overwhelming RL numbers. The RLAA does just this. Area analyses result in increased awareness of an area's cause(s) of flooding and offer possible solutions that reduce overall flood risk, reduce the cost of repairing flood damage, and ultimately keep residents safe.

FEMA Region VI has funded the University of New Orleans Center for Hazards Assessment, Response and Technology (UNO-CHART) to conduct RLAAs in some Louisiana and Texas communities. UNO-CHART has completed 14 RLAAs and six follow-up analyses as of this printing.

UNO-CHART is an applied social science research center that studies mitigation, specifically flood mitigation, on the spectrum of individual home structures to the community as a whole. Founded in 2001, this university-based center strives to enhance the knowledge of Louisiana communities and aid in increasing the understanding and ability of the residents to implement mitigation activities as a method of protecting themselves, as well as managing the risk to which the state and its residents are vulnerable. Collaborating with community organizations and local officials has helped UNO-CHART to emphasize the importance of issues around safety. This collaborative effort assists in spreading the message to even the most vulnerable populations around the state.

UNO-CHART prides itself in training graduate research assistants in disaster fields and guiding them through tasks that are representative of the types of tasks they may encounter in a professional setting. The center supports social scientists from a multitude of disciplines including, but not limited to, sociology, political science, public administration, urban planning, and anthropology. In addition, UNO-CHART employs scientists from applied physical sciences and civil engineers. Together, the collaborative team can contribute to a variety of funded projects. The center has always operated with the support of grants from federal, state, and local government entities, as well as foundations, for its work in mitigation and storm risk reduction.

Risk

The landmass that is Louisiana was formed on, around, and by water. As the City of New Orleans was created, floodwalls and levees were constructed to redirect the Mississippi River and other waterways. The human-made creations encouraged development near the water. The water became a vital component to the residents' way of life, whether it was for their livelihood, travel, shipping, or pastimes. Whatever the reason, the water encouraged development.

As more and more people build their homes near the water and behind levees, flood risk grows. This phenomenon is called the "levee effect." More and more people build homes and neighborhoods right outside the levees because of the space available for development and the erroneous assumption that it is safe (Kates et al., 2006). Continued high-volume development behind levees exacerbates the burden to the area when disaster strikes because new and existing developments will sustain damage.

Flood risks are often determined by watershed processes. These processes include rainfall intensity and duration, slope of the ground, area, land cover, the ability of the ground to absorb water, and obstructions along watercourses that impede flow. Each of these processes can be calculated for a more accurate determination of an area's flood risk.

Being informed of flood risks can aid decision making at all levels, from the individual to the federal government, when it comes to development. For homeowners, the decision could be to elevate a home. For a city, the decision could be to limit building permits. For the parish or county, acquisition of the whole neighborhood may be the answer. Without flood insurance studies or flood insurance rate maps (FIRMs), development could be allowed anywhere, possibly even in the most at-risk areas.

National Flood Insurance Program

The National Flood Insurance Act of 1968 created the NFIP as a mechanism for providing financial assistance to flood victims. The NFIP provides government-backed flood insurance to both homeowners and businesses who want it. FEMA is the federal agency in charge of the management of the NFIP. There are more than 90 private insurance companies that write flood insurance policies for the NFIP. Since 1968, there has been reform legislation to improve the program and its coverage.

In 1973, the Flood Disaster Protection Act ushered in the mandatory-purchase requirement for all properties that were in areas deemed susceptible to flooding and purchased using federally backed mortgages. The National Flood Insurance Reform Act of 1994 increased the mandatory-purchase requirements for all properties within designated special flood hazard areas (SFHAs) that carried mortgages from federally backed lenders. An SFHA is the land area anticipated to be covered by waters during a flood as indicated by NFIP maps. Floodplain management regulations of the NFIP must be enforced and flood insurance coverage is mandated within the SFHA. In 2004, the Bunning–Bereuter–Blumenauer Flood Insurance Act created and authorized grant programs that mitigate structures experiencing repetitive flood losses.

A community's participation in the NFIP is not mandatory. However, communities not in the NFIP do not gain the benefits of federally backed flood insurance. There are approximately more than 20,000 communities currently participating in the NFIP (GAO, 2010). To participate, communities must adopt and enforce floodplain management regulations, including the regulation of new development within the floodplain(s) and with the end goal of reducing flood losses.

Congress and FEMA intended the NFIP to be funded by premiums paid into the program by policyholders. However, recent catastrophic losses have

resulted in the NFIP borrowing money from the United States Department of the Treasury to pay claims. To date, the NFIP is indebted to the U.S. Treasury by approximately $18.8 billion (GAO, 2010). The NFIP faces the daunting task of providing affordable flood insurance while paying out claims to properties that may not be paying the proper "risk-based" premium.

Certain homeowners qualify for subsidized rates that do not reflect actual flood risk. Examples of properties that qualify for a subsidized rate include those properties constructed prior to the Flood Insurance Reform Act (FIRA) of 1973. These properties are known as "pre-FIRM." According to a report published by the Government Accountability Office (GAO), nearly 25% of policyholders pay a subsidized premium (GAO, 2010).

A pre-FIRM structure was built before the flood risk had been determined. A pre-FIRM structure must be brought into compliance once that structure is declared substantially damaged. Substantial damage occurs when the cost of repairing the structure reaches or surpasses 50% of the fair market value of the structure before it was damaged. A substantial damage declaration can come as a result of any hazard.

A property that has an NFIP policy may also be "grandfathered." A grandfathered rate is given to properties that were built in full compliance at the time but are in areas with updated risk determinations, usually due to a new flood insurance rate map (FIRM) being published. These subsidized and grandfathered rates are just small examples of the financial burden the NFIP must bear in carrying out its duties to provide affordable flood insurance.

Repetitive Loss Properties and the Cost to the National Flood Insurance Program

Another problem facing the NFIP is that of RL and SRL properties. Just as the NFIP cannot deny coverage to a building that is considered to be in a high-risk area, it cannot deny coverage to a repetitively flooded structure. An RL property is any NFIP-insured structure that has had two or more claims of $1000 or more in any rolling 10-year period since 1978.

There is an additional class of RL property that was created with the Flood Insurance Reform Act of 2004. An SRL property is a single- or multiple-family structure that has had four or more claims of $5000 or more, or two claims that cumulatively exceed the reported value of the building in any rolling 10-year period. Since 1978, RL and SRL properties have accounted for over $9 billion in flood insurance claims. In other words, although RL properties only account for 1% of all flood insurance policies currently in effect, they account for 25%–30% of all flood insurance claims (GAO, 2010).

With RL properties projected to account for 15%–20% of future losses to the NFIP, it becomes evident that more needs to be done to protect these properties from flooding. The NFIP imposes minimum requirements for the management of its nation's floodplains. By taking on extra floodplain management rules and regulations, community officials can make concrete steps toward reducing their citizens' flood risks and bringing down the cost of flood insurance in their communities.

National Flood Insurance Program and the Community Rating System

As mentioned, the NFIP offers flood insurance to communities that adopt and comply with minimum standards set forth by the NFIP for floodplain management. For communities that exceed minimum standards, the NFIP recognizes and rewards them with participation in the CRS. The CRS is a voluntary program that offers communities who are willing to adopt and enforce higher floodplain regulations and standards "credit points" for activities believed to reduce flooding. Credit points result in real-life savings on flood insurance premiums.

By completing some or all of the 18 floodplain management activities, credit points are assigned to a community, leading to a "class" designation. There are 10 CRS classes (1 to 10) and each class carries with it increased flood insurance discounts (Table 14.1). To participate in the CRS, a community that is in the NFIP completes the application and documents some or

TABLE 14.1 CRS classes by premium discounts

	Flood Insurance Premium Discount	
CRS Class	SFHA	Non-SFHA
1	45%	10%
2	40%	10%
3	35%	10%
4	30%	10%
5	25%	10%
6	20%	10%
7	15%	5%
8	10%	5%
9	5%	5%
10	0%	0%

all of the 18 different floodplain management activities available for credit in the CRS program.

The CRS has prerequisites for communities that have one or more RL properties (an RL community) in order to remain in good standing. One such prerequisite is that the RL community must review an annual RL list provided by FEMA to check the accuracy of addresses, the location of the property (in relation to the community's corporate limits), and if the property has been mitigated to reduce flood risk. The participating community must complete the necessary paperwork and submit it in order to document the accuracy of the FEMA-issued RL list.

Communities that have one or more RL property are divided into categories A, B, or C, as each designation carries with it certain responsibilities that pertain to RL properties. If a community has no RL properties, or if those properties have been mitigated, they are considered to be a Category A community. Category A communities have no prerequisites other than making sure the RL list is updated annually, if appropriate. If a community has one or more but fewer than 10 RL properties, it is considered a Category B community. A Category B community must perform the following:

- Review the RL problem and describe it.
- Develop a map of the RL area(s).
- Develop an RL address list and note which ones have been mitigated.
- Assume a yearly outreach project for those RL properties.

A community with more than 10 RL properties is considered a Category C community. Category C communities must complete the same projects as Category B communities and must prepare a floodplain management plan or area analyses for the RL areas. This activity is mandatory for Category C communities. The NFIP recognizes the financial burden that RL properties bring to residents in a community and wishes to require that communities address these properties through hazard mitigation planning. The RLAAs are worth credit points based on different CRS activities:

- 410 Additional Flood Data
- 430 Higher Regulatory Standards
- 440 Flood Data Maintenance
- 510 Floodplain Management Planning
- 520 Acquisition and Relocation
- 530 Flood Protection

Whether used to keep a community in good standing with the CRS or to address the repetitive flooding in an area, RLAAs are a mitigation tool that every RL community should utilize. In the following section, we examine the RLAA according to the FEMA-prescribed process and explain the importance of focusing on an RL area as a whole.

Selecting an Area: Area versus Buildings

For mitigation to be truly effective, it should cover an area of properties and not individual properties. For example, consider a street block with 10 houses that are slab-on-grade. Three houses employ a noticeable mitigation measure, such as elevation. Those three houses will stand out, given their new height in the midst of the other seven houses on the block. This not only gives the neighborhood a checkered look but can also lower the value of the property and cause more flooding for the next-door neighbor.

Note that properties found on the RL list are properties that have flood insurance claims. Properties that do not have flood insurance could flood repeatedly but are never listed and may not be considered as having a flooding issue. Using the "area" concept can benefit homeowners who do not have flood insurance through improved drainage systems among other large mitigation projects that may be used to correct flooding problems in a neighborhood where multiple homeowners do have insurance.

It is a common misconception that RL properties are only found in the more risky A, AE, V, or VE zones. This is simply not true. It is noted that RL properties are often found in the less risky X or X500 zones, as most FIRMs were completed in the late 1970s and 1980s, and the physical landscape has since changed. Whether because growth has led to an increase in impervious surfaces such as roofs and pavement or the floodplain has expanded naturally, the flood risk has likely changed over time. It is important to understand that repetitive flood insurance claims figures often understate the flooding problem for various reasons:

1. The NFIP records do not include claims data from before 1978, so there could have been additional losses not included in FEMA's RL list.
2. Policyholders may not have submitted claims for smaller floods for fear of such claims affecting their coverage or their premium rates.
3. There could be other properties that have been repetitively flooded for which the owners did not submit claims, or did not have flood insurance at the time of flooding.

Steps of Repetitive Loss Area Analysis: Federal Emergency Management Agency–Prescribed Process

Generally, an area analysis follows a FEMA-prescribed five-step process. However, UNO-CHART team has enhanced the five-step process by adding two more steps: (1) a preliminary comprehensive area selection step and (2) an ongoing collaborative relationship with the neighborhood after the

report is presented to the stakeholders. During the area-selection process, information about an area is reviewed, including the repetitive flood loss claims data as well as other relevant information about the neighborhood, such as its flooding history and the interest of its residents in learning more about flood mitigation. This is done through a collaborative effort with FEMA, local officials, and residents.

Once a neighborhood is selected, a smaller subset of properties within the neighborhood is selected as the analysis area based on the previously stated criteria, although the goal is to engage the entire neighborhood. Once the report and meetings are complete, the ongoing collaborative relationship is offered to the selected community. UNO-CHART will continually be available to provide homeowners with information concerning mitigation measures, policy issues, or other flooding-related matters as requested; if funding allows, a "follow-up" with the community will be conducted later.

Summary of Steps

Potential areas to be analyzed are discussed and reviewed in collaboration with local officials and residents using criteria that would suggest the need for risk reduction and the potential effectiveness of the effort. Below are the five FEMA-prescribed steps:

Step 1: Advise all property owners in the repeatedly flooded area that the analysis will be conducted.

Step 2: Collect data on the analysis area and each building in the identified study area within the neighborhood to determine the cause(s) of RLs.

Step 3: Review alternative mitigation approaches and determine whether any property-protection measures or drainage improvements are feasible.

Step 4: Contact agencies or organizations that may have plans that could affect the cause or impacts of the flooding.

Step 5: Document the findings, including information gathered from agencies and organizations, and relevant maps of the analysis area.

UNO-CHART offers an ongoing relationship with the community to provide information about flooding issues as needed. Sometimes, a follow-up visit is conducted. The reasoning for the follow-up is to encourage and support efforts to reduce flooding risk that might be initiated as a result of the initial area-analysis effort. Below are the FEMA prescribed five-steps:

Selecting the boundaries for the RL area to be analyzed presents a challenge. The analyst must select an area that best represents the larger area that is sized accurately to include the full range of flooding issues. As an

applied social science research center, UNO-CHART executes research methods systematically and collaborates with the community, maintaining a relationship with the area throughout and after the document has been created.

To begin the process of selecting an area, UNO-CHART gathers data from the Repetitive Loss Portal created by its partner Solutient, New Orleans, Louisiana, a technology contractor. The Portal provides a mapping tool that assists team members in locating high concentrations of RL and/or SRL properties. Using this method, the team then chooses several contiguous blocks of properties that serve as the study area and works with any active neighborhood associations and local officials in that area to get residents' approval and involvement so that they can have an active voice throughout the process.

UNO-CHART selection process differs from the requirements for communities seeking CRS credit. In order to qualify for CRS credit, the community cannot simply choose an area to analyze; the community must cover all the RL areas within its jurisdiction, in separate analyses if necessary. If multiple analyses are needed, the community can do them consecutively. The community must also complete yearly progress reports on the recommendations in the analysis and submit the progress reports to maintain credit.

Community officials interested in learning more about the CRS requirements for conducting RLAAs should consult the *CRS Coordinator's Manual.* The FEMA-prescribed five-step process is the same process followed by communities completing RLAAs for CRS credit. These steps do not need to be followed in any particular order.

Step 1: Neighborhood Notification

The first step of the FEMA five-step process is to advise the neighborhood about a project. The RLAA will include detailed information on how this notification is conducted.

As UNO-CHART conducts this step, a letter introduces UNO-CHART as a collaborator with the local government and provides a general time line for the study. This letter to residents explains their role in the process. The letter will say on "this date," the "chosen city" sent a notice to the homeowners introducing them to the project and informing them that researchers from UNO-CHART will be collecting data about their neighborhood.

A data sheet to be completed by the homeowners is included with the letter. The data sheet allows homeowners to share their flooding history with UNO-CHART, providing details that would otherwise be inaccessible. Furthermore, the data sheets bring residents into the process and allow them to gain a stake in the outcome. Copies of a letter and data sheet appear in this chapter after the Conclusion in Figures 14.3 and 14.4.

Step 2: Data Collection

The second step in the process is the collection of data relevant to flooding (i.e., the properties exposed to flooding and cause(s) of the repetitive damage). The data is collected by coordinating with several agencies and departments across multiple scales of data sources. Five primary sources of data and information include the following:

1. Community plans and studies
2. Flood insurance data
3. Drainage information
4. Flooding experiences of property owners
5. On-site data collection

They are explained as follows:

Community plans and studies: Floodplain or flood damage reduction ordinances, hazard mitigation plans, and land-use plans exemplify typical sources of information. There may be other plans or studies that would fall under this category as well, including watershed management plans. The focus here is to examine all plans or studies that have previously addressed or identified flooding problems or prevention activities in the study area.

Flood insurance data: This data includes the FIRM for the area, as well as the digital FIRMs (DFIRMs) where applicable. FEMA is updating the FIRMs for communities throughout the country. As part of the FEMA Map Modernization Plan, the Army Corps has been charged with updating and developing DFIRMs. Most FIRMs were created back in the 1970s and 1980s, but the floodplains in many areas have changed over the years: Increased development and improved drainage and flood protection measures have changed the shape of floodplains everywhere. By examining the FIRM or DFIRM for the community under analysis, a better understanding of the flooding situation is gained.

Drainage information: Similar to community plans and studies, this source of data examines any new drainage plans that may be in the works that would have an effect on flooding. This includes plans that may increase or decrease the frequency and severity of flooding. The goal here is to explore what has been done and what is being planned in order to be able to give solid recommendations to the community and homeowners to mitigate flooding.

Flooding experience of homeowners: This data is documented by the homeowners' data sheets that accompany the notification letters sent to every home in the study area. During the fieldwork process, some homeowners may approach the researchers in order to assess

their purpose and relay some information on the flooding history in the area. The purpose of obtaining and analyzing the experience of homeowners is to gain a clearer picture and "inside" information on the flooding situation in a study area. The homeowners in study areas often have valuable inside information that cannot be gained from the studies and reports that are analyzed.

On-site data collection: The fieldwork phase of the analysis yields data on the study area; the number of homes, types of structures, foundation conditions, height of a structure above grade and street, and photographs of homes are all examples of the types of information collected. UNO-CHART has modeled this information gathering on the National Flood Mitigation Data Collection Tool (NFMDCT) created by FEMA in order to assist communities seeking CRS credit. Researchers can gather all this information from the street or even their vehicles, and it is never necessary to enter the property or disturb the residents. An example of fieldwork is included in this chapter after the Conclusion in Figure 14.5.

Step 3: Alternative Mitigation Measures

Reviewing the drainage system, the flooding problem, and the types and condition of the buildings in the study area lead to the third step in the area analysis procedure—a review of alternative mitigation approaches to protect properties from future flood damage. Property owners should look at these alternatives but understand that they are not all guaranteed to provide protection from all floods. The following eight approaches are typically analyzed:

1. Drainage improvements
2. Acquisition of properties in the hazardous area
3. Elevating the houses above the 100-year flood level
4. Reconstruction
5. Constructing small levees or floodwalls around one or more houses
6. Dry floodproofing
7. Development regulations that reduce flood risks
8. Purchasing flood insurance coverage on buildings

Each approach has its pros and cons. Drainage improvements and development regulations need to be implemented by the city or parish/county. Property owners can implement the other measures, but city or parish/county funding can help, especially with acquisition and elevation where a portion of the cost must come from nonfederal sources. The approaches are explained as follows:

(a) (b)

FIGURE 14.1 An example of a homeowner-installed drainage channel to drain the rear of the yard to the street. (a) The owner ran perforated plastic drainage pipe around his patio in the back yard. Inlets collect water in the yard and from the downspouts. The drain pipes run to a solid plastic pipe that goes around the house and collects water from a similar pipe installed by the neighbor. (b) Water is then carried by the common pipe to the street.

Drainage improvements: These are determined by the problem statement and are site-specific. If the data suggests flooding is most often caused by poor drainage in an area, improving the drainage system is advised (Figure 14.1).

Acquisition of properties in the hazardous area: This measure involves buying one or more properties and clearing the site of development. If there is no building subject to flooding, there is no flood damage. Acquisitions are usually recommended where the flood hazard is so great or so frequent that it is not safe to leave the structures on the site.

Elevating the houses above the 100-year flood level: Raising the structures above the flood level is generally viewed as the best flood protection measure, short of removing the building from the floodplain. When a building is elevated, most parts of the building that can be damaged and the building's contents are high and dry during a flood; the floodwater flows under the floor instead of into the structure. Houses can be elevated on fill, posts/piles, or a crawl space. A house elevated on fill requires adding a specific type of dirt, called "structural fill," to a lot and building the house on top of the added dirt. Also, according to the Unified Development Code, fill can only be used if the use of such fill is mitigated by excavation and an engineering report states that the runoff created by the fill will not flood neighboring properties. A house elevated on posts/piles is either built or raised on a foundation of piers that are driven into the ground and rise high enough to elevate the house above the flood level. A house elevated on a crawl space is built or raised on a wall-like foundation

that elevates the house above expected flood levels. If a crawl space is used, it is important to include vents that are appropriately sized, that is, 1 in.^{2} for each square foot of the building's footprint.

Reconstruction: If a building is deemed unable to withstand the elevation process, demolishing the structure and replacing it with a new, safer structure is an option for the homeowner. The new structure will meet or exceed all flood and wind protection codes. This was formerly known as "demo/rebuild" and is now called "mitigation reconstruction." This option is available to homeowners under the SRL program.

Constructing small levees or floodwalls around one or more houses: Small floodwalls, levees, or berms could be constructed around one or more properties. Such barriers are not recommended for flood depths greater than 3 ft. Floodwalls are appropriate for homes with flood depths of less than 3 ft because of the large lot sizes commonly found in the area. If a floodwall is built around a house, it is important to include a sump pump with a backup generator so that rainwater can be pumped to the outside of the protected space. A flood prevention and floodplain management variance request form should be completed and submitted to the appropriate authorities prior to building the barrier.

If a homeowner is considering constructing a floodwall, there are certain requirements that must be considered:

- A method to close openings, such as the driveway. Generally, this requires "human intervention," meaning someone needs to be available and have enough time to take action.
- A system to prevent sanitary sewer backup from flowing into the building, such as a backflow valve.
- A system of drain tiles (perforated pipes) that collects water that falls or seeps into the protected area and sends it to a collecting basin or sump.
- A sump pump to send the collected water outside the barrier.
- Power to operate the sump pump around the clock during a storm.

Dry floodproofing: This measure keeps floodwaters out of a building by steps taken to protect the building directly. Walls are coated with waterproofing compounds or plastic sheeting. Openings (doors, windows, and vents) are closed, either permanently or with removable shields and sandbags. Dry floodproofing employs the building itself as part of the barrier to the passage of floodwaters and, therefore, this technique is recommended only for buildings with noncracked slab foundations, because the solid slab foundation of the building prevents floodwaters from entering the building from below. Also, even if the building is in sound condition, tests by the

U.S. Army Corps of Engineers have shown that dry floodproofing should not be used for depths greater than 3 ft over the floor because water pressure on the structure can collapse the walls and/or buckle the floor. Dry floodproofing is a mitigation technique that is appropriate for an area where flood depths do not exceed 3 ft.

Not all parts of a building need to be floodproofed. It is difficult to floodproof a garage door, for example, so many owners let the garage flood and floodproof the walls between the garage and the rest of the house. Appliances, electrical outlets, and other damage-prone materials located in the garage should be elevated above expected flood levels.

Development regulations that reduce flood risk: Many communities have adopted ordinances, deed restrictions, or neighborhood covenants that are intended to promote safety and order. Often, these restrictions may limit an owner's freedom to do whatever he or she pleases with the property or building. These restrictions can be enforced at the city level and/or the neighborhood level.

Many communities in flat areas with drainage problems require all new buildings to have their lowest floors elevated to a specified height above the street. This allows the streets to collect and store stormwater that cannot drain away fast enough, without flooding homes.

Ironically, neighborhood covenants or deed restrictions regulating development within a subdivision are intended to help the neighborhood maintain a sense of solidarity, distinct character, and residential quality. In certain instances, these deed restrictions may hinder residents' plans for a flood mitigation project.

The homeowners association can amend these covenants to allow for mitigation measures and continue to maintain a positive, unified neighborhood look by promoting crawl space–elevated foundations and allowing small floodwalls in front yards, to name a few examples.

Purchasing flood insurance coverage on buildings: Although it is not a mitigation measure that reduces property damage from a flood, an insurance policy from the NFIP has the following advantages for the homeowner:

- A flood insurance policy reduces a homeowner's financial expenses when flooding occurs.
- It is an excellent backup for a floodwall or elevation project in cases where the flood is higher than the protection level, as it helps transfer the financial risk.
- Repetitive, shallow flooding is unlikely to reach conditions severe enough for a disaster declaration, which allows for additional financial support. Therefore, flood insurance may be the only source of assistance that helps owners of damaged property to pay for cleanup and repairs.

TABLE 14.2 Summary of the alternative mitigation measures

Measures	Advantages	Disadvantages
Drainage Improvements	Little disruption of neighborhood Protects yards	May not work for large storms Dependent on free flowing channels
Acquisition	100% flood protection	High cost Need source of non-FEMA cost share
Elevation	More secure flood protection Flood insurance rate reduction	High cost Need source of non-FEMA cost share
Mitigation Reconstruction	More secure flood protection Flood insurance rate reduction	High cost Need source of non-FEMA cost share
Floodwalls	Effective for shallow flooding Soil types in Greenwell Springs are appropriate for floodwalls	Subject to seepage if water stays up for a long time No available funding
Dry Floodproofing	Low cost Effective for shallow flooding on slab foundations	Exposes homes to wall/floor damage Subject to seepage if water stays up for a long time No available funding
Flood Insurance	Always in effect Works for all flood levels Under ICC, can be a source of funds for elevation or mitigation reconstruction	Does not prevent flood damage (but does provide funds for repairs)

- Once a policy goes into effect, there is no need for human intervention except to pay the premium.
- Coverage is available for the contents of a home as well as the structure.
- Renters can buy contents coverage, even if the building owner does not buy coverage for the structure itself.

The advantages and disadvantages of each of these measures are summarized in Table 14.2.

Step 4: Coordination

The fourth step of the FEMA-prescribed process is coordination, but this is something that is happening from the beginning. In most municipalities, floodplain management responsibilities are spread over various local-level offices and departments, such as community development, public works,

public services, water boards, and engineering departments are examples. It does not cover the state and federal levels, such as the state hazard mitigation office, U.S. Army Corps of Engineers, and council of governments, as well as the various FEMA regions and offices.

It is easy to see that there are potentially many key players at the table, and it can be far too easy to leave someone off the list. This is why coordination is essential to area analysis. UNO-CHART begins the analysis process by meeting and discussing the project with FEMA officials to determine what areas have gained their attention. Most local officials will know which areas in their jurisdiction need attention and will not initiate coordination with FEMA. They may opt to bring in FEMA later in the process; this is acceptable.

Once an area is selected, local officials in charge of the analysis should consult any agency or department that may be developing plans that would affect flooding. As mentioned in the previous paragraph, there are many essential people and organizations who are key players in the area analysis, and coordination with each is important. The best way to go about coordinating with all these offices and groups is during data collection. In the data collection step, it becomes more evident which groups need to be contacted in order to receive the necessary information.

Problem Statement

Based on data collected from a study area, a problem statement is developed to summarize the flooding issues of the area and determine recommendations for residents and local officials to mitigate their flood losses. The problem statement identifies the key issues at work that are contributing to the repetitive flooding and are usually given in a bullet point format. The problem statement can best be thought of as an executive summary for the area analysis; it gets to the "meat" of the issues and describes them in summary fashion.

The following is an example of a problem statement taken from the RLAA of the City of Alvin, Texas:

> Based on the data collected from the five sources of information (community reports and plans, flood insurance data, drainage information, the property owners, and onsite surveying), the following list summarizes the repetitive flooding problems in the area:
>
> - Structures in the study area fall within the less risky X zone and in the more risky AE zone and the Mustang Bayou floodway.
> - Flooding is caused by heavy rains but aggravated by two problems:
>   - Mustang Bayou's channel cannot carry all the runoff that drains to it.
>   - The street drainage ditches are overgrown, or otherwise unable to convey water to the Bayou and out of the area.
> - Some drainage improvements were made to Mustang Bayou, but they have not stopped all flooding.

- There are 178 properties subject to flooding. Of them, 20 have been flooded to the extent that they qualify as RL structures under the NFIP. In the study area, 5 of the 20 RL properties are SRL properties. These 20 RL properties have made 48 flood insurance claims for a total of $794,126.00.

Step 5: Documenting the Findings

Documenting the findings is the last step in the FEMA-prescribed five-step process and, quite arguably, is the most important step. The required documentation comes in the form of the finished area analysis. For CRS purposes, this documentation is needed in order for the activity to be assessed and credit points awarded. For UNO-CHART, this documentation serves as a blueprint for other communities to use in order to create their own area analyses, either for CRS credit or just to address their repetitive flooding issues. The area analyses that UNO-CHART has completed are housed online and are accessible to the public at www.floodhelp.uno.edu.

As part of the agreement with FEMA, the area analyses and research methods must be shared with the public. UNO-CHART, with the assistance of its project partners, has created a Repetitive Loss Portal (the Portal) that has become a valuable resource to homeowners, local officials, and floodplain managers. There are two sides to the Portal: (1) a public side and (2) a private side. The public side has information that is useful to homeowners and officials, including important links to flood insurance and safety information; guides to floodproofing a home; and advice as to how to best prepare yourself, your family, and your home for a flood event.

The private side of the Portal houses all the RL data for the states of Louisiana and Texas. This information is protected by the Privacy Act and is kept secure from the general public. Officials must request access from FEMA Region VI through UNO-CHART and be given security clearance before accessing the information on the private side of the Portal. Once granted access, officials can search through the RL data by detail: city, community identification number (CID), date of loss, etc. There is also a geographical information system (GIS) mapping feature that plots RL and SRL properties. Not all communities in Louisiana and Texas have been mapped, but every community for which UNO-CHART completes an area analysis is mapped on the Portal. Depending on the GIS capabilities of a community, its drainage features, street names, major highways, soil types, and other details are added to the map.

Once the findings are analyzed, specific recommendations on ways to reduce the study area's flooding problem can be made to the city and/or residents of the study area, in addition to available funding sources to aid in meeting the cost of recommended mitigation measures.

Case Study Examples

Each area analysis has its own characteristics that make it as unique as the study area itself. Of the 14 analyses UNO-CHART has completed, there are certain steps that worked exceptionally well for some but not for others. In the following subsections, a few steps that worked well are highlighted.

Neighborhood Notification

In the area analysis currently being conducted in Alvin, Texas, UNO-CHART faced a situation that had never presented itself before. The area being studied was known to be a bilingual community. Rather than excluding those residents who spoke Spanish as their first language, UNO-CHART produced the notification letters and homeowner's data sheets in both English and Spanish.

The letters and data sheets were printed in English on one side and Spanish on the other. This allowed the residents the option to respond in whichever language they felt more comfortable. The Spanish response rate in Alvin is currently 16% of the total response rate. Typically, a response rate of 20% for studies such as the RLAA is considered to be "great."

Data Collection

Another area analysis is currently being conducted in Liberty, Texas. UNO-CHART was presented with a request from the local officials that UNO-CHART hold a "pre-meeting" with the residents of the study area introducing them to the project. Typically, UNO-CHART holds a meeting with the residents of a study area only at the end of the process to share the draft report and recommendations. UNO-CHART obliged and held a meeting on June 12, 2010, with the residents of the Oak Forest study area.

The entire study area comprises 40 properties, and 10 residents showed up at the meeting with UNO-CHART. After a brief presentation in which the process was explained, the residents shared in-depth information on the flooding situation in their area. They also brought with them their completed data sheets and even took some extra ones home to share with their neighbors who did not attend the meeting. After the meeting, UNO-CHART team members went into the field to collect the necessary data, and many residents who attended the meeting invited the team members to their properties to show them what they saw as things that contributed to the flooding. This forms the most productive fieldwork completed by UNO-CHART to date, and the in-depth information gained from the residents of Oak Forest has been most essential to the analysis itself.

Alternative Mitigation Measures

The Maplewood, Louisiana area is a prime example of creatively reducing individual flooding problems by way of alternative mitigation measures. Many residents reported that during a storm they get flooded from their backyard or their neighbor's yard, not from the street. Water flows to, or collects next to, the house's walls and does not drain to the street quickly enough. The result is very shallow water, usually less than 1 or 2 inches, sometimes only in one or two rooms.

Improvements to yard drainage can remedy this problem. Inlets and underground pipes can be installed. Several property owners have constructed such projects on their own. One was illustrated in Figure 14.1.

Coordination

In the Hollygrove, Louisiana area analysis, UNO-CHART came up against something for the first time: a source of floodwaters that belonged to two different parishes (counties). The Monticello Canal runs the line between Jefferson and Orleans parishes (Figure 14.2). On the Jefferson Parish side, the floodwall is approximately 6 ft higher than it is on the Orleans Parish side, which causes the Hollygrove neighborhood to be flooded when the canal overtops its banks. UNO-CHART had to coordinate between the two parishes in order to bring attention to the flooding problem being faced by the Orleans Parish residents living in Hollygrove.

UNO-CHART presented its findings and recommendations to the City of New Orleans City Council, where a representative from the Jefferson Parish Council spoke on behalf of Jefferson Parish and UNO-CHART's recommendations. It was the first time UNO-CHART had taken their analysis and findings so high within a city, as well as coordinating with another

FIGURE 14.2 The Monticello Canal near Airline Highway.

parish's officials in order to bring light to the flooding situation that could not be solved without having both parishes at the table.

To this day, Orleans and Jefferson parishes are in the process of partnering over the Monticello Canal in order to reduce flood losses to both parishes.

Complications

When working closely with communities and local officials, complications can arise. Sometimes, the research team may run into challenges in dealing with political cross fire or class and racial adversity within a study area. The best ways of handling such situations are unique to a community.

Another complication is not being able to get necessary documents in a timely fashion. As indicated by the UNO-CHART preliminary step of selecting the area, the research team collaborates with local officials from the very beginning. There is usually a time lapse between initial meetings and the actual beginning of fieldwork. Local officials have numerous ongoing projects at all times, and getting responses from them regarding the latest mitigation or drainage plans or getting signed letters from the parish to inform residents of the upcoming study can take weeks to months. This waiting period delays area analyses and can also require extensions from the grant funders.

Follow-up

Follow-ups are critical to the effectiveness of repetitive flood loss area analyses. A follow-up allows the research team and area residents to revisit the recommendations suggested in the final report of the original RLAA and gauge progress (if any) on the recommendations. The procedures for follow-ups include the following:

Step 1: Contact area leaders
- Local floodplain managers
- Residential leaders
- Political representation

Step 2: Collect data
- Homeowner data sheet
- Fieldwork
- Flood events and heavy rain events since analysis
- Drainage projects since analysis

Step 3: Analyze data
- Review previous findings and recommendations
- Assess progress
- Identify changes
- Identify challenges to mitigation

Step 4: Summarize data

- Identify additional needs
- Summary of solutions

Step 5: Draft addendum

- Post on UNO-CHART Repetitive Loss Web Portal
- Present to neighborhood
- Post link on neighborhood website (where applicable)

Follow-ups also allow UNO-CHART team to maintain a working relationship with the community and emphasize participatory action research (PAR). This method of community–university engagement has produced valuable results where local knowledge is incorporated in the research and the community has a voice to request improvements necessary for its residents' safety.

The follow-up is part of UNO-CHART's additional steps to RLAA. UNO-CHART makes itself available to the residents and local officials of a community for any help they may need along their mitigation journeys. Although UNO-CHART may not always have the answers, it is always present with information that can lead to the answers. This ongoing collaboration between UNO-CHART and the residents of the areas analyzed serves to strengthen the communities against future flood loss. It is UNO-CHART's operating belief that only an informed and educated resident population can lead to a safer and more resilient community.

Conclusion

The RLAAs help promote a culture of mitigation by increasing awareness of where area flooding stems from and some feasible options for reducing that flooding. Since the process of conducting an RLAA involves getting information and feedback from the whole community, including local officials, the residents of that area will talk about it. They will discuss it while waiting in line at the bank, when they see a neighbor at the grocery store, when they pick up their children from day care, or when they go to the community fitness center. The more people talk about mitigation and get positive reinforcement from a mitigation measure implemented by a neighbor the more others will talk and act to protect their homes. This will create a social culture—a culture that can help save lives.

The RLAA also encourages homeowners to be proactive about their flood safety. Too often, we hear of people whose flood damage costs were staggering. If homeowners apply just one or two of the nonstructural, low-cost mitigation measures, including removing carpet and adding tile to their homes, they could drastically cut flood loss costs as opposed to reacting to a flooding event that caused damage to the entire first floor of their home.

This ongoing collaboration is integral to what makes the RLAA a tool for mitigation. Through area analyses, UNO-CHART strives to make residents

aware of their flooding situation and the options that are available to them. UNO-CHART promotes an "act now, be saved later" mentality in that it suggests small projects that residents can take on themselves without grant assistance that will have a major impact on their future flood losses, or lack thereof. Samples of a letter to the community from the City of New Orleans' Mayor Ray Nagin's office, a sample flood protection data sheet, and the information gathered during fieldwork can be found in Figures 14.3, 14.4, and 14.5, respectively.

HOMELAND SECURITY AND EMERGENCY PREPAREDNESS: MITIGATION BRANCH

CITY OF NEW ORLEANS

C. RAY NAGIN
MAYOR

LT. COL. JERRY SNEED, USMC, (RET)
DIRECTOR

March 19, 2010

RE: Pines Village Repetitive Flooding Project

Dear Pines Village Resident:

The New Orleans Office of Homeland Security and Emergency Preparedness is reviewing ways to reduce some of our repetitive flooding problems. One opportunity we have identified is to partner with The University of New Orleans' Center for Hazards Assessment, Response and Technology (UNO-CHART) to conduct a flood risk assessment in Pines Village. CHART has already been visiting with neighborhood leaders about this possibility.

As part of this project, a team from UNO-CHART is preparing a "local area analysis" for this study area. The approach which they take includes collecting some data specific to your property. UNO-CHART staff will be in your area during the day between ***March 30 and April 1st*** collecting general information from the street, such as the type of foundation and approximate height of the house above the street. They will also photograph each property in the study area.

This work would be greatly improved with additional data that you might be able to provide. Attached is a data sheet that we hope you will complete and return by ***April 2nd, 2010***. After you fill the form out, please fold it, tape it, and mail it to the address on the flip side. A stamp has been provided.

After the analysis is completed, some preliminary recommendations will be developed. You will be invited to a meeting with us and the UNO/CHART team to review the findings. The meeting time and location will be advertised once the analysis is near completion.

If you have any questions about this project, please feel free to call Bradford Case, of the Homeland Security and Emergency Preparedness at (504) 658-8740; or Iman Adeinat at UNO/CHART, at (504) 481-0667.

Thank you for your assistance in helping us to complete this project.

Sincerely,

LtCol. Jerry W. Sneed
Director, NOOHSEP

Bradford W Case, CFM
Hazard Mitigation Specialist, NOOHSEP

Attachment

1300 PERDIDO STREET • SUITE 9E06 • NEW ORLEANS, LOUISIANA • 70112
PHONE 504.658.8740 • FAX 504.658.8651

FIGURE 14.3 Letter from Mayor Nagin's office to the community.

Pines Village Repetitive Flooding Analysis
Flood Protection Data Sheet

Name: ____

Property address: ______________________________________, New Orleans, LA

In what year did you move into the home at this address? __________

What type of foundation does your house have? ☐ Slab ☐ Crawlspace (please answer #3)
☐ Posts/piles (please answer #3)

If your house has a **crawlspace or post/piles foundation**, please indicate how high from grade your lowest floor of living space is. ____________________

Has the property ever been flooded or had a water problem?
☐ Yes ☐ No (if "no," please skip to question 8)

In what year(s) did it flood? ____

What was the deepest that the water ever got?
Over first floor: ____________ deep
In yard only: ____________ deep
☐ Water kept out of house or building by sandbagging or other protective measure

What was the longest time that the water ever stayed in the house? ___ hours or ___ days

What do you feel was the cause of your flooding? Check all that affect your building.
☐ Drainage from nearby properties
☐ Storm surge from nearby waterways
☐ Clogged/undersized drainage canal
☐ Overbank flooding from nearby canal
☐ Storm sewer backup
☐ Sanitary sewer backup
☐ Standing water next to house
☐ Other: ____________________

Have you taken any flood protection measures on your property?
☐ Moved utilities/contents to a higher level or parts of the building
☐ Regraded yard to keep water away from building
☐ Installed drains or pipes to improved drainage
☐ Sandbagged when water threatened
☐ Elevated all
☐ Waterproofed the outside walls
☐ Built a wall to keep water away
☐ Other: ____________________

Did any of the measures checked in item 9 work? If so, which ones? If not, do you know why they didn't work?

Do you have Flood Insurance? ☐ Yes ☐ No

Are you interested in pursuing measures to protect the property from flooding?
☐ Yes ☐ No (If "yes," please refer to our website (www.floodhelp.uno.edu) for useful information.)

FIGURE 14.4 Sample flood protection data sheet.

Address	Photo #	# of Stories	Occ	Elevated above grade	Elevated above street	Adeq Vents?	Structure type	Foundation type	Foundation condition	EC Diagram #	HVAC	Note: [MH = Mobile Home; CS = Crawl Spcae; BF = Brick Faced; S = Slab; BSL = Below Sea Level; AG = At Grade]
	1	1	Y	2	2 3		MH	CS	Fair	5	Elevated	Brown Mobile Home
	2	1	Y	2	1	Y	WF	Post	Good	5		Blue with ramp
	3	1	Y	3	1	Y	MH	CS	Good	5	E1;1 ft	Cream Mobile Home
	4	1	Y	3	1	Y	MH	CS	Good	5		White MH
	5	1	Y	3	1		BF	S	Good	10		Brown brick/garden
	6	1	Y	3	0 1	Y	MH	CS	Good	8		Blue/red MH
	7	1	Y	1	0	Y	WF	Piers	Good	5		Green & white
	8	1	Y	1	0 1	Y	WF	Piers	Good	5		Blue house
	9	1	Y	2 3	1 2	Y	WF	Post	Good	5		Dark blue trim
	10	2	Y	0 1	0	Y	MH	CS	Fair	5		Chain link fence
	11	1	Y	2	1 2	NO	WF	CS	Fair	8	Elevated	Church
	12	1	Y	2	0 1	Y	WF	Piers	Good	8	Elevated	Brown House
	13	2	Y	1	0 1	Y	WF	CS	Good	8	Elevated	White house
	14	1	Y	2	0	Y	MH	CS				
	?	1	Y	2	0	Y	MH	CS	Good	8		
	15	1	Y	2	0 –1	Y	WF	CS	Good	5		FOR RENT
	17	1	Y	2	0	Y	WF	CS	Good	5		
	16	1	Y	0	0		BF	S	Fair	1a		
	18	1	Y	0	0		WF	S	Poor	1a		Red Trim
	19	1	Y	0	0		WF	S	Poor	1a		Brown Door
	20/21	1	Y	0	0 1		WF	S	Good	1a		Fill yard
	1	1	Y	0	0 1		WF	S	Good	1a		White house/chain fence
	2	1	Y	1	0 1		BF	S	Good	1a		Roof damage
	3	1	Y	0	0		WF	S	Good	1a		Blue house
	4	1	Y	–1	0		WF	S	Good	1a		Converted Garage
	5	1	Y	–1	0		BF	S	Good	1a		Carport
	6	1	NO	0	1		WF	S	Good	1a		For sale
	7	1	Y	0	1		WF	S	Good	1a		Brown/Cream (Star)
	8	1	Y	2	2		WF	S	Good	1b		White
	9	1	Y	0	0		WF	S	Good	1a		Green trim
	10	1	Y	0	1		BF	S	Good	1a		Brown brick
	11	1	Y	1	1	Y	MH	CS	Good	5		Double Wide
	12	1	Y	1	1	Y	MH	CS	Good	5		Double Wide
	13	1	Y	2	1	Y	MH	CS	Good	5		Trailer

The addresses have been removed for privacy reasons.

FIGURE 14.5 An example of the types of information gathered during fieldwork.

End-of-Chapter Questions

1. How can an RLAA reduce risk?
2. What are the steps to completing a successful RLAA?
3. What are the different mitigation methods discussed in this chapter?
4. In what ways can an RLAA promote mitigation?

References

Government Accountability Office (GAO) (2010, September 22). GAO-10-1063T; *Continued Actions Needed to Address Financial and Operational Issues.*

http://www.fema.gov/library/viewRecord.do?id = 2434

http://www.fema.gov/plan/prevent/floodplain/data_tool.shtm

http://www.floodhelp.uno.edu

http://www.floodsmart.gov

Kates, R. W., Colten, C. A., Laska, S., & Leatherman, S. P. (2006). Reconstruction of New Orleans after Hurricane Katrina: A research perspective. *Proceedings of the National Academy of Sciences of the United States of America (PNAS), 103*(40): 14653–14660.

Managing Floodplain Development Through the NFIP: E273 Student Manual-FEMA 3-3. (2006, March).

UNO-CHART (2006, May 31). Repetitive loss area analysis #2: Jefferson Parish, Maplewood subdivision area. Retrieved from www.floodhelp.uno.edu.

UNO-CHART (2009, September 30). Repetitive loss area analysis #8: City of New Orleans, Hollygrove neighborhood. Retrieved from www.floodhelp.uno.edu.

UNO-CHART (2011, January 31). Repetitive loss area analysis #13: City of Alvin, Texas.

UNO-CHART (2011, February 1). Repetitive loss area analysis #14: City of Liberty, Oak Forest subdivision, Texas.

Chapter **15**

Tools for Hazard Mitigation

French Wetmore

Contents

Learning Objectives

After reading this chapter, you should be able to

- List the five general categories of mitigation tools.
- List examples of tools in each category.
- List examples of tools that can be implemented by property owners.

- List the pros and cons of using each example.
- Explain why some tools are difficult to implement due to their cost or political concerns.

Introduction

There are many tools of the mitigation trade. *Everything* should be considered when reviewing alternatives to reduce an individual's or a community's exposure to a natural hazard.

This chapter reviews the more common mitigation tools, organized under five general categories:

1. *Preventive* activities that protect new development and keep problems from getting worse.
2. *Property protection* activities that are undertaken on a building-by-building or parcel basis.
3. *Emergency response* measures taken during an emergency to minimize its impact.
4. *Flood control projects* that keep floodwaters away from an area.
5. *Public information* activities that advise people about the hazards and ways to protect themselves and their property from the hazards.

A Comprehensive Approach

The mitigator's mantra should be *Everything should be considered.* There is one pitfall that many mitigators fall into: thinking that only what a state or federal agency will fund is considered "mitigation." What an agency funds or promotes usually has more to do with the agency's mission and statutory authority than whether a particular measure is useful or appropriate.

Generally, agencies only invest the public's money in the more dependable approaches such as acquisition, elevation, and retrofitting public structures. For example, FEMA determined that it would only fund property protection measures that brought a building up to the same standards as the codes require for new construction. While it will not fund the less reliable approach of floodproofing residential buildings, FEMA does encourage floodproofing, where applicable, and has published guidance on how it should be done. FEMA also clarified that emergency management measures were not "mitigation," primarily because it had other funding sources for such programs and did not want to use up its mitigation funds for warning systems.

The fact that one agency or another will or will not finance a measure does not mean the measure is not useful. Obviously, funding is very important and outside funding always helps, especially if there is hesitation to mitigate.

However, many of the mitigation tools, especially the preventive measures, are inexpensive to implement, and many of them can, and should, be funded by the property owners rather than the public.

Most of the mitigation measures listed here relate to flooding. There are two reasons for this. First, flooding is more amenable to mitigation as it is more predictable, and protection measures are more affordable than for, say, tornadoes or severe earthquakes. Second, the United States has had more experience and has more government programs focused on flooding. On the other hand, there have been many lessons learned from using flood mitigation tools that can be applied to the other hazards.

Preventive Measures

Preventive measures are designed to keep the problem from occurring or getting worse. Their objective is to ensure that future development is not exposed to damage and does not increase damage to other properties.

The first measures reviewed—planning, zoning, and open space preservation—work to keep damage-prone development *out* of the hazardous or sensitive areas. The other measures impose standards on new developments to protect them from natural hazards, especially flooding and stormwater flooding.

Planning and Zoning

Planning and zoning activities direct development away from hazardous areas, especially floodplains, steep slopes, sinkholes, and other known problem sites. They do this by allowing land uses that are more compatible to the natural conditions of the land. Use of the land can be tailored to match the land's hazards, typically by reserving hazardous areas for parks, greenways, golf courses, backyards, wildlife refuges, natural areas, or similar compatible uses. They can also allow developers more flexibility in arranging improvements on a parcel of land through the planned development approach.

Comprehensive Plans

These plans are the primary tools used by communities to address future development. They can reduce future property damage by indicating open space or low density development within floodplains and other hazardous areas. In most states, a plan has limited authority. It reflects what the community would *like to see* happen. Its utility is that it guides other local measures such as capital improvement programs, zoning ordinances, and subdivision regulations. Unfortunately, most communities' comprehensive plans do not address natural hazards, a shortcoming that can be rectified when the plans are periodically updated.

Zoning

A zoning ordinance regulates development by dividing a community into zones or districts and setting development criteria for each zone or district. Zoning codes are considered the primary tool to implement a comprehensive plan's guidelines for how land should be developed. Zoning ordinances can limit development in hazardous areas, such as reserving floodplain zones for agricultural uses.

Zoning ordinances and other land use regulations can allow or encourage flexibility in lot sizes and location, so developers can avoid hazardous areas. One way to do this is through the planned unit development (PUD) approach. The PUD approach allows adjustment of site design standards and land use densities to preserve open space and/or floodplains from development (see Figure 15.1a and b).

Capital Improvement Plans

A capital improvement plan will guide a community's major public expenditures for the next 5–20 years. Capital expenditures may include acquisition of open space within the hazardous areas, extension (or withholding) of public services in hazardous areas, or retrofitting existing public structures to withstand a hazard. Most capital improvement plans are funded with local funds, but they can be augmented with FEMA mitigation grants.

Each year, the planned projects should be reviewed to determine if mitigation measures can be incorporated. For example, plans to replace a bridge could be revised to make the bridge higher, so that it will not flood as often, or wider, to be less of an obstruction to flood flows.

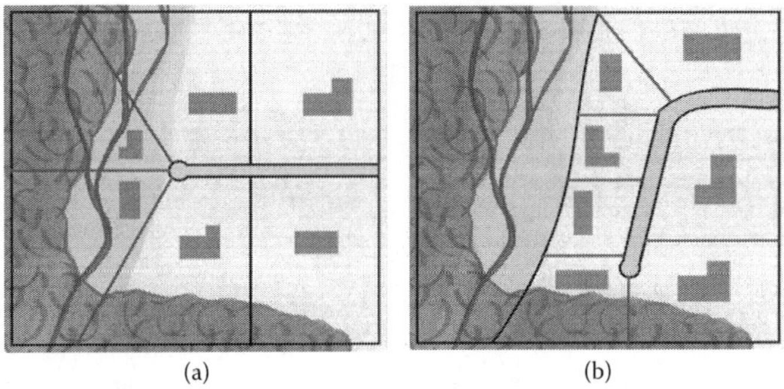

FIGURE 15.1 In the standard zoning approach (a), the developer considers six equally sized lots without regard for the flood hazard. Two properties are subject to flooding and the natural stream is disrupted. An alternative, flexible, PUD approach is shown on the right (b). The floodplain is dedicated as public open space. There are seven smaller lots, but those abutting the floodplain have the advantage of being adjacent to a larger open area. Four lots have riverfront views instead of two. These amenities compensate for the smaller lot sizes, so the parcels are valued the same. The developer makes the same or more income and the future residents are safer.

Open Space Preservation

Keeping the floodplain and other hazardous areas open and free from development is the best approach to prevent damage to new developments. Open space can be maintained in agricultural use or can serve as parks, greenway corridors, and golf courses.

Comprehensive and capital improvement plans should identify areas to be preserved by acquisition and other means such as purchasing an easement. With an easement, the owner is free to develop and use private property, but property taxes are reduced or a payment is made to the owner if the owner agrees to not build on the part set aside in the easement.

Although there are some federal programs that can help acquire or reserve open lands, open space lands and easements do not always have to be purchased. Developers can be encouraged to dedicate park land and required to dedicate easements for drainage and maintenance purposes. These are usually linear areas along property lines or channels. Maintenance easements also can be donated by streamside property owners in return for a community maintenance program.

Subdivision Regulations

Subdivision regulations govern how land will be subdivided and set construction standards. These standards generally address roads, sidewalks, utilities, storm sewers, and drainageways. They can include the following hazard protection standards:

- Requiring that the final plat show all hazardous areas
- Road standards that allow passage of firefighting equipment and snow plows (see Figure 15.2)
- Requiring power or phone lines to be buried
- Minimum water pressures needed for firefighting

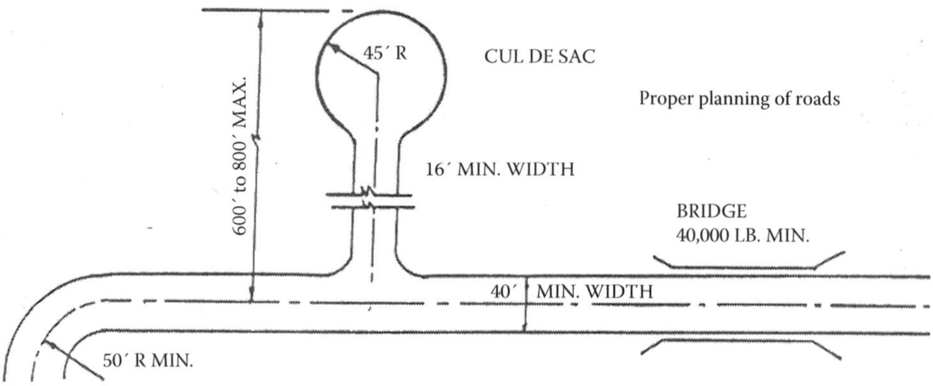

FIGURE 15.2 Subdivision regulations need to ensure that streets can handle emergency vehicles. (From *Wildland/Urban Interface Fire Protection*)

- Requiring that each lot be provided with a building site above the flood level
- Requiring that all roadways be no more than 1 ft below the flood elevation

Building Codes

The building code is the primary measure to protect new property from damage by fire, high winds, tornadoes, earthquakes, hail, and winter storms. When properly designed and constructed according to code, the average building can withstand the impacts of most of these forces.

Hazard protection standards for all new and improved or repaired buildings can be incorporated into the local building code. Provisions that should be included are

- Setting roof and chimney standards to minimize fire hazards
- Mandating hurricane protection standards for windows and doors
- Making sure roofing systems will handle high winds and there is adequate hurricane strapping
- Providing special standards for tying the roof, walls, and foundation together to resist the effects of wind
- Including insulation standards that ensure protection from extreme heat and cold as well as energy efficiency
- Regulating overhanging masonry elements that can fall during a quake
- Requiring new buildings to have tornado "safe rooms"
- Ensuring that foundations are strong enough for earth movement and that all structural elements are properly connected to the foundation

The national model building codes are the International Code series (I-Codes), promulgated by the International Code Council. Most states now require this code and most communities have adopted it.

While the I-Codes have incorporated many important hazard protection features, state and local governments could strengthen them. For example,

- Tornado safe rooms are not required.
- The Institute for Business and Home Safety (IBHS) has reviewed the I-Codes with respect to hazards such as hurricanes, floods, hail, and tornadoes. The IBHS recommends that the International Residential Code should be amended to increase design for wind loads to meet hurricane-resistant standards.
- IBHS has a set of recommendations to strengthen a building to better resist the impacts of natural hazards. The specific requirements for a "fortified" home are available at http://disastersafety.org/fortified.

The experiences of Hurricane Ike showed the value of these additional standards, as several "fortified" homes were left standing, surrounded by the debris of other demolished homes.

- While the I-Codes have sections on flood protection, they are optional in most states. Communities usually adopt separate flood standards.

Just as important as the code standards is the enforcement of the code. There were many reports of buildings that lost their roofs during Hurricane Andrew in Florida because sloppy construction practices did not put enough nails in them. Adequate inspections are needed during the course of construction to ensure that the builder understands the requirements and is following them. Making sure a structure is properly anchored requires site inspections at each step of construction.

There is a national program that measures local building code natural hazard protection standards and code administration. The Building Code Effectiveness Grading Schedule (BCEGS) is used by the insurance industry to determine how well new construction is protected from wind, earthquake, and other nonflood hazards. Every community interested in hazard mitigation should review its BCEGS report to identify where its code enforcement program could be improved. For more information, see http://www.isomitigation.com.

Manufactured Homes

Many states regulate manufactured or "mobile" home installation, which leads local governments to believe that they have no authority or responsibility for them. In fact manufactured homes are built in a factory in another state and are shipped to a site. They do have to meet construction standards set by the U.S. Department of Housing and Urban Development. As is well known, the greatest mitigation concern with manufactured housing is protection from damage by wind. The key to local mitigation of wind damage to mobile homes is their installation.

Following tornadoes in Oklahoma and Kansas, FEMA's Building Performance Assistance Team found that newer manufactured housing that had been anchored to permanent foundations performed better. They also found that newer homes are designed to better transmit wind uplift and overturning forces to the foundation. Unfortunately, the FEMA team found that building officials were often unaware of manufacturer's installation guidelines with respect to permanent foundations.

Communities with manufactured or mobile homes, even those in separate parks, should verify their authority to regulate or inspect manufactured home installation and then become familiar with the proper methods. Assuming that some other agency is taking care of their manufactured homes usually results in a lack of attention and, therefore, more exposure to wind damage (see Figure 15.3).

FIGURE 15.3 Dyersburg, Tennessee—Severe damage to a mobile home park resulting from a West Tennessee F-4 Tornado. (Photo courtesy of Mark Wolfe/ FEMA News Photo.)

Floodplain Regulations

Most communities with a flood problem participate in the National Flood Insurance Program (NFIP). As a condition of making flood insurance available for their residents, communities that participate in the NFIP agree to regulate new construction in the area subject to inundation by the 100-year (base) flood. The floodplain subject to these requirements is shown as an A or V Zone on a flood insurance rate map (FIRM).

The NFIP sets five major minimum floodplain regulatory requirements:

1. All development in the 100-year floodplain must have a permit from the community. The NFIP regulations define "development" as any man-made change to improved or unimproved real estate, including but not limited to buildings or other structures, mining, dredging, filling, grading, paving, excavation or drilling operations, or storage of equipment or materials.
2. Development along a river or other channel cannot obstruct flows so as to cause an increase in flooding on other properties. An analysis must be conducted to demonstrate that the proposed development will not adversely increase the water surface elevation of the base flood.
3. New buildings may be built in the floodplain, but they must be protected from damage by the base flood. In riverine floodplains, the lowest floor of residential buildings must be elevated to or above the base flood elevation (see Figure 15.4a–c). Nonresidential buildings must be either elevated or floodproofed.

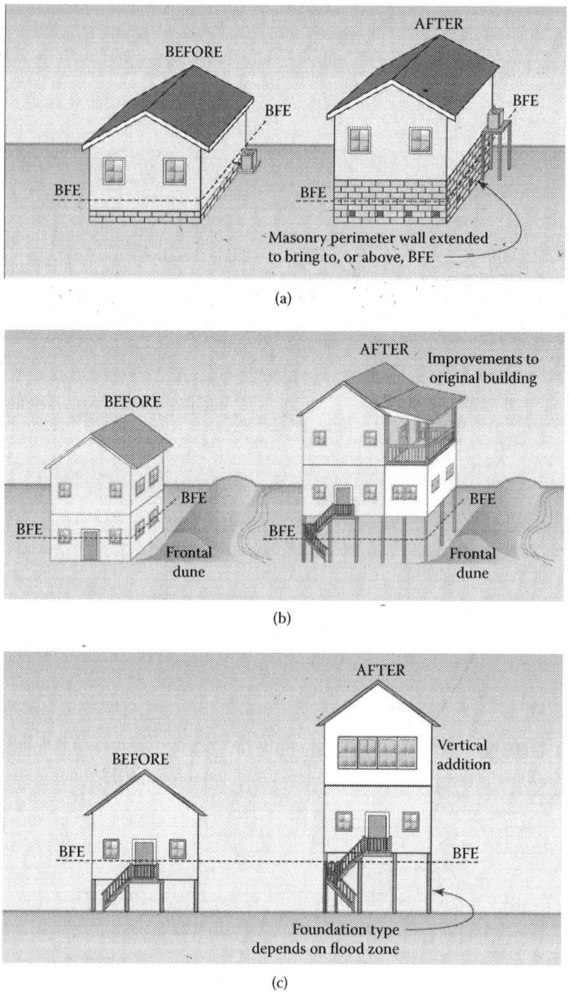

FIGURE 15.4 Common ways to elevate a house. (a) Rehabilitation with no increase in footprint to a home in Zone A—building must be brought into compliance with NFIP. (b). Lateral addition to a home in Zone V—both the addition and the original building must be brought into compliance with the NFIP. (c). Vertical addition (either new upper or lower floor)—in this case, the whole building must be brought into compliance with the NFIP. (From FEMA P-758, 2010a)

4. Development in the coastal high hazard area cannot obstruct the flow of waves, so the lower areas of an elevated building must remain open.
5. A "substantially improved" building is treated as a new building. The NFIP regulations define "substantial improvement" as any reconstruction, rehabilitation, addition, or other improvement to a structure, the cost of which equals or exceeds 50% of the market value of the structure before the start of construction of the improvement. This requirement also applies to buildings that are substantially damaged.

Communities are encouraged to adopt local ordinances that are more comprehensive or provide more protection than the federal criteria. The NFIP's Community Rating System provides insurance premium credits to recognize the additional flood protection benefit of higher regulatory standards (see Chapter 6 on the CRS).

To ensure that communities are meeting the NFIP standards, FEMA periodically conducts a Community Assessment Visit. During this visit, the maps and ordinances are reviewed, permits are checked, and issues are discussed with staff. Failure to meet all of the requirements can result in one or more consequences:

- Reclassification under the Community Rating System to a lower class
- Probation, which entails a $50 surcharge on every flood insurance policy in the community
- Suspension from the NFIP

Even though a community is in the NFIP, its floodplain regulatory program should be evaluated:

- The first step is to review the most recent Community Assessment Visit report to see if any problems still remain.
- The next step is to see how many staff members are certified floodplain managers, a program administered by the Association of State Floodplain Managers (www.floods.org).
- The third step would be to see how the community is doing or could do under the Community Rating System, which is discussed in Chapter 6.

Drainage Regulations

New development in mapped floodplains can be protected from overbank and coastal flooding by floodplain regulations. However, many communities have areas subject to inundation from stormwater runoff that has not yet reached the larger channels that have mapped floodplains.

There are three ways to prevent flooding problems caused by stormwater runoff:

- Ensure that new subdivisions and other development have adequate storm sewers and/or drainageways to carry the water away.
- Require new developments to hold their excess runoff on site, so that it will not overload the existing drainageways.
- Set construction standards so that buildings are protected from shallow water.

Drainageway standards are typically in subdivision regulations. Standards for storm sewers, ditches, culverts, and so on are best set when an area is laid out and developed. Traditionally, the national standard is to require that the local drainage system carry the 10-year storm. Recently, communities are finding that older estimates of the 10-year storm understated the true hazard, so they are addressing larger storms.

One problem with requiring the drainage system to carry water away is that runoff increases with urban development. The runoff equivalent of a 10-year storm occurs more frequently, from smaller storms. The problem is just sent downstream onto someone else's property.

Accordingly, modern subdivision regulations require new developments to ensure that the post-development peak runoff will not be greater than under pre-development conditions. This is usually done by constructing retention or detention basins to hold the runoff for a few hours or days, until flows in the system have subsided and the downstream channels can accept the water without flooding (see Figure 15.5).

If the storm sewers or roadside ditches cannot handle a heavy rain, the standard subdivision design uses the streets to carry excess runoff. If the flows exceed the street's capacity, adjacent properties will flood. Therefore, the third approach to protect from stormwater flooding is to make sure new buildings are elevated 1 or 2 feet above the street or above adjacent grade.

FIGURE 15.5 Many communities have made their stormwater management detention basins part of their parks or open space plans.

Property Protection

Property protection measures are used to modify buildings or property subject to damage. Property protection measures fall under three approaches:

1. Modify the site to keep the hazard from reaching the building.
2. Modify the building or property so that it can withstand the impacts of the hazard.
3. Insure the property to provide financial relief after the damage occurs.

Property protection measures are normally implemented by the property owner, although in many cases, technical and financial assistance can be provided by a government agency.

Keeping the Hazard Away

In some cases, properties can be modified so the hazard does not reach the damage-prone improvements. Keeping the hazard away is feasible for the hazards of flooding and wildfires.

Flooding

There are five common methods for keeping a flood from reaching and damaging a building:

1. Erect a barrier between the building and the source of flooding.
2. Move the building out of the flood-prone area.
3. Elevate the building above the flood level.
4. Demolish the building.
5. Replace the building with a new one that is elevated above the flood level (also known as "demo/rebuild" or "mitigation reconstruction").

Each approach has its advantages and disadvantages. For example, a barrier, such as a levee, floodwall, or berm, can be inexpensive and does not disrupt the house. However, it is only good for shallow floodwaters, where there is adequate room on a lot to ensure that water will not be diverted onto other properties.

Buying the parcel and removing the structure is the most secure way to protect against all flood hazards, but such a project may produce a "checkerboard" pattern in which nonadjacent properties are acquired. This can occur when some owners, especially those who have and prefer a waterfront location, prove reluctant to leave. Creating such an acquisition pattern in a community simply adds to the maintenance costs that taxpayers must support.

Wildfire

One way to defeat fire is by keeping fuel away from the building. This is called the concept of "defensible space." Defensible space involves providing sufficient space between the structure and flammable vegetation.

Within this space, the fire service has room to battle the wildfire before it reaches the structure or to stop a structural fire before it ignites the wild land vegetation. With sufficient defensible space, the structure even has a chance to survive on its own when fire service personnel and equipment are not available, as often happens during a significant wildfire (see Figure 15.6).

Retrofitting

An alternative to keeping the hazard from reaching a building is to modify or "retrofit" the site or building to minimize or even prevent damage. There are various techniques to do this.

Flooding

Flood retrofitting measures include dry floodproofing where all areas below the flood protection level are made watertight. Walls are coated with waterproofing compounds or plastic sheeting. Openings (doors, windows, and vents) are closed permanently, with removable shields, or with sandbags. Dry floodproofing relies on the structure's walls to withstand water pressure. Most buildings are not designed to handle such loads, so this measure is only recommended for areas subject to shallow flooding. The area also

FIGURE 15.6 (See color insert.) Boulder, Colorado, January 8, 2009—Houses were saved by a burnout operation. Having a defensible space around the house gave the firefighters this option. (Photo courtesy of Michael Rieger/FEMA.)

needs sufficient advanced warning time to close openings, place sandbags, and so on.

The alternative to dry floodproofing is wet floodproofing: water is let in and everything that could be damaged by a flood is removed or elevated above the flood level. Structural components below the flood level are replaced with materials that are not subject to water damage.

For example, concrete block walls are used instead of wooden studs and gypsum wallboard. The furnace, water heater, and laundry facilities are permanently relocated to a higher floor. Where the flooding is not deep, these appliances can be raised on blocks or platforms.

Wind

The high wind forces of tropical storms, hurricanes, and tornadoes can be resisted by securing the roof, walls, and foundation with adequate fasteners or tie-downs. These help hold the building together when the combination of high wind and pressure differences work to pull the building apart.

Another retrofit is to strengthen garage doors, windows, and other large openings. If winds break the building's "envelope," the pressures on the structure are greatly increased. Windows can be protected with storm shutters or special glass.

Air conditioning units, ductwork, and other equipment that is outside or on roofs should have their connections strengthened to keep them from becoming projectiles in high winds.

Tornado retrofitting measures include constructing an underground shelter or "safe room" to protect the lives of the occupants. Their worth has been proven by recent tornadoes in Oklahoma, as shown in Figure 15.7. They can be installed for approximately $3000.

Winter Storm

Winter storm retrofitting measures include improving insulation on older buildings and relocating water lines from outside walls to interior spaces. Windows can be sealed or covered with an extra layer of glass (storm windows) or plastic sheeting. Roofs can be retrofitted to shed heavy loads of snow and prevent ice dams that form when snow melts.

Thunderstorms

Retrofitting approaches to protect buildings from the effects of thunderstorms include

- Storm shutters
- Lightning rods
- Strengthening connections and tie-downs (i.e., wind retrofitting)
- Strengthening soffit and gutter attachments to minimize leakage

FIGURE 15.7 Shawnee, Okla., May 13, 2010 - All that remains of a country farmstead is a solitary "safe room" that helped save the lives of this family. Interior rooms can be reinforced and retrofitted to be tornado safe rooms. (Photo courtesy of Win Henderson/FEMA)

- Surge suppressors to protect delicate appliances during electrical storms
- Generators and backup power batteries to provide electricity to essential appliances such as sump pumps

Earthquake

Earthquake retrofitting measures include removing masonry overhangs that will fall onto the street during shaking. Bracing the building provides structural stability but can be very expensive.

Less expensive approaches may be more cost-effective in areas that face a relatively low earthquake threat. These include tying down appliances, water heaters, bookcases, and fragile furniture so that they will not fall over during a quake, and installing flexible utility connections that will not break when shaken.

Other Hazards and Measures

- Burying utility lines is a retrofitting measure that addresses the winds from hurricanes, tornadoes, thunderstorms, and the ice that accompanies winter storms.
- Installing or incorporating backup power supplies minimizes the effects of power losses caused by downed lines.

- Roofs can be replaced with materials less susceptible to damage by hail, such as modified asphalt or formed steel shingles.
- Wildfire retrofitting measures include replacing roofing with fireproof materials, installing spark arrestors on chimneys, and covering exposed surfaces with fire-resistant paint.

Urban Forestry

Trees are particularly subject to damage by wind, ice, and snow storms. Downed trees and branches break utility lines and damage buildings, parked vehicles, and anything else that were under them (see Figure 15.8). An urban forestry program can reduce the damage potential of trees.

Urban foresters or arborists can select hardier trees that can better withstand high wind and ice accumulation. Only trees that attain a height less than the utility lines should be allowed along the power and telephone line rights-of-way. Correct pruning after a storm is just as important as planting the right trees. If not done right, the damaged tree will not heal properly, decay over the next few years, and cause a hazard in the future. A trained person should review every damaged tree to determine if it should be pruned or removed.

By having stronger trees, programs of proper pruning, and ongoing evaluation of the trees, communities can prevent serious damage to their tree population. A properly written and enforced urban forestry plan can reduce liability, alleviate the extent of fallen trees and limbs caused by wind and ice buildup, and provide guidance on repairs and pruning after a storm. Such

FIGURE 15.8 Trees are the first victims of ice storms.

a plan helps a community qualify to be a Tree City USA (see http://www.arborday.org/programs/treeCityUSA/).

Insurance

Technically speaking, insurance does not mitigate damage caused by a natural hazard. However, it does help the owner repair, rebuild, and (hopefully) afford to incorporate some of the other property protection measures in the process. Insurance has the advantage that as long as the policy is in force, the property is protected and no human intervention is needed for the measure to work.

A standard homeowner's insurance policy will cover a property for the hazards of tornado, wind, hail, and winter storms. Separate endorsements are usually needed for earth movement (e.g., earthquake) coverage.

Although most homeowners' insurance policies do not cover a property for flood damage, an owner can insure a building for damage from surface flooding through the NFIP. Flood insurance coverage is provided for buildings and their contents damaged by a "general condition of surface flooding" in the area. Sample premiums are shown in Table 15.1.

Most people purchase flood insurance because it is required by the bank when they get a mortgage or home improvement loan. Usually, these policies just cover the building's structure and not its contents. Renters can buy contents coverage, even if the owner does not buy structural coverage on the building.

Governments can purchase commercial insurance policies. Larger local governments often self-insure and absorb the cost of damage to one facility, but if many properties are exposed to damage, self-insurance can be a major drain on the treasury.

TABLE 15.1 Pros and Cons of Structural Flood Control Projects

Advantages	Shortcomings
May provide the greatest amount of protection for land area used	They can disturb the land and disrupt natural water flows, often destroying wildlife habitat
Because of land limitations, may be the only practical solution in some circumstances	They require regular maintenance, which, if neglected, can have disastrous consequences
Can incorporate other benefits into structural project design, such as water supply and recreational uses	They are built to a certain flood protection level that can be exceeded by larger floods, causing extensive damage
Regional detention may be more cost-efficient and effective than requiring numerous small detention basins	They can create a false sense of security as people protected by a project often believe that no flood can ever reach them
	Although it may be unintended, in many circumstances, they promote more intensive land use and development in the floodplain

Communities cannot expect federal disaster assistance to make up the difference after a flood. Under Section 406(d) of the Stafford Act:

> If an eligible insurable facility damaged by flooding is located in a [mapped floodplain] ... and the facility is not covered (or is underinsured) by flood insurance on the date of such flooding, FEMA is required to reduce federal disaster assistance by the *maximum* amount of insurance proceeds that would have been received had the buildings and contents been fully covered under a National Flood Insurance Program (NFIP) standard flood insurance policy. [Generally, the maximum amount of proceeds for a non-residential property is $500,000.]

In other words, the law expects public agencies to be fully insured as a condition of receiving federal disaster assistance.

Emergency Response

Emergency response measures protect people before, during, and after a disaster. A good emergency management program addresses all hazards (human-made or natural) and it involves all departments; other local, state, and federal assets; and private sector organizations such as churches and the Red Cross.

This chapter reviews emergency response measures following a chronological order of responding to an emergency:

- Threat recognition—identifying an oncoming problem before it hits.
- Warning—getting the word out.
- Response—doing what can be done in the time available.
- Evacuation and shelter—getting people out of harm's way.
- Recovery and mitigation—cleaning up, repairing, and preparing for the next one.

Threat Recognition

The first step in responding to a hurricane, flood, tornado, or other natural hazard is knowing when weather conditions are such that an event could occur. With a proper and timely threat recognition system, adequate warnings can be disseminated.

Tropical Storms/Hurricanes

The National Weather Service's National Hurricane Center in Miami monitors all tropical storm and hurricane activity. It uses computer models to estimate where the storm will make landfall, the predicted wind speeds, and the likely storm surge levels. These predictions are updated periodically and disseminated to the media and through emergency management channels.

Riverine Flooding

A flood threat recognition system predicts the time and height of the flood crest. This can be done by measuring rainfall, soil moisture, and stream flows upstream of the community and calculating the subsequent flood levels.

On larger rivers, the measuring and calculating is done by the National Weather Service. On smaller rivers, locally established rainfall and river gages are needed to establish a flood threat recognition system. Some communities rely on local personnel to monitor rainfall and stream conditions and telephone their readings to the emergency center.

Severe Weather

The National Weather Service is the prime agency for detecting meteorological threats, such as tornadoes, fog, hailstorms, and winter storms. Severe weather warnings are transmitted through the NOAA Weather Radio System. As with floods, the federal agency can only look at the large scale, for example, whether conditions are appropriate for formation of a tornado.

For tornadoes and thunderstorms, local emergency managers can provide more site-specific and timely recognition by sending out trained spotters to watch the skies when the National Weather Service issues a watch or warning.

Severe snow storms can often be forecast days in advance of the expected event, which allows time for warning and preparation. Although it is more difficult, the National Weather Service can also forecast ice storms.

Wildfires

The Wildland Fire Assessment System is an Internet-based information system administered by the U.S. Forest Service in Idaho. It monitors weather conditions, such as moisture and wind, and provides a national view of weather and fire potential, including national fire danger and weather maps. Current conditions and predictions are available at www.wfas.net/. The Wildland Fire Assessment System predicts conditions favorable for wildfires. There must be a local observation system to identify and report local fires.

Dam Failure

A key part of a dam safety program is for the emergency management office to be in touch with the operators of upstream dams. There should be periodic communication checks and clear criteria for when a dam appears threatened and when the community should notify downstream properties.

Levee Failure

A levee can fail well before the waters reach the top, so levee patrols are usually needed to monitor their condition. As floodwaters rise, the emergency

management office needs to stay in communication with the patrols and the managers of levees who protect populated areas.

Warning

After the threat recognition system tells the emergency management office that a flood, tornado, thunderstorm, winter storm, or other hazard is coming, the next step is to notify the public and staff of other agencies and critical facilities. The earlier and the more specific the warning, the greater the number of people that can implement protection measures.

The National Weather Service issues notices to the public using two levels of notification:

Watch: conditions are right for flooding, thunderstorms, tornadoes, or winter storms.
Warning: a flood, tornado, and so on have started or have been observed.

A more specific warning may be disseminated by the community in various ways. The following are the more common methods:

- Outdoor warning sirens
- Commercial or public radio or TV stations
- The Weather Channel
- Cable TV emergency news inserts
- Telephone trees/mass telephone notification
- NOAA Weather Radio
- Tone-activated receivers in key facilities
- Sirens on public safety vehicles
- Door-to-door contact
- Mobile public address systems
- E-mail notifications

Telling people what to do is just as important as issuing a warning. A warning program should have a public information aspect. Citizens should know the difference between a tornado warning (when they should seek

NOAA WEATHER RADIOS

NOAA Weather Radio is a nationwide network of radio stations that broadcasts warnings, watches, forecasts, and other hazard information 24 hours a day.

NOAA weather radios can be very effective for notifying people, businesses, schools, care facilities, of weather threats. They have a monitoring feature that issues an alarm when activated by the National Weather Service.

NWS STORMREADY

The National Weather Service established the StormReady program to help local governments improve the timeliness and effectiveness of hazardous weather-related warnings for the public. Being designated as a StormReady community by the National Weather Service is a good measure of a community's emergency warning program for weather hazards. To be officially StormReady, a community must

- Establish a 24-hour warning point and emergency operations center.
- Have more than one way to receive severe weather warnings and forecasts and to alert the public.
- Create a system that monitors weather conditions locally.
- Promote the importance of public readiness through community seminars.
- Develop a formal hazardous weather plan, which includes training severe weather spotters and holding emergency exercises.

shelter in low spot), a flood warning (when they should stay out of low areas), and other appropriate warnings and responses.

Response

The protection of life and property is the most important task of emergency responders. Concurrent with threat recognition and issuing warnings, a community should respond with actions that can prevent or reduce damage and injuries. Typical actions and responding parties include the following:

- Activating the emergency operations center (emergency preparedness)
- Closing streets or bridges (sheriff or public works)
- Shutting off power to threatened areas (utility company)
- Passing out sand and sandbags (public works)
- Holding children at school/releasing children from school (school superintendent)
- Opening evacuation shelters (Red Cross)
- Monitoring water levels (engineering)
- Establishing security and other protection measures (police/sheriff)

An emergency action plan ensures that all bases are covered and that the response activities are appropriate for the expected threat. These plans are developed in coordination with the agencies or offices that are given various responsibilities.

Planning is best done with adequate data. One of the best tools is a map that shows what areas would be affected under different conditions (see Figure 15.9). A flood stage forecast map shows areas that will be underwater at various flood stages. Different flood levels are shown as color-coded

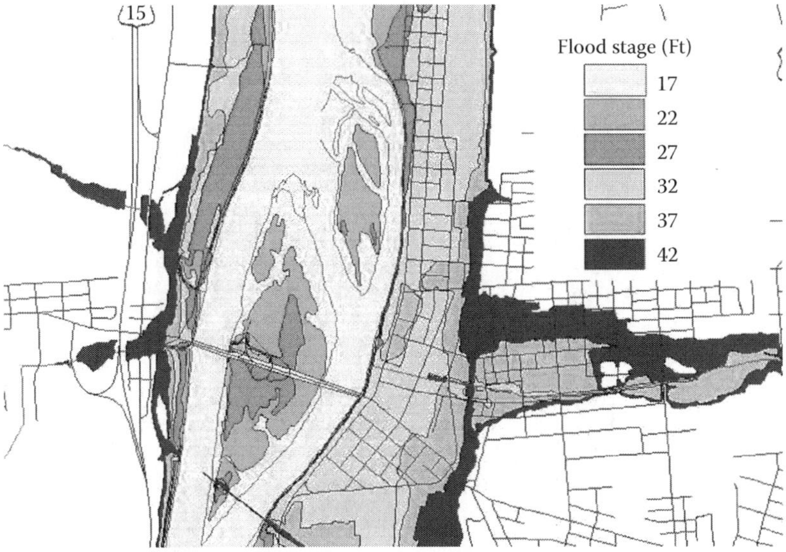

FIGURE 15.9 A flood stage forecast map relates predicted flood heights to areas that will be inundated.

areas, so that the emergency manager can quickly see what will be affected. Emergency management staff can identify the number of properties flooded, which roads will be under water, which critical facilities will be affected, who to warn, and so on. With this information, an advance plan can be prepared that shows problem sites and determines what resources will be needed to respond to the predicted flood level.

Emergency response plans should be updated annually to keep contact names and telephone numbers current and to make sure that supplies and equipment that will be needed are still available. They should be critiqued and revised after disasters and exercises to take advantage of the lessons learned and changing conditions. The end result is a coordinated effort implemented by people who have experience working together so that available resources will be used in the most efficient manner.

Evacuation and Shelter

In an area subject to the tremendous forces that accompany hurricanes, evacuation is a prime life safety concern (see Figure 15.10a and b). Given the 1–2 days of lead time provided by the National Hurricane Center, evacuation on a large scale is a realistic lifesaving task. In other situations, such as a tornado, it is safer to keep people where they are rather than expose them to danger from an event that gives little warning.

There are six key ingredients to a successful evacuation:

1. Adequate warning
2. Adequate routes

(a)

(b)

FIGURE 15.10 (See color insert.) (a) Adequate routes and (b) traffic control are two key ingredients for an evacuation.

3. Proper timing to ensure the routes are clear
4. Traffic control
5. Knowledgeable travelers
6. Care for special populations (e.g., handicapped, prisoners, hospital patients, schoolchildren, and those without transportation)

Those who cannot get out of harm's way need shelter. For most storms, a stick-built house (not a mobile home) often suffices, but for hurricanes, something sturdier is needed. That is why schools often serve as shelters during a storm as well as a place for those who have lost their homes after the storm.

Typically, the Red Cross will staff a shelter and ensure that there is adequate food, bedding, and washing facilities. Shelter management is a specialized skill. Managers must deal with problems like scared children, families that want to bring their pets in, and the potential for an overcrowded facility.

Post-Disaster Recovery and Mitigation

After a disaster, communities should undertake activities to protect public health and safety and facilitate recovery. Appropriate measures include

- Patrolling evacuated areas to prevent looting
- Providing safe drinking water
- Monitoring for diseases
- Vaccinating residents for tetanus and other diseases
- Clearing streets
- Cleaning up debris and garbage

Throughout the recovery phase, everyone wants to get "back to normal." The problem is, "normal" means the way they were before the disaster, exposed to repeated damage from future disasters. There should be an effort to help prepare people and property for the next disaster. Such an effort would include

- Public information activities to advise residents about mitigation measures they can incorporate into their reconstruction work
- Evaluating damaged public facilities to identify mitigation measures that can be included during repairs
- Identifying other mitigation measures that can lessen the impact of the next disaster
- Acquiring substantially or repeatedly damaged properties from willing sellers
- Planning for long-term mitigation activities
- Applying for post-disaster mitigation funds

Regulating Reconstruction

Requiring permits for building repairs and conducting inspections are vital activities to ensure that damaged structures are safe for people to reenter and repair (see Figure 15.11). There is a special requirement to do this in floodplains, regardless of the type of disaster or cause of damage. The NFIP requires that local officials enforce the substantial damage regulations. These rules require that if the cost to repair a building in the mapped floodplain equals or exceeds 50% of the building's market value, the building must be retrofitted to meet the standards of a new building in the floodplain. In most cases, this means that a substantially damaged building must be elevated above the base flood elevation.

There is a tendency for elected officials to waive permit requirements so that they can help people to get "back to normal" quickly. There are three problems with this attitude:

1. People with limited resources are likely to cut corners and repair in unsafe or unhealthy ways. For example, they may not thoroughly clean and dry out flooded areas, leaving their families exposed to mold or sediment in the ductwork.

FIGURE 15.11 After a disaster, all buildings need to be inspected to determine if they are safe to reenter. A substantially damaged building needs to be "red tagged" to stop repairs unless it meets the code requirements. (Photo courtesy of Adam DuBrowa/FEMA).

2. Getting "back to normal" means getting back to being exposed to damage by the next occurrence. Homes in floodplains will flood again. After the disaster is the time when people are most interested in protecting themselves. This is the best time to talk about redeveloping or clearing out a hazardous area.
3. Not enforcing its regulations can be a violation of the community's obligations under the NFIP. Local officials can waive permit fees, but not the requirement to get a permit to repair or rebuild a building in the floodplain, no matter what caused the damage.

This requirement can be very difficult for understaffed and overworked offices after a disaster. A good public information program can help explain the rules and procedures. In some areas, mutual aid agreements have been established so that building inspectors from a community not affected by the disaster can work in the communities that were hit the hardest.

Flood Control

Flood control projects have traditionally been used by communities to control or manage floodwaters. They are also known as "structural" projects that keep floodwaters away from an area as opposed to "nonstructural" projects, like preventive and property protection measures, which do not rely on structures to control flows.

These projects have three advantages not provided by other mitigation measures:

1. They can stop most flooding, protecting streets and landscaping in addition to buildings.
2. Many projects can be built without disrupting citizens' homes and businesses.
3. They are constructed and maintained by a government agency, a more dependable long-term management arrangement than depending on many individual property owners.

However, as shown in Table 15.1, they also have shortcomings. The appropriateness of using flood control depends on individual project area circumstances.

Levees and Floodwalls

The best-known flood control measure is probably a barrier of earth (levee) or concrete (floodwall) that is erected between the watercourse and the property to be protected (see Figure 15.12). Levees and floodwalls confine water to the stream channel by raising its banks. They must be well designed to account for large floods, underground seepage, pumping of internal drainage, and erosion and scour.

FIGURE 15.12 Velva, N.D., June 26, 2011 - A levee built around the town of Velva holds back the overflowing Souris River. One shortcoming of a levee is that the protected population is usually unprepared if it overtops or fails. (Photo courtesy of Andrea Booher/FEMA)

Key considerations when evaluating use of a levee include

- Design and permitting costs
- Right-of-way acquisition
- Removal of fill to compensate for the floodwater storage that will be displaced by the levee
- Internal drainage of surface flows from the area inside the levee
- Cost of construction
- Cost of maintenance
- Mitigation of adverse impacts to wetlands
- Loss of river access and views
- Creating a false sense of security (while levees may reduce flood damage for smaller, more frequent rain events, they may also overtop or breach in extreme flood events and subsequently create more flood damage than would have occurred without the levee)
- Whether the presence of the levee will encourage more development in the flood-prone area

Levees placed along the river edge degrade aquatic habitat and water quality. They are also more likely to push floodwater onto other properties upstream or downstream. To reduce environmental impacts and provide multiple-use benefits, a setback levee is the best project design. The area inside a setback levee can provide open space for recreational purposes and provide access sites to the river or stream.

Floodwalls perform like levees except that they are vertical-sided structures that require less surface area for construction. Floodwalls are constructed of steel sheet pile or reinforced concrete, which makes the expense of installation cost prohibitive in many circumstances. Floodwalls also degrade adjacent habitat and can displace erosive energy to unprotected areas of shoreline downstream.

Seawalls are barriers or retaining walls that are built facing a large lake or the ocean. They are intended to protect the land from erosion by wave action. However, they often have an adverse impact on the shore and on neighboring properties and the movement of sand. The natural forces that transport sand and replenish beaches are disrupted by the wall, often increasing shoreline erosion on adjacent properties. Therefore, they are not encouraged and are even prohibited in many areas.

Reservoirs and Detention

Reservoirs reduce flooding by temporarily storing floodwaters behind dams or in storage or detention basins. Reservoirs lower flood heights by holding back, or detaining, runoff before it can flow downstream. Floodwaters are detained until the flood has subsided, then the water in the reservoir or detention basin is released or pumped out slowly at a rate that the river can accommodate downstream.

Reservoirs can be dry and remain idle until a large rain event occurs. Or they may be designed so that a lake or pond is created. The lake may provide recreational benefits or water supply (which could help mitigate a drought).

Flood control reservoirs are most commonly built for one of two purposes. Large reservoirs are constructed to protect property from existing flood problems. Smaller reservoirs or detention basins are built to protect downstream property from the impacts of new development (i.e., more runoff). In urban areas, some reservoirs are simply man-made holes, excavated to store floodwaters.

Other considerations for reservoirs:

- Unlike levees and channel modifications, they do not have to be built close to or disrupt the area to be protected.
- Reservoirs are most efficient in deeper valleys where there is more room to store water or on smaller rivers where there is less water to store.
- There is the threat of dam failure, which would flood the area that is supposed to be protected by the reservoir.
- Sediment deposition may occur and reduce the storage capacity over time.

Diversions

A diversion is a new channel that sends floodwaters to a different location, thereby reducing flooding along an existing watercourse. Diversions can be surface channels, overflow weirs, or tunnels. During normal flows, the water stays in the old channel. During flood flows, the floodwaters spill over to the diversion channel or tunnel, which carries the excess water to a receiving lake or river.

Diversions are limited by topography; they will not work in some areas. Unless the receiving water body is relatively close to the flood-prone stream and the land in-between is low and vacant, the cost of creating a diversion can be prohibitive.

Dredging

Dredging (Figure 15.13) is often viewed as a form of conveyance improvement. However, it has the following problems:

- Given the large volume of water that comes downstream during a flood, removing a foot or two from the bottom of the channel will have little effect on flood heights.
- Dredging is often cost prohibitive because the dredged material must be disposed of somewhere.

FIGURE 15.13 Dredging can sometimes be effective but it has its disadvantages.

- Unless instream and/or tributary erosion is corrected upstream, the dredged areas usually fill back in within a few years, and the process and expense have to be repeated.
- If the channel has not been disturbed for many years, dredging will destroy the habitat that has developed.

To protect the natural values of the stream, federal law requires a U.S. Army Corps of Engineers' permit before dredging can proceed. This can be a lengthy process that requires much advance planning and many safeguards to protect habitat (and adds to the cost of the project).

Channelization

"Channelization" means straightening, deepening, and/or widening a stream channel or drainageway to remedy local drainage or flooding problems. There are concerns with this approach that need to be kept in mind:

- Channelized streams can create or worsen flooding problems downstream as larger volumes of water are transported at a faster rate.
- Channelized streams rise and fall faster. During dry periods, the water level in the channel is lower than it should be, which creates water quality problems and degrades habitat.
- Channelized waterways tend to be unstable and experience more streambank erosion. The need for periodic reconstruction and silt removal becomes cyclic, making channel maintenance very expensive.

However, properly sloped and planted channel banks are more aesthetically and environmentally appealing and can prove cheaper to maintain than concrete ditches. A combination of restored wetland detention, vegetated swales, infiltration trenches, and other best management practices that increase infiltration (reducing runoff) and improve water quality can be implemented in conjunction with stormwater system improvements.

Crossings and Roadways

Often, a culvert or bridge constricts flows and causes localized backwater flooding. One way to identify such places is to check the flood profiles, graphic portrayals of flood elevations.

The common solution to these problems is to raise the roadbed and enlarge the culvert or bridge opening. However, designers need to consider the potential for a raised road acting as a dam, flooding people upstream, and larger openings allowing more water downstream. Plans need to ensure that the projects do not worsen flooding on someone else.

Public Information

A successful hazard mitigation program involves both the public and the private sectors. Public information activities advise property owners, renters, and businesses about hazards and ways to protect people and property from these hazards. These activities can motivate people to take the steps necessary to protect themselves and others.

Information can bring about voluntary mitigation activities at little or no cost to the government. Property owners mitigated their flooding problems long before there were government funding programs. One university study in the 1980s found that people acted on information (see "Information Brings Results"). In fact, 31% of respondents from the study area had implemented one or more flood protection measures without outside financial assistance.

The usual approach to delivering information involves two levels of activity. The first is to broadcast a short and simple version of the message to everyone who could potentially be affected. The second level provides more detailed information to those who respond and want to learn more.

This section starts with activities that reach out to people and tell them to be advised of the hazards and some of the things they can do. It then covers additional sources of information for those who want to learn more.

Outreach Projects

Outreach projects are the first step in the process of orienting property owners to the hazards they face and the concept of property protection. They are designed to encourage people to seek out more information in order to take steps to protect themselves and their properties (see Figure 15.14). Outreach projects can include

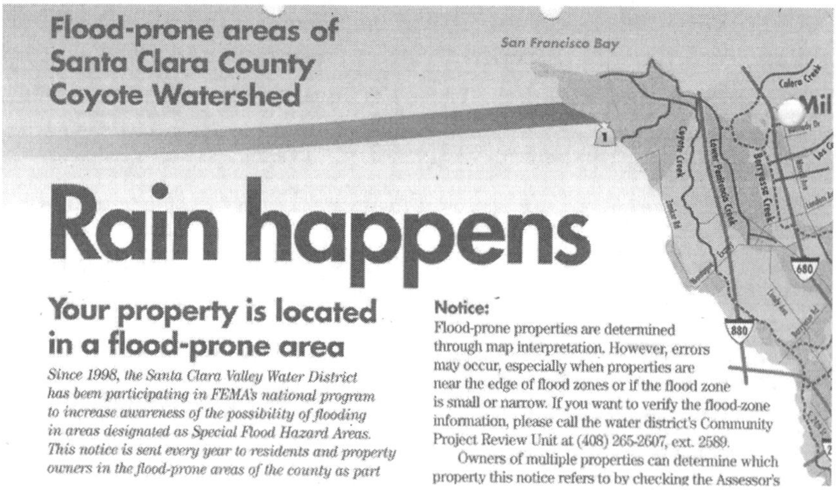

FIGURE 15.14 This outreach project is sent to all floodplain residents in the county.

- Community newsletters
- Direct mailings
- Local newspapers
- Press releases
- Presentations, interviews, etc., on local radio stations and cable TV channels
- Presentations at meetings of neighborhood, civic, or business groups
- Displays in public buildings or shopping malls
- Signs in parks, along trails, and on waterfronts that explain the natural features (such as the river) and their relation to hazards (such as floods)
- Brochures available in municipal buildings and libraries
- Special meetings, workshops, and seminars

Research has proven that outreach projects work (see sidebar "Information Brings Results"). However, awareness of the hazard is not enough; people need to be told what they can do about the hazard, so projects should include information on safety, health, and property protection measures. Research has also shown that a properly run local information program is more effective than national advertising or publicity campaigns. Therefore, outreach projects should be locally designed and tailored to meet local conditions.

Real Estate Disclosure

Many times after a flood or other natural disaster, people say they would have taken steps to protect themselves if only they had known they had purchased a property exposed to a hazard (see Figure 15.15).

FIGURE 15.15 Often homebuyers are not aware of the hazards their properties are exposed to. (Courtesy of St. Tammany Parish Emergency Management, St. Tammany, Louisiana)

INFORMATION BRINGS RESULTS

Dr. Shirley Laska, of the University of New Orleans, has studied various programs that encourage flood-prone homeowner "self-protective behavior." In her book she notes,

> The research reported herein demonstrates considerable interest among and effort by flooded homeowners to retrofit their homes to protect them from future flood damage. Several measures were undertaken by those who retrofitted. Moreover, they spent their own money – often considerable sums – to implement the measures....
>
> Having some source of retrofitting information appeared to encourage retrofitting, and the measures implemented by flooded homeowners who did consult an information source were evaluated by those owners as more protective than the measures implemented by homeowners who did not rely on a source [of information].

(Floodproof Retrofitting—Homeowner Self-Protective Behavior, University of Colorado, 1991, pages 221 and 223)

There are some federal requirements, but they have their limits. Federally regulated lending institutions must advise applicants for a mortgage or other loan that is to be secured by an insurable building whether the property is in a floodplain as shown on the community's FIRM. If so, flood insurance is required for buildings located within the floodplain if the mortgage or loan is federally insured.

However, because this requirement has to be met only 10 days before closing, often, the applicant is already committed to purchasing the property when he or she first learns of the flood hazard.

There are many state laws and local practices that rely on the seller disclosing his/her knowledge of the hazard. The shortcoming of these laws and practices is that the seller must be aware of the problem. Due to the sporadic occurrence of most hazard events, a property owner may legitimately not be aware of past or potential problems with a property being sold.

Libraries and Websites

The two previous activities tell people that they are exposed to a hazard. The next step is to provide information to those who want to know more. The community library and local websites are obvious places for residents to seek information on hazards, hazard protection, and protecting natural resources.

Books and pamphlets on hazard mitigation can be given to libraries, many of them obtained for free from state and federal agencies. Libraries also have their own public information campaigns with displays, lectures, and other projects, which can augment the activities of the local government.

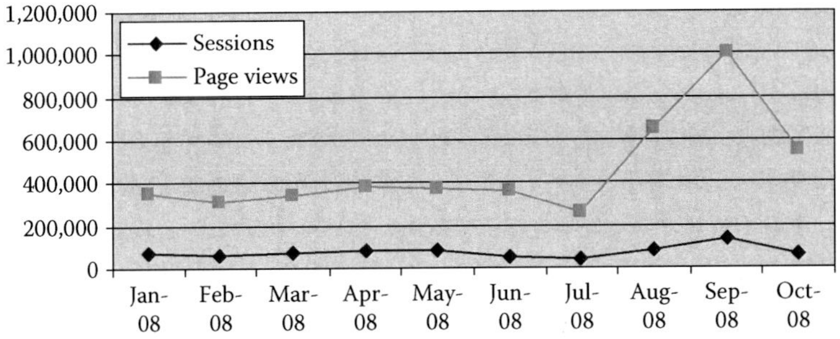

FIGURE 15.16 (See color insert.) The graph tracks hits and the number of pages viewed on the St. Tammany Parish, Louisiana, website. Usage increased dramatically in August and September 2008, when Hurricanes Gustav and Ike threatened the area. During the events, there were as many as 18,000 different users each day. Parish staff kept the information on vital topics, such as evacuation, reentry, and boil orders, updated 24 hours a day. (Courtesy of St. Tammany Parish Emergency Management, St.Tammany, Louisiana)

Today, websites are becoming more popular as research tools. They provide quick access to a wealth of public and private sites and sources of information. Through links to other websites, there is almost no limit to the amount of up-to-date information that can be accessed by the user (see Figure 15.16).

In addition to online floodplain maps, websites can link to information for homeowners on how to retrofit for tornadoes, earthquakes, and floods. There is a "FEMA for Kids" website that teaches children how to protect their home and what to have in a family disaster kit.

Technical Assistance

While general information provided by outreach projects or the library helps, most property owners do not feel ready to retrofit their buildings without more specific guidance. Local building department staff members are experts in construction. They can provide free advice, not necessarily to design a protection measure, but to steer the owner onto the right track.

Building or public works department staff can provide the following types of assistance:

- Determine whether a property is located within a mapped hazard, such as the floodplain
- Visit properties and offer protection suggestions
- Recommend or identify qualified or licensed contractors
- Inspect homes for anchoring of roofing and the home to the foundation
- Provide advice on protecting windows and garage doors from high winds
- Explain when building permits are needed for home improvements

FIGURE 3.1 New Orleans, Louisiana, 9/19/2005—Aerial view of flooded homes in a subdivision in St. Bernard Parish following Hurricane Katrina. (Photo courtesy of Andrea Booher/FEMA.)

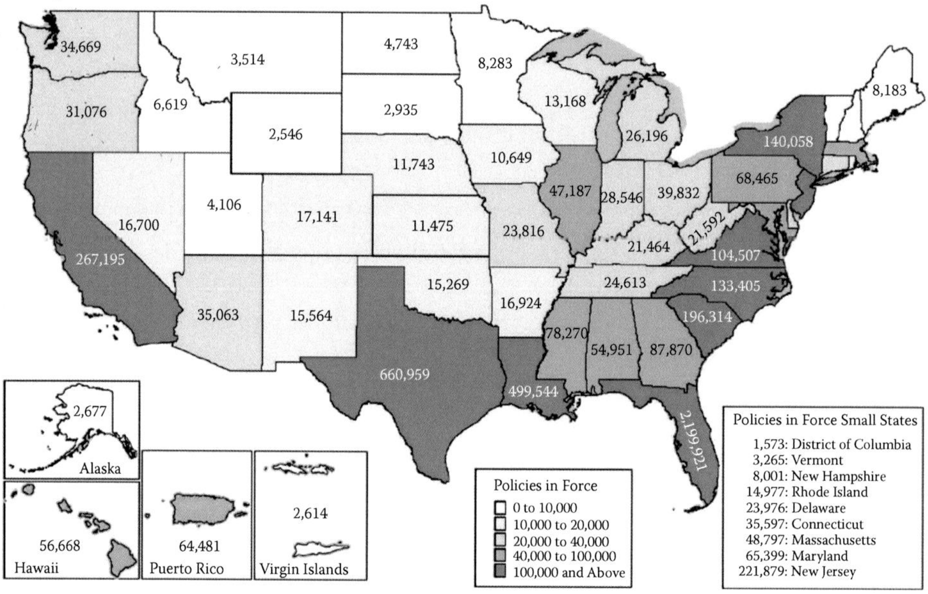

FIGURE 6.2 NFIP flood insurance policies in force by state, as of 9/30/2007.

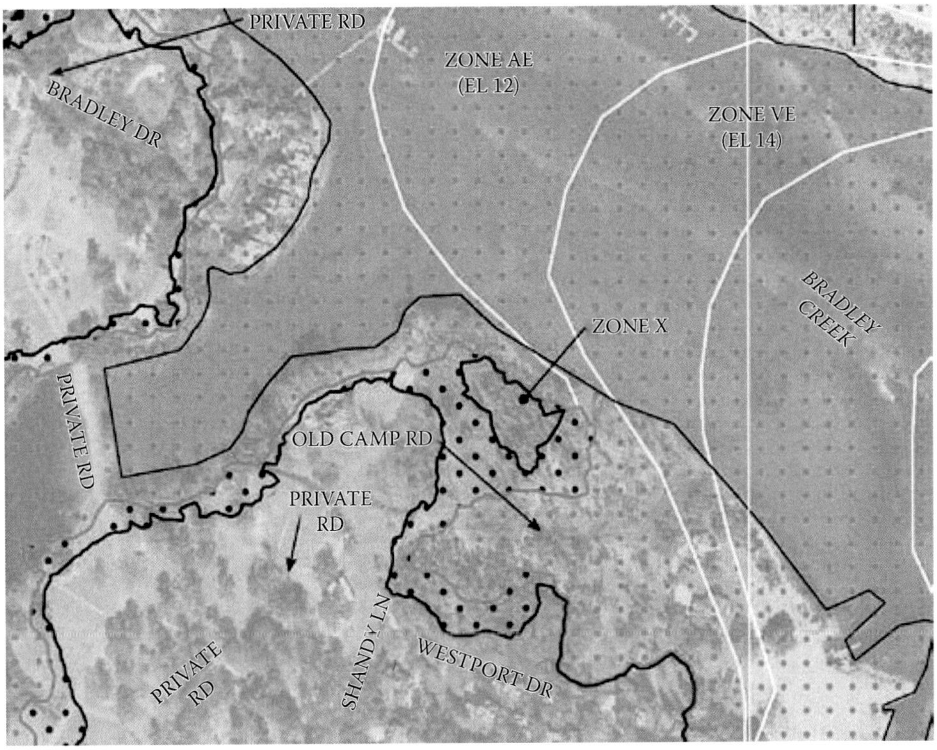

FIGURE 6.4 Excerpt from a digital flood insurance rate map (DFRIM). Recent FIRMs have been produced on a digital platform and are called DFIRMs. Many are on aerial photo base maps. For copies of FIRMs, see FEMA's Map Service Center at http://msc.fema.gov.

FIGURE 15.6 Boulder, Colorado, January 8, 2009—Houses were saved by a burnout operation. Having a defensible space around the house gave the firefighters this option. (Photo courtesy of Michael Rieger/FEMA.)

(a)

(b)

FIGURE 15.10 (a) Adequate routes and (b) traffic control are two key ingredients for an evacuation.

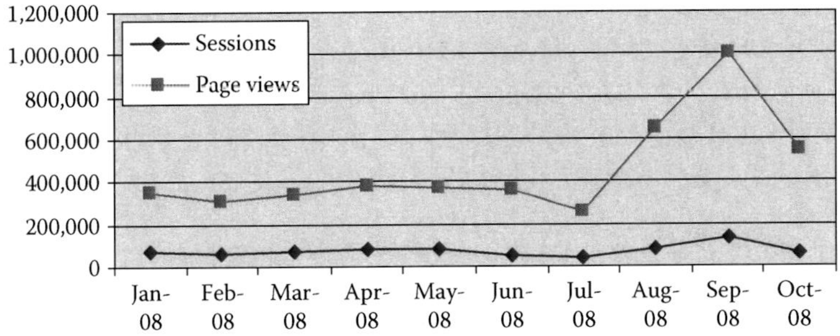

FIGURE 15.16 The graph tracks hits and the number of pages viewed on the St. Tammany Parish, Louisiana, website. Usage increased dramatically in August and September 2008, when Hurricanes Gustav and Ike threatened the area. During the events, there were as many as 18,000 different users each day. Parish staff kept the information on vital topics, such as evacuation, reentry, and boil orders, updated 24 hours a day. (Courtesy of St. Tammany Parish Emergency Management, St.Tammany, Louisiana)

Summary

This chapter shows that there are many different ways to mitigate the impacts of a hazard. They include

- Preventive measures, such as land use and construction regulations, that protect new development and keep problems from getting worse
- Ways to protect individual properties, including relocation, elevation, retrofitting, barriers, and insurance
- Emergency response measures, such as warning, response, and post-disaster recovery efforts
- Flood control projects like levees and reservoirs that control floodwaters
- Public information activities that educate people and encourage them to protect themselves and their properties

Some of these measures, like development regulations and emergency response, are the local government's responsibilities. Others can be implemented by individual property owners, such as retrofitting and improvements to a lot's drainage.

Some are difficult to implement because of their cost (flood control projects, acquisition) and some are difficult to implement for political reasons (setting higher standards for new development and regulating post-disaster reconstruction). Others, like public information programs, can be inexpensive and popular, but it is hard to see immediate results.

End-of-Chapter Questions

1. Name five preventive measures that can be implemented by a local government.
2. What is the biggest obstacle to implementing them?
3. Name the three general ways to protect existing buildings from damage by a hazard.
4. Which of the three ways can be implemented by the owners of the buildings?
5. This chapter reviews emergency response measures following a chronological order of responding to an emergency. What are the five general measures?
6. Name two advantages and two shortcomings of flood control projects.
7. What are the two levels of public information activities?
8. Name one measure that represents each level.

Resources

Preventive measures

- Coastal Construction Manual, FEMA 55, 2000.
- CRS Credit for Higher Regulatory Standards, 2006 (www.training.fema.gov/EMIWeb/CRS).
- Design and Construction Guidance for Community Shelters, FEMA, 2000.
- Manufactured Home Installation in Flood Hazard Areas, FEMA-85, 1985.
- *Subdivision Design in Flood Hazard Areas*, American Planning Association and FEMA, PAS Report 473, 1997.
- Wildland/Urban Interface Fire Protection, FEMA, 1989.

Websites

- Tree City USA—www.arborday.org/programs/treeCityUSA/
- Institute for Business and Home Safety—http://disastersafety.org
- Federal Alliance for Safe Homes—www.flash.org

Property Protection

- Engineering Principles and Practices for Retrofitting Flood Prone Residential Buildings, Federal Emergency Management Agency, FEMA-259, 2012.
- Homeowner's Guide to Retrofitting: Six Ways to Protect Your House from Flooding. Federal Emergency Management Agency, FEMA-312, 2009.
- *Local Flood Proofing Programs*, U.S. Army Corps of Engineers, 2005.
- Taking Shelter from the Storm: Building a Safe Room Inside Your House, Federal Emergency Management Agency, FEMA-320, 2008.

Websites

- http://floodhelp.uno.edu
- www.louisianafloods.org
- http://www.fema.gov/hazard-mitigation-assistance
- www.fema.gov/business/nfip

Emergency Response

- *CRS Credit for Flood Warning Programs*, FEMA, 2006 (www.training.fema.gov/EMIWeb/CRS).
- Emergency Management: Principles and Practice for Local Government, International City Management Association, 2007.

Websites

- Hydrologic Warning Council—www.hydrologicwarning.org
- International Association for Emergency Managers—www.iaem .com/
- National Weather Service—http://www.weather.gov
- River gauge information—www.weather.gov/ahps/
- StormReady communities—www.nws.noaa.gov/stormready/
- Wildland Fire Assessment System—www.wfas.net

Flood Control Projects

- *CRS Credit for Drainage System Maintenance*, FEMA, 2006 (www .training.fema.gov/EMIWeb/CRS).

Website

- National Association of Flood and Stormwater Management Agencies—http://www.nafsma.org

Public Information

- *CRS Credit for Outreach Projects*, Federal Emergency Management Agency, 2006. (www.training.fema.gov/EMIWeb/CRS).
- Floodproof Retrofitting: Homeowner Self-Protective Behavior, Shirley Bradway Laska, University of Colorado, 1991.

Appendix: Compendium of Links and Resources

Edward A. Thomas and Alessandra Jerolleman

Frequently Used FEMA Mitigation Websites

Comprehensive Data Management System (CDMS) version 2.5: http://www.fema.gov/library/viewRecord.do?id=3798
Flood Hazard Mapping: http://www.fema.gov/plan/prevent/fhm
Flood Smart: http://www.FloodSmart.gov
Flood Smart Risk Assessment Tool: http://www.floodsmart.gov/floodsmart/oneStepFloodRiskAddressSearch.action
Flood Recovery Maps—LA and MS: http://www.fema.gov/hazard/flood/recoverydata/index.shtm
Floodplain Management: http://www.fema.gov/plan/prevent/floodplain/index.shtm
Grant Programs: http://www.fema.gov/government/grant/index.shtm
HAZUS MH: http://www.fema.gov/plan/prevent/hazus
HAZUS Case Studies: http://www.fema.gov/plan/prevent/hazus/hz_casestudies.shtm
Map Service Center: http://msc.fema.gov
Map Modernization: http://www.fema.gov/plan/prevent/fhm/mm_main.shtm
Mapping Information Platform (MIP): http://www.hazards.fema.gov

Mitigation: http://www.fema.gov/about/divisions/mitigation.shtm
Mitigation Best Practices Portfolio: http://www.fema.gov/plan/prevent/bestpractices
Mitigation Planning: http://www.fema.gov/plan/mitplanning
National Flood Insurance Program (NFIP): http://www.fema.gov/business/nfip/index.shtm
National Flood Mitigation Data Collection Tool: http://www.fema.gov/plan/prevent/floodplain/Data_collection_tool.shtm
Plan and Prevent: http://www.fema.gov/plan/index.shtm
Pre-Disaster Mitigation (PDM) Grant Program: http://www.fema.gov/government/grant/pdm
Recover and Rebuild: http://www.fema.gov/rebuild/index.shtm
Repetitive Flood Claims (RFC) and Severe Repetitive Loss (SRL) Programs: http://www.fema.gov/government/grant/rfc/index.shtm
Stay Dry: http://www.fema.gov/library/viewRecord.do?id=3293

NOAA Websites

NOAA's Digital Coast: http://www.csc.noaa.gov/digitalcoast/
NOAA's Land Cover Change Program: http://www.csc.noaa.gov/landcover/atlas
NOAA's Sea Level Trends: http://tidesandcurrents.noaa.gov/sltrends/sltrends.shtml
NOAA's Vulnerability Assessment Tool: http://www.csc.noaa.gov/products/nchaz/htm/mitigate.htm

USACE Websites

Flood Risk Management Program: http://www.nfrmp.us
Risk Assessment: http://www.usace.army.mil/Pages/default.aspx
Silver Jackets Program: http://www.iwr.usace.army.mil/nfrmp/state

Other Useful Sites

American Society of Civil Engineers: http://www.asce.org
Association of State Floodplain Managers: http://www.floods.org
Google Earth: http://www.google.com/earth/index.html
National Earthquake Hazards Reduction Program: http://www.nehrp.gov/index.htm
National Institute of Standards and Technology: http://www.nist.gov/index.htm

National Interagency Fire Center: http://www.nifc.gov/
National Weather Service Risk Assessment: http://www.nws.noaa.gov/?bcsi_scan_1D1A7A50B174BA63=0
Natural Hazard Mitigation Association: http://www.nhma.info
Storm Smart Coasts: http://www.mass.gov/czm/stormsmart/
USGS Risk Assessment: http://www.usgs.gov/science/science.php?term=997

Glossary

Base flood elevation	Highest water surface elevation with a 1% chance of being equaled or exceeded in a given year.
Building code	A building code is a set of rules that specify the minimum acceptable level of safety for constructed objects such as buildings.
Capital improvement plans	A capital improvement plan will guide a community's major public expenditures for the next 5–20 years.
Channelization	"Channelization" means straightening, deepening, and/or widening a stream channel or drainage way to remedy local drainage or flooding problems.
Community emergency response team (CERT)	CERT teams consist of people who have received training in disaster preparedness for hazards that may impact their area, as well as basic disaster response skills, such as fire safety, light search and rescue, team organization, and disaster medical operations.

Community rating system (CRS) — CRS was initiated in 1990 to give communities an incentive to go above and beyond the minimum requirements of the National Flood Insurance Program (NFIP). A community can qualify for the CRS if it undertakes additional activities, such as providing flood protection information to residents, regulating areas not mapped by the NFIP, setting higher construction standards, helping insurance agents obtain flood data, and establishing a flood warning program.

Comprehensive plans — These plans are the primary tools used by communities to address future development. They can reduce future property damage by indicating open space or low density development within floodplains and other hazardous areas.

Detention — Flood detention is detaining and releasing flood water from a site.

Disclosure — Information regarding the flood zone must be disclosed when a home is being purchased.

Diversions — A diversion is a new channel that sends floodwaters to a different location, thereby reducing flooding along an existing watercourse. Diversions can be surface channels, overflow weirs, or tunnels.

Flood insurance rate map (FIRM) — An official map that has delineated both the special flood hazard areas and the risk premium zones.

Flood insurance study (FIS) — A source of technical data for adoption of floodplain ordinances and development of risk information used to establish flood insurance rates.

Flood Control Act of 1936 — This bill was the beginning of the federal movement toward structural projects, with authority given to the U.S. Army Corps of Engineers.

Flood hazard — Potential for inundation with risk to life, health, property, and natural value.

Floodplain	Any land that is susceptible to being inundated by water.
Floodplain management	The operation of an overall program of corrective and preventive measures for reducing flood damage, including but not limited to emergency preparedness plans, flood control works, and floodplain management regulations.
Floodway	Channel of a river or other watercourse and adjacent land areas that must be reserved in order to discharge the base flood without cumulatively increasing the water surface elevation more than a designated height.
Flood Mitigation Assistance Program (FMA)	Created by the National Flood Insurance Act of 1968 and amended as part of the National Flood Insurance Reform Act of 1994, the program's main goal is to provide grants to states and communities for long-term flood damage reduction projects in order to reduce or eliminate the claims under the National Flood Insurance Program.
Flood zone (Zone)	A geographical area shown on a flood hazard boundary map or a flood insurance rate map that reflects the severity or type of flooding in the area. A, AO, AH, AE, V, VE, and X are all examples of flood zones.
Freeboard	Freeboard is an additional factor of safety above the base flood elevation.
Grandfathering	An exemption based on previously existing circumstances. Any structures that were built in compliance with the floodplain management regulations in effect at the start of construction will continue to have their flood insurance rate set as if they were in compliance, even if higher base flood elevations or more restrictive risk zone designations are enacted.
Hazard mitigation	Any sustained action taken to reduce or eliminate long-term risk to life and property from a hazard event.

Hazard Mitigation Grant Program (HMGP)
Created by the Stafford Act, the program is intended for post-disaster declaration cases and offers grants for long-term mitigation projects before and after a disaster. The program is the largest source of federal funding for communities after a disaster declaration, which is distributed proportionally with the damage loss estimates.

HAZUS
HAZUS is the Federal Emergency Management Agency's basic risk analysis methodology and technological tool to analyze potential losses from natural disasters such as floods, hurricanes, and earthquakes. The methodology comprises the latest engineering as well as geographic information systems knowledge and tools.

Increased cost of construction (ICC)
To help with the cost of meeting the substantial damage requirement, the National Flood Insurance Program has the ICC provision. This is an additional flood insurance claim payment of up to $30,000 to help meet the code requirements.

Levees and floodwalls
Probably the best known flood control measure is a barrier of earth (levee) or concrete (floodwall) erected between the watercourse and the property to be protected. Levees and floodwalls confine water to the stream channel by raising its banks.

Mandatory purchase requirement
Buildings located in flood hazard areas must have flood insurance coverage as a condition of federal aid (e.g., Housing and Urban Development [HUD], Veterans Administration [VA], and Environmental Protection Agency [EPA] programs), federal disaster assistance, and loans from federally insured banks and savings and loans.

National Dam Safety Program
This program was created through Water Resources and the Development Act of 1996; the program focuses on dam safety projects against natural and man-made hazards. The program offers grant assistance to states, dam safety technical and archival research, and dam safety training for state staff and inspectors.

National Earthquake Hazards Reduction Program (NEHRP)	Established in 1977 by Congress, the program is a coordinated approach to address, identify, reduce, or eliminate the earthquake-related risks through basic or applied science and engineering measures. Specific goals include the development and implementation of earthquake loss-reduction policies and strategies, improvement of techniques to reduce seismic vulnerability, improvement of seismic hazard identification and risk assessment methods, and improvement of understanding earthquakes and their impacts.
National Flood Insurance Act of 1968	This Act initiated the National Flood Insurance Program, making federally subsidized insurance available in many flood-prone regions for the first time.
National Hurricane Program (NHP)	Established in 1985, the program focuses on hurricane risk assessment and provision of relevant tools and technical assistance to local and state agencies in regard to development of hurricane evacuation plans. The program is a partnership of several agencies including the National Oceanic and Atmospheric Association, National Weather Service, U.S. Department of Transportation, and U.S. Army Corps of Engineers.
No adverse impact (NAI)	A type of floodplain management in which the actions of one property owner do not adversely affect the flood risks for other properties.
Planning and zoning	Planning and zoning activities direct development away from hazardous areas, especially floodplains, steep slopes, sinkholes, and other known problem sites. They do this by allowing land uses that are more compatible to the natural conditions of the land.
Planning Pilot Grant Program (PPGP)	The PPGP was a pilot established in Louisiana following Hurricane Katrina. It provided a funding source for localities not only to update their existing comprehensive hazard mitigation plans, but also to scope and prioritize hazard mitigation projects.

Pre-FIRM structure A building that was constructed in an area before the flood insurance rate map was published and the true flood risk known.

Public–private partnerships Collaborative, cooperative groups with the aim to proactively address community issues, such as pre-disaster mitigation, which include a governmental agency working in tandem with any private entity (e.g., non-profit, chamber of commerce, a club, etc.) as no one sector can accomplish the task in question on their own.

Repetitive loss area analysis An approach that identifies repetitive loss areas, evaluates mitigation approaches, and determines the most appropriate alternatives to reduce future losses.

Repetitive loss property (RL) Any insurable building for which two or more claims of more than $1000 were paid by the National Flood Insurance Program (NFIP) within any rolling 10-year period since 1978. An RL may or may not be currently insured by the NFIP.

Reservoirs and detention Reservoirs reduce flooding by temporarily storing flood waters behind dams or in storage or detention basins. Reservoirs lower flood heights by holding back, or detaining, runoff before it can flow downstream.

Response The response phase involves efforts and activities targeted at saving life and property during emergency situations.

Retrofitting Retrofitting involves making modifications to an existing structure, such as hardening the structure to withstand higher wind loads.

Safe room A safe room is a hardened structure specifically designed to meet FEMA criteria and provide “near-absolute protection” in extreme weather events, including tornadoes and hurricanes.

Severe repetitive loss program (SRL)	Authorized by the Bunning–Bereuter–Blumaneauer Flood Insurance Reform Act of 2004 and amending the National Flood Insurance Act of 1968, the program provides funding for long-term flood damage and the risk reduction or elimination of projects encompassing SRL structures (as defined by the National Flood Insurance Act).
Severe repetitive loss property	As defined by the Flood Insurance Reform Act of 2004, severe repetitive losses are 1–4 family residences that have had four or more claims of more than $5000 or at least two claims that cumulatively exceed the building's value. The 2004 Act creates new funding mechanisms to help mitigate flood damage for these properties.
Special flood hazard area (SFHA)	The land area covered by the floodwaters of the base flood on National Flood Insurance Program (NFIP) maps. The SFHA is the area where the NFIP's floodplain management regulations must be enforced and the area where the mandatory purchase of flood insurance applies.
State coordinating agency	As a requirement of participating in the National Flood Insurance Program (NFIP), each state governor designates a state coordinating agency. These are often in the water resources or natural resources department, but some are in the emergency management agency, the local government affairs department, or the state planning office. The state coordinating agency provides technical assistance to communities and coordinates the activities of various state agencies that affect the NFIP.
Subdivision regulations	Subdivision regulations govern how land will be subdivided and set construction standards. These standards generally address roads, sidewalks, utilities, storm sewers, and drainageways.

Substantial damage	Damage to a structure in which the cost of restoring the structure to its prior condition would equal or exceed 50% of the market value of the structure before the damage occurred.
Substantial improvement	Any reconstruction, rehabilitation, addition, or other improvement to a structure, which equals or exceeds 50% of the market value of the structure prior to the improvement.
Urban forestry	The care and management of tree populations in urban settings.
Warnings	A warning is issued by the National Weather Service when a particular weather situation is imminent, such as a tornado spotted on the ground.
Watch	A watch is issued by the National Weather Service when conditions are favorable for the development of a particular weather situation, such as a severe thunderstorm.
Wildland urban interface	The transition zone between developed lands and forested lands.
Write-your-own (WYO)	The WYO is an agreement with the insurance industry that allows private insurers to write National Flood Insurance Program policies.
Zoning	A zoning ordinance regulates development by dividing a community into zones or districts and setting development criteria for each zone or district. Zoning codes are considered the primary tool to implement a comprehensive plan's guidelines for how land should be developed.

Index

A

B

G

H

N

O

P

W

Z